Dear Dave,

Your daughter spent most of her life savings to buy this book for you. Kate is one of my favorites & does an outstanding job at our firm. I'm sure you're as proud of her as I am. I hope you enjoy this book – lots of silly musings from a crazy dad.

Sincerely,

SURE DAD,
YOU KNOW EVERYTHING

SURE DAD, YOU KNOW EVERYTHING

A Father's Whimsical Guide To His Children
(And Then Some)

Lawrence N. Rosenblum

Illustrated by Hillary Miles

Published by Sure Dad Publishing, LLC
www.suredad.com

Printed by Signature Book Printing
 www.sbpbooks.com

All characters appearing in this work are fictitious. Any resemblance to real persons, living or dead, is purely coincidental.

ISBN: 978-0-578-15117-5 (Hardcover)

Illustrated by Hillary Miles
Edited by Maureen A. Vincent
Layout execution by Allegra – Design • Marketing • Print – Rockville, MD

Printed in the United States of America

To my one and a half wonderful children
(the other half depends on the day)

FOREWORD

Our dad began this book when we were both in middle school. We never knew how he came up with this idea, but we knew Dad was a bit odd. He started carrying a notepad everywhere and would stop at red lights—or sometimes mid-sentence—to write down things like "belly button lint" or "farts." We found the house littered with napkins and scraps of paper covered with unrelated topics. It was then that we realized that Dad was losing it. He was never really like other dads though, so it shouldn't have surprised us. This was the father who locked himself out of a running car (multiple times, although he swears it was only once) and left outgoing voice messages about self-answering desks and smartphones taking over the power grid.

One of the strangest things our dad does is his annual holiday newsletter. Instead of sending a normal holiday message to friends and family, Dad decided to make fun of people who send out a yearly report. He started writing his own version for our family, but with extreme exaggerations. He pretended we were astronauts or winners of the lottery and Nobel Peace Prize. The newsletter began with half-truths that actually gave a vague idea of what we were up to, but has since morphed into something like the eighth Harry Potter book. Dad seems to like writing down his crazy ideas, and thinks that people really enjoy his sense of humor. We hope he's right.

Regardless of how many people read it, we know how much this book means to him. It might actually come in handy if we ever get around to reading it ourselves. Actually, we hear it's pretty good. In all seriousness, our dad has spent a lot of his time and effort working on this amorphous blob of a book, and we could not be any more ~~embarrassed~~ proud.

Love,
Sam and Amy

PREFACE

There's an old Yiddish expression which loosely translates as follows: "Opinions are like tushies; everybody has one." (I cleaned this up a little; OK, so maybe something got lost in the translation.) Now as for me, I only have one tush, which is plenty. But I've got a million opinions and lots of advice to hand out. Give me a subject and I've got something to say. It's like a disease—I just can't keep things to myself.

You see, this book was originally intended to be an essay for my children—15 years ago (oy!). It was to be a kind of whimsical ABC guide to life through a father's silly, passionate, cynical, sensitive, offbeat, serious and sometimes jaded eyes. The children are both young adults now (at least chronologically), so they are still not supposed to pay much attention to anything I have to say. But before they put me into the home, I decided to impart my precious wisdom, handed down from generations (well, not really), and commit my pontifications, witticisms and quips to writing. You know, my dos and don'ts, my philosophies, my observations and perceptions, my musings on life's unanswered questions, etc. Anyway, some people I respect encouraged me to turn all this into a book, suggesting that others might be interested in reading about my take on the universe. (Ultimately, you'll decide if that was a good idea—or not). So I took their advice and, lucky for you, I've got lots to discuss. If you're interested in tongue-in-cheek humor and a veritable cornucopia of useless information, with a little bit of stream of consciousness and plenty of cross-references thrown in, you've come to the right place. There is something for everyone here, so you're bound to find a section of interest.

In my subtle and not so subtle ways, I'm offering lots of advice; not just to my children, but to anyone else reading. So you might want to take some copious notes. I'm like a volcano, with my creative juices flowing, endlessly spewing my incessant ramblings and diatribes (see *Diarrhea*). I can riff about life's inconsistencies with sarcasm, cynicism, racy language and a touch of irreverence (well, maybe more than a touch). Hoping not to offend anyone, I can rant and rave about anything and everything (see *Freedom*)—and being completely ignorant about a subject doesn't stop me at all. Oh, and you may want to check out the innuendo; I'm big on innuendo. And by all means, please read between the lines; there's plenty there too. It's a lot of fun. But you shouldn't take me too seriously. I don't.

When I was a little boy, I was quite inquisitive. My uncle would answer my endless series of questions with: "What, are you writing a book?" Well, I guess now I am. But I should have paid a lot more attention (see *Remembering*).

Please don't look here for heavy themes like the purpose of life. But I do wax poetic about hundreds of other topics. Sorry, I don't have all the answers, and I'm not always right; I'm just mostly right. Fortunately, I was the product of good parenting, learning the difference between right and wrong. Unfortunately, I'm afraid that many struggle to really understand the difference today.

When I was growing up, I had a boss who took great pleasure in teasing me relentlessly, pointing out everything I was doing wrong. I guess I wasn't too offended, as I came back to work each day. So when he would find me loafing somewhere, not doing anything, he would berate me to "do something, even if it's wrong." That always stuck with me, as it was good advice (see *Do Something*).

Even though the subjects are arranged in alphabetical order, they actually appear randomly on the pages (they call that dichotomy). Serious follows stupid, which follows self-deprecation, and on and on. Open the book anywhere and read away, as there really is no beginning and no end. I'm sure you will find it quite riveting. But reading this book from cover to cover will drive you absolutely crazy (see *Overkill*). Would you read an encyclopedia from beginning to end? Of course not. It's best to pick it up, read a few pages and then find something else to do. Trust me on this. My head has already exploded several times. It took me 15 years to write this, so it will likely take you 10 years to read it.

I'll sum up my redundant and rambling themes this way: do the right thing, be nice, be smart, be yourself, chase your dreams, make a difference and be proud. Simple enough, right? Just always be satisfied that you are doing the best you can. That may sound trite, but it's a great way to live. You can't fool yourself, you know, as you tend to be your biggest critic.

It's easy to sit on the sidelines and whine and complain (usually to yourself) about life. So I'm writing down what I think is right and wrong, with plenty in between. But maybe someone, even my children, will read this and find it enjoyable, entertaining, thought provoking and possibly just a little bit helpful. Who knows? Stranger things have happened. Now be my guest. Go take a seat in your easy chair (no idea what that is), relax, enjoy and read on. I'm sure you will be spellbound, hanging on my every word. You might even be inspired to do something.

At least now I'm doing *something*.

ACKNOWLEDGMENTS

I am extraordinarily fortunate to have a happy, lovely, caring and responsible daughter, along with a smart, quick witted, friendly and (mostly) loving son. A broad smile comes to my face every time I think of them (well, most times). When I was ready to settle down and have a family, I looked forward to having children someday. To say that they exceeded my wildest dreams is an understatement. My daughter Amy and my son Sam have grown up to be the kind of adults any father would be proud to have raised, and I am the proudest dad I know. I bore lots of people with my constant bragging about them. (God knows, I am completely unbiased in my assessments, of course.) My children have been such a source of joy for me over many years. By no means are they perfect—and clearly they have their moments— but overall I think they are great. And besides all their attributes, they are both finally off the parental payroll. I really enjoy that.

I would love to take all of the credit for successfully bringing up my darlings. I would love to, but I can't. At least half of the credit goes to their mom, who did most of the heavy lifting while I was building a career, and she continues to be a great mother to them.

My hope is that every dad could be as lucky as me, and be so proud of their children (see *Count Your Blessings*).

≈

Thanking is something I really enjoy doing, and there are plenty of people who really helped me with this book.

I never would have gotten this damn thing done if not for the tremendous help and support of three very special ladies. First, my editor Maureen Vincent (see *Last Names*) has more patience than anyone I know. She was able to polish my various messages while (more than) gently guiding me in the direction of final completion—not an easy task. Her persistence has really paid off, as I fought her most of the way with lots and lots (and lots) of last-minute changes.

Second, I'm blessed to have Hillary Miles, whom I've known since before she was born, as a very close friend. She is by far the most brilliant and talented artist I've ever seen. Her level of imagination is limitless, and she has truly enhanced this book with her outstanding illustrations.

And most importantly, I want to thank my sweetheart Nancy. She has put up with so many distractions and interruptions while I was writing this book. Her unbridled support and encouragement have been most appreciated by me, especially when I really needed them.

There are others to thank, and in my attempt to protect the innocent, I'll just use the initials of those who've helped and supported me (or pretended to be supportive)—some, who may not even know it, simply by their inspiration. Here they are. And take it from me, they are (were) some of the coolest people on the planet:

AAA	EKP	LAG	RCL
AER	FXB, Jr.	LFG	RER
AK	GAM	LJD	RLL
AMB	GSN	LRR	SJM
BFK	HNK	LSR	SJR
BLM	JPB	ME	TJR
CFW, Jr.	JR	MSW	WTL
DFH	JRF	PLR	

CONTENTS

M

HERE WE GO

So here's how this works. I pick a topic and write something serious/ cute/ silly/ stupid/ funny/ sarcastic/ whimsical/ personal about it. And you're quite moved and impressed that it is so thought provoking/ profound/ perceptive/ insightful/ stupid/ uproariously funny/ clever/ nutty/ subtle/ not so subtle/ charming/ enlightening, which causes you to read on. You get the idea; I'll do my job and you'll do yours. Fasten your seatbelt and enjoy the ride. Just read, read, read (see *Reading*), for God's sake.

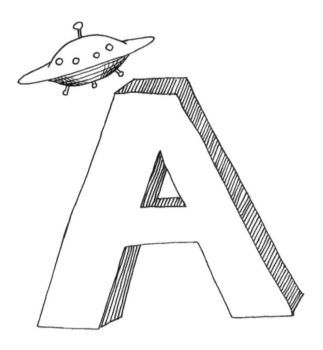

AARDVARK

Please pardon my ignorance, but as for aardvarks, I don't know much about them, except they're weird looking. One thing has always bothered me, though. Who was in charge of deciding how to spell this word? It should be oddvark, right? Look, this is the beginning and that's the best I could come up with. Sue me.

ABANDON

You can't abandon your friends or your family; it's a law. Sure, you sometimes get mad and even nasty with the ones you're close to, because they can drive you crazy. But turning your back or walking out is never an option, especially when they need you. (So how am I doing so far; see *Patience*?)

ABERRATION

Yeah, we're all aberrations. Good luck in finding an average person (see *Normal*). They don't exist. (Read on; I'm just getting warmed up.)

ABLE

Like most things, there are good able's and bad able's (or ible's—or apples).

These able's (and ible's) empower you:

Acceptable
Accessible
Accountable
Adaptable
Adorable
Advisable
Affordable
Agreeable
Amiable
Amicable
Attainable
Avoidable
Biodegradable
Cain and Abel
Capable
Catchable
Charitable
Compatible
Credible
Curable
Debatable
Deductible
Defendable
Delectable
Dependable
Desirable
Digestible
Doable
Edible
Enable
Fixable
Flexible
Foreseeable
Formidable

Fungible (I don't know
    what that means, but
    it's probably OK)
Honorable
Hospitable
Huggable
Identifiable
Impeccable
Incredible
Indescribable
Indispensable
Intangible
Laughable
Likable
Lovable
Marketable
Personable
Pliable
Portable
Predictable
Presentable
Preventable
Redeemable
Reliable
Remarkable
Replaceable
Responsible
Retractable
Reversible
Saleable
Sensible
Treatable
Understandable
Unforgettable
Usable

Vegetable
Verifiable
Veritable (strange word,
   but I think that's OK too)

Viable
Winnable

These are the ones that tend to disable you:

Arguable
Avoidable
Contemptible
Culpable
Deplorable
Despicable
Disagreeable
Disposable (see *Recycling*)
Distractible
Enable
Excitable
Forgettable
Gullible (like *Gullible's Travels*)
Illegible
Impenetrable
Impossible
Incapable
Incompatible
Incomprehensible
Inconceivable
Inconsolable
Incorrigible
Indefensible

Inevitable
Inoperable
Insatiable (see *Dieting*)
Insufferable
Insurmountable
Intractable
Invincible
Irreparable
Irresistible (resist already)
Irresponsible
Irritable (especially
   irritable bowel syndrome)
Penetrable
Perishable
Predictable
Regrettable
Reprehensible
Unbelievable
Unconscionable
Unforgivable
Unmanageable
Unrecognizable
Unreliable

ABORTION

Abortion is a tough subject, so pay attention here. When does life begin? Are you killing a baby? I have no idea. But do you really know what it's like to have something very unwanted growing inside your body? I wouldn't be so insensitive as to compare it to a cancer, but maybe to some women it is. I do know this: it's not my body, it's not my choice and it's not my business. It's none of yours either. No one should interfere, because it's a very private issue.

5

Let's keep it that way. However, I've certainly noticed that our feelings about abortion tend to change when we are no longer childless or want to be childless.

ABRASIVE

There's really no reason to be abrasive to anyone. Save it for the sandpaper. (Work with me here; I'm still warming up.)

ABS

You want flat abs? Just lie on your back; they'll flatten right out. Not only are those washboard abs unnatural looking—try maintaining them when you're over 40.

ABSENCE

Does absence make the heart grow fonder? Yeah, it usually works that way. You tend to take lots of things for granted when you're with someone all the time. However, absence or no absence, either they're in your heart or they're not (see *Love*). Now if you're talking about an abscess, that's something entirely different.

ABSOLUTES

Because there are no absolutes, nothing is ever absolute, not even these words of wisdom (see *Generalizations*).

ABSTAIN

There are typically two choices: You're either for it or you're against it. If you don't care, you're giving up your right to vote (see *Cop Out*). Care! And politicians who abstain from any vote are not being responsible to the position for which they were elected. They aren't chosen to hold office to vote "I don't really know, so can somebody else please decide" on an issue. Not an option.

ABSTINENCE

It's OK to wait, as some things are worth waiting for, like babies. But remember that: it's your choice to hold off, not someone else's (see *Peer Pressure*).

ABUSE

We all get mad—sometimes very mad. But NEVER, NEVER, NEVER, EVER take it out verbally or physically or any other ally on someone else or yourself. Get a punching bag, go run around the block, jump in a lake—or something. Abuse can always be prevented. If you can't stop, get some help. And while we're at it, abusing drugs or alcohol is one of the most idiotic things anyone can do.

ACCENTS

So you think it's perfectly OK to make fun of other people's accents? How well do you think you'd do speaking their language? Can you converse in two languages like they can? Knock it off, as it's not funny; at least they're trying (see *Speak The Language*).

ACCEPTING

Instead of spending time trying to change someone, accept them for what they are: imperfect, just like you. Be accepting of others and, above all, accept yourself.

ACCIDENTS

Of course it's an accident; otherwise they'd call it an on-purpose. Preventable accidents are not accidents; they're just examples of not being careful.

ACCIDENT WAITING TO HAPPEN

Taking unnecessary risks is dumb. Not doing something about unsafe places is even dumber. (Take a hint here.)

ACCOMPLISHMENT

It's a great feeling to know that you did something well, especially if it's something particularly good. Self-satisfaction is a wonderful feeling, so sit back and admire your handiwork.

ACCOUNTABILITY

No one "makes" you do anything unless they have a gun to your head. So you can't always blame someone else, as we are all accountable for our own actions. You want to take full responsibility for your actions, both good and bad. That goes both ways, so you should hold others accountable too.

ACCUSATIONS

If you accuse someone of something, you'd better make damn sure you can back it up. Making false accusations will get you into big trouble—and won't do much to help your credibility (see *Reputation*).

ACKNOWLEDGMENT

Always know who to thank; you know, that giving credit where credit is due stuff. They'll always appreciate it. And you'll feel better for it. (Pay attention here.)

ACTIONS

Words can come rather freely to our lips, but it's our actions that really do most of the talking. They speak volumes, and much more loudly than the sounds emitted from our lips. Remember: talk is very cheap, so make sure your actions match your words. Don't talk about it; be about it. And while you're at it, make sure you take responsibility for your actions.

ACTIVE

The benefits of being active far outweigh the comfort (or laziness) of being passive. So if you're not already, get active and stay active, as a sedentary life will probably kill you (see *Exercise*).

ACTORS

Could you imagine being in a serious relationship with a professional actor? If they were really good at their craft, how would you know if they were ever being truthful with you or always just acting? They could be very convincing, right *(see Orgasm)*? That probably explains why most actors marry other actors and then divorce each other. Maybe their performances weren't that good after all.

ACTS OF GOD

Because acts of God can be very nasty, you don't want to rile Him—or Her. (Yes, thank you, Mr. Obvious.)

ADAPTING

Roll with the punches, will ya? Stop being so set in your ways, because the world is changing way too fast. Get with it already.

ADDICTION

Fortunately, addiction is one of the few problems I don't have, unless you consider always shooting your mouth off an addiction (then I guess maybe I do). But if you're really addicted to something and just can't stop, get help or get into some program. You're not going to be able to beat this by yourself. But deep down inside, you already know this, right?

ADMITTING YOU'RE WRONG

Admitting you're wrong is never very easy (see *Ego*), but believe me, you'll sleep better at night if you have the strength to do it (strength being the operative word.) This exercise often takes plenty of muscle. Keep in mind that it's highly unlikely that you're always right and the world is wrong.

ADO

What's an ado? You know, "much ado about nothing," "without further ado"? How come there isn't an adon't?

ADOLESCENT INDISCRETIONS

Who didn't do any stupid, embarrassing, hurtful or regrettable things growing up? Boring people, that's who. As long as you didn't go to jail because of it, these indiscretions shouldn't haunt you for the rest of your life. Even if you did go to jail, you paid your debt to society, right? Those who can't get over it (and constantly bring it up to you) clearly never advanced past their own adolescence. Maybe they were too boring to have committed any learning experiences.

ADOPTION

There is nothing more unselfish than adopting a child. These are people who really want to be moms and dads (see *Heroes/Heroines*). Talk about choice. Well, they really make one—and it's a great one.

ADRENALINE

What a rush! Too bad they can't bottle that adrenaline up and sell it. Somebody would make a lot of money. Oh wait, maybe it's already in coffee.

ADULT

I always thought that adult and a dolt were the same thing. Through some eyes, maybe they are. How old do you have to be, to be considered an adult? No idea. However, it is sad but true that at some point you have to at least act like an adult. This is one of the harsh realities of life, as being an adult comes with lots and lots of responsibilities. I really hate this (see *Growing Up*).

ADVENTURE

For some, every day is an adventure—which may be inadvertent. Just use your head and don't take any unnecessary risks.

ADVERSITY

We all have to deal with adversity sometime in our lives. And sometimes it's a lot of sometimes. No one can really escape it, so just do the best you can.

ADVERTENT

I understand how things can be inadvertent, but how exactly does one go about being advertent?

ADVERTISING

Most of us are often advertising, whether we know it or not. The way we dress, our body language and the things we say allow us to subtly (or not so subtly) display our wares. We are advertising for friendship, jobs, love, lust—and new car discounts. Sometimes we subconsciously do this, so don't be surprised when others react to your inadvertent overtures. Yes, another reason to see yourself as others see you (see *Cleavage*).

ADVICE

If you find yourself constantly asking others what they think, then you're not thinking enough (see *Confidence*). If you're really unsure, don't go to your friends for advice, as they are probably just as ignorant as you. The best place to go is to an older, more experienced person. The older, the better, as you usually can't beat the life lessons they've learned. Chances are, whatever it is, they've been there, done that. And sure, you can listen to their advice, but ultimately you're the one who has to make the decision.

ADVOCATE

Don't ever be afraid to stand up for whatever or whomever you believe in. If you're waiting around for someone to be your advocate, you may have a long wait. So at least be an advocate for yourself.

AFFAIRS

So you can't keep your hands off Ms. Hotsy Totsy or Mr. Studley? Oh, wouldn't you know it: they or you are already in a committed relationship. How inconvenient! And if you think Prince Charming will dump his wife and marry you, and you'll go off into the sunset together, think again. Listen genius, he cheated on her. But of course he would never cheat on you, right (see *Changing Their Stripes*)? Having an affair is the ultimate act of betrayal to your mate and a terrible reflection on your character (or lack thereof). Either un-commit from your current partner and have your precious fun, or deal with your real problem: your current relationship (see *Counseling*).

AFFECTION

There are so many ways to show affection. Use them all.

AFRAID

It's OK to be afraid. We all have our fears, and it's nothing to be ashamed of. The ones who say they are afraid of nothing are absolutely afraid of something (see *Bullshit*). However, you want to make sure these fears don't take over your whole life. If they really get in the way, you might want to get some help to confront and deal with them. Above all, never be afraid to do what's right. Never.

AFTERBIRTH

I can't stand to see things being wasted (see *Recycling*). After a baby is born, they have no further need for the placenta or umbilical cord. But it's filled with rich stem cells that science is now finding very valuable in treating lots of diseases. So don't just have the hospital throw that bloody, gooey stuff away; let the doctors and scientists put it to good use. If you have a religious objection to this, get over it.

AFTERLIFE

Of course there's an afterlife. Otherwise, what the heck's the point of all this? Boy, will I be very angry and disappointed if there's nothing after. I'll be dead, but very angry. However, by the time we find out, it's likely too late to do much about it. The words naughty or nice come to mind here. But if there is reincarnation, I would definitely want to make some changes the next time around, if I have anything to say about it. Being born into a rich family would be number one. Otherwise, given the choice, coming back as a dog would be OK (except for Pavlov's dog); either that or as a sports bra (see *Sexist*). Going to hell is probably being reincarnated as a doormat or a toilet or something. Anyway, I've got a deal with some of my friends that whoever goes first will put in a good word for the others. Can't hurt, right? So look me up when you get to the other side. I won't be too hard to spot—just look for the guy with the tarnished halo who thinks he knows everything. On second thought, maybe I would be hard to find.

AGE

You're only as old as you feel because, after all, age is a state of mind and just a number. But here are a few questions I have: Why is it that when we're younger, we want to be older, and when we've been around for a while, we long for those younger days? If you're 50 and expect to live to be a hundred, does that make you half dead? And since the average age in America is 39, if you're over 40, does that make you above average? Some people grow old gracefully and, like a fine wine, get better with age (see *Late Bloomer*). Others—oh well; sometimes it's the miles, not the years. Remember: the older you get, the smarter you get (they call that experience). You also become more sure of yourself and more set in your ways. That's good and bad. But no matter how old you are, it's best to be young at heart. Which is why you always want to surround yourself with youth and their energy: it tends to rub off on you.

AGENDA

Having an agenda is a good way to plan your life. Just don't make it too hidden.

AGGRESSIVE

Aggressive behavior will only allow you to score points in sports. Being aggressive with anything or anyone else likely won't work for you.

AHA MOMENT

Yes, we all have those times when the light bulb finally goes off, and everything seems so clear. We love epiphanies. Too bad we often have to practically hit someone over the head until they finally get it. Get it?

AHEAD

Quitting when you're ahead is usually a good idea. Knowing when you're ahead isn't always so easy. Therefore, it's best to know your limits—and theirs. Now quitting when you're a leg or a foot ahead isn't so smart.

AIDS

AIDS is one of the most horrible and gruesome diseases known to man or woman, and if not treated is an automatic death sentence. Africa is being ravaged and destroyed by it, but we really don't seem to care because it's so far away and we think they speak funny languages. We better care! Researchers and scientists need lots of funding to find a cure, and we've got to help make it happen. However, there is something called prevention. So for God's sake, practice safe sex. And never share needles. You shouldn't be using needles anyway (see *Addiction*).

AIM HIGH

Go ahead and aim high, and swing for the fences; what do you have to lose (see *Risks*)? If you don't aim for the stars, you'll never know how high you can go.

AIR

How can gas stations, in all good conscience, charge for air? It's free almost everywhere else, isn't it? I guess capitalism has reached a new low.

AIR GUITARS

Come on. Why on earth would anyone want to pretend to be playing a guitar? And in public yet? Do you see anyone pretending to play a piano or trombone? Well, maybe you do, but that's weird too. Do you think they know how ridiculous they look? Probably not.

ALBATROSS

We all carry around lots of stuff in life. You really want to get rid of that nasty albatross around your neck though. Please do something about it, as it looks rather silly (see *Fashion*).

ALCOHOL

A little wine or a stiff drink now and then won't hurt you (see *Moderation*). But don't use it as an excuse to do something stupid, like driving. It impairs your judgment, and you may regret doing anything you wouldn't do otherwise. Who are you kidding? Alcohol is a drug, and a very dangerous one at that. Unfortunately, it gives some people liquid courage. And there's no such thing as a happy drunk. The only happy one is the one who takes advantage of you when you're tipsy.

ALIENS

Why the hell are we searching for other life forms? Don't our esteemed scientists ever go to the movies? We should lie very low, because if they find us, that means they are more advanced than we are. And in that case, they will eat us. Who is doing the thinking here? I worry about things like this. Somebody has to. Maybe you should too.

ALIMONY

Yes, I know all too well that the concept of alimony is an attempt to somewhat equalize income between two ex-spouses. It's a shame that when it's over, it usually all boils down to money (alimoney).

ALIVE

Because it's so great to be alive, live it with gusto (whatever that is). It beats the alternative—at least I think it does.

ALL CONSUMING

Whatever it is that's bothering you, don't let it take over your life—it'll drive you crazy (see *Perspective*). Lighten up already.

ALL GOOD THINGS

All good things don't always have to come to an end, you know. If nothing else, they can stay alive through your memories. Nothing wrong with that.

ALL OF YOUR EGGS IN ONE BASKET

It's always best not to have all of your eggs in one basket. First of all, if you drop it, they all break. Not that I care, mind you, as I don't like eggs. But if you've got too much riding on someone or something, there's a good chance you'll be disappointed in the end. Then what would you do? That's why it's best to spread out your risk (see *Plan B*).

ALL OVER THE MAP

You always want to stay focused, as you'll save a lot of gas, time and energy if you're not all over the map.

ALLOWANCE

Children should get a weekly allowance in exchange for doing their daily chores. It's the best way for them to learn the value of money and the responsibilities involved in helping to maintain a household. Start 'em early on the American way (see *Capitalism*). However, paying them $300 per week seems a bit excessive to me.

ALL'S FAIR IN LOVE AND WAR

Who says that all's fair in love and war? Nothing is fair in war. War really sucks. And when love is blind, it's usually not very fair either.

ALL'S WELL THAT ENDS WELL

So is all well when it ends well? That would be yes, as the end is way more important than the beginning. It's all about how you wind up.

ALL YOU CAN EAT

What a horrible idea this "all you can eat" is. If it's all put out in front of you so you can eat like a pig, you will (see *Portion Control*). Some people take this term very literally and actually end up eating all of everything. Be careful, as you don't want to get between them and their food, as you may be taking your life in your hands.

ALL YOU NEED IS LOVE

All you need is love? Can you live on love alone? Hardly, so get your head out of the clouds (see *Reality*). Love will only get you so far. You need lots of things—food, shelter and money, for instance. Love sure helps though.

ALONE

Being alone and being lonely are two different things. Solitude can be a great time to sit back and reflect, as you can always use some alone time to get introduced to yourself. However, loneliness is never fun. Just remember that you're never really alone. Even when you think you're alone, you're not alone. Someone or something is always with you. You just gotta look around.

ALONG FOR THE RIDE

No one likes to be used all the time, so keep your eyes out for hangers-on, as sometimes it's hard to lose them. And it's usually a very one-way ride. At least make sure they wear a seatbelt.

ALTER EGO

We all have this image of ourselves that no one else can see. We think of ourselves as the one who will stand up to some asshole boss or chase down the bad guy who just stole that lady's purse. We can run a marathon if we want to or lose those extra 20 pounds in a week and a half. It's always nice to dream, and it's good to have those creative juices flowing. You just don't want to get too carried away with the other you, as you may be disappointed.

ALWAYS

The best ways are to always:

Aim high.
Avoid staring straight into oncoming headlights.
Back up your files.
Be clean shaven (girls too—you know what I mean).
Be fair.
Be faithful.
Behave yourself.
Be honest with yourself.
Believe.
Believe in yourself.
Be on time (or mostly on time).
Be on your best behavior.
Be you.
Blot stains before trying to rub them out.
Bus your own trays.
Carry some cash with you.
Check the expiration date on your medicine.
Check your fly after visiting the bathroom.
Clean up after yourself.
Clean your outdoor grill before reuse.
Clear the snow off your car before you drive away.
Cover your mouth when you cough.
Double-check the recipient's address before you send an e-mail.
Do what you say you'll do.
Do your chores.
Finish what you start.
Flush when you're done.
Follow your dreams.
Follow your heart.
Give a good tip.
Go down swinging.
Have a daily routine.
Have an exit strategy.
Have an open mind (well, usually anyway).
Have a spring in your step.
Have some blueberries (best fruit for you).
Hold your ground.

Hug and kiss your mom and dad.
Keep your car doors locked while driving.
Keep your head up (and your chin too).
Keep your room clean.
Kiss your children goodnight.
Kiss your life mate goodnight.
Knock before entering any closed door.
Know the value of a dollar (one hundred cents).
Know your limitations.
Know yourself.
Lead with your strengths.
Leave the house expecting to meet your boss.
Leave well enough alone.
Listen to your heart.
Look both ways before crossing the street.
Look like you know what you are doing.
Look presentable.
Make your bed after you get up.
Mind your manners.
Pass on the left.
Pay attention.
Pick up after yourself.
Play nice.
Proofread your work.
Put the toilet seat down when you're done.
Put things back where you found them.
Put your napkin on your lap.
Remember who your friends are.
Repeat your phone number when leaving a voicemail message.
Respect authority (especially if they're bigger than you are).
Respect boundaries.
Respect intelligence.
Respect other's privacy.
Respect other's privates.
Respect other's time.
Respect your elders.
Replace toilet paper to roll over the top (paper towels too).
Return borrowed items.
Sit back and admire your work.
Speak authoritatively (even if you don't know what you're talking about).
Speak the truth (or almost always).

Stand and sit up straight.
Stay grounded.
Stay to the right (in America anyway).
Stretch before and especially after exercise.
Take a mint when it's offered.
Take the high road.
Take your hat off indoors.
Take your time.
Tell your children you love them.
Tell your honey you love them too.
Think before you speak (reversing this order is a big mistake).
Tip the wait staff (unless the service is horrible).
Treat people as you'd like to be treated.
Tuck your shirt in.
Turn off the light when you leave the room (TV too).
Use spell-check before sending an e-mail.
Use sunscreen when you're outside.
Use those tushie protectors when sitting on a public toilet.
Use your turn signal when changing lanes.
Wait your turn.
Wash your hands after using the bathroom.
Wash your hands before you eat.
Wear safety goggles when using power tools.
Wipe off your shoes before you come into the house.
Yield the right of way.

AMBIVALENCE

Ah, who cares about ambivalence (see *Voting*)?

AMBULANCE CHASERS

Attorneys who are attracted to tragedies like vultures, with a very self-serving agenda, are the ones who give this very worthy profession a bad name.

AMBULANCES

You're supposed to stay out of the way of ambulances, not hold up traffic and gawk at them, you know. That goes for fire trucks too (see *Rubbernecking*).

AMERICAN

It's great to be an American, and we're lucky to live here. Be proud. Be very proud.

AMERICAN DREAM

The American dream is one of the things that make this country great. Of course, it's unique to our country, and the opportunities here are absolutely limitless. Keep the dream alive.

AMERICA THE BEAUTIFUL

America is the best country in the world (see *Patriotism*). Or so I'm told, as I haven't been to any other countries (see *Travelitis*). But that's what they say, and I don't doubt them for a minute. God knows, we're all not so beautiful, but this country sure is, so keep it clean. Land of the free, home of the brave.

AMUSEMENT RIDES

I guess there are people in this world who like to throw up. That's my only explanation for the strange attraction of so many to being flipped upside down and in circles, in unnatural positions and at Mach speeds. And they call that fun? Maybe the fun happens when the ride is finally over. If they enjoy that feeling so much, wouldn't it be easier (and cheaper) to simply stick their fingers down their throats?

ANAL

This word is used to describe lots of types of behavior. My guess is that it's not a compliment, as it doesn't have such a lovely connotation. They're really calling you a bad name—but don't get all anal about it.

ANAL SEX

Yeech! The tush was designed to be an exit, not an entrance (see *Hygiene*). Guide yourself accordingly.

ANGELS

You can see angels every day; you just may not know it. Look at the face of a baby; look into their eyes. No, they're not very angelic when they're crying or pooping; but just listen to that giggle. If that's not the sound of an angel, I don't know what is. Even the worst ones are really angels, especially when they're asleep. Plenty of smart people believe in angels—I mean the flying around kind. You know, special angels that watch over you, and all. Until someone can prove to me that they don't exist, I kind of believe in them too (see *Guardian Angels*).

ANGER

There is way too much anger is this world. Sure, we all get mad, and some get very mad far too often. But the key is to control it and keep it in check (that's a chess term). If you have an anger management problem (someone will tell you), get help. Anyway, anger never solves the problem; it just adds to it. Nobody likes people who are mad all the time. So keep that in mind if you plan to get along in our society.

ANNIVERSARIES

I don't care much for anniversaries. It's typically a date set aside to commemorate an event that occurred in the past. We celebrate the number of years we are married (or divorced), at our job or in our house. We also recognize the date someone passed away, a hurricane wiped out a neighborhood or a war began. Why must we schedule a date to be happy each year to commemorate a joyous event? Shouldn't we be happy about that all year? Same with a sad occasion. Do we need to set aside a day every year to remember to be sad? If we really miss the people we lost, that sadness often comes to us when we think of them. And what should we do if we have a scheduled day to be happy on the same day we're supposed to be sad? See what I mean?

ANNOYING

Yes, some of us go out of our way to be annoying, as that's one way people probably won't forget us (see *Pain In The Ass*). Ask my children all about that.

ANONYMOUS

If you're somebody, others tend to have high expectations of you. That may be good or bad, so sometimes you may just want to consider being a nobody.

ANOREXIA

Eat, for God's sake. There's such a thing as being way too skinny.

ANSWERS

No one (especially me) has all of the answers. If anyone says they do, they don't. As for me, it's all I can do just to know the questions. Now you want to be careful, as every question usually does have a solution, but it might not be the one you're looking for. Remember: the smartest people in the world are those who admit they don't always know the answer. That would make me smart, in my book. (This is my book, you know).

ANSWER TO

Ultimately in life there is only one person you really have to answer to: That's you, silly (see *Fooling Yourself*).

ANTAGONIZE

If you're going to start a fight, you better be ready to finish it.

ANTICIPATION

Sometimes it seems like it takes forever for your birthday to arrive, the workday to end or the ketchup to come out of the bottle. The anticipation (and the waiting) can drive you crazy. Especially when, after all of the pent-up demand, the prize ends up being rather underwhelming. Oh well.

ANYBODY CAN DO THAT

If anybody can do it, then they would, right? Most things look much easier to do than they really are. Just ask a magician.

ANYTHING

Unless you know everything and have everything, anything really is possible (see *Optimist's Creed*).

APPEARANCES

Seeing can be very deceiving, as things aren't always as they appear. So don't take everything at face value or judge a book by its cover (see *Silly Phrases*).

APPEASING

It's good to get along, but it's another thing to really bend over backwards (or frontwards) for someone just to make them happy (see *Self-Respect*). Appeasement didn't work for Neville Chamberlain (look it up); it won't work for you either.

APPETITE

If your eyes are bigger than your tummy, close your eyes (see *Moderation*).

APPLE A DAY

Does an apple a day really keep the doctor away? It likely does, as it's a step toward healthy eating habits (see *Fruits and Vegetables*). Just a step, mind you.

APPRECIATION

We often don't appreciate things or people until we don't have them. Sure, it's always nice to have more; but remember that you could always have less. Be thankful for what you have.

APPROVAL

The one you ultimately have to please is yourself. So don't spend all your time looking for someone else's approval. Living your life shopping for nods and acknowledgements and being dictated by another's opinions will get you nowhere.

ARCHITECTURAL PLANS

I can look at building plans until the cows come home (whatever that means) and still never know what it's going to look like. Some people have the knack of visualizing these plans, which is very cool, and some don't. I don't.

ARE

You are what you are, and some things just can't be changed. So be proud and show everybody what you're made of. And stop concentrating on what you're not. After all, it's what you are that makes you, not what you aren't.

ARGUING

There's an art to arguing which I haven't quite mastered, but here's what I know. Good preparation is the key—and you don't want to underestimate your competition. A good arguer will know when to zip it and when to fold (that's an origami term). Make sure you have a backup argument, sometimes called Plan B. Occasional blinking is OK, but excessive blinking is not recommended, as it's a sign of losing. Raising your voice is also not the winning way. Always remember that some things just aren't worth arguing about. If you argue about everything, nobody will want to be in your company (see *Pick Your Battles*).

ARGUING WITH YOURSELF

Yup, we all have two of us inside; and those two constantly argue with each other. Should we go to work or school today or should we call in sick? Should we eat that very tempting piece of chocolate cake or stick to our diet? It's a wonder we ever get anything done with all of that internal dialogue and noise going on. In the end, we should just listen to the one who's right. And deep down inside, we always know which one that is, don't we now (see *Conscience*)?

ARM TAPPERS

Don't you just hate it when someone is talking to you and they insist on tapping your arm as they're speaking? Like there is any way to ignore their incessant ramblings when they are right in front of you. I guess they already know they are going to bore the hell out of you and have to keep hitting you to make sure you haven't fallen asleep.

AROUND THE CORNER

You never know what's around the corner—which could be good or could be bad. They call that exciting. So do I.

ARRESTED DEVELOPMENT

Some people never grow up. Something happened at the end of their teen years, and they just stopped growing, maturing and learning. Fortunately, it's never too late to pick up where you left off. Problem is, these people are the last to know they're still living inside an 18-year-old noggin.

ARROGANT vs. COCKY

Being cocky means that you're sure of yourself, which can be OK. Being arrogant just means that you're a jerk. If your shit doesn't stink, if you're better than everybody else, if you're God's gift to the world, then by all means let everyone else know it. Show them what an asshole you can be. Don't be shy.

ART

How do they do it? Talk about creativity; talk about imagination; talk about perfection. The skills and abilities they possess are truly exceptional and remarkable. Paintings that look like photographs, abstract pictures with glorious colors, sculptures that can pass for the real thing. It's a gift, which makes it an art, not a science. Sure, what one person considers a masterpiece, another may view as dreck (see *Yiddish Expressions*). But true art is someone's interpretation and expression of the world around them. The best are exceptional in their depiction and imagination—and God bless them. Simply genius. Thank goodness we have art galleries and museums to house their treasures forever (hopefully), representing a commitment to preserve a civilized society. Way to go, art.

ARTICULATE

I sure do admire those who speak well and have a real way with words. To be able to put the right words and phrases together, and having them effortlessly roll off the tongue, is truly a rare talent. Another art, I guess. As for me, I've got way too many marbles in my mouth. So do most of us.

AS GOOD AS IT GETS

It can always get better, as there are really no limits on good. Good is good.

ASHAMED

Anybody who says they've never done anything to be ashamed of is either deluding themselves or lying. We've all done things we should be ashamed of.

The key is to admit it, try to rectify it, not repeat it and move on. Doing that is nothing to be ashamed of.

ASK

It rarely hurts to ask. Got a question? Ask away. Need something? Ask for it. Just don't keep asking the same thing over and over. After all, you typically don't get what you don't ask for. And remember: if you don't ask, the answer is always no. The response may really help and surprise you (see *Learning*).

ASK FOR HELP

You know, you don't have try to do everything yourself. Go ahead and ask for help; the person you're asking might even like it. People usually enjoy feeling needed, you know. But going overboard and always asking for aid is probably not a good idea. You could lose a lot of friends that way.

ASK HIM/HER OUT

Go ahead, be daring and give it a shot (see *Adventure*). You never know unless you try, right? What's the worst thing they can say? No? Then you'll know they have bad taste. It won't be the first no in your life; and it won't be the last.

ASLEEP AT THE WHEEL

If you're driving and nodding off, for God's sake, pull over and get out of the car. Walk around, do some jumping jacks, breathe in some fresh air—whatever. Then get back in and drive until you're tired again. The driver always has to be alert; otherwise you're going to get into some big trouble. Caffeine helps too.

ASPIRE

Yes, aspiring and perspiring are two different things. However, if you truly aspire to better yourself, you may end up perspiring along the way.

ASSAULT WEAPONS

There is absolutely no reason on God's green earth that anyone needs to possess assault weapons. Not sports enthusiasts, not hunters, not criminals, not little old ladies—no one. To fire an automatic clip of 30 rounds into a target, animal or little old lady is simply asinine. These weapons often get into the hands of angry, nutty people, resulting in horrible disasters. Owning assault weapons to protect our homes is ludicrous. We don't need that kind of protection (see *Overkill*). If you follow that logic, maybe it's best to have a Sherman tank sitting on your front lawn. It's no surprise to me that these weapons have a name that begins with ass.

ASSERTIVE

Stand your ground and let your voice be heard. Just know when you've been standing there too long.

ASSES

The human ass is a very durable piece of equipment. And contrary to popular belief, you can't freeze, work, scare, sneeze, sweat or laugh your ass off. You can't bust your ass either, even though it's already cracked (some are more cracked than others). And making an ass out of yourself is always a possibility, especially for those with oversize cabooses. There's also no such thing as a dumb-ass (there is such a thing as a dumbwaiter, though), because most of us don't have any brains there. And if you have to ask: yes, your ass does look big in that. However, you could wipe your ass off (see *Hemorrhoids*), so be careful. All this means that your ass will likely always be there. That's not necessarily good news, as some of us could do with a little less ass and a little more brains.

ASSHOLES

Being called an asshole is far from a term of endearment. It's mostly association with one of the more disgusting of bodily functions. And that part of the body is the grossest on even the loveliest of beauties. For most of us, it takes way too much effort to be an asshole. Best to use all of that energy to do something productive—like being nice. Now if you don't pay attention to anything else in this book, listen closely to this: Don't be an asshole (see *Exclamation Points*)!

ASSUME

They say that when you assume, you make an ass out of u and me. No, you don't. You just make an ass out of you. Same with presume.

Asses

ATE

Just like everything else, there are good ate's, and there are bad ate's. (Remember: you are what you eat.)

These are good, and good for you:

Accentuate

Ameliorate

Arbitrate

Articulate

Authenticate

Bifurcate

Calculate

Calibrate

Celebrate

Chocolate

Coagulate

Cogitate

Collaborate

Commiserate

Communicate

Concentrate

Considerate

Consolidate

Consummate

Contemplate

Coordinate

Copulate

Create

Dedicate

Delegate

Deliberate

Delicate

Dinner date

Dissipate

Donate

Don't be late

Duplicate

Educate

Ejaculate

Elaborate

Elucidate

Emulate

Enumerate

Excavate

Exfoliate

Exonerate

Fascinate

Fornicate

Fortunate

Fumigate

Go out on a date

Hesitate

Hydrate

Illuminate

Immaculate

Incorporate

Ingratiate

Innovate

Inseminate

Insinuate

Integrate

Investigate

Masticate

Masturbate

Matriculate

Medicate

Meditate

Moderate

Motivate

Must be something I ate

Navigate

Negotiate

Only eat one plate(ful)

Open the gate
Originate
Ovulate
Participate
Passionate
Percolate
Populate
Postulate
Pontificate
Prefabricate
Procreate
Pronate
Propagate

Punctuate
Reciprocate
Refrigerate
Regenerate
Regulate
Resonate
Saturate
Speculate
Stipulate
Tabulate
Tolerate
Urinate
Validate

Stay away from these ate's, as they will likely give you indigestion:

Agitate
Aggravate
Alienate
Annihilate
Barbiturate
Berate
Can't wait
Capitulate
Confiscate
Decimate
Denigrate
Desecrate
Desperate
Deviate
Dominate
Don't eat the whole plate
Don't know what I ate
Eliminate
Emasculate
Eradicate
Evaporate
Exacerbate
Exaggerate
Exasperate
Hibernate
Humiliate

I can't believe what I just ate
Inaccurate
Inappropriate
Incarcerate
Incinerate
Infatuate
Interrogate
Intimidate
Intoxicate
Inundate
Irate
Irritate
Jailbait
Just plain late
Liquidate
Mandate
Manipulate
Must've been something I ate
Mutilate
Nauseate
Probate
Obfuscate
Obliterate
Overstate
Prevaricate
Regurgitate

Renegotiate
Stuck at the gate
Suffocate
Terminate
Underestimate

Unfortunate
Vegetate
Violate
Watergate

AT LEAST

Well, at least you're not in a wheelchair, at least you're not starving, at least you didn't finish last. For some reason, we all use those facing difficulties to put things into perspective and realize that suffering is all relative. However, "at least" rarely has its desired results. The pain, disappointment, fear and anger are still paramount in their minds and difficult to reduce by intellectualizing. Keep trying (see *Cheering Section*), but don't be surprised if your well-intended attempts fall on deaf ears. Try to tell a child with a scraped knee that it doesn't hurt (good luck with that). Of course it's not hurting you, so it really is all relative.

ATMs

Whoever invented ATMs had a wonderful idea. Getting money without going to the bank—who'da thought (see *Impersonal*)? No standing in line or waiting for the bank to open. Get your money at midnight on Sunday, holidays, whenever. What's not to like?

ATROPHY

If you don't use it, you're going to lose it. Sitting around too much makes your muscles (and everything else) turn to mush. You don't want to be mushy, do you (see *Exercise*)?

ATTENTION

Some of us crave attention way too much, but it's the little babies who really need it. We should just settle for being noticed once in a while. Those who insist on always being the center of attention have a genuine problem. Now standing at attention is usually unnecessary, but paying attention is very important. Listen, am I just talking to myself or what?

ATTITUDE

When it comes right down to it, they say it's all about attitude and that attitude is everything. It really is. A positive attitude and a strong will can get you through some very rough spots. Your mind is very powerful and can get your body to do some pretty amazing things. Think about that the next time you're hurting and your body needs to heal. Your attitude affects everything you do or say during your entire life, so make it a good one. Have an attitude of gratitude (see *Count Your Blessings*).

ATTRACTION

Do opposites attract? Well, in physics they do. With humans it often happens too; otherwise it's hard to explain why some people are attracted to each other. The docile one needs the pushy one to get anywhere, and the pushy one needs the docile one to keep things calm. That's just the way it is, I guess.

AUTHORITY

We have to have authority in this world. Otherwise, everyone would just do whatever they wanted whenever they wanted. That's why you should respect authority and not undermine it. If you complain too much, they may put you in charge; then we'd all be in big trouble.

AUTOGRAPHS

Now let me get this straight. A complete stranger (see *Celebrities*) puts their name on a piece of paper and that becomes a cherished possession? They don't know who you are, as you mean nothing to them, but somewhere along the line we were taught that this souvenir should mean so much to us. I'd much rather collect something useful, like IOUs. So by all means, hold onto those autographs, as they might be worth nothing someday. Go figure.

AUTO RACING

OK, call me stupid (you won't be the first one), but I don't get it. You watch a bunch of cars going around and around in circles for hours and hours on end. And they call this a sport? Is that a lot different from watching flies fly? I guess the attraction is waiting for the crashes (see *Morbid*).

AVALANCHE

Why, oh why do we let things pile up or ignore obvious problems and end up with an avalanche falling on us (see *Procrastination*)? If we deal with the here and now, here and now, we'll avoid all that insufferable snow.

AVERAGE PERSON

If there is such a thing, the average person must be pretty boring. Which is why I challenge you to find me one. They don't exist. So being average isn't something you'd want to aspire to. Now being above average—I'm all for that.

AVOIDANCE

You can try to avoid your problems, but they'll never get solved (or go away) that way (see *Reality*).

AWAKENING

Awakening isn't always about getting up from a snooze. Sometimes life hits you smack in the face and you see things very differently. That's called an awakening. You heard it here.

AWARENESS

Use those eyes in the back of your head. Pay attention, and always know what's going on, where you are and how you got there. Be aware of your surroundings, or they might simply envelope you.

AWAY

You usually want to put things away. This sounds stupid, but it really does help you find things later. You know, a place for everything and everything all over the place (see *Neatness*).

AWESOME

We are very complicated beings. That's pretty awesome when you think about it. I think about it.

BABE RUTH

I don't care what anybody says. Babe Ruth had the most influence and impact on any sport ever—ever. Baseball was never the same after Babe. He was the most popular sports legend there ever was. More people knew his name than the president's, for Pete's sake. (Who's Pete, anyway?) Babe Ruth walked the walk and talked the talk and struck out plenty too. And I believe he did call that home run dedicated to the sick child. Even if it isn't true, it makes a great story. We've got to believe in something, don't we?

BABIES

Where do babies come from? You have to look in a different book for that. Let's just say they come from the miracle of birth. Think about it: they are so special, as they virtually define innocence. And so huggable. So it's no surprise that they're called bundles of joy. But having them and watching them smile and giggle is the easy part. They are only little toys for a short time. The daunting task is to help mold, nurture and raise them into mature, productive, happy and healthy adults. It's a lifelong project; not for them, but for you (see *Parenting*).

BABYING

This probably sounds obvious, but don't baby your children when they are no longer babies. It's normal to want to be protective and shield them from life's difficulties, but you've got to let them fly on their own after a while (see *Spoiled*). Otherwise you can end up stymieing their growth, making them destined to never be able to do anything on their own (see *Enabling*). And stop babying yourself, for goodness' sake; you're way too old for that.

BABY-SITTING

So who sits on babies, anyway? That would clearly get you into trouble (see *Abuse*). It should really be called baby-watching or child-watching, right?

BACKED INTO A CORNER

Sometimes it feels like the world is closing in on you and there's no way out. There always is, of course, especially if you think ahead and give yourself plenty of options. Staying out of corners couldn't hurt either.

BACK-SCRATCHING

No one really knows why, but having your back scratched just feels indescribably good. Maybe it's got to do with carving away dead skin. You can't get into too much trouble with this, especially if they scratch your back and you scratch theirs (see *Friends*).

BACKSTABBER

It's not a good idea to be a backstabber—or a backstab-ee, for that matter, as this is illegal in most states. Being a frontstabber probably isn't a good idea either. Another reason it's best to always know who your friends are.

BACTERIA

When you think of bacteria, you think about those nasty germs and such. However, there are plenty of good bacteria which each of us needs to survive. Does that mean we shouldn't strive to stay squeaky clean? No, but I'm sure it means something. I just don't know what.

Babying

BACK TO NORMAL

Whether we admit or not, we all crave order in our lives. Disruptions and distractions tend to unsettle us. However, it's hard to know what normal is in our quickly changing world.

BACK TO SQUARE ONE

When all else fails, it's not so bad to just start over. Sometimes you have no choice, and that's OK too.

BACKWARDS NAMES

Even I can spell these names—can't go wrong here. (The fancy term is palindrome.) Isn't it nice to know they can go backwards and forwards anytime they like?

Ada	Elle	Pop
Ana	Eve	Sis
Anna	Hannah	Tot
Asa	Ma'am	Yay (not a name,
Ava	Mom	but should be)
Bob	Nan	
Dad	Otto	

BAD

Take the good with the bad, or the bad with the good. Your choice (see *Balance*).

BAD APPLE

Does one bad apple spoil the whole bunch? Of course not. If you find a bad apple, just cast it aside and move on to the good ones. That goes for people too.

BAD BREATH

Try to always keep a mint handy, as you never know when you'll need it. If it looks like your present company is in pain every time you open your mouth, take that as a dead giveaway. One sure cure: hydrate, hydrate, hydrate (see *Water*).

BAD CALL

No team ever loses a game because of a bad call. They lose because they didn't capitalize on all of the other chances they had to win (see *Sports*).

BAD CHILDREN

There is no such thing as bad children—just bad moms and dads (see *Parenting*).

BAD DREAMS

You think you're the only one who dreams about falling, your teeth coming out or running around naked? You don't have that market cornered, you know. We all dream about that weird stuff. Keep away from pickles and ice cream late at night and those dream interpreters, because more than likely your bad dreams mean absolutely nothing.

BAD HABITS

Bad habits are so easy to fall into and so difficult to break (see *Discipline*). That's why they say that old habits die hard. It's a force of habit, you know.

BAD INVESTMENTS

It's always best to know when to fold 'em (see *Cut Your Losses*).

BAD MOODS

So they're in a bad mood. Ah, don't take it personally, as it likely has nothing to do with you. Everybody gets in a bad mood once in a while. If you leave them alone, they'll eventually get over it (see *Hope*).

BAD NEWS

We all have to deliver and receive bad news from time to time. It's part of life, and no one is immune. The key is to be as caring and sensitive as possible if you're delivering the message (see *Diplomatic*). If you're the recipient, remember that the bearer of bad news is just delivering the message, and it's best not to kill the messenger.

BAD TASTE

The higher the class level of the group you're with, the better chance you'll have of offending them with the stupid things you say. Best to know your crowd. If you say or do something in bad taste, no one will think you taste very good anyway.

BAD THINGS

Just because something bad happens to you, don't assume you deserve it or that you did anything wrong. Yes, bad things do happen to good people. That's just the way it is. Call it the law of averages. Try to make the best of it and learn from it. And always look for the silver lining; although sometimes you have to look real hard—sometimes extra real hard.

BAGGAGE

Boy, we all sure do carry around plenty of baggage (see *Living in the Past*). It's best to try to leave it with the other unclaimed luggage or it will really give you a very sore back. Actually, a sore lot of things.

BALANCE

I'm a big believer in balance. You know, what goes up always comes down; what goes around, comes around; take the good with the bad. Get the picture? Now pessimists will be dreading their good fortune, expecting bad things to be around the corner. Optimists will look at a bad day today and hope for a better one tomorrow. It has to work that way—it's balance. Think of it as a happy (or not so happy) medium. You want to lean toward the optimists.

BALDNESS

Some people have short legs, some have big ears and yes, some have little or no hair. So what? Putting a rug on your head won't turn you into someone else, just like lengthening your legs or cutting back on those elephant ears won't. (It didn't help Van Gogh now, did it?) Anyway, who are you kidding? We still know you're bald. And you are not fooling anyone with those stupid hair plugs, wearing hats all the time or other silly disguises (see *Comb Overs*)? And how come so many bald guys (not girls) grow beards? Are they trying to compensate or just hide their faces (see *You Are What You Are*)?

BARK

If your bark is worse than your bite, you may want to tone down the bark.

BASEBALL

Ah, the national pastime. Baseball sure is some sport. Think about it. It's got all of these parallels to life—first base, second base, third base, home run (see *Sex*). You're safe, you're out, double play, strike three, pop-up, extra innings. And every player has a chance to star. What's the matter, the game's too slow for you? Got a plane to catch or something? Sit back and take a load off—it's fun to play or watch baseball. But who thought up that stupid designated hitter rule in the wimpy American League? Since when do we have one-dimensional players? It's bad enough that the pitchers are so specialized—closers, semi-closers, only pitch to righties, only pitch to lefties, only pitch if it's sunny, only pitch on Thursdays. What's next? Baseball players who throw but don't catch? Come on, make those pitchers hit. Don't get me started. And what's with all that crotch grabbing—some ancient pagan ritual? Oh yeah, and don't forget: there's no crying in baseball. Ask Tom Hanks.

BASEBALL CAPS

I'll never understand why some guys (and gals) don't know how to wear a baseball cap. The brim is in the front, silly. To keep the sun out of your eyes, not to keep you from getting a red neck. That is, unless you have something against red necks (see *Prejudice*). You don't see them putting their pants or jerseys on backwards, do you? Why baseball caps?

BASEBALL COACHES

What is it that causes grown people to exhibit such childlike behavior when an ump's call doesn't go their way? They'll kick the dirt, yell and scream and stomp around like three-year-olds. Have you ever heard the umpire say, "Gee, I'm terribly sorry; on second thought, you're right—that really was a strike"? Dream on. Save your tirade for something that's important or productive (if there is such a thing).

BATED BREATH

I know what bad breath is, but bated breath? No idea. Maybe that's what you use to catch fish.

BATHROOM

Your bathroom isn't a library or an office; so keep the books (including this one) and magazines somewhere else. Unless you really like the ambiance in there, just take care of business and get out. I can think of much nicer places to spend my time, as the bathroom not really conducive for reading. Your tush will thank you (see *Hemorrhoids*).

BATTLES

Most of us seem to always have some battle or another going on. Sometimes it's even with ourselves. Although it may not seem like it at the time, most of these battles are unimportant. Lighten up, move on and give it a rest.

BE

To be, or not to be? Given the choice, I would recommend that you be:

Accepting
Accountable
Active
Adaptable
Affectionate
A gentleman (unless you're
    a girl)
A good friend
A good listener
A good sport
A good tipper
A leader
Alert
All that you can be
Altruistic
Amazing
A mensch (see *Yiddish
    Expressions*)
An advocate
Appreciative
A sport (pick up the tab once
    in a while)
Assertive

At peace
Attentive
Authentic
Available
Awake
Aware of your surroundings
Brilliant
Brave
Careful
Caring
Cause (that's why)
Cautious
Charitable
Charming
Classy
Clever
Comfy
Compassionate
Concise
Confident
Considerate
Consistent
Content

Content with your own company
Conversational
Cool
Cordial
Courageous
Courteous
Cozy
Creative
Credible
Cuddly
Curious
Dalton
Decisive
Dedicated
Definitive
Deliberate
Delicious
Determined
Dependable
Devil
Different
Diplomatic
Disciplined
Discrete
Distinctive
Dynamic
Effective
Efficient
Empathic
Empowered
Energetic
Energized (beam me up, Scotty)
Enlightened
Erotic
Ethical
Exotic
Expressive
Fair
Faithful
Fall
Firm

Flexible
Forgiving
Forthright
Forward
Free
Friend
Friendly
Frugal (not cheap)
Fruitful (and eat a lot of fruit)
Fulfilling
Funny
Gallant
Gentle
Generous
Genuine
Good
Good to yourself
Gracious
Grateful (full of grate)
Great
Gregarious
Grounded
Handy
Happy
Hardworking
Have
Helpful
Hind
Hive
Hold
Holden
Honest
Honorable
Human
Humble
Independent
Industrious
Informed
Inquisitive
Innovative
Inspired

Inspiring
In the moment
In tune
Jesus
Just
Kind
Lieve
Long
Loved
Loving
Low
Loyal
Mannerly
Mindful
Mine
Motivated
Mysterious
Natural
Neat
Neath
Nice
Nimble (thanks, Jack)
Noteworthy
Nurturing
Objective
Observant
Open
Organized
Orgasmic
Particular
Passionate
Patient
Perceptive
Persistent (but not annoying)
Personable
Polite
Positive
Practical
Pragmatic
Prepared
Proactive

Productive
Profound
Progressive
Prolific
Prompt
Proud
Prudent
Persuasive
Prompt
Quick (thanks again, Jack)
Ready
Real
Realistic
Reasonable
Reassuring
Reliable
Remarkable
Resilient
Resourceful
Resolute
Respectful
Responsible
Responsive
Right
Righteous
Safe
Satisfied
Selfless
Sensible
Sensitive
Silly
Simple
Sincere
Smart
Special
Specific
Speckled
Spectacular
Spiritual
Spontaneous
Somebody

Successful	Understanding
Supportive	Understood
Sure	Unique
Sure of yourself	Utiful
Sweet	Ware
Sympathetic	Warm
Tenacious	Way cool
Tender	Welcoming
Thankful	Well
Thoughtful	Well groomed
Tolerant	Well read
True	Wholesome
True to your school	Y.O.B.
Trusting	Yond
Trustworthy	Yourself
Unbiased	Y.U.

Be all of these things and you'll be going to heaven for sure. They may even make you a saint.

BEACH

Is it me, or is the beach much hotter than it used to be (see *Global Warming*)? And how about all of that beautiful, burning sand? It's so special to have it sticking to your skin, getting on your food and blowing in your eyes. Not to mention its uncanny ability to find its way into your most intimate of areas. Lovely.

BEANS

Beans, beans, they're good for your heart; the more you eat, the more you fart; the more you fart, the better you feel; so eat some beans with every meal. Well—no thanks for me. I don't like beans.

BEAT 'EM

So if you can't beat 'em, join 'em, right? Nah—just get the rules changed, or play a different game. But whatever you do, don't cheat.

BEATING A DEAD HORSE

I'm an expert at beating a dead horse (see *Obnoxious*). So go ahead and beat away, if that's your idea of a good time.

BEATING AROUND THE BUSH

It's great to be sensitive to others' feelings, but get to the point already. We don't have all day, you know.

BEATLES

The Beatles simply defined synergy: the whole is much greater than the sum of the parts. Wow, talk about group chemistry; they were clearly much better together than they were as individuals. The Beatles made a lasting impression on an entire generation, as their music was groundbreaking and extraordinary. When they were together, they lived up to their legend. And after they broke up, the best thing they ever did was not reunite. It would've been a huge disappointment, as it would be almost impossible to live up to the hype and expectations. I never understood their way of counting the days of the week though.

BEAUTY

Is beauty only skin deep? You bet it is, and those are wise words (unfortunately, not mine). Think of it as packaging. We're often disappointed at what's inside after we take off the wrapper, as looks can be very deceiving. But beauty isn't necessarily something you see. It's something you feel deeply within your soul, and comes from your mind and from your heart. Beauty really is in the eye of the beholder, and we know it when we see it. Don't forget that everyone has some beauty in them. Sometimes you just have to look real hard.

BEAUTY PAGEANTS

I have one question about beauty pageants: Why? It all seems rather silly and pointless to me (see *Beauty*).

BECAUSE I SAID SO

That's not an answer; it's more like a nasty statement or threat. Best not to answer a question that way.

BEGGING

Ask, don't beg. Begging is not very becoming.

BEGGING YOUR PARDON

I'd still ask, but remember: only governors can grant pardons. Beggars can't be choosers, you know.

BEGINNINGS

Every day is a new beginning. Good thing. Embrace it and enjoy it. That always gives you something to look forward to, you know (see *Tomorrow*).

BEHIND CLOSED DOORS

Yes, what people do in the privacy of their own homes is no one else's business. However, bomb making and other dastardly illegal activities become police business.

BEHIND THE CAMERA

Never volunteer to be the photographer, especially at a family event. Trust me, you really can't enjoy yourself if you're stuck taking pictures or shooting video the whole time. Volunteer someone else or hire a professional. That way the precious memories will be recorded and (hopefully) you'll get to have a good time. Otherwise disappear for a little while so no one will volunteer you.

BEHIND YOU

You'll never know how inspiring it is to have someone behind you until it happens. They can provide the extra spark of support you need to get you through the tough times, or to just get you through the day. Find someone to get behind and find someone to get behind you. Oftentimes, they're the same person (see *Angels*).

BEING FOLLOWED

If you're driving alone (especially at night) and fear that you're being followed, it's best to play it safe. Drive to the nearest police station or firehouse and lean on your horn. That will likely scare away the bad guys and/or get someone's attention (see *Safety*).

BEING HONEST WITH YOURSELF

One of the toughest things in life is to be honest with yourself. We can make all kinds of excuses and try to explain things away (see *Rationalizing*). But in the end, when it's just you and you, and no one else is around, it's very hard to escape the truth.

BELIEVE

Believe in something or someone. Start with yourself.

BELITTLE

To belittle anyone is to be very little. Very little. Why go that low?

BELLY BUTTON

Innies, outies—how do you really know if it's buttoned or not? Imagine going out of the house without your belly button buttoned? What would the neighbors think? And whose idea is that belly button lint?

BELLY SHIRTS

Oh girls? Little belly shirts should only be worn by those with little bellies. Boys? Don't bother.

BELONG

Join a group or organization and get active in it. It will give you a wonderful sense of belonging. You want that.

BEND DOWN

When you talk to little children, kneel down to their level. They really can't relate otherwise. Some of us find this easier than others—bending down, that is. Getting back up is usually the hard part.

BENEFIT OF THE DOUBT

Give them the benefit of the doubt already. It won't cost you anything. But remember: Screw me once, shame on you. Screw me twice, shame on me. Or something like that. Either way, you don't want to be screwed. But I digress (get used to it).

BE NICE

It never hurts to be nice. Well maybe sometimes it hurts a little. But still be nice. And play nice (see *Manners*).

BE PREPARED

To be prepared isn't just some Boy or Girl Scout thing. You'll never know when you'll need those extra batteries, emergency flares, protective gear (see *Condoms*) or that spare tire. Not the one around your gut though. You don't need that. Anyway, think ahead.

BEST

Whatever you do, you want to always try your best. Can't go wrong there. As hard as it is to become the best, it's a lot harder to stay the best. And it sure can be very lonely at the top. The steeper the climb, the harder the fall.

BETRAYAL

Never betray a friend. Never betray your family. Never betray your country. Never betray a confidence. Otherwise, have a good time.

BETTER

No matter what you have, do or say, someone will always have, do or say something better, maybe even much more better. So what? It's a big world, and there's room for them too. No need to let it diminish what you have, say or do.

BETTER PLACE

Every day we should all try to make this world a better place. You sinners and transgressors might want to aim for at least twice a day. It's certainly a challenge, but it's our job. That's why we're here, you know.

BETTER YOURSELF

Keep striving to better yourself. It's not easy, but you should try to gain the wisdom, will and strength to be better. Set goals every day or you'll become quite stagnant and boring (see *Mediocrity*). Stagnant people smell. And they just don't smell through their noses.

BIBLE

Yes, there is a reason they call the Bible the Good Book. It's because you can learn a lot by reading it. But you shouldn't take everything in it too literally, as I believe it was written to be an anecdotal guide to life's lessons. Unfortunately, some try to follow the words too specifically and miss the real points of the stories. Just be good to your fellow man (and woman)—that's the whole point. There must not have been too many people in the world in those days, and things must have been rather informal, what with everybody being on a first-name basis and all. And talk about big families. How on earth did Jacob feed 13 children back then? Oy!

BIBLE BELT

How does one wear a Bible belt? It's probably a chastity belt or something. Anyway, I don't think they're very fashionable anymore.

BICKERING

All that sniping is a complete waste of effort, as it accomplishes absolutely nothing. Ever hear of holding your tongue? Well try. You know, it takes two, so it's very hard to bicker if one party won't bicker back.

BIDDING

Don't get stuck doing someone else's bidding. Let them bid for themselves (see *Self-Respect*). That goes for auctions and everything else.

BIG BANG THEORY

The Big Bang Theory makes lots of sense to me and shouldn't conflict with any belief, concept or explanation of creation. Everything started somewhere and somehow, right? Boom!

BIG BROTHER

Yes, Big Brother is everywhere. He's hiding in our computers, GPS devices and cell phones, to name a few. Speed cameras watch us, our buying habits get tracked and our banking activities are closely monitored. Another reason to be on your best behavior.

BIGGER

Bigger isn't always better. Take it from me, a vertically impaired guy—less is sometimes more. And the bigger they are, the harder they fall. They really do.

BIGOTRY

There ought to be a law against bigotry. Actually, there are plenty of laws against it, but unfortunately, it's very hard to legislate morality. Prejudice is the result of some deep-rooted ignorance. Do all you can to prevent it, as it has no place in this world.

BIG PICTURE

Can't see the forest for the trees? That's a problem. So stop getting lost in the details, and step back and look at the big picture. Trust me—you don't want to be the type that is happy re-arranging the deck chairs on the Titanic.

BIG SHOT

Be my guest; go ahead and act like a big shot. Just remember that there are always lots of bigger shots.

BIKE HELMETS

Why are bike helmets typically mandated only for those under 16 years old? Are we too smart to fall from our bikes and hit our heads when we become adults? Hardly. Who cares how stupid you look in them (and you do look stupid in them)—it works. How good do you think you'll look in a casket or, worse yet, in a wheelchair for the rest of your life? Don't be an idiot—wear a bike helmet (see *Risk*).

BILLBOARDS

Talk about a blight on our environment. Take those billboards down already. They really make an ugly area uglier.

BINGEING

Bingeing is a completely absurd and controllable type of behavior that serves no redeemable purpose. Unless you call sticking your finger down your throat and throwing up redeemable.

BIODEGRADABLE

We are a wasteful society, believing everything is disposable. When we're done, we just throw it out, right? When it comes to food residue and such, instead of clogging the landfills, just leave it out and let Mother Earth recycle it. Just put it in a neat place where she can find it.

BIORHYTHMS

Of course there's something to biorhythms. Our bodies are constantly talking to us; unfortunately, we're not always listening. And we can make them do all kinds of important and cool things if we just try. Too bad the mainstream medical establishment hasn't embraced this concept yet.

BIRDS

I like to admire birds from far away—very far away. They must go to some special military school to learn to fly in those cool formations when they're part of a flock. How do they know which one is the leader? Probably the one with the biggest beak.

BIRD SHIT

You can usually walk around dog shit or horse shit. But bird shit? It's like the lottery: you never know when you'll get kissed by the lucky stick. If it hits you, you'll surely know it. And don't you just love it when those dive-bombers hit the windshield? Can't they just poop in the woods like the bears?

BIRTH CONTROL

We all have lots of choices in life. If you don't intend to bring a baby into this world as a result of your wild lovemaking, use some protection. It's not that complicated. However, if you're waiting until you are nice and settled and are ready to have children, you never will. Have them before you're ready, but after you know what you are doing. Just know what you are getting yourself into (yes, the pun is intended; see *Parenting*).

BIRTHDAY CARDS

You're not going to get cards unless you send them. So here's my latest brainstorm: Because it's so hard to remember everyone's birthday, I'm going to send all the people I know a birthday card on January 1 of each year. It's up to them to decide when to open it, because they probably know when their magic day is. We'll call it the lazy approach to birthday card giving. I'll use some innocuous, generic, pre-printed card, and everyone would be included in this very special mailing (see *Insincere*). What's not to like?

BIRTHDAYS

Although some of us may deny it, having a day that's unique and special to you is rather nice. The fact that you share that day with millions of others is of little consequence. It's at least one day of the year when it's mandatory for everyone to be nice to you (see *Rules*).

BITING OFF MORE THAN YOU CAN CHEW

Sometimes your eyes are bigger than your stomach. It's best to only put on your plate whatever you can consume. Therefore even people with big mouths (and/or big stomachs) have their limits. It's always good to know yours.

BITING THE HAND THAT FEEDS YOU

Always know where your bread is buttered. It's one thing to be a person of principle; just make sure it doesn't interfere with being pragmatic.

BITING YOUR TONGUE

It's really hard to say something nasty when your teeth are clenched on your tongue. And you're probably much better off. The worst that can happen is that you get a bloody mouth. At least that way it's self-inflicted.

BLAME

So it's better to give than receive, huh? Well, here's the exception. Where applicable, blame is something you should take but not give (see *Do The Right Thing*). Now don't let your guilty conscience completely overcome you. Hurricanes, tornadoes, wars—those you can blame on somebody else. Feel free.

BLANK CHECK

No, you really don't want to give a blank check to anybody or for anything (see *Taking Advantage*).

BLASTING MUSIC

It's lovely that you enjoy your music (or what you call music). However, just because you like it doesn't mean that everyone else likes it or wants to hear it. Actually, we really hate to hear your music blasting out of your speakers, shattering our eardrums. And God knows why it's always our luck to be stuck behind you in bumper-to-bumper traffic, no less. Turn it down or suffer your own consequences (see *Hearing*).

BLESS YOU

Why is it that when someone sneezes, you're supposed to wish them well? Is having snot coming out of your nose something to celebrate? Whoopee! In any case, I prefer to use the German term, "goes-in-tight." Or should that be tightly?

BLIND FAITH

It's one thing to have very strong beliefs that are very near and dear to you, and can't be (and shouldn't be) changed very easily. It's an entirely other thing to blindly follow someone or something without any rational reason. That kind of blind faith will prevent you from seeing the obvious.

BLOOD PRESSURE

Want to see your blood pressure go up? Just sit impatiently in the doctor's office; the longer you wait, the higher it gets (see *Anxiety*). It's called the directly proportional rule. But here's where most doctors make a mistake. They should always check your pressure after the physical, not before. Your blood pressure goes way down after they tell you you're not dying. This is called the indirectly proportional rule.

BLOWING IN THE WIND

If your attitudes change by whichever way the wind blows, you're missing something (see *Substance*). You're actually missing a lot of things.

BLOWING YOUR BRAINS OUT

Blowing your brains out is not a very good idea (see *Suicide*), as it's very messy. Find a better way to deal with your frustrations, as ending things doesn't solve much. And it will really ruin your nice clothes.

BLOWING YOUR NOSE

Ever see those professional athletes standing on the sidelines, blowing their noses without a hankie? One-handed, no less. That takes real talent—I can't do it. However, nobody wants to see them or you spewing snot everywhere (see *Hygiene*), so use a tissue. Use a couple of tissues. Don't you just hate seeing someone using a napkin (a linen one, naturally) to blow? And what's with those people who have to look into their handkerchief after they're done? What do they expect to find in there? Yesterday's news?

BLOW JOBS

Why do you suppose they call them blow jobs? I think I missed the blowing part. Shouldn't they be called suck jobs? And I don't get the job part either.

BLOW-UP DOLLS

C'mon guys (or girls), what are you thinking? I really get the no-talking-back quality, but having your way with vinyl dolls? They really don't make good friends, you know. To each his own, but definitely not this guy.

BLUE

Too bad that for such a beautiful and vibrant color, blue often has such a negative connotation. You know, I'm feeling blue today or singing the blues. Go figure. Of course, everybody sees a different shade of blue.

BLUE BALLS

Having blue balls is very uncomfortable, as it is both painful and preventable (see *Cock Teasing*). However, it's really a guy thing, so most girls don't have to worry about it (see *Penis Envy*); unless of course they're the instigator.

BLUE EYES

Yes, blue eyes are very pretty. But like most things, color doesn't really matter.

BLUE SKIES

Behind all of those clouds, rain, snow, sleet and hail is the bluest of skies. Always.

BLUNTNESS

Being blunt isn't always so bad, as people at least know where you stand. It's surely better than beating around the bush (see *Diplomatic*).

B.O.

I have one thing to say about B.O.—P.U. (see *Hygiene*).

BOB

Who is this guy Bob, and why does he get so much named after him? Bobbing for apples, bobcat, bobwhite, Bob-ra Anne, shish kebob, bobsled, bob-tailed deer, etc. What's up with him?

BODY

Very few people are satisfied with their bodies, especially if all of their parts are still original and un-retouched. All of us know our bodies better than anyone else, as well we should. We know where all of our visible (and not so visible) imperfections are, and assume that everyone is constantly focused on them. Well guess what? Because the rest of us are so wrapped up worrying about our own appearance, we rarely even notice your little zit popping out. Now if you have one big eyebrow—that we'd notice. Some things are clearly worth fixing. Remember: your body is like a temple; if you take care of your body, your body will take care of you.

BODYBUILDERS

I think bodybuilders' real purpose in life is to make the rest of us look (and feel) inadequate. They succeed.

BODY LANGUAGE

People don't only speak with their mouths. Sometimes their bodies speak volumes. You can really tell a lot by listening to their bodies, so be observant. That would be figuratively, you nut, not literally (see *Farting*).

BODY PIERCING

First of all, body piercings have gotta hurt. Second of all, they look stupid. And how practical is it? Could you imagine getting your nipple ring or your nose ring caught on something? Or worse yet, your nipple ring caught on your nose ring. Or even your nipple ring caught on someone else's nose ring; not to mention their tongue ring getting in the way. Ouch! So why do people do it? I don't have the slightest idea.

BOLD

Go ahead and be bold. And be proud while you're at it (and be a Marine if you want to). Just don't make an ass out of yourself. That would be too bold.

BOOGER CHECK

So you can't pass a mirror without looking at yourself? Well, while you're spending countless hours admiring your gorgeous profile, it's best to always check to make sure that nothing is hanging out of your nose (see *Free Samples*).

BOOGERS

What possible purpose can boogers serve? They clog your nostrils, put you in embarrassing situations and are just generally gross and disgusting. I don't know what anyone was thinking when they invented them.

BOOKS

Reading a book can be such a magical experience. If you let it, your imagination will run wild, as your visualizations of the scenes and events are not influenced by anyone or anything. Sometimes TV and movies can rob you of that special treat and treasured ability. Give your imagination some exercise—go curl up and read a good book. Or a bad book. Or this book.

BORROWED TIME

From the day we are born we are on borrowed time, as our days on this planet are definitely limited. I guess the amount of time we spend often depends on our credit report. Now I'm talking about our ultimate credit report, not the one from our credit card companies. Pay attention.

BORROWING

When you borrow something, you want to return it in better condition than you got it. That way they'll let you borrow something else, like their child, for example; which may not always be such a good thing. Of course, there are limits here. If you borrowed an old car, don't give them a new car back (see *Overkill*). And when it comes to borrowing money, some people confuse that with burrowing and end up getting in over their heads

BOSSES

Everyone has a boss. Hell, even bosses have bosses. Our bosses include our parents, employers, customers, police, politicians and on and on. If you can't tolerate the thought of someone telling you what to do, you better think about starting your own planet.

BOTH ENDS

If you try to play both ends against the middle, you'll likely lose. You can lose things like your friends, the game or your dignity. It's not worth it, so play fair (see *Rules*).

BOTTLED WATER

Now I know I'm a trusting soul, but how many people really believe all of this pure water stuff? Have you ever gone to visit the "spring" they use for that special water? I can't be the only one who thinks someone is sitting in their basement filling up these bottles from the tap and charging big bucks for it. And the BPA in those bottles will probably end up killing you anyway. You think it's any coincidence that Evian spelled backwards is naïve? It's the same feeling I get when I've meticulously separated out all of my recyclable waste, only to see the trash people dump it in with the rest of the garbage.

BOTTOM

Once you've hit bottom, there's really only one way to go. The good news is that it can only get better from there (see *Tomorrow*).

BOTTOM FEEDERS

Bottom feeders only want one thing: to drag you down to join them (see *Company You Keep*).

BOXERS vs. BRIEFS

Boxers. Got to let the boys breathe, you know. Anyway, if you're ever caught with your pants down, it looks like you're wearing a bathing suit, not your birthday suit.

BOXING

Can there be a more barbaric sport than boxing? This isn't much different from the Roman gladiators, except they had to kill their opponents to win. Two guys pounding away at each other, savagely beating their brains in—I don't get it. And they have the nerve to call it a sport. Worse yet, women's boxing is also allegedly a sport (see *Degrading*).

BRA

What do I know about bras? Not much, as I don't wear them. However, my brilliant and creative illustrator designed the B chapter heading with a bra on it, so I needed to include this topic. As you'll find, not really knowing about a subject doesn't deter me from having an opinion or writing about it. It's a long book for a reason. But I digress. I'm told by several baby boomers that they wish they had some foresight when they were busy burning their bras during their formative years. It seems that those braless days, while demonstrating their support for feminist issues, have accelerated the drooping effects of aging. Oh well.

BRAGGING

If you have to tell everyone how great you are, you probably aren't (see *Modesty*). Leave the gloating to the Gloats (I made that up).

BRAIN

Your brain needs exercise, just like your muscles. If you sit around watching mindless TV all day, your brain will turn to mush, just like your tush (OK, so that doesn't rhyme; sue me). Like many other things, you better use it or lose it, so clear out those cobwebs and stimulate your mind already. What are you waiting for? You're not getting any younger, you know. Are you taking this down?

BRAIN FREEZE

Oy, talk about an uncomfortable feeling. You want to eat or drink that cold stuff slowly. Very slowly. My brain hurts just thinking about it. Nobody can afford a frozen brain.

BRAINS

Sure, lots of people are smart, and many of them aren't very shy about telling us. However, even though they think this makes them better than you, they're wrong, as it's not all about brains. It's the ones with more compassion, caring and concern for others that deserve a higher standing in our society. They can really put those brainiacs to shame.

BRAINSTORM

Nothing like a good idea once in a while. But don't think too hard or your head might explode (or implode). There's only so much room in there (see *Memory*).

BRAINWASHING

I have plenty of dirty thoughts all the time, but I don't think washing my brain would do any good. And trying to fill someone else's brain solely with your beliefs or ways of doing things won't work either. Washing hands, faces and clothes is much more effective. Leave the brain alone.

BRAVERY

Being brave is relative, as there are lots of different ways to show courage. It's not always about saving someone's life, you know. Riding a bike without training wheels for the first time usually takes plenty of guts. Speaking in front of a group or facing a difficult medical decision can also require lots of courage. So does standing up to injustice, inequality and bullying. Everyone can be brave; it makes for strong hearts. And we all need strong hearts, right?

BREAD

The darker the bread, the better it is for you. Don't ask me why.

BREAKING INTO SONG

OK, so this will really display my ignorance. I completely understand that musicals and operas are art forms that attempt to tell a story in an enjoyable and entertaining way. However, the realistic and pragmatic part of me has trouble understanding an important scene in a musical when they simply break into song. It's even worse in an opera, as there is only singing and no dialogue at all. That's simply lost on me, since people don't do that in real life. Give me a *Star Wars* or *Indian Jones* movie anytime. Now that's what I call realistic. I can really relate to those stories. (Yes, I am a confirmed idiot.)

BREAKING UP

Yes, breaking up is usually very hard to do. Of course, it all depends on which side you're on. If you're the dumper, it's best to be gentle, understanding and considerate of the other's feelings (see *Class*). If you're the dumpee, it's perfectly OK to be hysterical and carry on like a lunatic. Just remember that breaking up with you is probably a reflection of their bad taste. And they likely taste bad too.

BREAST-FEEDING

Breast-feeding is the best feeding, as lots of the mother's nutrients and other goodies get to the baby. That helps to build up the immune system, you know. Now it may be uncomfortable and inconvenient at times (or so I'm told), but apparently it's very natural and worth it. You should probably watch out for deflation though, if you know what I mean (see *Bra*).

BREAST IMPLANTS

I don't have breasts (actually, I kind of have man breasts), but I do know something about the relationship between one's appearance and one's self-esteem. If you have become disfigured through disease or some other tragedy, then by all means have as much cosmetic surgery as you need. But listen, ladies: if breast implants are the result of strictly elective surgery, you're probably kidding yourself about it making you feel like a different person. And according to countless (exactly how many are "countless"?) surveys, breast implants look and feel fake. Remember: happiness comes from within (see *You Are What You Are*), so deal with it. Of course, any time they put you under, it's dangerous; so why risk it? You'll also end up saving a lot of money.

BREASTS

Where would we be without breasts? There'd be lots of hungry babies and unfulfilled guys and girls, that's for sure. Not to mention foreplay would certainly suffer. But I digress (yet again). Now gents, in polite company it's best not to use these euphemisms (or mephemisms):

Babies	High beams	Puppies
Cans	Honkers	Rack
Coconuts	Hooters	Rocks
Cupcakes	Jugs	Tatas
Girls	Knobs	Tits
Hangers	Knockers	Titties
Headlights	Melons	

These are OK:

Boobs	Breasts (of course)	Chest
Bosom	Bust	Mammaries

BRIEFCASE

If you're a professional, you've got to look the part to play the part. Carry around a briefcase, even if you've got nothing in it. If you look important, you are important. It's all about image.

BRIGHTER DAYS AHEAD

It doesn't really matter what happened today or yesterday, as there are always brighter days ahead. Therefore, you should try to keep your eyes looking forward. That will save you some eyestrain as well.

BRIGHT SIDE

There's always a bright side. It may be hard to find sometimes, but it's best to keep your sunglasses handy.

BRILLIANT

It's not just the geniuses who are brilliant. If you radiate happiness and warmth, you're brilliant. Shine on.

BRINGING A HORSE TO WATER

Sure, you can bring a horse to water, but you can't make it drink. There's only so much you can do for someone. Ultimately, they have to live their own lives, not you. Anyway, living your own life should keep you busy enough.

BRIS

Well, I'm all for traditions, but sometimes enough is enough. Yes, all boys should be circumcised (see *Hygiene*). But who needs that public (or pubic) spectacle. It's a wonder that more boys don't grow up with some kind of weird bashful complex. Actually, most do (see *Cause and Effect*).

BROKE

If it ain't broke, don't fix it? Sure, some things are best left as they are (see *Leaving Well Enough Alone*). But what if it's broken, and no one but you knows it? Then by all means, fix it. And be quick about it.

BROKEN HEART

Too bad scientists haven't found an easy way to mend a broken heart. It's often hard to avoid, it's very painful and it can last a while. But like most things that get broken, even hearts can eventually be repaired. So there is hope (see *Time Heals*).

BROKEN RECORD

If you find yourself saying the same thing to the same person over and over, either they're not listening or you're not being very effective in your approach. It's best to simply change your message—or find someone else to talk to.

BROWNNOSING

Think of the image brownnosing conjures up. Pretty disgusting, huh? Hard to really see what's going on with your nose way up there anyway. Kissing ass or kissing up don't sound too pleasant either. Try being yourself (see *Honesty*).

BRUSHING YOUR TEETH

You're supposed to brush after every meal, but nobody does. Twice a day is OK—when you get up and before you go to sleep. You've got to at least brush your teeth every morning if you want to appear civilized. And don't forget to floss.

BUDGETS

A budget should not be just some set of numbers representing unattainable goals. Use your head and start with reasonable expectations of income and absolutely necessary expenses. Then expand from there. Most people are amazed at the amount that remains on paper to either spend or make up (as in deficit). A budget is a great tool to keep you out of trouble (see *Living Within Your Means*).

BUFFETS

It's this simple and all very mathematical: going to buffets equals overeating (see *Discipline*). Do yourself a favor and order off the menu. It's much easier to control yourself that way. And no eating the leftovers off your neighbor's plate either.

BUGS

I'm sure bugs have some extreme importance in the food chain, but they really bug me.

BULLFIGHTING

What's up with bullfighting? Aren't we in the civilized 21st century for God's sake? What's the point anyway? Let's see how those matadors would do if we gave the bulls some swords too. Then it would be closer to a fair fight.

BULL RUNNING

And how about those lunatics that let the bulls chase them down those narrow streets? There must be some allure to being trampled to death (see *Adventure*). You got me.

BULLSHIT

Now I've never actually seen bullshit, since I don't hang around bulls. But I must have some innate ability to recognize it, as I sure know it when I hear it. Bullshit does have its useful place in our language though, as it tends to add some punctuation to conversation (see *Cursing*). However, if you don't know what you're talking about, it's best to just shut up.

BULLYING

Bullies think they have something to prove by picking on those smaller or weaker than them. They do prove something: they prove they are idiots. This is just their way of hiding their own insecurities and, in a warped way, trying to feel better about themselves. Want to drive bullies crazy? Ignore them. Reacting to their taunts has a way of simply empowering them. Don't.

BUMPER STICKERS

Our Constitution guarantees that we can say or write almost anything we want; it's our freedom of speech. Some choose to use their cars as traveling billboards (see *Obnoxious*). Bumper stickers can be funny, clever, stupid or serious. That's what free expression is all about—especially the stupid part.

BUMPS IN THE ROAD

Yes, life's journey can be a bumpy ride sometimes. There is no such thing as a perfectly even, flat road, so you can't just cruise along at a constant speed and expect to get anywhere. The trick is to find your way around all of those bumps in the road. It may take a bit longer to maneuver around them, but it's really the only way to ensure a successful future.

BUNDLE OF JOY

A bundle of joy represents the essence of all that is good in this world (see *Children*). Where would we be without them? Nowhere, that's for sure.

BURNING BRIDGES

It's not a good idea to ever burn your bridges. First of all, you probably couldn't actually burn one down, and if you could, remember that arson is illegal in most states (see *Playing With Fire*). But most importantly, you shouldn't burn bridges because you don't know if you'll ever have to cross back.

BURPING

A little slip here and there can't be helped. But some slobs insist on making such a big production out of belching. We call them pigs.

BUSINESS

Getting into business is like getting into trouble. It's so much easier to get into and much harder to get out of (see *Exit Strategy*).

BUSY

Stay busy. It's when you've got nothing to do that you get into trouble. There's no such thing as being too busy, because you can always find time to do what you really want to do (see *Priorities*). It's all about choices. You sure can be very busy though.

BUSYBODY

Of course everyone's body is extremely busy. We've got lots of little guys (non-gender-specific) in there putting in plenty of overtime, day and night, keeping our innards working smoothly. Those unnamed and unheralded beings work so hard making sure that all systems are running properly. They deserve a raise.

BUSY PEOPLE

Yes, if you absolutely need to get something done, give it to a busy person to do. They're used to finding a way.

BUT

"Everything was really spectacular, but…." "You look great, but…." "I'm on my way, but…." For a little word, but can sure undo a lot of things.

(However isn't far behind.) It tends to negate everything that's said before it. We should eliminate but from the English language—which would make this book a whole lot shorter.

BUTT

A butt is the end of a cigarette. I fail to get the association between a cigarette and one's hind parts (see *Asses*). The preferred term is tush (or tushie for you purists). Yes, we all know that crack is a design flaw. But just because it's cracked doesn't mean it'll break. Anyway, I understand this will be corrected in the next model. There's also talk of a recall; however, I'm the only one I've heard this from. Other acceptable tush terms are:

Backside	Keester
Behind	Posterior
Bootie	Rear
Bottom	Rear end
Bum	Rump
Buns	Rumpelstiltskin (probably not)
Caboose	Rusty dusty
Cheeks	Seat
Duff	Scuttlebutt (never mind, that's
Fanny	something else)
Gluteus maximus (some are	Tuchus (see *Yiddish*
more maximus than others)	*Expressions*)
Hind parts	
Hynie	

Even ass is OK, but don't use the word butt unless you have a habit of lighting up your tush. Ouch.

BUTTERFLIES

Talk about some awesome creatures (see *Beauty*). Butterflies are so relaxing to watch, and they don't buzz in your ear either. On the other hand, those people skipping around with butterfly nets really scare me.

BUTTERFLY STROKE

The butterfly stroke sure looks like a very unnatural and uncomfortable way to swim. Way too much drag for all of that effort, so what's the point?

BYGONES

Sure, I would let bygones be bygones. They can be anything they want—it's not my business (see *Gay*).

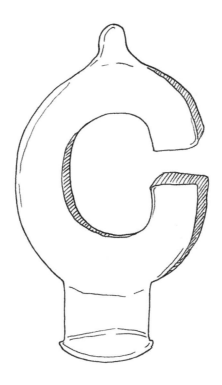

CABIN FEVER

Ah, togetherness. Imagine the quality time you can spend with those special to you during a bad storm. There's a blizzard or hurricane outside, but you are nice and safe in the warm confines of your abode. Then the power goes out. Nothing to do, nowhere to go, no air conditioning or heat—for days; maybe weeks. Those close to you become way too close. The walls close in, you're lucky if you don't kill each other and it becomes more like house arrest. I last about five minutes in those situations. Way too much togetherness for me. I'll take my chances fighting the elements.

CALL WAITING

Now, whose idea was call waiting? How rude can you get? Let's see. Somebody's on the other line. So maybe they're more important than you are. "Whoops! Need to see who that is, gotta go—bye." Now if you're the one who initiated the call, it's really quite rude to succumb to your click (see *Selfish*).

CALLER ID

Having Caller ID is a great way to screen your calls so you don't have to talk to people you don't like. Now if you have caller ID and call waiting, you don't even have to click to piss everyone off.

CALM BEFORE THE STORM

It's not always calm before the storm. Sometimes there's just a long streak of bad weather and not much calm at all.

CALM, COOL AND COLLECTED

Follow these three Cs and you'll live longer. Not only that, but you'll smell nicer and be much more likable.

CAMARADERIE

Camaraderie is a good thing. Being on the same team, working together, helping each other—what's not to like?

CAMOUFLAGE UNIFORMS

What's up with our military? Those weird green or ugly tan uniforms are not working, as they're not really blending with the background. We can still see you.

CAMP

If you can afford it, every child should go to camp. Those of us lucky enough to have gone have such fond memories of summers at camp, even if we hated it back then (see *Selective Memory*). There's just nothing like running around in that miserable sticky heat and humidity, with bugs flying up your nose and sweating like a pig. Nothing like it. And bug juice, of course. Oh, and you've gotta love those very inventive camp songs. They were usually kind of silly and never made much sense, but you sang them anyway (see *Peer Pressure*). At least it was one way to get your mind off those bugs flying up your nose.

CAMPAIGN TV ADS

I can't think of a bigger waste of money than running political campaign TV ads; although it does help keep the media in business. Anyone who makes their decisions based on these should lose their right to vote. Can you actually believe those venomous and ridiculous things the candidates say about each other? Read, learn, find out—don't just vote for the one with the prettiest smile. It's probably fake anyway.

CAMPING

Ah, the call of the great rustic outdoors. What a wonderful way to commune with nature. My only question is: How natural is it with portable gas stoves, comfy cozy cots, bug-proof tents, easy chairs, TVs, fancy meals and battery-operated hair dryers? That's really roughing it, right? (I made up the part about the hair dryers.)

CANCER

Cancer is a shockingly scary word today—justifiably very scary. However, contracting cancer is not necessarily a death sentence, as plenty of people live long, happy, healthy and productive lives after dealing with it. Attitude and treatment play a huge role in recovery. If your mind stays positive, your body will follow. Stay positive.

CANDLESTICKS

Why do they call them candlesticks? Shouldn't they really be called candlestick holders?

CAN DO

We spend too much time and effort finding ways we can't do things (e.g., too tired, too busy, too lazy). Often our natural first reaction is no. Instead, look for ways you can say yes. With few exceptions, you really can do whatever you set your mind to, and you'd be amazed at the level of abilities you actually possess. Having a can-do attitude is a great way to live, so keep it up. Yes, you can. That's the spirit.

CANDY

For some overeating candyholics (I made that word up), spare your body the digestion issues and just tape the candy to your ass. It's just going to end up there anyway (see *Moderation*).

CAN'T BUY LOVE

You can shower someone with gifts and attention, but if it isn't there, it isn't there. Sorry. And no, money can't buy love, although it can sure buy lust. And maybe money can't buy happiness either—but it can come awfully close sometimes.

CAN'T GO HOME AGAIN

Who says you can't go home again? It likely isn't the way you remember, but of course you can go back there, any time you want. It's a free country, you know.

CAN'T WIN

Boy, you sure can't please everyone. You can say that again (I think I just did). With some people, no matter what you say or do, or how you do it, it's never enough and they'll always find a way to let you know it (see *Five Percenters*). Just do the best you can and the heck with them.

CAPITALISM

Yes, despite the efforts of some, capitalism is alive and well in America (at least for now) and has a long history of working better than any other ism. We need to remind our politicians of this from time to time (see *Freedom*).

CAR COLORS

There are two schools of thought about car colors. The brighter and more distinct, the easier it is to be recognized and therefore easier to find your car in a parking lot (which is an age-old problem). However, it also makes it way easier for the boys and girls in blue to catch you doing something you shouldn't be doing (see *Nose Picking*). Your choice.

CAREER

If you love what you do, you'll always do what you love. Remember though: ultimately a career is only a means to an end, as it's just a job (see *Perspective*).

CAREFUL

You can't be too careful in life, as you never know who or what you'll step into.

CARING

Give a shit about something, somebody—anything (see *Conviction*). Let that be your trademark. And you shouldn't be discouraged if someone doesn't care for or about you the way you care about them. There's no accounting for taste, so there's little point in wasting your time with them.

CAR GAUGES

Car gauges are there for a reason, so keep an eye on them. And don't forget those very aptly named idiot lights either. They're not just there to blink at you. It's rather idiotic just to blink back at them.

CAR MAINTENANCE

Wouldn't it be quite helpful to teach you how to take care of your car in school? It sure would save lots on maintenance costs. The experts tell you that if you change the oil every 3,000 miles and keep the tires properly inflated, your car will last forever. However, they forget to tell you to change your windshield wiper blades every six months. And remember to change the air in your tires at least once a year (see *Gullible*).

CAR POOL

I prefer a swimming pool to a car pool. Too bad most drivers do as well (see *Traffic*).

CAT

Sorry, cat lovers, I don't get it: what do cats do? They don't fetch, they don't poop outside and they don't protect you. What do you say? "Here, kitty, kitty, go attack that big bad home invader." They'd look at you like you're crazy. It's not all their fault though. What would you do if you had a sissy name like Fluffy or Muffin? They must be embarrassed. Try naming them Fido or Rover and see what happens. I bet plenty of them don't like their names, so it's no wonder they have nine lives. Oh, and I'm sure those prissy little poodles are part cat.

CATAPULT

Yes, a <u>cat</u>apult is a very good use for <u>cat</u>s. I'm all for that.

CAT GOT YOUR TONGUE

Cat got your tongue? Serves you right. You've got no business having a cat in your mouth anyway.

CATHOUSE

I understand there are lots of strange noises coming from these cathouses. Must be those cats doing all of that moaning and such. Here's another reason to stay out of cathouses—too much cat litter. Why do you think they call it a catastrophe?

CAT'S AWAY

When the cat's away, you should act as if the cat were there. It's not simply an excuse to do something stupid (see *Taking Advantage*). And don't play around with those mice either—way too dirty.

CAUSE

Find a cause—it'll give you something to do, and you'll feel good about it. Why? 'Cause it's the right thing to do.

CAUSE AND EFFECT

Yes, most things in our world are related. Very related. It's all about actions and reactions.

CAVEMAN SYNDROME

Like the dinosaurs, those macho, unfeeling, uncaring, chauvinistic males should be long extinct. If you see any still roaming the earth, you may want to remind them that their time has passed.

Cat Got Your Tongue

CELEBRITIES

People become famous for lots of reasons, both good and bad. Whether they are entertainers, movie stars, athletes or musicians, we tend to revere them and shower them with attention and adulation. Every move of theirs is scrutinized and chronicled. They have this star quality, and we just idolize them. And God knows why. They are basically ordinary people, albeit (you be it) some with special talents. They likely perform the same bodily functions as us mere mortals. So when they fall from grace like the rest of us, we're shattered and crushed. It's too bad we don't hold the real heroes in such high esteem. I'm talking about the scientists and doctors trying to eradicate those horrible diseases; and our public safety personnel; and soldiers who are willing to sacrifice their lives to protect us. Somewhere along the line we just let our priorities get way out of whack. The good news is that it's never too late to get them back in whack. (I think I've beaten this into the ground.)

CELLOPHANE PACKAGING

Now I know I can't be the only one who's constantly fumbling with all of that cellophane, trying to open up packaged products. You'd think those items were so valuable that all the extra protection was necessary. They can put plenty of those little arrows and tags on them, but I still have trouble. Oh well, such is life. Maybe I'm the only one who has trouble with this.

CELL PHONE ETIQUETTE

Technology is great, isn't it? You can have your phone with you and talk to anybody, check your email, text and surf the Internet anywhere, anytime. Unfortunately some people believe this is their lifeline and treat the phone like an umbilical cord. They can't part with it morning, noon or night. Guess what? We all don't want to hear your endless, one-sided conversations. Imagine talking to someone who's on their cell phone and hearing the toilet flush? Yeech! Don't flush, silly, or you're busted. So if you're in a group with lots of company around, turn the damn thing off (see *Socialization*).

CELLULITE

Cellulite isn't so pleasant to look at and isn't real healthy to have either. There's nothing "lite" about it. Either exercise it off or cover it up.

CEMETERIES

Do you know how this special tradition of building cemeteries got started in the first place and why they buried dead people in ancient civilizations long ago? Because corpses stank, attracted animals and bugs and spread nasty diseases, that's why. This custom is quite outdated today (see *Cremation*). Why ruin a perfectly good piece of land? Anyway, we plant things in the soil to grow, right? Human remains are dead, so there's no more growing for them. There was also the thought that dead people needed their bodies after they were gone. Well, they don't (see *Organ Donors*). They're dead. And people actually go to the gravesite to talk to them. Guess what? They're not there. They're in your heart and in your mind—or in the dog that's licking you (see *Afterlife*). After they're done removing all of my very valuable guts and assorted goodies, I've given strict instructions to have what's left of me stuffed and mounted. And clothed.

CHALLENGE

Challenge your mind and challenge your body. It's a good exercise and they will both thank you. Unfortunately for some though, every day is a challenge. The real challenge for us is to help them (see *Charity*).

CHALLENGING AUTHORITY

Sure you can challenge authority. Just do it respectfully—and not all of the time (see *Picking Your Battles*).

CHANCE OF A LIFETIME

There is no such thing as a chance of a lifetime, because you never know what's around the corner (see *Tomorrow*). So stop beating yourself up already. Anyway, who cares? You never really know how things would have turned out; maybe it would have been a disaster. Move on.

CHANGE

Ah, just having the opportunity to do things differently from our normal, inflexible ways is always something we look forward to, right? Wrong. People aren't resistant to change; they are just resistant to changing. We typically despise and dread change, and fight it tooth and nail (never understood that one). Why? Because we're afraid, that's why. It's the unknown. The more things change, the more they stay the same? No, silly, the more they change. Change is constant and usually good in the long run anyway. If you're not going to embrace it, at least accept it. So get on the train or be run over by it. Sometimes the winds of change come on like cyclones or hurricanes. And change for the sake of change is a complete and utter waste of time (that's a cow phrase). Slowly and methodically is the best way to go, as gradual change is usually preferable to drastic change. That goes for dieting, getting wrinkles and saving your money, just to name a few.

CHANGING DIAPERS

OK macho boys, changing diapers is no big deal. There are way more disgusting things in life, and the good news is that the diaper stage doesn't last forever. Take the good with the not-so-good. Girls, you already know about all this stuff (see *Sexist*).

CHANGING THEIR MINDS

Sure, you can influence others, but you can't change someone else's mind. Ultimately only they can.

CHANGING THEIR STRIPES

This comes under the sad-but-true department, as ultimately most don't really change their stripes. As much as dedicated and disciplined people try to overcome themselves, they often revert back to their old ways. Under lots of pressure their true selves often reappear. It's just the way it is.

CHANGING THE WORLD

You never know the impact you can have in the world. Just the thought of changing it sounds rather daunting. However, we all have the capability to change it, either individually or collectively. And it often starts with just one person. Don't forget, changing something can begin to change everything; so don't stop trying (see *Hope*).

CHANGING YOUR MIND

Of course you can change your mind; just make sure you know the consequences. And this isn't simply a woman's prerogative (see *Sexist*). So change away. It's a free country, you know.

CHANGING YOUR UNDERWEAR

Please—you need a fresh set of underwear every day. None of this inside-out-the-second-day stuff.

CHARITY

Charity begins at home? Well maybe that's where you're supposed to learn about it, although some use this as an excuse not to help others. Giving to help those less fortunate is a moral obligation and requirement for being a dues paying member of the human race. The most genuine form of charity is to do it anonymously, which shows no hidden or selfish agenda. So you don't have to tell the whole world about it. Go ahead and put your money where your mouth is. You really want to give, give and give some more. Give till it hurts? No, it's not supposed to hurt. Just give till you feel it. Didn't your mother teach you to share?

CHARM

You don't have to go to charm school to amaze them with your special magic and appeal. All you have to do is use your God-given talents to flash that special smile, be sincere and use your charisma to knock down those barriers. Lay it on them (see *Class*).

CHASE

Oftentimes the chase is more exciting than the prize (see *Disappointment*). Sometimes the things we believe we want the most don't seem to be all that important when we finally get them. It's then that we realize it was the sport of the chase that we enjoyed more.

CHASING RAINBOWS

There's nothing wrong with chasing rainbows. But just know you'll never catch them. And good luck getting that pot of gold at the end too (see *Reality*). Nobody's found it yet, and you won't be the first.

CHEAPER BY THE DOZEN

If you need it, and can store it, you normally want to buy in bulk.

CHEATING

So, you think you got away with something? Nobody caught you? Everyone does it, so that makes it OK, right? Who will know? Well, guess what? Someone will always know; yeah, you, silly. If it was a big deal, and you have a conscience, it may haunt you for a long time. The pleasure you derive from cheating will never erase the guilt; that is, if you are any kind of a decent person. Oh, and oral sex is definitely cheating. (Sorry, Mr. Clinton; sex is sex, adultery is cheating and is is is). And cheating death usually doesn't work either. It can be a hollow victory knowing your achievement wasn't really earned (see *Loser*). Anyway, cheaters never prosper. They may think they do, but in the long run, they don't. Save the guilt for something else; don't cheat.

CHEERING SECTION

We all have a cheering section. It's just that some are louder than others. If you can't see or hear yours, keep listening and looking; you'll find it.

CHEMISTRY

When it comes right down to it, the chemistry is either there or it isn't. Face it, if there is no attraction, all the chemicals in the world won't change that. You gotta have that spark (see *Love*).

CHEWING THEIR CUD

What a charming way cows consume their food. They eat what they've already eaten—many times. Can you imagine if they hadn't stopped that at least three stomach business further up the evolution ladder? On second thought, don't imagine.

CHICKEN OR EGG

Which came first, the chicken or the egg? No idea. Who cares!

CHILD

We should always listen to the child in us. Sometimes, they're the only one who actually makes sense. Can't find the child? The may be well hidden, so just keep looking; they're in there—for real.

CHILDREN

I'm a huge fan of children. Love and life are the most extraordinary gifts children bring. Since they are our future, we can never do enough to invest in theirs. They start out so innocent and cute and say the coolest things (until about age five). Some parents treat them as toys and love to show them off. However, that gets old fast, as they soon become even more of an awesome responsibility. Remember: it's a lifetime commitment, and they're not always so cute. Gotta love 'em, though. And where the hell do they get all of that energy?

CHIP ON YOUR SHOULDER

Too bad you're pissed off at the world. Wonder why no one wants to be around you? Well, it could be that grotesque chip on your shoulder, which is invisible to you, but obvious to all others. It's like so many things: you know it when you see it, and it is quite unattractive and a big turn off. Whatever the cause, have a chipectomy performed and get over it.

CHOCOLATE

Chocolate must've come out of the Garden of Eden, because it's way too tasty (see *Temptation*).

CHOICES

Sometimes having the opportunity to choose can be dangerous, as we don't always choose wisely (see *Buffets*). Too many choices often require too many decisions, which can cause way too much brain overload, among other problems. It won't kill you but can sure give you a headache.

CHRISTMAS/HANUKKAH

The true meaning of Christmas is to commemorate the birth of Jesus. And Hanukkah, which is a relatively minor holiday by Jewish standards, commemorates the Maccabees' success and the miracle of the long-lasting lights. These are supposed to be religious observances. Unfortunately, today the spiritual significance is almost entirely overshadowed by the ultra-commercialization of these holidays. We purists should stop bemoaning that fact, recognize the reality and do something about it. We should limit Christmas and Hanukkah observations to strictly religious celebrations. Let's just create a new holiday, conveniently dated December 26, and call it Happy Day or something. Then we can all overindulge ourselves in gift giving and merriment and not feel the slightest bit guilty about ignoring the holiness of the religious holidays. Better yet, let's make every day the Happy Day! Just think how much the world would be changed by that idea alone.

CIRCUITOUS

You can keep going around and around in circles if you want, but the shortest distance between two points is a straight line. Save your strength, and use your head.

CLASS

Never be afraid to show your class. If you don't have any, get some. A touch of class is always welcome.

CLASSICAL MUSIC

You know why classical music is so great? Because it has so much class, that's why. Listening to it can be so uplifting and inspiring. No, I'm not talking about those symphonies that put you to sleep. Anyway, where else would you find all of those crescendos? Whatever those are.

CLEAN AS A WHISTLE

Exactly how clean are whistles? Lots of germs in your mouth, right? I rest my case.

CLEAN CARS

Clean cars not only look nice but they drive better. Less wind resistance.

CLEANING

Few of us like to clean. It defies human nature (see *Messes*). Cleanliness is next to godliness, you know. No idea what godliness is; best to go somewhere else to find out. I can't know everything.

CLEANING YOUR ROOM

A clean room is a happy room. And look at all of the time you can save, as you'll suddenly find all of that real important stuff you're looking for. Imagine finding that hundred-dollar bill, last week's lunch or a long lost relative.

CLEAN LIVING

Nothing wrong with clean living, but being squeaky clean is really overdoing it. You've got to live a little, you know.

CLEAN PLATING

In my generation, our parents insisted that we not leave the table until we finished everything on our plates. It had to do with children starving in Europe or Africa or some other place, which I never understood. How would my eating or not eating make them any less hungry? Consequently, our moms and dads raised a generation of overeaters. It's a disease, as we not only have to eat everything on our plate, but also on our child's plate and the plate of the person to our immediate right or left (see *Pigs*). Using a little less plate will likely result in a little less waste. And it's a good idea to leave some food on your plate for someone else; let them clean your plate. That way, at least you can keep your girlish figure.

CLEAN SLATE

Wouldn't it be nice if we could start off fresh, without being bogged down by any past mistakes? Well, guess what? You can, because every day is a new day. So go ahead and start off tomorrow with a clean slate. You heard it here.

CLEAVAGE

Sure, you want to sneak a peek. So look, but don't touch (see *Discreet*). That is, of course, unless you're invited to. I think they call this advertising. And ladies, when you're obviously displaying your rather ample wares, you shouldn't be upset when the guys are talking to your knockers and not your face.

CLEAVERS

The Cleavers were not a family to emulate, as they weren't real (see *TV*). Now did June wear those pearls when she went to bed, since she always had them on? And what was up with Lumpy (and who'd name their child that anyway)?

And how come they never went to the bathroom? "Hey, Dad, the Beave's been in the can for over an hour; what do you think he's doing in there?" These are difficult questions that sadly will never be answered. Such is life.

CLEVERNESS

Go ahead— use your wit, your smile, your innovative thinking and your personality. Lead with your talents. Clever is always appreciated.

CLINGING

So stop clinging to old memories, boyfriends, girlfriends, ex-spouses and trees already. Live for tomorrow, not yesterday, and leave the clinging to peaches.

CLINTON FINGER POINT

You know how Bill Clinton used to point without using his index finger? He would make a slight fist, with his thumb and index finger sticking out. Then he would flap it around for emphasis. It was a semi-point, and plenty of others now emulate him. Great. Maybe he should've patented it. So this is one (no, not that one) of his legacies. Pretty wimpy, if you ask me. Your mother told you never to point your finger, but if you need to point to get your point across, use your index finger like a real person, for God's sake.

CLOCKS

Clocks are manufactured by human beings. They are not naturally created elements like rocks and trees. However, we build clocks but can't control them, as they have minds of their own. Of course, they claim to always be correct and on time. As for me, I believe they are either too slow or too fast, depending entirely on my mood at the time.

CLOSED DOORS

Lots of doors get closed to you in life. When that happens, there's usually another door, a key or at least a window that opens. All you have to do is find one, as they're not always clearly marked. So keep looking.

CLOSE ENOUGH

Lots of things are close enough. Sometimes close enough is quite close enough. Sometimes they're actually way too close.

CLOSE TALKERS

Don't you hate it when certain people insist on getting right in your face to tell you something? As for me, give me my space.

CLOTHES

Do clothes really make the person? Nah, the person makes the person. Clothes or the lack thereof can get you noticed (sometimes very well noticed), but clothes really just keep you from getting cold. However, you can tell a lot about someone by the clothes they wear (or don't wear). So you don't want to run around in dirty, torn rags unless you have to (even if that's in fashion).

CLOUDS

Clouds may seem to stay around forever, but they eventually go away (see *Balance*). They don't all have a silver lining, but plenty of them do. And sometimes it's hard, but you should try to keep your head out of the clouds, as it's difficult to breathe in there.

COCKFIGHTING

No, I'm not talking about male bonding here. Anybody who is involved with cockfighting must be really sick. What idiot would enjoy watching two birdies trying to kill each other (see *Boxing*)? Get a life.

COCKLES

You know how some things just warm the cockles of your heart? So how can you be sure that your cockles are working properly? Do you tell the doctor that you think you have a cockle problem? Do they have to do something invasive, like peek-a-boo into your heart to check? I worry about things like that. You probably should too, unless you're really in touch with your cockles. What you do in the privacy of your own home is, of course, your own business.

COCK TEASING

Now being a cock teaser is not something you want to aspire to (see *Reputation*). If, for whatever reason, you can't deliver, then don't advertise. Fellas, this usually doesn't apply to you.

CODES

We've got codes up the wazoo (wazoo?). We're in password overload. Passwords for e-mail, ATMs, Internet porn sites (or so I'm told), answering machines—you name it, we've got it. Codes for everything. Codes for locks, codes to get into men's rooms, codes to get out of men's rooms. So here's the quandary: what passwords should we use? There are two schools of thought on this (there are probably some who get degrees in this field). You either use the same code for all of them or different passwords for each. If you use the former and some code hacker unveils your closely guarded secret, you're finished. That hacker then knows all of your passwords and can probably even break into your bathroom. If instead you use different codes for everything, good luck remembering them, especially when you really have to (see *Gotta Go*). If you kept a list of all of your secret codes, where would you put it? Probably in some password-protected file or something.

COINCIDENCE

You'll drive yourself crazy if you try to read anything into some situations. It's just a coincidence, so let it go (see *Fate*).

COLLAR STAYS

When you buy dress shirts, make sure you get the ones with the collar stays sewn in. God knows why anyone would want the kind with the removable ones. It's just something else to lose. Why the hell do they make them that way in the first place?

COLLECT YOUR THOUGHTS

You always want to collect your thoughts before you say anything. The key is always to think *before* you talk, especially if you're upset. That way you'll at least make some sense.

COLLEGE

Going to college shouldn't be optional for anyone, as we all need plenty of education. Completing high school just doesn't prepare you enough for life. College can, and should, be a life-changing experience. While some colleges are better than others, the name of the school isn't as important as what you do with what you've learned. When you choose your college, remember: you can make a big school smaller, but you can't make a small school bigger.

COLLEGE YEARS

Your four years (sometimes more) in college can be the most memorable of your life. It's a time when you can really grow up (or in my case, grow some). You can make lifelong friends and experience things that will stay with you forever. That may be good or bad, but it should mostly be good. Be a sponge and enjoy learning.

COLOR

What would life be like if there weren't any colors (see *Boring*)? Whoever thought up this concept really knew what they were doing. Think about it. You can't really describe color, and you can't explain it to someone who can't see. So count your blessings.

COLOR-BLIND

Being color-blind doesn't necessarily mean you can't distinguish between colors. It can also refer to those who don't make decisions based on a person's race or color (see *Tolerance*). The best don't even notice those superficial differences.

COLORING

Oh, by all means, color outside the lines (see *Imagination*). It's those drab conformists who insist on taking no risks and staying between the lines.

COMBATIVE

Sure, you can go around picking fights with everybody (see *Chip on Your Shoulder*). You won't make many friends that way, and odds are you'll underestimate your competition once in a while and get your ass kicked. Try being nice.

COMB OVERS

Really? Don't you think we notice that your entire head is covered by a few strands of hair from the back of your head? You might want to look in the mirror to see how ridiculous you look. The sad part is that you probably do, but you clearly don't see what we see.

COMFORT

We all want to be comfortable, but never sacrifice safety for comfort. Those seat belts may be annoying but they do save lives.

COMMERCIALS

I think that most TV commercials are simply designed to insult your intelligence. Those stupid jungles ring around in your head, hypnotizing and torturing you. Do they really think we blindly believe what they tell us and that will make us run out and buy whatever they're selling? Unfortunately, they do and we do.

COMMON COURTESY

Everyone's entitled to common courtesy. That means everyone; even people you don't like (see *Manners*).

COMMON SENSE

You either have common sense, or you don't. They can't teach this to you in school, which is a shame, as common sense is more uncommon than you'd expect. If you have it, you can do almost anything; so consider yourself blessed. If you're not sure whether or not you have any common sense, you probably don't; so hang around somebody who does. You want to stay real, real close to them. Unfortunately, it won't wear off on you, but the proximity will certainly help.

COMMUNICATION

Wars have been fought, marriages have crumbled and friendships have been ruined over bad communication. That's why it's so important to choose your words carefully, as they can be so easily misunderstood. Here's a guide from the best (and most effective) to the worst forms of communication:

Face-to-face verbal	Yelling
Non-face-to-face verbal	Carrier pigeons
Handwritten	Smoke signals
E-mail	Nonverbal
Group e-mail (see *Insincerity*)	Mind reading
Jumping around and waving your hands like a nut	

COMMUNITY

The best people don't just buy a house; they buy a neighborhood. You have to live somewhere, so you might as well get active in your community and make an impact (see *Neighbors*). You learn that it really does take a village, but better yet, you develop a sense of belonging. And you can't beat that.

COMMUNITY SERVICE

Our criminal justice system has it backwards. Performing community service shouldn't be viewed as a punishment; it can and should be a very rewarding experience. There are plenty of lessons to be learned, which is why no child should be allowed to graduate from high school without performing some community service.

COMMUTE

Yes, sitting in traffic is an incredible waste of time. Stress levels can skyrocket—and that's before you even get to work. Better if you can use that time to just ponder and think. Let your mind expand and gear up for your day. The trip home can also be more beneficial if you take the time to decompress and think some more. It's probably not a good idea to get too relaxed and close your eyes though. That would be bad form.

COMPANY YOU KEEP

Are you defined by the company you keep? Unfortunately, to a large extent yes. If you hang around a bunch of losers, you do end up suffering from guilt by association. It's too easy to be painted in broad strokes, so you may want to take stock of your associations.

COMPASSION

Be proud of, ignite and enflame your compassion, because it's fundamental to being a human being. So go ahead and let it show. And while you're at it, let it snow—like you have any control over the weather.

COMPELLING

Compelling is such a neat word, one of my favorites. It's just so riveting.

COMPETITIVE

It's good to be competitive, but some people really go overboard and treat everything like a competition. Life is just not like that. However, when you're in the game, know when you're on the same team, as some have to be reminded not to compete with their teammates, but against the other guys.

COMPLACENT

Being complacent will quickly make you fat, stupid and lazy. Always strive to be and do better (see *Trying*).

COMPLAINING

If you're always complaining and don't have any friends, add two and two together; it's not a coincidence. So save your voice—nobody really wants to hear you pissing and moaning all of the time (see *Pain in the Ass*). I really need to pay attention to this stoic advice.

COMPLICATED

Yes, the world is very, very complicated. Therefore, you'd be wise to uncomplicate whatever and wherever you can.

COMPLIMENTING

There's an art to both giving and receiving compliments. The key for both is to make sure you mean them and are gracious when receiving them. Who wants to be known as an Eddie Haskell (see *Sincerity*)?

COMPROMISE

Achieving compromise is often very difficult, as there's rarely such a thing as a happy medium. The true measure of a good compromise is when all parties walk away equally unhappy. That's why they call it give and take. Now why do you suppose promise is included in this word? I guess it's to make sure everyone lives up to their end of the bargain.

CONCENTRATION

The look of concentration is often confused with the look of constipation. They shouldn't be confused, as they are not the same.

CONCLUSIONS

As with your artwork, you want to draw your own conclusions. It's best to connect the dots yourself and not be so influenced by everyone else.

CONDESCENDING

Unless you have an unusually large proboscis, it's not acceptable to look down your nose at anyone. Being condescending smacks of elitism, which won't make you any friends. You're no better than they are.

CONDOMS

Use condoms whenever you're in the throes of lovemaking, as there is nothing *dumb* about con*doms* (see *AIDS*). Some claim that using condoms desensitizes men's erectile feeling and inhibits their sexual experience. They're idiots. Yes, you always want to practice safe sex (practice is the fun part). If you think you may be getting lucky, you won't be surprised (see *Parenting* and *Consequences*). Best to keep 'em fresh, just in case you happen to stumble upon someone who wants you. It could happen, you know.

CONFIDE

If you can't confide in a friend, it's probably because they're not one. Another reason to know who your friends are.

CONFIDENCE

Confidence is not something you're born with; it kind of grows inside you (completely dissimilar from germs). Like everything else, it needs proper care and feeding. So give yourself plenty of credit, as success breeds success. Exude confidence whenever you can. Ooze confidence from your pores. But be careful, because being confident and being arrogant are two very different things. We don't like arrogant.

CONFLICT

Show me a relationship with no conflict, and I'll show you a relationship that's going nowhere. Just learn how to deal with it.

CONFRONTATION

Although some relish it, most of us don't like confrontation, and we avoid it like the plague. You shouldn't be afraid to confront someone, but it may not always be the best way to resolve an issue (see *Picking Your Battles*).

CONFUSING

Life can be very confusing, as all isn't as obvious and predictable as one might hope. That's not an excuse; it's a fact.

CONFUSING WORDS

Why do words that are spelled absolutely identically, and even pronounced the same, mean completely different things? Are you going to swim in the pool or shoot some pool (see *English Language*)? What were they thinking when they wrote all of this down? It's got to be some kind of conspiracy. There's no other possible explanation.

CONGRESS

So whose idea was it for Congress to only have two-year terms? It's a wonder they can get anything done, since they're always in a perpetual re-election mode. Come to think of it, maybe that's not so bad (see *Accountability*). Sometimes less is more, but not here. To be more effective, change it to staggered four-year terms. Yes, you heard it here first.

CONNECTION

Being able to have that special bond and level of understanding with someone is a thing to cherish, nurture and protect. This type of connection can be described in other ways too (see *Love*). However, if you simply can't connect with people, you might want to consider returning to your home planet.

CONSCIENCE

You know that annoying voice inside your head that's always warning you when you're about to do something stupid? Well, it wouldn't hurt to listen to it every so often. Now if you don't have a conscience, you'd be wise to go out and get one (usually next to the laundry supplies in the grocery store), and keep it clean. Let your conscience be your guide.

CONSEQUENCES

No matter what you do, there are almost always consequences, both good and bad. Here's the only thing I learned in physics: For every action, there is an equal and opposite reaction. (Actually, I never took physics class, but somebody told me this.) Consequences don't have to be opposite or equal, but if you gotta play, you gotta pay.

CONSERVATION

We have a limited amount of natural resources in this world of ours, and we're now running out of everything (especially toilet paper). So think about that the next time you take that ninth trip to the grocery store on the same day or leave the TV on all night. Conserve, conserve, conserve (see *Selfish*). Leave something for the next group coming into this world, will ya? Oh, and conservation and conversation are two completely different things.

CONSIDERATION

Considering another's feelings before your own will make you a better person. You want to be a better person, right? So stop being so selfish; you may even get used to being considerate.

CONSIDER THE SOURCE

No one likes to be constantly berated and criticized, as it's quite unpleasant and annoying. However, if those beraters are real jerks, it shouldn't bother you at all. If you have no respect for them, it doesn't really matter what they say.

CONSISTENT

One of the hardest things to do in life is to be consistent. That goes for exercise, diet and lovemaking. Now some of us are consistently inconsistent, which isn't so horrible. You don't want to be totally predictable, but consistency does have its pluses (see *Reliable*).

CONSPIRACY THEORIES

There are those who believe in conspiracy theories to explain lots of weird things. I don't. Conspiracies require lots of secret planning and cooperation. Most people can't keep secrets or play nicely together.

CONSTIPATION

Yeech, constipation is no fun. Load up on fiber and lots of water (the eternal cure-all). Bulk, bulk, bulk. Go, go, go.

CONSTITUTION

Could you imagine starting from scratch, writing a document to set up the laws, basic concepts and parameters for a brand-new country? Our forefathers (my guess is that there were probably more than four) had such a daunting task, with little or no precedent or history to guide them. If you ask me, they performed some miracles getting consensus and getting this done. We've lived under the Constitution for well over 200 years and built the strongest and best country in the world. And those Amendments aren't too shabby either. Good job, fellas.

CONSTRUCTIVE CRITICISM

This takes a bit of work, but you really do someone a favor if you can sugarcoat your criticism just a little (see *Diplomatic*). Of course, don't overdo it, as you want to make sure they get your message. But constructive sure beats the hell out of the destructive kind.

CONTENTMENT

If you're lucky enough to ever achieve contentment, share your secret. Unfortunately, it's not so easy.

CONTESTS

Most of us will win very few contests during our lives. I believe there is only so much lifetime luck allocated to each one of us. If you use it up on little things, you likely end up being out of luck. So I'm holding out for winning the lottery or some other big money. That's why I don't enter all those different little sweepstakes and contests, as I don't want to waste my chances. My luck, I'll still end up winning a free soap dispenser or something. Whoopee!

CONTRADICTIONS

Yeah, life is full of contradictions (see *Oxymorons*). But you want to at least try not to contradict yourself. Not too often anyway.

CONTRARY

To argue just for argument's sake is a complete waste of time. Too bad some people make a career of it. Contrarians are those who find fault with everything. Stay away from them, as they'll just bring you down to their level.

CONTROL

Take control of your life, and don't let the wind just blow you around. That's why it's important to pay attention when you're in the driver's seat. Well, another reason, that is.

CONTROL FREAKS

There are those who insist on having to make all decisions regarding everything. They have no confidence in anyone else's ability and feel they must control everything. Hard to expect someone can be right all of the time, as it's not possible. There's another name for them: assholes.

CONVENTIONAL WISDOM

Save conventional wisdom for the conventions. Who cares what everybody else thinks; we're all entitled to our own opinions. Anyway, it doesn't matter what they think; it matters what you think. They call that freedom.

CONVERSATION PIECE

Why do they call it a conversation piece? There must be something wrong with mine. It doesn't say a word.

CONVICTION

Do things with conviction, and say things with conviction. Believe in yourself and others will too. If you sound like you know what you are talking about, they'll think you do. Only you will know when you're full of shit. Here's a helpful hint: always throw some statistics in your discussions. Make them up if you have to. Who cares? If it sounds authoritative, people will rarely challenge you (see *Lying*).

COOLING OFF

Cooling off is often the best way to deal with your nasty anger. Get sprayed with water if you must. Sometimes it really helps.

COOL NAMES

My friends swear that these are real names. Not only do my friends swear a lot but they also lie.

Al B. Back
Al B. Late
Al B. Seanya
Al B. Tross
Al Capella
Al Catraz
Al Fresco
Al G. Bra
Al Gee
Ali Money
Al O. Kate
Alma Mater
Al Paca
Al Truist
Al Vira
Amanda B. Reconwith
Amanda Huginkiss
Anita Bath
Anita Break
Anita Hugg
Ann A. Rexic
Art A. Fact
Art Deco
Arthur Scopic
Aunt Arctica
Barb Wire
Bea True
Beau Leemia
Ben Dover (husband of Ilene)
Ben E. Factor
Ben Nicetonoya
Bill Board
Bill E. Club

Bill E. Ruben
Buster Cherry
Buster Hyman
Charlie Horse
Chester Drawers
Chip Monk
Clair Voyant
Claude Balls
Cliff Hanger
Colin Ascopy
Crystal Clear
Dee Cups
Dick Hurtz
Dick Trickle
Dixie Recht
Drew P. Balls
Drew P. Nutsack
Eileen Dover
Emma InyetFlip Iton
Fonda Peters
Frank Lee
G. Barry Fartzalot
Harry Armpits
Harry Legs
Harry P. Ness
Hava Tampa
Hazel Nut
Helen Wheels
Hugh G. Erection
I. P. Daly
I. P. Freely
Ida Hoe
Ima Hogg

Ivana Tinkle
Izzy Worthit
Jack B. Nimble
Jack B. Quick
Jack Meoff
Jay Walker
Jean Poole
Jen Italia
Jerry Rigged
Jim Nasium
Jim Nastics
Johnny B. Goode
Jose Canusi
Justin Kase
Justin Thyme
Karen Feeding
Kay Nine
Lettuce Pray
Manny Paws
Margo Rita
Marina Peer
Mel Encolly
Mike R. Phone
Mike Rotch
Miss Tory
Mona Lott
Nick Name
Nova Kane
Olive Greene
Ophelia Butts
Ophelia Pane

Paige Turner
Patty O'Furniture
Pearl E. Gates
Perry Winkle
Phil Anthropy
Phil D. Basket
Phil E. Buster
Phil E. Cheesesteak
Phil O. Dendron
Phil R. Monic
Polly Esther
Pop Aratzi
Rick Shaw
R. T. Choke
R. Thritis
R. U. Inyet
Rocko Gibralter
Rufus Leeking
Sara Bellum
Seymour Beaver
Seymour Butz
Shirley U. Gest
Simon Sezz
Sir Cumference
Skip Jack
Tom Ato
Tom Foolery
Van Guard
Violet Blue
Will B. Back
Will Power

From the military, of course, we have:

Admiral Quality
Colonel Lingus
Commander Cody
Corporal Punishment
General Appearance
General Confusion
General E. Speaking
General Impression

General Ledger
General Mayhem
General Motors
Major Disaster
Major Payne
Major Trouble
Major Woodie
Private Parts

97

And we can't forget the infamous Schitt Family, can we?

Crock O. Schitt	Jack Schitt
Fulla Schitt	Loda Schitt
Ho Lee Schitt	Needeep N. Schitt
Giva Schitt	Pisa Schitt

COORDINATION

Coordination is another one of those things you either have or you don't. I truly admire people who have good coordination. The good news is there are degrees of coordination, so you don't have to lose all hope. For instance, maybe you can't dance, but you can play ball. Now for God's sake, if you can't dance, spare us, and just sit down and envy those who can (see *Making A Fool Of Yourself*). There is nothing worse than watching people who have no rhythm try to dance. Trust me, you can't fake this. And don't assume that after you've had a couple of drinks, you automatically become John Travolta (or Mrs. Travolta). Doesn't happen.

COP-OUT

No, a cop-out isn't some sort of police picnic. But using some lame excuse to get out of something does reveal a lot about one's character (see *Spineless*) or lack thereof.

COST OF DOING BUSINESS

Well, sometimes you've just got to pay it. It's just the cost of doing business.

COUCH POTATO

One of the wonderful by-products of the TV generation is the propensity to lay in front of mindless programming for hours and hours on end. If you want to have an early death, then by all means be a couch potato and sit around all the time.

COULDA, WOULDA, SHOULDA

Talk about an exercise in futility. Stop beating yourself up already; it's not healthy and you'll drive yourself crazy. So you didn't—big deal. You can't change the past. Just learn from it and do better next time. Move on, for gosh sake's, and keep those eyes forward (see *Tomorrow*).

Cool Names

COUNSELING

If your relationship isn't working and you're having trouble repairing it, go to counseling—both of you. A referee (or intermediary) will either help the salvage operation or suggest it's time to move on.

COUNT ON

This has nothing to do with numbers. Just be the kind of person that everybody can count on. It's the best kind of math.

COUNT YOUR BLESSINGS

Appreciate what you have, as you could be much worse off than you are right now (see *Perspective*). Remember that you're better off than most people on the entire planet—you really are. So quit complaining and count your blessings. Hopefully you can't count that high.

COUNTRY MUSIC

Country music has way too much twang in it for me. Sorry, I don't do twang.

COVER YOUR MOUTH

As nice as you are, nobody really wants your germs. So when you're coughing, sneezing and hacking away, do us a favor and shield your mouth from everybody else.

COWARDICE

It's perfectly acceptable to be afraid once in a while—we all are. However, it's a whole other matter to run away from all of your problems. You don't want to make a career of it.

CRACK OF DAWN

Things that are cracked usually break. I guess that's why the crack of dawn (poor Dawn's crack) is followed by daybreak.

CRANKY

Cranky people are usually tired (see *Babies*). So go take a nap and don't be such a Grumpelstiltskin. It's best to make sure you get up on the right side of the bed when you awake. I don't know which one that is, since I get up on the left side. Maybe that explains some things. Maybe not.

CRAVINGS

So why do we tend to crave and desire the things we can't or aren't supposed to have? And it seems that once we get what we wanted, the craving isn't completely satisfied (see *Disappointment*).

CREATIONISM vs. EVOLUTION

Is it possible to believe in both evolution and creationism? I think so, because I do. Yes, Darwin was right. We all grew out of the same place (the Garden of Eden?), bringing us to our current model. But do you think all this happened by itself? Something or someone pressed that button to get it all started (see *Big Bang Theory*). Hopefully we're still evolving, as we can stand plenty of improvements.

CREATIVE

Where would we be without filmmakers, artists, composers, songwriters, inventors and scientists? My hat's off to all of them. I don't know how they do it, but God bless them. (I really don't wear hats, by the way.) Everyone possesses the necessary skills to be creative; it's not just a God thing. Some of us create art, some of us create music—and some of us create messes (but they are creative messes). Use your untapped talents and you'll surprise yourself. Getting those creative juices flowing can be a real kick.

CREDIT

Credit isn't always about borrowing money. It's also about not taking credit for something that someone else did, either good or bad. Oh yeah, and don't forget to give credit where credit is due (see *Humble*).

CREMATION

Do us all a favor and tell your loved ones to torch you after you're gone and scatter your ashes in your favorite place. No need to waste all of God's green earth by planting your bones in the ground (see *Cemeteries*). You're not there anyway (see *Afterlife*).

CRIME DOESN'T PAY

Of course crime doesn't pay. And crime does have its resulting costs: insurance increases, stolen items have to be replaced and prison is expensive. So unfortunately we all end up paying for crime one way or another.

CRISIS

If you seem to always live your life going from one crisis to another, something is wrong; probably more than something. You might want to consider stepping back and taking stock, as the fault may actually lie with (see *Fooling Yourself*).

CROSS-DRESSING

It's a free country, so you can dress anyway you'd like. However, because so many of us are rather easily confused, it's best to wear boys' clothes if you're a boy and girls' clothes if you're a girl. If you're not sure, pick one— but not both. Boys' clothes for me.

CROSSING YOUR LEGS

Girls, I can't really help you here, but they say you need to cross your legs in a ladylike fashion. Sure, I like ladies (get it—ladylike?), but I have no idea what that means. Now boys, don't be crossing your legs with one knee over the other like old men do. People will think your penis is gone. You could also get a bad case of crushed nuts that way. That's why it's always best to have your ankle placed over your opposite knee. Just be careful when you're wearing shorts, as you don't want your goodies to hang out. OK, maybe you do (see *Advertising*).

CROWDS

I don't like crowds; way too crowded.

CRUEL

There's never anything to gain here by being a meanie, so don't be cruel. Thank you, Elvis.

CRYING

We live in a society where it's only cool for ladies to cry, right? Wrong. We all can laugh, so there's nothing wrong with crying too (see *Balance*). It's very OK to cry; just don't start another Niagara Falls. Although crying never really solves anything, a good cry oftentimes makes you feel better. It kind of purges your body (see *Puking*). If you see someone cry, it sometimes becomes contagious. I have no idea why—same thing with laughing. Remember: everybody cries, even (especially) those really tough guys who won't admit it. Don't believe me? Just see what happens when they get kidney stones; they cry like babies. So no one is too big to cry.

CRYING WOLF

If you keep crying wolf, people will eventually stop believing and listening to you (and that's not a good thing). That is, of course, if they ever did.

CULTURE

Ah, a little culture once in a while won't kill you. You might even learn something; or, better yet, like it.

CUPBOARD IS BARE

What's a cupboard, and why doesn't it have any clothes on?

CURES

The old saying goes: They can send a man to the moon, but they can't find a cure for the common cold. Notice they never sent a woman up there (see *Sexist*)? Who cares about the common cold? You get over it, right? But there are a whole lot of deadly diseases that should have been cured by now. During the dawn of the space age, with all of the vast problems in the world, this country was united in our quest to reach the moon. Lots of money was spent, lots of technology was invented, lots of people were involved and the dream was realized. We need to commit that same level of funding, national attention and enthusiasm to conquering these horrible diseases. Just throwing more money at a problem doesn't always solve it, but in this case, it helps. I'm getting off my soapbox now. Have you ever seen a soapbox? I saw two guys box once. However, it wasn't very pretty (see *Digressing*).

CURIOSITY

Curiosity killed the cat. That's perfectly OK—I don't like cats (see *Cats*).

CURSING

Cursing has its place in this world. It's very therapeutic to sprinkle in a swear word now and then, usually when you're alone. It does tend to add some spice and a little extra emphasis to a conversation, but should probably be used sparingly, especially around children. I don't follow that advice too well, but shit, no one's perfect. Color me guilty.

CURVE BALLS

Sure, life throws us lots of curve balls. So you get out of the batter's box, dust yourself off and take a deep breath. Then you go back in, swinging for the fences.

CURVES

Life rarely goes as planned, nor should it. That's why it's always best to keep your eye out for the curves ahead. No, not those curves (see *Cleavage*).

CUTTING BAGELS

Many brave souls have had their hands sliced to bits while cutting a bagel in half. Why? Because they did it wrong, that's why. The proper way to cut a bagel is very simple: Lay the bagel flat (not on its edge) on a cutting surface, with one hand on top to steady the bagel and the other hand slicing from right to left (or left to right—your choice). Halfway through, with the knife still in, turn the bagel on its edge and cut it the rest of the way in a downward motion. Safety first, as bagel injuries can be life-threatening (and quite embarrassing), you know.

CUTTING IN LINE

Unless your intestines or kidneys are about to explode or a baby is on its way out of the hatch, cutting in line is strictly prohibited.

CUTTING YOUR NAILS

Girls, I have no idea what you do to keep your nails looking so pretty. But boys, keep those nails trimmed. Best to cut them after a shower when they're soft. And don't leave those clippings on the floor for people to step on; they go in the trash. Or flush them down the toilet.

CUTTING YOUR LOSSES

As with lots of things in life, there comes a time when you have to be practical and honest with yourself. Hope can only go so far until reality stares you in the face. That's the time to get out while you can.

DAMNED IF YOU DO

Damned if you do and damned if you don't. So you might as well do (see *Do Something*).

DAMSEL IN DISTRESS

It doesn't matter if she's in dis dress or dat dress—help her anyway (see *Open the Door*).

DANGLING

Fish or cut bait; don't leave people dangling. It's very unfair and selfish to keep someone on the hook, not knowing if they are going to be dumped or not. That goes for lovers, employees and soon to be ex-friends.

DARE

Daring someone to do something is pretty dumb. Taking someone up on their dare is even dumber.

DARKEST HOUR

Yes, the darkest hour is just before dawn. This is done on purpose. It's to show us that when things seem bleakest, a little ray of sunshine appears to signal better times ahead (see *Hope*).

DARK SIDE

We all have a dark side. When it's telling you to do something you shouldn't, just don't pay attention to it. Listen to the bright side.

DAY

Because you can't control everything, each day is like a new adventure. Embrace it and enjoy is, as you never want to take a day for granted.

DAY OF RECKONING

The rotten things you do will catch up with you sooner or later. So sleep tight.

DAYS

Seven days in a week? Hardly. Consider these:

Bad Day	Happy Day
Birthday	Heyday
Black Day	Ice Cream Day (I made that up)
Dog Day	Judgment Day
Doomsday	Nice Day
Dennis Day	Off Day (or Day Off)
Doris Day	Rainy Day
Field Day	Someday
Good Day	

And of course you can't forget these seven days (they make a week, you know):

A Month of Sundays (don't ask)	Thirsty Thursday (I made that up too)
Monday, Monday	
Tuesday Weld	Gal Friday
Wednesday's Child	Saturday Night Live

DAYS ARE NUMBERED

Of course everyone's days are numbered. All you have to do is look at the calendar. Those aren't letters next to each day, silly; they're numbers. Sheesh!

DEAD

They say you should never speak ill of the dead. That makes no sense to me. Why glorify someone simply because they're dead, especially if they were a real asshole the whole time they were alive? Go ahead and blast them. What's the worst that can happen? You'll get hit by lightning? Well, maybe you should reconsider blasting them too hard (see *Pragmatic*).

DEADLINES

Nothing dead about deadlines, as we all live by them and can't escape them. We have work deadlines, school deadlines, bill-paying deadlines and having-baby deadlines, to name a few. Maybe it's not such a bad thing, because without deadlines nothing would likely ever get done. So if no one else sets them, you may want to. However those self-imposed deadlines are typically the hardest to meet (see *Procrastination*).

DEATH

Death is a part of life and inevitable; we simply have to accept it. When it's time, it's time. Actually, we start dying on the day we're born, which is a rather morbid thought, but true. They call death the great equalizer. I don't know what that means, but they say lots of things I don't understand (see *They*). On many levels, death really does bring the ultimate peace. However, I think it's just another chapter in life, and it may actually be a different beginning. Life may be practice for something bigger and better (see *Rationalization*). We're all afraid of death because we really don't know what happens. As for those who've passed, we can always keep them alive through our memories, right? And our parents are always with us, even if only in spirit, because that's their job (see *Parenting*). So they're never really gone. They just speak to us in a very different way.

DEATH AND TAXES

Yeah, we all die, but we all don't pay taxes. Trust me on this one.

DEATH PENALTY

I know that all life is precious. But killing the killer will never compensate for the loss of the victim and will never bring them back. An eye for an eye is looking for vengeance, which won't get you anywhere, right? I'm torn on this issue because there's only one way to absolutely guarantee a killer will never harm another, and that's capital punishment. If they take someone's life deliberately and maliciously, I don't think they deserve to keep theirs.

DEATH WARMED OVER

Come on ladies, you don't ever want to leave the house looking like death warmed over. Men, however, often can't help it (see *Shaving*).

DEATH WISH

Death wish? Try wishing for something else or you might wake up dead one day (see *Risk*).

DEBT

Our society relies heavily on debt. We are constantly encouraged to borrow money to buy things that we can't otherwise afford (see *Instant Gratification*). To follow the American Dream of owning a house, everyone has to get a mortgage. Need a car? Take out a loan. And use your credit cards to buy everything else. It's so easy—way too easy. All of a sudden we've got brand-new DVD players, TVs, IPods, computers, and we owe a lot of money. Here's a news flash: Don't borrow any more than you can afford to pay back. Period (see *Discipline*). Is that too complicated?

DECISIVE

Once you make a decision, stick to it; or at least give it a chance. Assess all of the available data, get opinions from others (if you must), then go for it. Don't look back, as second-guessing is a complete waste of time. However, this doesn't mean that you can't change your mind at some point and cut your losses if you have to (see *Admit You're Wrong*).

Death Wish

DECLUTTER

Our incoming crap tends to significantly outweigh our outgoing crap. We therefore tend to accumulate all kinds of useless junk. After a while, the excess trash propagates and crowds you out. So take the time and just declutter your life. Start now, before you are forced to get a big place to house all that ridiculous stuff.

DECOMPRESS

After those rough meetings, a very long day or taking that nasty test, you may want to sit back and recharge those batteries. Never mind the maybe. Lots of deep breaths and some other relaxation exercises should really help (see *Yoga*).

DEEDS

Ultimately, your value in this world is not usually based on the things you hope to do, intend to do or want to do. It's all about the deeds you accomplish. And the only one to stop you is you.

DEER

Sorry, Bambi fans, but deer are actually overgrown rodents. They eat your flowers, carry those malicious ticks (see *Lyme Disease*) and smoke cigarettes while playing poker in your driveway. Just like underarm hair, they have no redeemable qualities.

DEFEATIST ATTITUDE

If you've already decided you can't win or succeed, why bother trying? Bother (see *Giving Up*).

DEFER

When in doubt, it's often best to defer to someone who knows more than you. Plenty do, as even you can't know everything. This doesn't excuse you from making your own (not urine) decisions. It just gives you an opportunity to collect information and get some advice from trusted and respected individuals.

DEFIANT

If you defy authority, be prepared for the consequences. And there are lots of consequences.

DEFINE YOURSELF

Don't' let someone else define you. That's your job (see *Reputation*). It's what freedom is all about.

DEGRADING

You don't want to degrade anyone or let anyone degrade you. It's all about respect, which everyone (including you) deserves.

DEHYDRATION

There are studies which seem to indicate that many of our everyday maladies are the result of dehydration. Headaches, sore throats, joint pain, etc. I think there is something to this. So drink, drink, drink, until your pee is clear. You want to flush all of the nasties out of your body. All day, every day. Nighttime—not so much (see *Wetting Your Bed*).

DÉJÀ VU

What's déjà vu all about? Maybe it's a parallel universe. It's so eerie though, like you've been down that road before. I would so much like to control my déjà vu's; maybe even go down different roads. Wouldn't you?

DELIVER

If you're all talk and no action, you're going to wind up being the only one who listens to you. Don't just talk—deliver.

DELUSIONAL

If you always know what's real, you'll always stay grounded. Wishing is one thing; living in a fantasy world is another. Sure, everyone has delusions of grandeur, and those delusions aren't necessarily bad (see *Hoping*). Oh, we can dream, can't we? Just don't quit your day job.

DEMOCRACY

Despite all of our whining and complaining (and we do plenty of whining and complaining), democracy is still the best form of government there is (see *Perfection*). Those Four Fathers must have been pretty smart. But whose idea was it to allow presidential campaigns to last four years? Why didn't they have the foresight to at least ban those stupid and mindless TV commercials? And what happened to those Four Mothers anyway (see *Sexist*)? Just remember that democracy is not a spectator sport.

DENTIST

Suffice it to say that just hearing that high-speed drill is enough to send shivers up and down your spine. And don't you just love the wonderful smell of burning teeth? I'll never know why they insist on having those long, drawn out, one-way conversations with you. Your answers are just gurgles that they can't possibly understand. Maybe they really don't care what you have to say, as they're probably telling the same story to patients all day. But remember that when it comes to your teeth, your dentist is your friend.

DEODORANT

If in doubt, always load up on that fragrant masking stuff. B.O. is P.U. (pretty ugly).

DEPENDABLE

The more people can depend on you, the more powerful you become. Go ahead and flex your dependability.

DEPRESSION

The blues got you down? Well that happens to everybody, as we all get depressed from time to time. If it gets real bad, don't fool around. Go ahead and seek some help (see *Psychotherapy*). There is no shame in seeking treatment—absolutely no shame. No stigma is attached to this anymore, as it's become a very popular malady, so don't let that stop you. Exercise can really help tone down the symptoms (it releases lots of endorphins), so you might want to try that too. Also, if you're depressed, excessive sleep is not your friend. You think it's an escape, but too much sleep is your enemy. Remember: mental illness is a disease that can be treated.

DESPERATE

Desperate people do desperate things. Don't allow yourself to be put into that situation, and stay away from those who are. You can spot them a mile away, as they growl a lot.

DESSERT

Dessert is something you can afford to pass up once in a while. But not always—you gotta live, right (see *Moderation*)?

DESTINY

If you're waiting for things to happen by themselves, they won't. For the most part, you control your own destiny.

DESTRUCTIVE

You don't want to be known as someone who's always destructive, so try being *con*structive. You might even like it.

DETAILS

If you're the kind of person who remembers to take care of the details, then you're the kind of person that others will remember. It's the little things that make you stand out the most.

DEVIL

Don't forget: there's lots of <u>evil</u> in the d<u>evil</u>. That's what makes him (or her) bad.

DEVIL IS IN THE DETAILS

Seemingly great ideas can be completely sidetracked when you get enmeshed (I so like that word) in the details. Maybe that tells you it wasn't such a good idea after all. If so, you may want to stick with the big picture (see *Perspective*) and leave the details for someone else. Anyway, doesn't the devil have better things to do than bother with your details?

DIARRHEA

Couldn't our stomachs find a nicer way to let us know when they're sick? How about a more subtle and less embarrassing message to the brain after all of that chili and onions? Like "Don't eat that crap again." That would work for me.

DICTATORS

Can you think of a better way to describe a real dick?

DIETING

So you get frustrated because you can't lose your gut after one day of diet and exercise. You might want to jot this down: it took you a while to develop that lovely physique, and it will take a while to get rid of it (see *Perseverance*). Yes, dieting is often an exercise in futility. Unless you're big on the Ds in diet (discipline and determination—OK, there's only one D in diet), you lose weight and then you gain it back. You lose some more; you gain back some more. Here's a hint: in general, the better something tastes, the worse it likely is for you. Doctors tell you to watch what you eat; and they don't mean to watch as you shove all that garbage into your mouth, you know. If you really want to lose weight and get healthier, then you've got to change your lifestyle— permanently. Sorry, there just is no easy way around it. Stay away from junk food, don't smoke, don't drink too much (except water), eat less and move around a lot (see *Exercise*). The longer you put this off, the harder it gets, so start now. Don't procrastinate, as there is no time like the present. It's not just the best way; it's the only way.

DIFFERENCE

So here's your choice: you can be a nobody all of your life, or you can make a difference in this world. Make a difference. The world will be a better place because of you.

DIFFERENT

Don't ever be afraid to be different (see *Unique*). Otherwise, you'll be just like everybody else. And who wants that; there's already too many of them around.

Dieting

DIGESTING

Always give your body time to digest your food (see *Mastication*). The slower you eat, the faster you get filled up, which also tends to keep you from overeating. You also want to have time to digest the facts, as it's best to do that *before* you react.

DIGNITY

Above all, everyone deserves their dignity. Think about it: If you don't have your dignity, you don't have anything. You can give it up if you want to, but no one else can take away your dignity. No one.

DIGRESS

Oh yes, I digress plenty. It's a disease and comes with talking (or writing) too much.

DINGLEBERRIES

Dingleberries are mostly a male phenomenon (see *Hygiene*). They are not a fruit of any sort and therefore not ripe for the picking.

DINOSAURS

Dinosaurs are extinct. If you keep thinking and living like a dinosaur, you'll be extinct too. Get with it already (see *Caveman Syndrome*).

DIPLOMA

Fortunately for many, they don't put your grades on your diploma. So no matter what, getting a diploma is an achievement. For some, it's a huge achievement. Congratulations!

DIPLOMATIC

You don't have to have a career in the Foreign Service to be a diplomat. You just have to be careful and considerate of the things you say and the way you say them.

DIRECTIONS

Men don't often follow (or take) directions very well. But this is nothing new. Maybe it's a macho thing, but it's so hard for us to ask, as we're on a quest and it's almost like giving up. And following directions can take all the fun out of the adventure. If you're a woman passenger in a car, it's best not to yell at us when we're lost (see *Ego*). We already know we're lost, so it doesn't help to point this out, especially at an elevated decibel level. Try to calmly get us un-lost. After all, you want to get there in one piece, don't you? Now I have no idea why we tend to turn down the volume of the radio when we are trying to figure out where we are. Maybe our brains can't take that extra stimulation. And of course, some of us get lost going around the block but won't admit it (I freely admit it). Anyway, if you don't know where you're going or what you're doing, at least get someone who does to point you in the right direction. It's a start.

DIS

Dis's and dat's are a part of life. You want to stay away from deese dis's:

Disagreeable
Disappear
Disappoint
Disarray
Disaster
Discard (or dat card)
Discombobulate
Discomfort
Discontent
Discord
Discourage
Discourteous
Discredit
Disdain
Disease
Disenchant
Disengaged (unless the
    wedding is off)
Dis-function
Disgraceful
Disgruntled
Disgusting
Dishearten

Dishevel
Dishonest
Dishonor
Disillusion
Disingenuous
Disinterested
Disjointed
Dismantle
Dismay (dat-may is fine)
Dismember
Disobedient
Disorderly
Disorganized
Disorient
Disparaging
Dispel
Dis-picable
Dis-pising
Disqualified
Disregard
Disrespect
Disrupt
Dissatisfied

Dissect   Distrusting
Dissent   Disturbing
Distractions

DISABILITY

Some people can't do things like the rest of us. Some can't walk, some can't hear, some can't see. But they're all human beings who deserve to be treated with dignity and respect (see *Compassion*). Your job is not to pity them, but to be as supportive and helpful as possible.

DISAPPOINTMENT

Yes, life is full of disappointments, as things don't always go the way you want or expect them to. It's not fun to feel let down, but it's best to learn from your disappointments and get over them. Not having high expectations helps, and not setting yourself up for the fall helps even more. Disappointing others—now that is something you can control (see *Reputation*). Try not to do that.

DISASTER

Unfortunately, it sometimes takes a disaster to bring people together. If you live through one, you can at least build on it. Some good often comes from adversity.

DISCIPLINE

There's discipline, and then there's discipline. So what is it about our society? We can have the best of intentions: to lose weight, exercise or watch what we say. But sticking to our guns and staying with it is most often the hard part. I am convinced that discipline is inversely proportional to age; the higher the age, the lower the discipline. God knows why. For instance, the potential benefits of staying on a rather strict regimen to drop some excess poundage should be enough incentive to be well disciplined. One would think that the prospect of good health and long life would be enough to give you the discipline you need. It's not. Damn.

DISCRIMINATION

The only part of you that should ever discriminate is your palate. Otherwise, there's no place for it. No place. Ever. Are you getting this?

DISHING IT OUT

If you can't take it, don't dish it out.

DISINGENUOUS

Oh, for goodness' sake, only be genuine. Everyone can tell when you're not.

DISRESPECTFUL

We're all human and it's hard to keep from being irreverent at times; and some people are just plain hard to get along with. But being disrespectful is not really excusable. It's OK to think it; just don't say it or let your facial expressions give you away (see *Temptation*). How can you expect anyone to respect you if you act in such a disrespectable manner? Well?

DISTRACTED DRIVING

Are you crazy? Put that stupid phone away, turn off the DVD player and pay attention to how you're driving. Whatever emergency text message you're getting about the latest episode of your favorite TV show can wait (see *Instant Gratification*). You can't possibly concentrate on driving when you're distracted by your portable devices. Remember: you can kill someone (or even yourself) with that car if you're not careful. And it's not just about keeping yourself out of trouble; you're trying to be safe from all those other idiots on their stupid phones.

DISTRACTION

It's often very difficult to avoid distractions when you're trying to get anything done, especially something important. You need lots of determination, discipline and focus, which often seems to be in short supply (see *Eye On The Ball*).

DIVINE INTERVENTION

We usually know how things happen, but often can't explain why. So you tell me: Could it be the Guy (Gal) upstairs? I say yes.

DIVORCE

No one can really know what goes on inside a marriage except the participants, so being on the outside looking in doesn't tell you anything. All I know is that it takes a lot of work to get along with anybody, much less the person you are married to. There is no such thing as an amicable divorce, especially when money and/or children are involved. If there are young children involved, find a way to do what's best for them (see *Selfish*). Having to finally give up and become divorced is very sad, embarrassing and difficult to do. Sometimes it's the only option. Ultimately, you need to be happy—and that's not a selfish goal. Just know if that goal is possible after divorce.

DO AS I SAY

Do as I say, not as I do? Nonsense; that's backwards. Don't you want to be a good role model? A lot of people are watching, you know.

DO BEE

OK, it's a little outdated, but it's still better to be a "do bee" than a "don't be." Well, maybe a lot outdated.

DOCTORS

Well, doctors aren't in the profession for the money anymore, as managed care has killed that. Come to think of it, managed care has killed a lot of things. And just like everything else in this world, there are good doctors and there are not so good doctors. But most really care and try to heal the sick, and that puts them way up in my book (they're in the Ds, for gosh sake). And they have so much influence over us. Just some reassuring words from them tend to put us at ease (such as "No, that hangnail likely won't kill you"). However, an occasional "I've never seen this before" or "Yech" would have quite the opposite effect. We'd be in pretty bad shape without doctors. Go docs!

DOCTOR'S OFFICE

If you walk in and see a lot of magazines in the doctor's office, chances are you're in for a long wait. Look on the bright side: a crowded waiting room usually means it's a good (or cheap) doctor (see *Rationalizing*).

DODGING A BULLET

A bullet always has the advantage, as it travels much faster than you. So you actually have a better chance of dodging a ball. Play nice.

DOG DROPPINGS

Since I'm not real good about picking up after the dog, I rationalize that it's good fertilizer. This is perfectly OK, as long as it's not me who steps in it.

DOGS

I find it so fascinating that dogs can lick their hind parts, a talent most of us don't have. When everybody else is mad at you, a dog will jump and lick you all over (of course, in only the most appropriate places). So it's not a bad idea to get a dog to keep you company, as long as you properly care for it. But what's up with that dog food—yeech! Do they really like that stuff? And why can't they pee all at one time? They've got to tinkle a little here, and tinkle a little there. I guess it has something to do with spreading the wealth around. I know that dogs wag their tails when they're happy, but how come you never see them smile? And, contrary to popular thinking, you *can* teach an old dog new tricks (see *Change*).

DOING IT ALL

You may think that you can do it all, but nobody ever can. It's not humanly possible. That's why they invented friends and family.

DO IT RIGHT

If something's worth doing, do it right. Otherwise, don't bother. And while you're at it, try doing it right the first time.

DO ME A FAVOR

You don't tell someone to do you a favor, you ask them. Unfortunately, when you hear these words, it's usually not a request or question, but more of a demand or expectation. So if you have that phrase delivered as a non-question, it's best to start running.

DO THE RIGHT THING

You'll never go wrong doing the right thing. Never. But it's not always easy to know the difference between right and wrong. And sometimes it's very convenient to be confused (see *Rationalization*). However, it's very difficult to lie to yourself, so you usually know the right way, deep down inside, don't you?

DONE

Even though you think you're done, you're never completely done. There's always something else to do. But what's done is done. So move on.

DON'T KNOW

We don't know a whole lot more than we ever knew. And that's OK (see *Learning*).

DON'T POOP WHERE YOU EAT

Besides getting rather messy (and in this case rather disgusting), mixing business with pleasure can make things quite complicated.

DONUTS

Don't you just love a good donut? (Like there's such a thing as a bad donut.) Too bad it's one of the worst fat pills you can take.

DOOM AND GLOOM

Getting caught up in doom and gloom does nothing but breed more doom and gloom. It's infectious. Stay away.

DO OR DIE

I'd go with do, every time (see *Do Something*). Dying may not be too pleasant.

DOORMAT

If they're constantly walking all over you—it's not them, it's you (see *Self-Esteem*). Tell them to wipe their shoes somewhere else.

DOs AND DON'Ts

Try to follow these simple rules in life.

Do:

> It (listen, you procrastinators, just do it, and stop with the excuses already).
> It right.

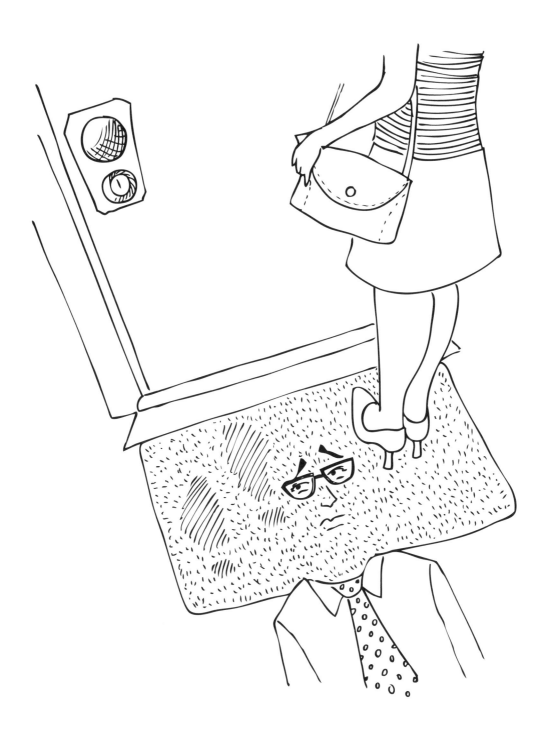

Doormat

It your way (put your signature on it).
It yourself (you usually get lots of satisfaction that way).
Kind things.
Something.
Something nice.
The best you can (only you will know).
The right thing.
Unto others before they do unto you (nah, just making sure you're paying attention; treat others as you would like to be treated).
What you say you'll do (there are already too many empty promises in this world).
You think I'm made of money?

Don't:

Abuse anything or anybody.
Anger the people who prepare your food.
Answer a question with a question.
Apologize for something that's not your fault.
Appear overanxious.
Argue with someone carrying a gun.
Ask, don't tell.
Ask the same question a hundred times.
Badger (gentle questioning is OK).
Beat yourself up.
Be petty.
Berate.
Betray a friend.
Betray anyone's confidence.
Bite the hand that feeds you.
Bother Wellanuf (it's best to leave Wellanuf alone).
Break your promise.
Burn any bridges.
Buy what you can't afford.
Cheat (it's never worth it).
Cut in line.
Cut off another driver.
Cut off your nose to spite your face (you would look very silly without a nose anyway).
Dawdle (some kind of dance, I think).
Depend on someone else for your happiness.

Dillydally (at least don't dally).
Discipline your children in front of others.
Dish it out if you can't take it.
Do something stupid.
Drink and drive.
Drink on the job.
Eat between meals (it will spoil your dinner).
Eat right before you go to sleep.
Eat the yellow snow.
Eat where you poop (yech).
Eat while driving.
Enable
End a sentence with a preposition.
Ever lose hope.
Ever pass up a chance to pee.
Exaggerate.
Feed the animals.
Feel sorry for yourself.
Fidget (oh, who can help it?).
Flaunt.
Forget to brush.
Forget to change your oil.
Forget to check the air in your tires.
Forget to flush.
Forget to say thank you.
Forget to shower (every day, please).
Forget to wash behind your ears.
Forget to write.
Forget where you came from.
Forget your manners.
Forget your rubbers (see *Sex*).
Forsake your friends.
Forsake your health.
Fret (unless you're a guitar).
Get in your own way.
Give into peer pressure.
Give up the ship.
Give up without a fight.
Go grocery shopping when you're hungry.
Go near animals with very large teeth.
Go out without shaving (this is mostly for boys).

Gossip.
Go there.
Grope.
Hire a friend or relative.
Hitchhike.
Impose.
Intentionally hurt someone's feelings.
Interrupt (guilty as charged).
Invade someone's privacy.
Jaywalk.
Keep a lady waiting.
Kick 'em when they're down.
Knock it 'til you try it.
Leave the house without brushing your teeth (and your hair too).
Leave your keys in the car.
Lend money to a friend or relative.
Let anyone push you around.
Let anyone take advantage of you.
Let down your friends and family.
Let the facts get in the way of a good argument.
Let them dangle.
Let the sun catch you crying.
Let your children talk to strangers (unless you're there).
Lick your lips in the cold weather.
Lie.
Litter.
Live your life in someone else's shadow.
Look down.
Lower yourself.
Make a mess.
Make a promise you can't keep.
Make fun of the elderly.
Marry the rebound girl or guy.
Mess with Mother Nature.
Mow the lawn when the grass is wet.
Nitpick.
Open a door you can't close.
Outsmart yourself.
Overdo it.
Paint with your good clothes on (OK to paint naked).
Pander.

Park there.

Pass go.

Pass on the right.

Patronize.

Pick a fight.

Pick on anyone.

Pick your nose (while in your car).

Placate.

Play dumb.

Play favorites.

Play in traffic.

Point.

Provoke.

Put all your eggs in one basket.

Put your nose where it doesn't belong (see *Brownnosing*).

Quit.

Raise your hand to anyone (raising your hand to ask a question or for permission to go to the bathroom are both OK).

Raise your voice.

Reward unacceptable behavior.

Risk more than you can afford to lose.

Rock the boat.

Rubberneck

Rub it in.

Run alone.

Run red lights.

Run with lollipops.

Run with scissors.

Rush to judgment.

Self-medicate.

Send emails you don't want the whole world to see.

Settle.

Slurp your soup.

Smother.

Sniff your armpits in public.

Spend money you don't have.

Squander.

Start something you can't finish.

Step on someone's toes.

Stop moving (see *Exercise*).

Stop thinking about tomorrow (sorry, couldn't help it).

Sweat the small stuff (it's mostly small stuff).
Swim alone.
Tailgate.
Take advantage.
Take anyone for granted.
Take any wooden nickels (what are wooden nickels?).
Take a ride from strangers.
Take candy from strangers.
Take crap from anyone.
Take unnecessary risks.
Take something that doesn't belong to you.
Take yourself too seriously.
Talk back.
Text while driving.
Think twice (it's alright).
Threaten.
Touch that.
Try this at home.
Try to live up to others' expectations.
Underestimate the power of the force.
Underestimate yourself (ever).
Use your cell phone while driving.
Use double negatives (don't never).
Use sex as leverage.
Use the same word more than once in the same sentence (unless
    you're me).
Use your napkin as a tissue.
Use your sleeve as a napkin (or tissue, for gosh sake).
Use your tissue as a napkin (or sleeve).
Wait until the last minute (I've really got to work on that).
Walk alone.
Walk on the grass (it's just for viewing).
Waste anyone's time (especially your own).

Don't be:

A bump on a log.
Abusive.
A crank pot.
A deadhead.
A doormat.

A follower (not blindly
    anyway).
A grandstander.
Afraid.
Afraid of the dark.

Afraid of the truth.

Afraid to apologize.

Afraid to ask.

Afraid to be yourself.

Afraid to reach out to someone.

Afraid to take risks.

Afraid to tell the truth.

Aggressive.

A glutton for punishment.

A hermit.

A jerk.

A knucklehead.

Ambivalent.

An airhead.

An asshole.

An enabler.

An idiot.

Annoying.

Antagonistic.

A pervert.

A punching bag.

Arbitrary.

Ashamed.

A shrinking violet.

A sitting duck (probably don't want to be a standing duck either).

A stick-in-the-mud.

A stranger.

A Sunday driver (except on Sunday).

A two-timer.

Cheap.

Cluttered (a cluttered mind is a wasted mind).

Combative.

Complacent.

Condescending.

Cruel (sorry).

Dismissive.

Deceptive.

Delinquent.

Desperate.

Destructive.

Disrespectful.

Duped.

Embarrassed.

Frivolous.

Fuddled.

Gratuitous.

Greedy.

Grudge.

Guile.

Hurtful.

Impatient.

Impolite.

Impossible.

Impractical.

Impudent.

Inappropriate.

Indifferent.

Insensitive.

Insincere.

Intolerable.

Jealous.

Judgmental.

Labor.

Late for dinner (or any other meal).

Lazy.

Little.

Loud.

Misleading.

Moan.

Nasty.

Negative.

Oblivious.

Obnoxious.

Offensive.

Over-protective.

Paranoid.

Phony.

Pompous.

Pushy.

Presumptuous.

Ridiculous.

Reluctant to apologize.

Ridiculous.

Rude.

Sarcastic (well, don't be too sarcastic).

Scammed.

Selfish.

Shallow.

Showy.

Silly (OK, you can be silly).

Solicitous.

Something you're not.

Stifling.

Stingy.

Stupid.

Suggestive (unless you really have a suggestion; see *Cock Teaser*).

Too serious.

Tray.

Ungrateful.

Vain.

Vengeful (no one wants to be full of venge, anyway).

Wasteful.

Your own worst enemy.

Don't say:

Anything racially insensitive, including racial epithets.

Don't make me come back there/stop the car/turn around/use my belt.

I brought you into this world, and I can take you out.

I hate you.

I'll give you something to cry about.

I'll kill you.

These are words you can't take back, so you're better off not saying them in the first place.

DO SOMETHING

It's much better to do something, rather than do nothing. Sitting around just coasting through life and complaining will only get you so far. But if a job is worth doing, you want to do it right; don't just go through the motions. Think about it: if not you, who? And if not now, when?

DOUBLE CHINS

Do double chins serve any real purpose? We're supposed to have two eyes, two ears, two arms, etc. But only one chin, right? Another design flaw, I think. Hopefully, it will be corrected in the next model.

DOUBLE Ds

God knows why someone would choose to expand their breast size to such high proportions. I'm told by some who come by it naturally that it's a real problem to haul those things around everywhere. If that's what God gave you, you're likely stuck with it (them). Sure, for us boys, it's nice to look at, but it may not be worth all that trouble (see *Consequences*).

DOUBLE STANDARDS

Two sets of rules? One for you and one for everyone else? Hardly. Very few of us are allowed to follow our own set of personal rules (see *Not-Me Syndrome*). Sorry, you're just like the rest of us.

DOUBTS

We all have doubts, even those who seem very self-assured (although they're usually the last ones to admit it). You just don't want doubts to rule your life. If you constantly doubt yourself, buy up some of that self-confidence juice and drink lots of it. Doubters do fill a wonderful role in our society; they typically make you work harder to prove them wrong. Oh, and stay away from that Doubting Thomas guy, whoever he is.

DO WHAT YOU SAY

And say what you do. Good words to live by.

DOWN PAT

Poor Pat. She (or he must be of the rather large variety to be able to ingest all of that stuff that goes down them.

DOWN THAT ROAD

If you've been down that road before, there's no excuse for making the same wrong turns this time (see *Mistakes*).

DREAMS

Go ahead and follow your dreams. Just make sure they're at least mildly attainable, as some people spend their time chasing too many rainbows. Dreams really can come true, and it surely can happen to you.

DRESS FOR SUCCESS

Yes, you can dress them up, but you can't take them out, right? Sometimes. But if you want to act the part, you've got to look the part. If you look good, you feel good, and good things can't be too far away. Successful people tend to look successful. I'd start there.

DRESSING

Sorry, gents, but girls are generally better dressers (see *Sexist*). Anyway, guys look silly in dresses. However, ladies—unlike boys, you can't dress right or left (see *Penis Envy*). Like it matters to us either.

DRINK LOTS OF WATER

Water is your friend and is very good for you (see *Water*). Keep drinking, and keep peeing. It's great for your plumbing—and for your skin, as it enhances your complexion. Remember to drink so your pee is always clear. OK, so that's rather personal, but it's important. If you only drink when you're thirsty, you've waited too long.

DRINK MORE WATER

Are you paying attention here? Keep drinking. You really can't drink too much water.

DRIVE

Being driven isn't necessarily a bad thing. Just don't let it consume you.

DROWNING YOUR SORROWS

If you think drowning your sorrows is productive, knock yourself out. However, when you wake up from your stupor, your problems will likely still be there.

DRUGS

Good drugs, taken properly, can do wonders for you. But if they're illegal or not prescribed, stay away from them. No exceptions—it will only get you into trouble. Big trouble.

DRUNK DRIVING

Drunk driving can cause the single most preventable form of destruction there is. If you drink too much, you're too stupid to know you can't drive. So either limit your drinking or get somebody else to drive. And for God's sake, if you see someone is too drunk to drive, TAKE THEIR KEYS! (Can you hear me?) How hard is that? Are you worried that they might get mad at you? Worry that they might get killed or, worse yet, kill someone else (see *Risk*). Use your head.

DUCT TAPE

When all else fails, duct tape can usually do the trick. It's the universal go-to product. It can do anything.

DUMB THINGS PEOPLE SAY

Like somebody is going to say "Sure I will" to any of these:

Bite your tongue.	Go play in traffic.
Break a leg.	Go pound sand.
Eat me.	Go soak your head.
Eat my shorts.	Go to hell.
Get lost.	Kiss my ass.
Get outta here.	Knock 'em dead.
Go fuck yourself.	Knock yourself out.
Go jump in a lake.	Sit on it.
Go lay an egg (good luck with	Stick it up your ass.
that one).	Stick it up your nose.

DYEING YOUR HAIR

Women generally dye their hair to be fashionable. Men dye their hair to look younger. Gentlemen, you're not fooling anybody—and you look stupid. Gray is OK.

DYING

Here's an uplifting observation: Of course you start dying the day you're born. Some of us benefit from a very, very slow death.

DYSFUNCTIONAL FAMILIES

Being in a dysfunctional family used to carry a stigma. Unfortunately, this is now becoming the norm. So much for progress.

EACH OTHER

Here's how to make a long-term commitment with your mate:

Be nice to each other.
Be warm with each other.
Cry with each other.
Eat with each other.
Hug each other.
Kiss each other.
Laugh with each other.
Listen to each other.
Love each other.

Nap with each other.
Play with each other (take that any way you want).
Shower with each other.
Sing to each other.
Sit with each other.
Talk to each other.
Wait for each other.

EAR HAIR

Come on, guys, do you know how disgusting ear hair is to look at? Shave it, mow it, pluck it, cut it—whatever you do, just get rid of it. Same with nose hair.

EARLY BIRD

So you think the early bird catches the worm, do you? Well, guess what? The early bird catches hell for waking up all the other birds while looking for those darn worms.

EARLY DECTECTION

If you see or have even the slightest signs of anything wrong, find out for sure and get it fixed (see *Early Intervention;* oh, and how convenient—that's next). That goes for your body, your child, your job and your relationship.

EARLY INTERVENTION

Nip it in the bud. The earlier you deal with a problem, the better chance you have of getting it solved. Rarely does it fix itself, and the longer you wait, the worse it typically gets. If it's a medical issue, don't put it off; go to the doctor already.

EARLY vs. LATE

If given a choice, I'd go with early. So what if you're the first one there? At least you won't miss anything—especially any of the food.

EARN

When everything is handed to us, we tend not to appreciate much of what we have. If we earn it instead, then it tends to mean a whole lot more to us. You earn what you learn.

EARRINGS

Come on, fellas. You guys look silly with earrings. It's a girlie thing.

EASY

Oh please. If it were so easy, everybody would be able to do it (see *Accomplishment*). And yes, it's way easier said than done. Ah, if it were only that easy.

Early Bird

EASY WAY OUT

Don't just take the easy way out (see *Giving Up*). The easy way isn't always the best way. It's just the easy way.

EATING TOGETHER

Eating alone has its drawbacks. You can develop nasty table manners (that is, if you even eat at a table), gorge yourself and become antisocial. Dining with others, especially your family, allows for lots of opportunities to interact, eat more wisely and eliminate bad habits at mealtime (see *Farting*).

EAT LESS

Eat less and move around more. If you don't need it, don't eat it. Just think small portions. Lots of us eat because we're bored, so find something else to do with your spare time. If it goes past your lips, it will likely get to your hips (see *Blubber*).

EAT YOUR WHEATIES

Ninety-seven percent of all American nutritionists say that your breakfast is the most important meal of the day. I made that up (see *Statistics*), but it sure makes good sense to me. Breakfast gets you going and gives you the right fuel to start your day. Now who in our busy society has time for a healthy, leisurely daily breakfast? I don't, but we all should.

ECHO

Who thought up this echo business, anyway…anyway…anyway? It sure is cool…cool…cool.

EDIBLE UNDERWEAR

Is it proper to use a knife and fork when dining on edible underwear? Erotica is fine, but count me out on this one (think skid marks). I'll pass—likely not enough protein.

EDUCATED

Being educated doesn't necessarily make you smart. Possessing knowledge and experience—now that makes you smart. There is such a thing as an educated idiot, you know.

ELBOWS ON THE TABLE

So you can't you put your elbows on the table? Why not? It's the best way I know to keep your head from falling into your food, right?

ELDERLY

Do you know why the elderly are so revered in many cultures? It's because they have so many life experiences from which to draw. They are admired by younger generations and sought after for guidance and counsel. In this country, because we all think we know everything, we never have to ask for their opinions or guidance. We just ship them out to die when they get in the way (see *Humiliation*). So respect your elders; they deserve it.

ELECTORAL COLLEGE

I'd close down the Electoral College; blame budget cuts. Know anyone who's graduated from there? Not me. In the early days of our country, an elite group of men (see *Sexist*) chose the president, allegedly by taking into account the desires of their constituents. Now it's an all or nothing deal. The candidate who gets the most votes in a state gets all of that state's electoral votes. Theoretically, a candidate can win the election for president while getting only a minority of the country-wide popular vote. Right, President Gore? That's stupid and causes some candidates to decide to abandon a state and not campaign there at all. But he or she will eventually govern the whole country, so what good does that do? The popular vote should decide the winner, as the Electoral College has outlived its usefulness.

ELECTRICITY

I don't know how it works, but you can sure feel the electricity in a room without putting your finger in a socket.

ELEVATORS

Proper elevator etiquette dictates that you've got to stare at the ceiling, the changing numbers or the floor, and absolutely not look strangers in the eye. Don't even think about smiling or saying hello to anyone you don't know. We ought to get those rules changed.

E-MAILS AND TEXT MESSAGES

E-mails and text messages are the bane of our existence. We are clearly in overload mode today. They are so intrusive, and the response expectation is unnatural and usually unattainable. People simply expect instant access 24/7, which is contributing to the downfall of our society (see *Socialization*). Anyway, make sure you don't e-mail or text anything you'd rather not have the whole world see. That goes for videos and pictures as well. You never can be too sure where they might end up. Actually, if it's especially embarrassing or personal, you can be sure it will turn up everywhere.

EMBARRASSING MOMENTS

You want to keep embarrassing moments to a minimum, as no one, especially you, will likely forget them. Here are some tips:

> Always do a booger check when you're near a mirror.
> Carefully re-check (and check again) the recipient before sending your messages (see *E-mails And Text Messages*).
> Don't walk around with toilet paper stuck to your shoe.
> Don't tuck your dress in your panty hose (boys, not to worry here).
> Keep your farts to yourself.
> Keep your fly closed (unless you're in the act, so to speak).
> Keep your shoes tied (but not together).
> Try to keep your bathing suit on at all times, especially while swimming or diving.

EMBARRASSMENT

Do you think the fact that "bare ass" is included in embarrass is a mere coincidence? I think not. And if you go out of your way to embarrass someone, they likely won't get over it. Which means you'll have to keep looking over your shoulder for a very long time (see *Paybacks*).

EMBELLISHMENT

So who doesn't stretch the truth a little now and then? It can really add to an otherwise rather boring account of an event. Just make sure your story is mostly grounded in reality (see *Lying*).

EMERGENCY

Unfortunately most of us have very different definitions of the term emergency. Some think getting a splinter or expecting a phone call qualifies. Not even close. Emergencies are usually life-threatening events. Try to keep that in mind the next time you're tempted to use the word.

EMOTIONS

Like many other things, you either have them or you don't. You therefore can't create emotions you don't possess. Unfortunately, lots of people have trouble controlling their emotions, as we're all human (most of us anyway). We just have to make sure they don't get in the way of our better judgment.

EMPOWERMENT

If someone intimidates you, it's only because you've empowered them to be able to. If you have no respect for them, don't give them the satisfaction of getting to you. They can't hurt you if they're powerless (see *Consider The Source*).

EMPTY HANDED

Whenever you're invited to someone's house, never go empty handed. Bring flowers, wine, desert, a box of paper clips—bring something (see *It's The Thought That Counts*).

EMULATE

Emulate is good. Just make sure you emulate the good ones, not the bad ones.

ENABLING

An enabler may have good intentions, but they delusionarily (that's not a word, by the way) hate to say no, and often end up actually paralyzing the one they are trying to help. They just become a conduit for the enablee (that's not a word either, but should be) to get from point A to point B. Stop helping, already; especially when they don't need it.

ENCOURAGEMENT

It's probably no surprise that there is "courage" in encouragement. How hard is it to give someone that little extra push they may need to succeed?

ENDINGS

Sometimes endings can be rather bittersweet. That goes for relationships and just about everything else (although happy endings can be fun). Just look at them as new beginnings. Something generally begins when something else ends.

ENDS

Do the ends justify the means? Not always. Sometimes it's not so much where you end up, but how you got there.

ENEMIES

It's been said (by Michael Corleone) that it's best to keep your friends close and your enemies even closer. That's great, except no one should really have any enemies (except in wars and such). You don't have to like everybody. But enemies? Nah.

ENERGY RECOVERY

You ride a bike for a while and get tired. You rest for a couple of minutes and you're good to go. If you are out running and get tired, you can rest all day and you're still tired. Probably not enough smiling (see *Running*).

ENGAGED

When you are in a conversation with someone, stay engaged with them, as it tends to keep you (and them) awake (see *Look 'Em In The Eye*). Pretend if you have to.

ENGINEERS

Why do you have to go through four years of college and get a Bachelor of Science degree just to drive trains? I guess that Casey Jones guy must have been pretty smart.

ENGLISH LANGUAGE

So what kind of drugs were they taking when they decided to write down the English language? For starters, why would anyone go through all the trouble of adding silent letters into words (sword—what the heck is the w for)? And spelling two words identically that are pronounced differently and mean two completely different things (wind a clock—and wind, brrr)? Not to mention having the same sound come from different (or a combination of different) letters (see *Enough*). Do we not want anyone else to be able to read or write English? And why should Bud Abbott get an extra b and t in his last name? Was he so special? Does Illinois really need those extra letters? And enough with the gh's and ph's already. I'm all for having challenges in life, but this is ridiculous (see *Overkill*).

ENOUGH

How much is ever enough? Whatever it is, it's often never enough for some (see *Satisfaction*). Close enough and good enough usually suffice. Too much is usually better than not enough, and it's always best to leave well enough alone. However, if it's enough for you, then it's probably enough.

ENTHUSIASM

Show some signs of life, and don't just be a bump on a log. Enthusiasm is very contagious and even infectious, you know. Infect away.

ENTITLED

Some think that they're God's gift to the world and therefore entitled to everything. Not so. In our society, we should all be entitled to food, love, fresh air, life, medical care, shelter and clothing. The rest we should have to work for.

ENVIRONMENT

Our environment is the only one we have, so we would all be wise to protect it.

EQUALITY

In our never-ending quest for equality, there are limitations. Mothers will never be fathers and fathers won't ever be mothers. They each lack the proper parts, you know.

ER

Er, uh, er, ah…. Stop and think. Nobody wants to hear you stalling to answer a question. They may inadvertently jump to the wrong conclusion (see *Lying*).

ERASING IMAGES

Remember how you inadvertently walked in on your mom or dad when they were getting dressed? Or worse yet, when you saw grandma in the shower? You know how those images stay with you and make you sick every time you remember them? Well, maybe they can dull over time, but good luck with permanently erasing them. Too bad we weren't born with a delete button; maybe it will be an option on the next model. I'm such a big fan of selective memories.

ERECTIONS

Girls, you'll never know what this is like—a blessing and a curse. Boys, keep it in your pants (see *Modesty*). Your flag is up.

ESCAPE

You can escape lots of things, but it's very hard to escape your own mind, as it follows you everywhere. That is, unless you get some chemical help, which is not necessarily a good idea. Sorry.

ESCALATOR ETIQUETTE

This is very important, as it will keep you from getting trampled. Even though escalators are designed to take you up and down with no effort on your part, there are those who insist on walking on them anyway. You see, in their haste they will likely arrive at their very important destination at least five or six seconds ahead of you. Time is very precious, you know, so you have to understand that these are life and death ticks on the clock for them. If you wish to avoid unnecessary and nasty encounters with complete strangers, and if you desire to use an escalator solely for its intended purpose, you really want to stand on the right.

ESOTERIC THINKING

Esoterica—I'm lost here. Keep it simple, so even I can understand (see *Taking Yourself Too Seriously*).

EULOGIES

I'm all for respecting the dead, but why do some people go overboard in their eulogies? Now I'm not suggesting that they say the guy was a real rotten son of a bitch and we're much better without him; but come on. Sometimes, I sit back and listen and wonder who they're talking about, because their descriptions bear no resemblance to the person I knew. Keep it real.

EUPHORIA

Sometimes you've got to pay for those high highs with some very low lows (see *Balance*). To me, it's not worth it. I enjoy being happy; I don't need euphoric.

EVERYBODY DOES IT

Sometimes we have this mob mentality and just follow along, regardless of the consequences. Everybody downloads music and movies illegally, cheats on their taxes and exceeds the speed limit. It's great if everybody does it, but that doesn't make it right. It really doesn't.

EVERYTHING

You can do a lot of things, you can know a lot of things and you can even have a lot of things. But face it: you can't do everything, you can't know everything and you can't have everything. That's why you have to rely on others. And there's nothing wrong with that; it's a good thing.

EVIL

Evil stands for Extraordinarily Vile Insipid Loser (among other things). Words can't adequately describe the horrible nature of this word. Do all you can to stay away from it.

EVOLUTION

Of course we evolved from apes. At least the men did. The women, of course, evolved from that pretty lady named Eve (see *Patronizing*). Want proof? Watch the monkeys dance, and then watch us dance. Want more? Notice how we scratch ourselves (see *Inhibitions*). Enough said.

EXACERBATE

Talk about making a bad situation worse, even if you have the best of intentions. If you're dead in a hole, stop digging.

EXAGGERATION

The more you exaggerate, the less people will believe you (see *Reputation*). Using words like everybody or nobody doesn't help, as there are no such things as absolutes. Now this advice would come under the "do as I say, not as I do" category. Always.

EXAMPLE

Because the little ones are always watching, it's best to set a good example. It's the preferred and easiest way to teach.

EXCEPTIONS

Yes, there are always exceptions. Just don't always be the exception.

EXCLAMATION POINTS

Exclamation points are way too overused!!!!!!!! Just my opinion!!!!!!!!

EXCRUCIATING DETAILS

Stop! We don't want to know every insignificant detail of your story. Spare us from hearing about the color of the shirt you were wearing or the amount of humidity that day. Just stick to the basics. Learn to summarize and be succinct. We don't have all day, you know. Who, what, where, when and sometimes why. Otherwise, the mere telling of the story will take as long as the event itself did. We'll wait for the movie.

EXERCISE

Every day you exercise, you add a day to your life. I made that up, but it's probably true. We all need exercise, and it will rarely kill you. If you sit around and do nothing, you're going to get fat, plain and simple. If you're kind of chubby now, this is something that you already know. So get up and get moving. It's usually best if you can find an exercise partner, and start off small like taking a walk. If nothing else, the fresh air will do you good. Walk up the stairs instead of taking the elevator (I'm not talking 70 stories here, you know). Ride a bike; anybody (or almost anybody) can ride a bike. Now if you suddenly decide to join a gym and plan on going every single day, you won't. You'll quickly become discouraged and quit. That's why it's best to try to work up to a good regimen. But at least start. A little today, a little more tomorrow and bing, bang, boom, you'll be in better shape in no time. After you exercise, you'll feel like shit, all sweaty and smelly. But after a while, you'll begin to feel better, and look better and be healthier. It's also a great way to get rid of some of the blues we all have. Remember those endorphins in the brain? Exercise will help you think more clearly too, as it tends to blow out those cobwebs. It will always be an effort to exercise; there's no getting around that. You likely will never love it, but you don't have to despise it either, and it could actually be fun (maybe?). Now people who really love to exercise have their own problems (see *Lunatics*). So go ahead and give it a shot.

EXERCISE IN FUTILITY

An exercise in futility is an exercise in stupidity.

EXES

What can it be more gut-wrenching than to think of the one you loved (who dumped you) being with someone else? (Although for the ones we now can't stand, that's a pleasant thought.) When you are the jiltee, you get sick just thinking about it. And when the feelings are still raw, it's hard to stop torturing yourself. Just take some solace in knowing that someone who had the bad taste to let you go will likely never be happy and is now driving someone else crazy. Find something new to occupy your mind.

EXHIBITIONISM

Some things are best left to one's imagination. Don't be so sure that everyone wants to see all of your goodies hanging out. Before you go anywhere, look in the mirror and think about whether you would want your father or mother to see you look like that. Yes, it's nice not to have any inhibitions, but it's usually best to keep some things to yourself.

EXIT STRAGETY

Wherever you go and whatever you do in life, it's always a good idea to be able to find a way out. That goes for business ventures, relationships and going to grandma's house. Leave bread crumbs if you have to. You gotta know when to move on (see *Cut Your Losses*).

Exit Strategy

EXPECTATIONS

The expectations you want to meet are yours and not someone else's. They don't all have to be great. If you set yourself up to expect the moon, you'll likely be disappointed. So tone it down some and you'll be better off. Unfortunately, most people don't always do what they say they'll do (see *Disappointing*). Too bad, but that's something you want to keep in mind.

EXPENSIVE WEDDINGS

Talk about a waste of money. If you have to put on such an opulent wedding affair, you have way too much wealth. Either give the cash to the new Mr. and Mrs. for a new house or something, or donate it to charity. Who needs the caviar? It looks disgusting anyway.

EXPERIENCE

You can read about it, watch it or be told about it, but the best way to learn it is to experience it. Whatever you do, experience the thrills life has to offer. And the ones who have the most experience deserve our respect and should be our go-to people.

EXPERTS

An expert is someone from out of town who says they're an expert.

EXPIRED MEDICINE

Always check the expiration date on the labels of all medicine. You may be taking nothing.

EXPONENTIAL

Having two children is not two times the work of having one. The job is exponentially higher, more like ten times. Having three—forget about it. I think Mother Nature is trying to tell us something. Probably telling us to stop screwing around, that's what.

EXPRESSIVE

Speak your mind, as no one can express your thoughts better than you. No one can read your mind you know, unless they have ESPN or something.

EXTEND

Extend a hand and extend yourself, as it's almost always appreciated. However, it's overextending yourself that becomes a problem, because you usually can't deliver. And I wouldn't fool with hair or penis extensions either (see *You Are What You Are*).

EXTINCTION

Extinction—now that really stinks (see *Dinosaurs*).

EXTREMES

If you spend most of your time in any extreme (either high or low), you don't get a chance to enjoy the middle. I like the middle. Extremists are usually crazy lunatics and really scare me; they scare lots of people. But I digress yet again. Anyway, extreme highs are rarely worth the extreme lows (see *Balance*).

EYE ON THE BALL

If you keep your eye on the ball, you'll rarely strike out (see *Perspective*).

EYES

Your eyes are the most sincere and expressive part of your body, as they never lie. They are the windows to your soul. So don't be afraid to look them in the eye or have them look into yours. It tends to be the best way to know the truth.

EYES FORWARD

Pay attention to what's in front of you and leave the past behind.

FACE-LIFT

Why is it that some men and women insist on trying to recapture their youth by tinkering with their looks (see *Age*)? Really? We're not fooled by some of you ladies, with your skin pulled so tight you can barely move your lips. I understand all about self-esteem, but you can't change what's most important—nor should you. What's inside is what's most important.

FACIAL EXPRESSIONS

It's so easy to read facial expressions, and often hard to hide them. You know, being wide eyed or the look of shock and horror. One can sure tell a lot by observing these expressions, and they can usually give you away. Yes, they can be louder than what comes out of your mouth.

FACIAL HAIR

Facial hair is rather unattractive on women. However, when it comes to men, I've come full circle on this. Full beards are generally scruffy looking and tend to put some age on you. Mustaches are fine, of course, but goatees are just OK—they make some guys look like goats.

FAILURE

Failure is such an overused and misunderstood term. It typically doesn't mean that your life is over. It just means that you didn't succeed this time, and you can learn from it (see *Lessons*). Big deal, so try again. Failure is not falling down; real failure is falling down and not attempting to get back up. And the truest example of failure is someone who stops believing in themselves. Believe already.

FAIRNESS

Life is usually fair, but sometimes it's not. That's just the way it is. However, that doesn't give you an excuse to break the rules (see *Rationalization*). Being fair minded will get you very far in life. Oh, and there's no such thing as being more than fair. Fair is fair.

FAIR-WEATHER FRIEND

Being a fair-weather friend is a nasty contradiction. And it makes for a really bad friendship, especially in bad weather.

FAITH

Faith has very little to do with organized religion. It comes from the deep recesses of the heart. No matter what, you should always have faith. Have faith in your friends, have faith in God (if that's your thing) and have faith in your family. They'll usually come through. But above all, have faith in yourself. Keep the faith, baby.

FAKE FIREPLACES

Is anyone so stupid as to think fake fireplaces are real? The logs never burn up, for gosh sakes. So what's the point? Either replace it with a real one or wall it up. If you're cold, just turn up the heat.

FALLING FROM GRACE

Falling from grace doesn't always have to be permanent. Although it may take lots of work, you can usually climb back up, you know (see *Fortitude*). Who's Grace, by the way, and how can you fall off her?

FALLING OFF YOUR BIKE

If you fall off your bike, it's best to get right back on the seat and ride again. This goes for falling off lots of other things that don't necessarily come equipped with a seat (or a saddle).

FALSE ADVERTISING

It's not just businesses who advertise. We may not be aware, but we are always advertising something: our ability, knowledge, sex appeal, lack of sex appeal. You just want to make sure you can back up your implied or stated claims.

FAME

Who needs fame? It's usually fleeting anyway, as fans are usually shallow, with short attention spans. Fortune—now that I'll take.

FAMILIAR

Isn't it nice to encounter a welcome sight, especially if you're lost? Kind of warms those cockles in your heart, doesn't it? How are your cockles?

FAMILY

Your family should be very important to you. But is blood really thicker than water? Should you blindly side with and follow your family no matter what? Doubtful; they're human too and can be real screwups like anyone else. Hopefully, your family will always be there for you; however, that's not always the case. Embrace your family when you can, but if it is not reciprocated or appreciated, move on. The world has changed over time, and the clan mentality is long gone. Closeness is no longer defined only by blood lines. I don't necessarily think that's a bad thing (see *Friends*).

FAMOUS PEOPLE

So you (a complete stranger to them) get to stand next to some celebrity and have a picture taken to capture this auspicious moment. Does that make you especially important (see *Autographs*)? Do you think it was quite memorable for them, as you were No. 1000 that day? If you really need this picture on your wall to make your life complete, you're clearly missing something. Probably missing a lot.

FAN

It's good to be a fan, but if you get too carried away, you can become a fan-addict (get it—fanatic?). Not fantastic.

FANCY CARS

Where, oh where did we get so lost and forget that cars are simply a mode of transportation, not a member of our family? Many people look at their cars as extensions of themselves. I hope they're not, as cars are all metal, plastic and rubber. Are you? Cars are a means to an end, getting you from here to there. If you're spending all of your life in a car, get a life. You can buy a house for the money some people spend on a car, for gosh sake. Comfort is one thing, but excess is excess. If you've got that much money to spend, buy a reasonable auto and give the rest to charity. They need it more than you do. At least then you won't cry bloody murder when you get a tiny scratch or, God forbid, even a dent on it.

FANTASIES

It's always cool to fantasize—you know, that spectacular vacation, being with Prince/Princess Charming, winning the lottery. It's a nice way to exercise the imagination. Unfortunately, reality tends to get in the way and often doesn't live up to our dreams (see *Disappointment*).

FARTING

The average person farts 14 times a day. Let's just say that puts me a bit above average (OK, maybe a lot above average). In most situations, good discipline dictates that you try to hold it in (see *Manners*). However, sometimes nature just won't cooperate and you have to let it rip. So be discreet—or stand near a dog. Going to the bathroom also helps. Stay away from the ones who say they never fart, because with all of that built-up gas, they will probably explode at any given moment. (That's my own version of the Big Bang Theory.) Oh, and girls don't fart; they simply fluff (see *Pandering*).

FASHION

Sure, nobody wants to look like they're wearing their grandparent's clothes. But going through a new wardrobe the way everyone else goes through toilet paper is just an incredible waste of money. If you try to keep up with the latest fashions, you'll be broke and behind the trends before you've paid the bills.

FAST CARS

Great, so you can go from zero to sixty in five seconds. Where's that going to get you, except into an accident or out of favor with law enforcement personnel? Anyway, where's the fire (see *Smell The Roses*)?

FAST FOOD

Fast food serves a purpose and isn't always bad for you. It's just mostly bad for you (see *Instant Gratification*). It gets its name for the speed at which it leaves your body.

FAST WOMEN

I've heard of fast women, but the only ones I've ever seen are the ones who run faster than me. Actually, that would be most of the women I've seen.

FAT

If you eat too much fat, you will get and stay fat. It's almost that simple.

FATE

Things happen for a reason. We might not always understand it, but there's almost always a reason. They call it fate when there isn't a better explanation. It could be something about being in the right place at the right time or in the wrong place at the wrong time. You also want to be careful about tempting fate, even when it's very tempting.

FAT FREE

Fat free food is usually taste free. Even if it doesn't have any fat, it's not necessarily calorie free or good for you. Sometimes you end up gaining, not losing weight, because you have this false sense that you can eat plenty and not get fat(ter) (see *Assume*).

FAT POLICE OFFICERS

Ever notice the difference between some of our (mostly male) veteran police officers and this country's military service personnel? Take a look at their waistlines, as our police can get rather round in the middle (see *Donuts*), while our armed forces must stay fit and trim. Why do you suppose it's a requirement for the military and not for the police? We need to change that, as our police officers need to be healthy, so they can run after Mr./Ms. Bad Guy/Gal when necessary. It's probably a criminal conspiracy to keep some of our boys in blue on the chubby side.

FAVORITES

Try as we may, we all play favorites. It's just human nature and we can't help it. Just don't be too obvious, as the nonfavorites are bound to notice.

FEAR

If you let yourself become a captive of fear, then fear won and you lost. Fear can be very paralyzing and will eat you alive. Anyway, the things we fear the most tend to never happen or not to be as bad as we thought. So don't even fear the Reaper. Let him fear you.

FEARLESS

Don't look at me. I don't fear less; I fear plenty.

FEDERAL HOLIDAYS

Admit it, how do you really celebrate Presidents' Day, Columbus Day or Labor Day? No real special salutes, just another day off, right? Nothing like Christmas or Thanksgiving, is it? Are we really supposed to commemorate all of the presidents and Columbus too? (The Vikings get cheated.) Oy, that's a lot of presidents. I just send them a card and relax. And who really celebrates birthing babies on Labor Day?

FEELINGS

It has become very twenty-first century to be in touch with your feelings. Everybody has them, but some have trouble showing them. That's really no one's business as long as you understand and know them.

FEELING SORRY FOR YOURSELF

If no one else is feeling sorry for you, chances are you shouldn't either. Anyway, wallowing in self-pity won't get you very far.

FEEL RIGHT

If it doesn't feel right, it probably isn't right. Go with your gut (see *Instinct*) and remove yourself from that uncomfortable situation.

FEMININE SIDE

Boys, don't be afraid to show your feminine side; and do it often. Girls, you shouldn't have much trouble doing this.

FENCES

Fences do make good neighbors. It tends to cause us to respect others' privacy and boundaries. However, mending them isn't always so easy.

FICTION

Whoever made this word up had it backwards. Fiction should be true and nonfiction should be untrue. Right?

FIGHTING A LOSING BATTLE

It's hard to know when it's in your best interests to walk away. But if you're not getting anywhere after repeated attempts, you may want to consider it.

FIGHTING FIRE WITH FIRE

Do you fight fire with fire? Of course not; you fight fire with water. Always try to get the advantage. Thank you, Captain Obvious.

FIGHT OR FLIGHT

Unfortunately, fighting is a natural reaction to lots of things. However, it's best to use your smarts and your words during an altercation, and leave your fists at home. But stand your ground, especially when you know you're right. Now if it's a fistfight, you might want to walk (or run) away. There are two reasons for this. First, if you're bigger and stronger, what do you have to prove? Second, if they're bigger and stronger, why stick around to get your ass kicked? In that case I'd definitely go with flight. Are you then running away from a fight? Damned right you are (see *Pragmatic*).

FINAL FAREWELL

There are two ways to leave this world: suddenly or long and drawn out. Going suddenly leaves little opportunity to say good-bye to loved ones (see *Unfinished Business*). However, if they're clearly on their way out, you do get to bid them a final farewell. The downside of course is that you see them in a suffering, degraded state. Either way, it's a very difficult situation. Yet another reason to be nice to people. How many reasons do you really need?

FINDERS KEEPERS

Possession is nine-tenths of the law? Maybe, but if it's not yours, someone else is missing it. Finders should find out who it belongs to and return it. Yes, losers are usually weepers, but finders don't have to be keepers.

FINDING YOURSELF

For some, finding yourself isn't very difficult. For others, it may be more of a challenge, so just keep looking. You'll get there; but hang on, as it may be a lifelong quest.

FIND OUT

Read the paper. Watch the news (if you can fit it in between the cartoons, sports and video games). Find out what's going on. Wouldn't you feel pretty stupid if you were the last one to know that the world is ending tomorrow (see *Embarrassment*)? You know how you are glued to the news when it's snowing out or there's a hurricane coming? Just pretend you have to follow the news every day to find out if the world is still there and if you still have to go to work. That should be plenty of motivation.

FINE PRINT

There's another old Yiddish saying: What the large print giveth, the fine print taketh away. I lied; it's not really a Yiddish expression but, nonetheless, always read the fine print. It's usually way more important than the big print.

FINGER

It's OK to lift a finger, but you shouldn't give (them) the finger. And make sure you have a clear view of the mirror and your reflection when you're pointing fingers, as you may want to point them at yourself.

FINISH

You don't want to start something you can't finish, so it's best to finish what you start. They call this follow-through (see *Reputation*).

FINISHING TOUCHES

Your finishing touches tend to distinguish you. They can be part of your special signature, and people will remember your uniqueness. Sometimes it's those little things that really matter.

FIRE

It's so hard to believe that we depend on fire to give us warmth when it's cold and heat to cook our food. But it can pose such an incredible danger. That's why you shouldn't play with fire unless you're prepared to get burned. This sounds rather obvious, but so many of us can't quite get it right and end up getting burned anyway.

FIRE LANES

Don't park in fire lanes. Do you want to be the idiot who gets in the way of a fire truck when there's a real emergency? That's why you shouldn't park there. Being stupid is not an excuse.

FIRST BITE

Why does the first bite usually taste better than the last bite? I think it has something to do with the law of diminishing returns. Too bad we can't all just learn to be satisfied with the first bites.

FIRST IMPRESSION

So you only have one chance to make a first impression? Maybe—but so what? Suppose you make an ass out of yourself the first time. That means that you either are an ass or you made a mistake. If they're any good, they'll stick around for a second impression (see *Benefit Of The Doubt*); otherwise they're not worth it.

FIRST STEPS

The key to success often involves that first step. Sometimes it feels like a giant leap; it can involve plenty of risk and require lots of guts. But once you get past that, the next steps become easier and easier. They really do.

FIRST TIMES

Ah, your first kiss, your first love, your first sexual exploits, your first speeding ticket. We all remember our firsts, but that's not what really matters. It's not how you start out, it's how you end up. Your firsts are just practice. Your most recent kiss should be way more important than your first one. If not, you better find out why.

FISHING FOR COMPLIMENTS

If you spend lots of time asking those around you if you are looking beautiful or doing a great job, you likely aren't. (And your ass probably does look fat in that.) Do you really need all of that positive reinforcement? If so, no level of compliments will ever be enough. Remember: if you spend a lot of time fishing for compliments, you might end up being thrown back into the water.

FISH OR CUT BAIT

Decide already. We don't have all day.

FIVE-PERCENTERS

There are those who have 95 percent of their lives going exceptionally well, but insist on focusing on the five percent that isn't. Hell, I'd be overjoyed at 80 percent. Anyway, you want to stay away from them, as their ability to find something wrong with everything can be catching. Don't let them bring you down with them and take the fun out of life. If you can't appreciate what you have, you likely don't deserve it—all 95 percent of it.

FIVE-SECOND RULE

If it falls on the ground or is mistakenly put in the trash, you have five seconds to retrieve and still use (or eat) it. I don't make these rules; I just report them.

FIXING 'EM

Going into a relationship thinking you're going to change someone is an exercise in futility. It's not going to happen. If they can't fix themselves, you can't fix 'em.

FLAG BURNING

Yeah, yeah, I know all about the First Amendment and freedom of speech. But find something better to do with your time than burning the American flag. Too many people died trying to protect Old Glory (see *Freedom*).

FLAG-WAVING

It's finally fashionable to wave the Stars and Stripes, so knock yourself out and let your patriotism fly once in a while. So when you think of it, go ahead and put the flag up (not that flag).

FLATTERY

Flattery will get you everywhere? I don't think so; it will probably get you something, but not everything (see *Sincerity*).

FLEETING THOUGHTS

Too bad some thoughts go away so fast, although in some cases that may be a good thing. (This happens way more often as you get older.) Just stick around and pay attention; they're bound to come around again, especially if they're any good. Yet another reason to keep an open mind.

FLEXIBLE

Keep your plans flexible and keep your mind flexible; everything doesn't have to be done your way. And above all, keep your body flexible (see *Exercise*).

FLIPPING A COIN

When all else fails, flipping a coin isn't such a bad way to decide matters. You'll usually get the right answer (see *Fate*). Pick heads.

FLIRTING

Go ahead and flirt away. Just know the consequences (see *Cock Teasing*).

FLOWERS

If you don't believe in God, then please tell me where all the gorgeous flowers come from (see *Miracles*). Just think: they define beauty, smell so good and make great gifts. What's not to like? Flowers are nature's way of showing us how wonderful the world really is. By the way, giving flowers to someone doesn't always have to involve romance. It's a great expression of friendship, appreciation and kindness. Just another way of bringing beauty and joy into someone's life.

FLUSHING

You want to save water, don't you? If it's yellow, let it mellow; if it's brown, flush it down. Good words to live by.

FLYING

There seems to be something unnatural about taking a plane, as I don't think man (or woman) was meant to fly. We can crawl, walk, swim, glide, even skateboard, but not fly. A big heavy box takes you in the air and gets you someplace. How do they do it? It doesn't sound too safe to me. I much prefer walking—or at least staying on the ground.

FOLK SONGS

"Blowin' in the Wind" and "This Land Is Your Land" are still pretty relevant today, if you ask me. You asked, right?

FOLLOW

If ever in doubt, always follow your heart; and your conscience (see *Directions*). They won't lead you astray.

FOLLOWING ORDERS

Yup, I'm just doing my job and following orders. Good excuse. When did you hear that before (see *Nazis*)? If your job forces you to do things you know in your heart of hearts is wrong, use your head. Find another job.

FOOD

We all tend to forget that food is merely a means to an end—the end being nutrition for our bodies. We make such a big deal about every aspect of a meal: preparation, presentation, texture, aroma, taste, you name it. If we spent as much time and effort worrying about important issues like war and disease, we would be able to solve all of society's ills in no time. Unfortunately, the level of taste in our meal is directly proportional to the amount of extra pounds we carry around. We are a nation obsessed with food and eating: fast food, eating out, eating in, gourmet food—and it goes on and on. We lose sight of the fact that eating is just another bodily function. And food is simply fuel for our bodies; it goes in and comes out. It's those damn taste buds that create so many of our problems (see *Dieting*). Here's a rule of thumb: If it's fried, sweet, creamy or salty, it's generally not good for you (see *Disappointment*). We need to find a way to dull our taste buds and desensitize our minds to the visual attractiveness of decadent delights. We would be a much healthier (not to mention skinnier) country. It's really all about making good choices. Just remember: after those first few delectable bites, the novelty and excitement quickly wear off. I think that's another Garden of Eden punishment. Thanks a lot Eve (and Adam too).

FOOD FOR THOUGHT

Brain food is the best kind of nourishment anyone can have. It's not fattening, so you can really gorge yourself. And it keeps your noggin in shape. What's not to like?

FOOLING YOURSELF

You can fool lots and lots of people, but there's one person you can never fool: that's you. Your conscience will always be haunting your head, as ultimately you have to live with yourself. It's very hard to hide from yourself, so make your decisions and choices carefully.

FOOTSIES

It's fun to play footsies, especially if you have a willing partner. Unrequited footsies can be a problem, however. Boys, you may not want to do this in the men's rooms while you're sitting in your stall. You may inadvertently be sending a very wrong message to someone (see *Gay*). Or it may be the right message, which is completely up to you.

FORBIDDEN ACTS

Under no circumstances should you:

Abuse
Cheat
Commit violence (of any kind)
Complain
Dance on someone's grave
   (except on dictators')
Deface
Degrade
Hit
Humiliate
Kill
Lie (try not to)
Maim
Mayhem (I don't know how
   you mayhem, but you're not
   supposed to)
Murder
Pillage (don't know what that is
   either)

Point
Punch
Rape
Riot
Run out of gas
Slap
Smack
Smoke
Spit
Steal
Strike
Take a day for granted
Taunt
Throw things at anyone (OK
   in sports though)
Whine

FOREVER

Nothing is forever and nothing lasts forever—which is usually a good thing, because forever can last a very long time. Maybe that's not necessarily a good thing. Now forever and a day—that's really a long time.

FORGETFUL

So you forget things once in a while. Big deal, we all do. In today's world, with so much information bombarding us constantly, it's a wonder we can even remember our names (see *Name Tags*). There's only so much stuff we can cram into our brains, you know.

FORGIVE AND FORGET

Some of us aren't very good at either forgiving or forgetting. Forgiving is hard enough, but it's not always so easy to forget (see *Impossible*). It should come as no shock that giving is part of forgiving. Best to get over it already. If it were only that easy.

FORK IN THE ROAD

There are forks in the road almost everywhere you turn; they're usually called choices. And those signs can be terribly confusing. If ever in doubt, just take the high road. Can't go wrong with that.

FORM OVER SUBSTANCE

Form over substance? I'd go with substance. Anybody can put on a show, but real results are accomplished with plenty of effort. Form often masks what's hidden underneath, which often has very little depth.

FORTITUDE

It sometimes requires plenty of guts to accomplish things and get somewhere. However, the ones who really stick to it and employ lots of fortitude are the ones who do. As for having intestinal fortitude, I think that's some kind of stomach ailment.

FORTUNE-TELLERS

Maybe fortune-tellers have special talents to predict the future, but I'd rather be surprised. If they were any good at their craft, they'd be spending their lottery winnings instead of reading tea leaves.

FORWARD

If you're not going forward, you're going backwards and the whole world is passing you by. Nothing ever stays still. So turn around already and try to catch up.

FORWARDING ADDRESS

It sure would be nice to have a forwarding address for loved ones who have passed away. It could easily facilitate getting rid of some of that nasty guilt (see *Unfinished Business*), and it sure would help in finding that hidden stash of cash. OK, so addresses may be a problem, as postal employees may not be particularly interested in delivering those special messages. How about at least a new phone number?

Fortune-Tellers

FOUR-LETTER WORDS

Forget about swear words. The worst four-letter words are: hate, evil and kill. Love is one of the best ones though.

FRECKLES

Those who have freckles often don't like them. But to the rest of us, they're so cute and distinctive (see *You Are What You Are*).

FREE

Don't kid yourself. Nothing is really free. Everything has a price tag and there's always a catch. Are the best things in life free? Sorry, I don't think so. Hell, they even charge for air at gas stations. Sometimes it's not very obvious, but what looks free at the onset can have a very long-term cost (see *Fine Print*).

FREE COUNTRY

Thank your lucky stars our country is free. Unfortunately, we usually take our hard-fought liberties for granted. Those in other countries, especially the unfree ones, sure wouldn't.

FREEDOM

What were they thinking when they put "dom" in this word. There's nothing "dumb" about freedom. Unfortunately, freedom is one of those things that you don't appreciate until you lose it. Protect it, as there's nothing "free" about it either. Too many people paid with their lives to keep us free, so treasure your freedom and don't ever forsake it.

FREE SAMPLES

Lord knows why we enjoy free samples so much. Who can resist taking them? And it doesn't really matter what they are; if they're handing them out, we'll take them. Most of them usually end up stuffed in a drawer somewhere or thrown out, never to be seen or used again. But at least they were free.

FREE WILL

Free will is a God-given right and should be strongly defended. Except for some very basic laws—no killing, stealing, raping (see *Ten Commandments*)—

we really are free to do whatever we want. We can go almost anywhere we desire, make our own choices and take the job of our choice. This is just another thing that makes this country great. It's a right that everyone should greatly preserve and cherish.

FREE WILLY

Yes, Willy should be free, but not only the one in the movie. All willies should be free. Going commando may be one way, but discretion dictates that the zipper needs to stay zipped most of the time. Our society has a thing about that.

FRENCH FRIES

Those damn French. We save their asses in two World Wars and the best they can do is give us French fries? That's the thanks we get? Those delicious, irresistible little hunks of fried potatoes do nothing but clog our arteries and fatten our behinds. And the only French we Americans understand is: "Do you want fries with that?" How do you say thank you in French (see *Gesturing*)?

FRENZY

Don't you just hate it when those TV and newspaper reporters try to whip us all into a frenzy over something that has either happened, is about to happen or may never happen? "It may snow, there's a blizzard coming, it's probably going to be bad, there's a less than even chance, oh, the sun is coming out—never mind." All they usually accomplish is to scare the pants off of us (and very few of us look good without pants). I guess it's all about justifying their existence (see *Ratings*).

FRESH AIR

Oftentimes, the best way to get out of a rut is to take a stroll outside and suck in a few deep breaths. The therapeutic value of a nice break outdoors, coupled with a little exercise, is easy to overlook. The key is to find the fresh (and not polluted) air.

FREUDIAN SLIP

You want to watch out for the proverbial Freudian slip. But I think this is a girl thing, because most boys don't wear slips.

FRIENDS

Good friends are family you choose. So yes, you absolutely, positively, without a doubt gotta have friends; and I would be completely lost without mine. This is one of the most important Fs there is—family being the other. And remember that you can't pick your family (but you can, of course, pick your nose). Sure, you can be very choosey in selecting your friends. Your trusted confidants will always stand by you through thick and thin, as you would stand by them. But like anything else that's worthwhile, you have to work at friendships. Never take your friends for granted, and never let them down or forsake (or even five-sake) them. Because, unlike family, they don't have to be there. Be a foul-weather, not a fair-weather friend, as it's usually when you go through some very hard times that you really know who your friends are. Your job is to embrace them in sadness (help them cry, if you'd like) and celebrate them in joy (laugh and dance together). Some people rank friends: best friend, second-best friend, close-friend-but-not-best friend, acquaintance, jerk. You get the idea. I have a different way: close friends, and all other friends. BFF (best friends forever) relationships are often way too weird and unnatural (see *Overdoing It*). You see, you don't always have to be in constant contact for them to be your nearest and dearest. If you can simply pick up where you left off, whether after a five-minute or five-month absence, and don't have to get reacquainted, then they're your closest friends. Everybody needs a friend—and you can never have too many. If you don't have one, find one. Find a few! Now (see *Exclamation Points*)!

FRIENDSHIP

There's no better way to travel than to sail on the S.S. Friendship. Take a ride on that boat and your life will be forever enhanced.

FRIENDS IN HIGH PLACES

You can be the best of the best, but once in a while, it does help to have friends in high places.

FRIVOLOUS LAWSUITS

Ah, if only frivolous lawsuits were just another thing to wear. No such luck. Too many of us are quick to sue people, abusing and clogging our judicial system. Like an idiot, you spill coffee on your lap or jump in front of your neighbor's lawn mower; filing a lawsuit is almost becoming a natural reflex. It's one thing to seek retribution or to make yourself whole when it's someone else's mistake, but trying to profit from an unfortunate situation is inexcusable, especially if an accident is due to your own negligence (see *Taking The Blame*). Sure, it keeps lawyers in business; but we can find better things for them to do (I don't know what though).

FROM THE MOUTH OF BABES

If we spent more time listening to the little ones instead of ignoring them (and having the TV babysitter occupy their time), we might actually learn something. Maybe a lot of somethings. Oftentimes children make a whole lot more sense than we do. Very often.

FROWN

It takes more muscles to make a frown than it does to make a smile. (Someone told me that once; I don't know if it's true, but it works for me.) So why sate the energy? Anyway, a frown is just a smile turned upside down (I borrowed that from a song), so either walk around standing on your head or lose that nasty facial expression.

FRUITS AND VEGETABLES

Eating fruits and vegetables promotes good health and will likely cause you to live longer. However, I'm of the belief that those really nasty veggies like Brussels sprouts and cauliflower are probably the exception, as I can't stand them.

FRUSTRATION

Frustration is something we all have to deal with. You can often minimize life's irritations, but you can't eliminate them. The key is not to let them drive you crazy.

FUL

You can always fill up on these:

Artful	Cheerful
Bashful (oh, too cute)	Delightful
Beautiful	Eventful
Bountiful	Faithful
Careful	Fanciful

Fearful
Flavorful
Fruitful (might as well
    multiply, while you're at it)
Graceful
Grateful (full of grate?)
Helpful
Hopeful
Insightful
Joyful
Lawful
Masterful
Meaningful (nothing mean in
    that)
Mindful
Mouthful
Niceful (I made that up;
    sounds kinda nice, doesn't it?)

Peaceful
Playful
Plentiful
Powerful
Resourceful
Respectful
Spoonful
Successful
Tactful
Tasteful
Thankful
Thoughtful
Useful
Watchful
Willful
Wishful
Wonderful
Youthful (see *Age*)

Don't fill up on these, as they'll likely get you sick:

Awful
Bellyful
Boastful
Disgraceful
Disrespectful
Distasteful
Doubtful
Dutiful (see *Constipation*)
Earful
Forgetful
Frightful
Harmful
Hateful
Hurtful
I'm very ful (see *Moderation*)
Lustful

Mournful
Nastyful (I made that one up
    too)
Painful
Pitiful
Regretful
Remorseful
Resentful
Shitful
Sinful
Snootful
Spiteful
Tearful
Ungrateful
Vengeful
Wasteful

FUN

Have fun. Have lots and lots of fun. In our busy and very complicated world we sometimes forget to make time to kick back and enjoy ourselves. Life is supposed to be fun; not all of the time, but a lot of the time (see *Lighten Up*). You just don't want to have fun at someone else's expense. Actually, you may want to, but it's not a very nice thing to do. So enjoy yourself, sing a song (to yourself please) and put a smile on your face. It may be contagious. In fact, it really is contagious.

FUNDAMENTAL

When you break down most complicated things, they tend to be rather fundamental. Even fundamental things can be difficult to understand, but sometimes they're all you've got. Back to basics for me.

FUNERAL

Where is the fun in funeral? Well, I guess it's in the beginning of the word, but that doesn't make any sense to me.

FUNNY BONE

Don't you just hate it when you hit your funny bone and it reverberates and goes numb? It's so annoying. I don't know why they call that bone the humorous, as there's nothing very funny about it. Ouch!

FUTURE

The future is all new, and the exciting part is that you never really know what it will bring. Sure, you can try to plan for it, but you certainly can't control it. It's all about tomorrows, not yesterdays. Some people fear the future. There's really no point in that. Just welcome it and embrace it (see *Change*).

GAMBLING

Never, ever gamble more than you're ready to lose. Don't be fooled, as the odds are always against you (see *Risk*).

GAMES

Sure, we all play games, although sometimes we don't know it. Just make sure the other side knows what game you're playing and that the rules are clearly spelled out.

GARLIC

The health nuts tell us that garlic is very good for you. I doubt it, as it stinks to high heaven (see *Redundant*). It doesn't just get on your breath, but it seems to come out of all the pores in your body. You tend to reek of it. So if you really want to keep your friends and neighbors away, by all means eat plenty of garlic.

GAY

The world is a very diverse place. People come in different shapes, sizes and colors. If we were all the same, it would be a very boring planet. That's why everyone's different. I think they call it gay because they deserve happiness, just like everyone else. I don't understand people being attracted to others of the same sex, because I'm not. But plenty of people are for a variety of reasons. That's life, and that's what makes the world go around. As long as innocent people aren't hurt and laws aren't being broken, people's sexual orientation is their own business—not mine and not yours.

GAY MARRIAGE

Marriage is more than just a piece of paper. It's a lifelong commitment between two loved ones. This union and way of life is more important than a written document. However, if that's what someone needs to solidify their forever relationship, that's fine with me. Gay, straight, white, black, tall, short—count me in as an advocate. Why should anyone be denied the same opportunities as heterosexual couples to be miserable (see *Divorce*)?

GENERALIZATIONS

You should probably stay away from words like always, never, everything, nothing, everybody and nobody. I don't, but you should (see *Do As I Say*).

GENEROSITY

Want to feel great? Give someone something they need. Give them your friendship, give them a gift, give them your love. Give of yourself. But remember: you can be generous without having to tell everybody about it (see *Bragging*). So give, give, give. Share, share, share.

GENTLEMAN

Boys, you always want to act like a gentleman ("act" often being the operative word). Girls, you probably don't (see *Penis Envy*).

GENTLENESS

The gentler you are, the more special they feel. Pile it on.

GERMAPHOBIC

You know those odd folks who always wash their hands after they touch something? Cleanliness is one thing, but these are some very strange people (see *Overkill*).

GERMS

Some things should be shared and others should not. Germs are from the should-not category and are best kept to yourself.

GESTURING

Oftentimes flapping your arms around adds punctuation to what you're saying. You usually seem more passionate about a particular topic that way. Be careful of some types of hand gestures though, as these may inadvertently (or advertently) get you into trouble. Watch out for excessive flapping though, as it may actually cause you to fly away. Maybe that's OK.

GETTING AWAY WITH IT

Yeah, you may think you know what you can get away with. And you may never, ever get caught, and then think you got away with something. But you never really do (see *Conscience*). It is very difficult to fool yourself, you know.

GETTING BETTER

Sure try to do things just a little bit better every day, whether it's work, play, love or being sick. After a while, you'll be a lot better. You want to be better, right?

GETTING EVEN

We all want to get back at someone who wronged us, and we may even enjoy seeing them squirm. But you won't ever get even. Why give them the satisfaction of knowing they got to you anyway? Lowering yourself by taking a page from their book and giving them some of their own medicine may make you feel better. But your hurt, loss or embarrassment won't be the same as theirs. Yours will probably be worse, since you have character and class; they likely don't.

Germs

GETTING FIRED

Getting fired really sucks. It's easy to blame the one who canned you, and you may be right. But you want to take a good hard look in the mirror before you begin your job search, just to be sure (see *Fooling Yourself*).

GHOSTS

Are ghosts real? How would I know? But when I do find out, I'll try to let you know (see *Afterlife*).

GIANT

Being a giant in someone's eyes usually has more to do with standing out and being exceptional, rather than having anything to do with height (except for basketball players, of course).

GIFT CERTIFICATES

Now don't get me wrong, a present is a present. And I understand the intent of giving a gift certificate, as this way the giftees can get something they really want. But it just doesn't seem that special to me. I look at it as a fast and dirty way to fulfill an obligation. As for me, I'd rather give someone a goofy thing that they probably don't need and can't exchange. At least they would remember me when they are cleaning out the garage.

GIGGLES

It's fun to get a case of the giggles once in a while, although it could be embarrassing to be giggling away at inappropriate times (see *Funeral*). Too bad you can't buy giggles by the case, as I would certainly stock up on them. Anyway, children are by far the best gigglers, especially the real little ones.

GIRLS MATURE FASTER THAN BOYS

Sorry guys, but girls do mature faster than boys. For example, in the most traditional of Jewish households, a girl goes through the rite of passage to adulthood at age twelve. The boys aren't recognized as adults until thirteen. It takes us guys a while to catch up in the maturity department (see *Late Bloomers*), although some of us never do. And that's not always a bad thing.

GIRLS ROOM ETIQUETTE

Can't help you here. I'm a boys room kinda guy.

GIVE

Yeah, it is better to give than to receive. Much better.

GIVERS

There are givers. There are takers. And there are give-and-takers. In life, if you give more than you take, you win the ultimate contest and will leave this world a better place.

GIVING BLOOD

Giving blood doesn't hurt. You can't get AIDS, and you really do save someone's life. So what's the question?

GIVING IN

Giving in is not the same as giving up, because sometimes it's the most prudent thing to do. The key is to know when (see *Pragmatic*). Hint: If you're fighting a losing battle with no chance of winning, you might want to think about it.

GIVING SOMETHING BACK

If this isn't an overused concept, I don't know what is. Just because someone's made a lot of money, their guilty conscience tells them to give something back. Where have they been? How about always doing charity work because it's the right thing to do, and not because you now have some wealth. Anyway, it's not always about dollars (see *Giving Your Time*).

GIVING UP

There's no future in giving up, but never ever give up? That's really impossible, as we're not all superhuman. Just don't give up too easily or without a fight. Quitters never win, you know (see *Trying*).

GIVING YOUR TIME

Giving someone or something your time is often way more valuable than giving your money. Don't get me wrong; plenty of people and worthwhile organizations need your money, so don't stop. However, time is very precious, and typically in short supply, and can't be replaced. (It's a nonrenewable resource.) That's why the time you give someone should be highly appreciated. If not, you're just wasting your time.

GLOATING

Big deal, so you were right and everybody knows it. You don't have to rub their noses in it.

GLOBAL WARMING

Of course the world is getting hotter. Can't you tell? How much more proof do you need? You can't just explain away and dismiss melting icecaps and rising ocean levels as nothing to worry about. I don't know if we're causing all of it (see *Farting*), and I'm not smart enough to know what to do about it, but we have to do something. We either need to adapt or find ways to minimize its effects. It's probably due to some terrorist plot.

GLORY

There is nothing wrong with basking in the glory of a big achievement. Go ahead; you deserve it. But like most things, just don't overdo it (see *Gloating*).

GO

"I go, no, you can't have one. And she goes, but I want one. So I went, OK, go ahead and have one, but only one. Then she goes, thanks for nothing." So where's everybody going and wenting anyway? Aren't going and went action words? Try using the word said—that works much better (see *English Language*).

GOALS

Setting goals every day is very important. The key is to make them attainable without making them too easy to achieve. If your goal is to get out of bed in the morning, that's probably not too hard to do. If it's to climb Mt. Everest, you may have a problem. Here's my rule: If you can hit 75 percent of your goals each day, you're doing pretty well. Even 70 percent isn't too bad.

GO AROUND ONCE

You only go around once in this world and it's all about choices. Some choose to be an asshole; some choose to be a mensch (see *Yiddish Expressions*). It's completely up to you. I would strongly suggest mensch—but that's just me.

GOD

If there is a God, why do so many bad things happen? No idea. But I firmly believe that there's definitely someone or something out there. Call it God, call it the Force, call it divine intervention, call it a higher power or being—call it whatever you want. And if you believe, you can have any relationship you want with God (see *Choice*). You can talk to Him (or Her), pray, yell, ignore, whatever. Your communication or connection is completely up to you. It can be in a formal, structured way through organized religion or in an informal, free thinking way. Whether you adhere to the Big Bang Theory, evolution, the Bible or anything: somebody must have pushed the start button (which is why evolutionists and creationists don't have to be mutually exclusive). Nothing happens by itself or without a purpose. It's probably no coincidence that God and good are so closely related. Don't believe me? Then how do you explain beauty and color and sound and scent? And listen, genius, who do you think taught those birdies such pretty songs? And why does it smell so sweet in the spring? How come snow doesn't make any noise when it falls? And what makes trees change to their brilliant colors every year? Huh? Huh? Huh? All I know is that someone (or something) puts the sun away at night and takes it back out in the morning. I think it's God.

GOD BLESS AMERICA

God knows, we need all the blessings we can get.

GOD-GIVEN RIGHTS

I borrowed these from someplace, but the only God-given rights should be life, liberty and the pursuit of happiness. What you do with those is completely up to you (see *Free Country*).

GOD KNOWS

"God knows" is usually a good response when you don't know the answer to a question and all else fails. Chances are, God does know. He (or she) just might not be telling you.

GO DOWN SWINGING

Don't just stand there when you are one strike away from being out. At least go down swinging (see *Trying*). That goes for baseball and life in general. It's always best not to give up without a fight.

GOD WILLING

God is always willing. You just have to know how to ask (see *Prayer*).

GOING

If you don't like the way things are going, get off your ass and do something about it. We can all change our direction.

GOING FOR A RIDE

Sometimes when the world feels like it's closing in on you, just hop in the car and take a ride. It can help clear your head, especially if you roll the windows down and get some fresh air. (You may want to reconsider that window business if it's cold and rainy though.)

GOING FOR BROKE

If you're going for broke, you'll usually find it.

GOING NOWHERE FAST

Make sure you're in gear when you're trying to get somewhere. Otherwise, you'll just be stuck in neutral, idling away (see *Wasting Time*).

GOING THE EXTRA MILE

Well, it doesn't have to really be a mile, but most will remember the extra touch you put on things. That special effort is usually well appreciated.

GOING THROUGH THE MOTIONS

You're not doing anybody any favors if your heart isn't in it and you're just going through the motions. If it's worth doing, do it right; otherwise, don't bother.

GOING TO HEAVEN

There are some in this world who have an automatic pass to go to heaven (see *Teachers, Doctors and Nurses*—the good ones, that is; don't see *Lawyers*). The rest of us have to gain entry the old-fashioned way: we have to earn it (see *Golden Rule*).

GOING TO HELL IN A HANDBASKET

What the hell is a handbasket? And why would you go on a trip to that nasty place in one? My guess is that there are plenty of other modes of transportation to hell. All you need is a one-way ticket. Actually you may not have a choice, as round trips aren't likely available.

GOING TO THE DOCTOR

Does anyone enjoy going to the doctor? Do you think we like to have our privacy invaded, not to mention our most intimate of private orifices investigated? How about the cold hands and freezing stethoscope? Fun? Of course not. Which is why some of us avoid going to the doctor until our legs are falling off or we're bleeding profusely out of both ears. Silly, if you wait that long, it may be too late. So go already, and don't be such a baby (see *Ounce of Prevention*).

GOING TO THE PRINCIPAL'S OFFICE

Dum, da dum, dum. When you know you're in trouble, those rotten guilt feelings come flooding in. Time for a reality check. If you're wrong, you're wrong, and you have to face the music (likely not very pleasant tunes either). But if you didn't commit any transgressions, stand up for yourself and don't just take it (see *Hold Your Ground*).

GOING TO YOUR HEAD

Always remember that success can be fleeting. Savor it and enjoy it. But when you peel your good fortune away, you're just like everyone else: still human.

GOLDEN RULE

Yes, do unto others as you would have them do unto you, and treat people the way you want to be treated. Those are outstanding words to live by. If you're only going to follow one rule in life, this should be the one. Be good to your fellow man and fellow woman. And just because someone acts like a real ass toward you, that's not an excuse to violate this rule. You're better than that (see *Class*). And don't treat others well because you expect to get something special back. You do it because it's the right thing to do.

GOLF

Sorry, I think golf is a suck-ass sport. I'm with Mark Twain on this one: what a way to spoil a good walk. Why do they call it a sport anyway? Just because you sweat? You're in the sun, for God's sake; of course you're going to sweat. And what's with those golf carts (see *Exercise*)? Golf takes forever to play, it's boring as hell and the clothes they wear are ridiculous. All you do is hit this little ball, chase it around the course and spend a lot of money. And why do they always talk about a handicap when discussing golf? Handicapped brain, maybe. I just don't get it. Call me stupid; it won't be the first time.

GONE

They're not gone if they're not forgotten (see *Memories*).

GONE FISHING

Lots of people really enjoy fishing, and they claim it is very relaxing. It's allegedly a sport also, but of course I wouldn't know, as I don't fish either. They do suggest staying away from the brown trout, which makes sense to me. If I were a fish eater (which I'm not), it would seem to be much easier to go to the store and just buy the damn fish, right?

GOOD

Yes, good almost always triumphs over evil, although sometimes it takes a long time. If you're the betting type, go ahead and put your money on the good ones. Best chance of winning.

GOOD-BYES

I'm not real good at good-byes (neither are a lot of others), as it seems way to final. "See you later" works best for me. When you really mean it, good-bye is often very hard to say. Maybe that's a good thing.

GOOD CAUSE

You should always give to a good cause. It's 'cause they need you. Pay attention here.

GOOD DEEDS

Here's a no brainer. Do at least one good deed each day. Since the good deeders are in the clear minority in this world, they have to take on the extra work of not only doing their good deeds, but also chipping away at the backlog of good deeds everybody else is supposed to do. Somebody's got to pick up the slack because we need more, not less, good deeders. The saying "no good deed goes unpunished" is not only terribly inaccurate, it disparages the value of these actions. But remember: thinking about doing something nice is a start, but it doesn't really mean much unless you actually go through with it. And good deeds don't get repaid; they just get passed along. So hurry up and get going. Now! Put this stupid book down and go out there and start (see *Do Something*).

GOOD DIE YOUNG

You think the good die young? Doubtful. If so, then that doesn't say much for the rest of us ancient ones, does it? Nah, the good, or the good we all do, lasts forever.

GOOD GRACES

If you spend most of your life trying to stay in everyone's good graces, you won't have much of a life. And anyway, you'll never please them all, so why try?

GOOD GUYS

No, good guys don't finish last. They'll always be first in most of our eyes.

GOOD IDEAS

Some say that most good ideas have already been taken. That just shows they don't have any imagination and gives them an excuse to be lazy. Good ideas are everywhere, simply waiting to be discussed.

GOODNESS

Sometimes you have to look pretty hard, but there really is goodness in everyone. It's typically right next to godliness.

GOOD NIGHT

Always say good night to those near you before you go to sleep. A kiss won't hurt either, as no one's too old for that. Of course, you want to have good dreams and sleep well, don't you (see *Cranky*)?

GOOD OLD DAYS

I wish I had known the good old days were so good when I was living them. I probably would have enjoyed them more. Yes, we all tend to embellish the past. And it seems the more distant the memories, the more they become the good old days. However, if we're really honest with ourselves, those days probably weren't much better than these days. Instead, we should probably be focused on today and tomorrow (see *Eyes Forward*).

GOOD SAMARITANS

I'm sorry—they should be called Great Samaritans.

GOOD THINGS

Good things are worth waiting for (see *Patience*) and sometimes do come in little packages. Rarely is there too much of a good thing (see *Moderation*). Just remember that, contrary to conventional wisdom, all good things don't have to come to an end. Not ever.

GOOD TIMES

If you concentrate on the good times, the bad times tend to fade. No, they don't disappear altogether (see *Selective Memory*), but fade and become way less important.

GOOSE BUMPS

Now exactly what purpose do you suppose goose bumps actually serve? To tell you that you're cold? Don't you already know that?

GOTTA GO

Why is it that when you've really got to pee, you can't think of anything else but peeing? When you gotta go, you gotta go, so eliminate all obstacles and take care of business. I guess that's why they call it relieving yourself. Yes, it's such an indescribable feeling to make your bladder gladder (see *Relief*).

GPS

I swear GPS stands for Getting People Stupid. Great, now we'll forget how to even read a map or follow someone's directions. We have to listen to this not-so-nice voice telling us where to go. And of course we blindly obey, even if they are sending us off a cliff. Don't you get enough of those instructions already (see *Marriage*)?

GRACIOUS

Sometimes it's difficult to appear to be appreciative of someone else's efforts, especially when you're not (see *Sincerity*). So learning to be gracious is something to strive for. Keep striving.

GRADUAL vs. DRASTIC

If you slam on the brakes, you'll wear them out fast. If you lose lots of weight on some fad diet, you'll likely gain it all back and then some, pretty quickly. Instead, if you come to a gradual stop, your brakes will last forever (not really, but they'll last longer). And if you slowly and gradually change your eating habits, the weight will come off and stay off. Take a hint.

GRANDPARENTS

Everyone should be fortunate enough to have grandparents—especially good ones. They can dote on you and spoil you, and then go home and leave it to your parents to practice the proper discipline. They can be a resource to help you solve your problems and give you some confident advice when you need it.

Never underestimate the value of their years of experience. Going to Grandma's (or Grandpa's) house should always be a treat. If not, find other grandparents.

GRAND PLAN

For centuries, people much smarter than me have tried to understand the Grand Plan. Everyone has their theories and ideas, but I know one thing: There *is* a Grand Plan. I'm not sure what it is, but my guess is that we probably find out at some point (see *Afterlife*).

GRASS

Why is it that grass is often like hair and tends to grow where you don't want it?

GRASS IS GREENER

Everything is not as it appears, so the grass isn't always greener on the other side. Just use more fertilizer on yours (see *Count Your Blessings*).

GRATUITOUS COMMENTS

To say something just to say something is a waste of time. If you've got nothing to say, save your breath and don't say anything.

GRAY

No, everything isn't either black or white. Sorry, there's lots of gray in this world (see *Gray Hair*).

GRAY HAIR

Hair gets gray—so what? It makes you look very extinguished (or was that distinguished?). Consider the alternatives and talk to your bald-headed friends. Do you think they'd complain about gray hair?

GRAY SKIES

Gray skies will eventually clear up, so go on and put on a happy face. How silly, but true.

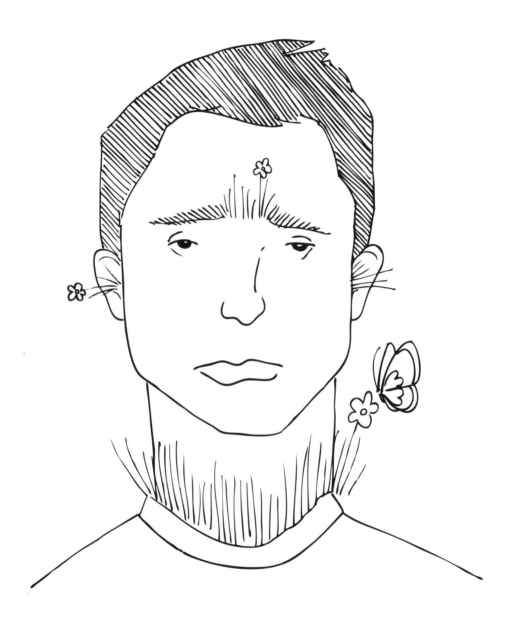

Grass

GREED

Greed is a bad word and drives a lot of people. Don't let it drive you.

GREEN LIGHT

Green means go, so don't dawdle; get going. It's the dawdlers that always get passed by. You don't want the whole world to be honking at you, right?

GROOMING

Everyone likes those who are well groomed. You not only look better, but you smell better too (see *Hygiene*).

GROPING

Nope on grope. That is, not unless you're invited.

GROUND RULES

It's always best to find out the rules *before* you play. After is usually too late. Way too late.

GROUP E-MAILS

Group e-mails are a rather impersonal form of communication. Do I want to get the same message a hundred other people get? Unless it's a critical news alert like "Oh gosh, you should've seen him running around with his fly open," it just seems to lack sincerity. At least pretend it's a personal message meant only for me.

GROWING UP

I'm sticking with Peter Pan on this one: I never want to grow up (see *Neckties*); so there! Being a child forever would definitely have its advantages. Now growing old and growing up are two different things. You don't really have a choice with the former, but you kind of do with the latter (or ladder).

GUARANTEES

When it comes down to it, there really aren't many guarantees in this world. Even the written ones have holes in them (see *Fine Print*). Yet another reason to live life to the fullest. How many reasons do you need?

GUARD

You probably want to let your guard down in the most familiar of circumstances. However, new acquaintances should have to earn your trust. Of course, it makes no sense to walk around paranoid all of the time, but you never really know what someone else has in mind until you get to know them (see *Taking Advantage*). That's why it pays to keep your guard up in the beginning.

GUARDIAN ANGELS

We all have guardian angels—someone's always looking out for us. They may be hard to spot without those wings and all, but they're out there. Oftentimes they're dressed up as friends.

GUILT

Most of us with any feelings carry around lots of guilt, and it will follow us as long as we let it. However, guilt isn't always so bad, as it usually forces us to do the right thing. But don't let your guilty past cause you to worry about the future (see *Wasting Time*). I'm an expert on Jewish guilt, and I'm told that guilt instilled by any mother is very much the same.

GUILTY CONSCIENCE

That damn conscience. A guilty one can really gnaw at you and keep you up at night. But you can fix it, change it, admit to it or do whatever you have to do to de-guilt yourself. It's usually completely within your own control.

GULF WAR I

War is hell and there's no glory in it. People get killed and homes are destroyed. But the first Gulf War was a time when the whole world came together to kick out a horrible tyrant who invaded a defenseless country. The free world really needed to see a clear example of good defeating evil.

GULLIBLE

If you believe everything you hear, you'll find that you're hearing more and thinking less. And others will enjoy feeding you all kinds of nonsense.

GUN CONTROL

Which is more important, the Sixth Amendment or that "Don't kill" commandment? I'm going with the "Don't kill." Too bad there just isn't a way to keep the guns out of the hands of the bad guys and only in the hands of the good guys, but it's the crazy angry ones who really shouldn't have access to firearms. I just don't buy that right-to-bare-arms stuff (as I don't like wearing short-sleeved shirts). So the horrible foreign monarchs are long gone, and anyway, if the military ever takes over, our little popguns won't stop their tanks. When our Founding Fathers drafted the Constitution, they only had those muskets that took half an hour to load and didn't hurt and maim lots of innocent people (see *Assault Weapons*). And don't forget, guns don't kill people; people kill people (but guns help).

GUT

You want to listen to your gut; it's almost always right. Now as for those noises it makes that everybody else can hear, it's trying to tell you something too: Feed me.

GUTS

I admire people with guts (we call that intestinal fortitude). Some have more guts than brains, but I admire them anyway (see *Do Something*).

GYNECOLOGIST

I think the proper term should be groinocologist. After all, what's a GY (guy) doing in this business, right? Anyway ladies, wouldn't you be more comfortable having a female doctor peek-a-booing down there?

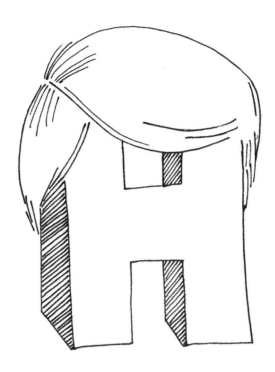

HABITS

Yes, we are all creatures of habits—especially nuns (I couldn't resist). Whether we like it or not, we tend to default to the same responses, routines and attitudes. But all habits aren't bad; for instance, it's a good habit to clean up after yourself. And creatures don't have to be scary. However, those zombie creatures really do scare me; but I digress (again). Anyway, old habits do die hard, especially the bad ones. Unfortunately, habits are easy to get into, and often hard to break.

HAIRCUTS

We boys seem to be rather finicky about our haircuts. First, we always look goofy after we get them. And it takes more than one shower to get all of those scratchy little hairs off. Naturally, we put those haircuts off as long as we can, which leads to other consequences (see *Samson Effect*). So who needs it? Why does hair have to grow anyway? Your bones stop growing, your teeth stop growing, your nose stops growing (unless you're Pinocchio; see *Lying*). Can't hair stop at your desired length? I think this is a hair stylist conspiracy; otherwise they would have figured out a way to stop hair growth by now. And how come your definition of "not too short" is always very different from the haircutter's? Same with "a little off the sides." The good news is that even a bad haircut will not last forever.

HAIR STYLES

Women typically change their hairstyles and colors many times throughout their lives. Men, on the other hand, usually stay with the same style forever, only altered by thinning and graying hair. That's what helps make men boring. When it comes to our hairstyles, we love to be boring.

HALF-ASSED

Half-assed is better than no-assed at all. Something is better than nothing (see *Do Something*).

HALF-ASSED INVITATIONS

A half-assed invitation isn't necessarily insincere; it just isn't definitive (see *Round Tuit*). You know how you can ask someone if they are busy? Or free on Saturday? Or had lunch yet? Well, don't, as we call this a loaded question. You don't want to box them in when they innocently tell you they're not busy, and then it turns out they have no desire to do whatever it is you wanted to do (see *Wiggle Room*). It will save plenty of embarrassment (yours and theirs) and awkward moments if you just ask a more direct question. Try this instead: "Can you have lunch with me on Saturday?" This way they can more graciously lie and decline your invitation. They may have some other pressing business to attend to—like having to re-arrange their sock drawer or something.

HALF BATH

I never understood why they call it a half bath. Does it mean that you can only pee in there? Or maybe just poop. But not both, I guess.

HALF FULL

Here's the age-old question: Is the glass half full or half empty? I say six of one, half a dozen of the other. Anyway, what difference does it make when you're really thirsty? Again, half is better than none.

HAND-HOLDING

Handholding doesn't always have to be a romantic thing. Taking someone by the hand can also be a very reassuring sign of friendship—for boys and girls.

HANDICAP

Making fun of people with special needs shows that your handicap is far larger than theirs. Don't be an asshole.

HANDICAPPED PARKING SPOTS

I'm often tempted to let the air out of the tires of cars illegally parked in handicapped spots. But that would also be illegal, and it would really tie up the space for someone who needed it. Don't be so lazy and inconsiderate. Park somewhere else; the walk will do you good. And be thankful you don't need a handicapped tag.

HANDIWORK

After you've completed a project, it's often a very rewarding feeling to sit back and admire your handiwork (see *Accomplishment*). Go ahead, take it all in. Smile; you deserve it. See, you can do it after all.

HANDLE

In the big picture, you're rarely given more than you can handle (see *Grand Plan*). Sometimes you'll be surprised at what you can ultimately deal with.

HANDS

Unless otherwise invited, keep your hands to yourself. And don't put them out the car window either.

HANDSHAKE

The way you shake hands makes a lasting impression. Make your handshake a firm one, for God's sake, as there's nothing worse than one of those wimpy, dead fish ones. Some people grab a hold and shake incessantly for five minutes; they're either nervous or just plain nuts. Others try to squeeze everything out of you, making it clear that they are of a dominant species; they're nuts too. There was a time when most business deals were done with a simple handshake. Too bad those days are gone.

HANDWRITING

They say that you can tell a lot about a person by their handwriting; you can tell they have messy handwriting, for one. I wouldn't know about this, as I usually can't read my own. I'm often very envious of people with good handwriting, both girls and boys. Anyway, the handwriting isn't always on the wall; which is OK, as staring at a blank wall probably won't do you any good.

HANDY

Don't be so quick to pay someone to take care of your minor repair and maintenance needs. You'd be amazed at how handy you can actually be. So give it a shot (see *Trying*). Remember: your tool is your friend.

HAPPEN

There are those who find ways to make things happen. And there are those who find lots of reasons why they can't. And of course, there are those who complain that things always happen to them (see *Blame*). Make things happen. There's always a way.

HAPPENS FOR A REASON

It may not always be very apparent, but everything happens for a reason. Everything. Sometimes it just takes a while for the reason to reveal itself.

HAPPINESS

Everyone deserves to be happy—you included. However, happiness is severely lacking in many areas, and is often very elusive. But finding happiness is extremely important. After all, life, liberty and the pursuit of happiness are in our Declaration of Independence; that's pretty powerful. How many other countries are founded on those principles (see *America The Beautiful*)? But I digress. Real happiness comes from inside, as no one can "make" you happy. So don't depend on others for your happiness, as you are entirely responsible for it. Go ahead, put on your happy face and spread as much happiness around as you can—all day, every day. Treat happiness like a disease and infect everyone with it. Some people spend so much time looking everywhere for happiness when it's often right there next to them, staring them in the face. Just open your eyes a little—or maybe a lot. You'll find it.

HAPPY MEDIUM

Sometimes, in our lifelong quest for peace and serenity, it's really just a happy medium we seek. I'd be happy with that.

HARD WORK

You can't go wrong with hard work, as it almost always pays off. Sometimes it takes a while, but keep at it.

HARM'S WAY

It's a very good idea to stay out of harm's way. They usually have the right-of-way, you know.

HAS-BEEN

I'd rather be a has-been than a hasn't-ever-been. At least that way, I guess, you were something at some point. That's better than being nothing.

HASTE

Does haste make waste? No, haste usually makes a mess. Wasters make waste.

HATE

Hate is the worst word in the English language. It's the nastiest four-letter word there is. I think it stands for Have All The Evil. It requires so much energy to hate. Talk about wasted effort. Can you imagine if we redirected all of that hateful energy into something productive? We could power the entire world. Sure, you can dislike someone, you can loathe, detest and despise them, you can never want to see them and you can even wish you never met them. But you shouldn't hate anyone. It's a way too powerful and final expression. If you really have to despise someone, hate what they are, not who they are. However, you can hate asparagus, baths, school, rainy days, cigars and work. That's perfectly OK. Some even hate to complain, although they probably really love it.

HATRED

You aren't born with hatred, as it's not in your genes. It's a learned trait and, unfortunately, it is taught to you as you grow up. Some things are not worth learning or teaching, and this is one of them.

HATS

If you insist on wearing a hat while you're inside, you're not fooling anybody. We know you either don't have any class, or there's nothing under there (see *Baldness*), or both. And you look stupid. Do you really expect it to rain inside? There's only one exception to this rule: You want to always have your thinking cap on.

HAVE

We usually don't realize what we have, or how good we have it, until we have to do without (see *Appreciation*). That goes especially for ice cream, friends and electric toothbrushes.

HAVE A NICE DAY

Do you think that voicemail message that's set up to greet anonymous callers really cares if I have a nice day (see *Insincerity*)? I think not.

HAVE A WAY WITH WORDS

Yes, some of us have it and some of us don't (see *Sure Dad, You Know Everything*).

HAVE-NOTS

Instead of whining about all of the things you don't have, how about appreciating the things you do have (see *Count Your Blessings*)?

HEAD

You know that big lump between your shoulders? It's your noggin. Here's your choice: use it or lose it. Otherwise it will atrophy like unused muscles. And guys, always think with the upstairs one.

HEADACHE

Now here's something mankind and womankind can easily live without. To me, headaches serve no useful purpose. At least other aches and pains warn your body that something's wrong. But headaches? What do they tell you? That you feel miserable? You already know that, so what's the point (see *Pain In The Ass*)?

HEAD IN THE SAND

If you insist on keeping your head in the sand when it comes to dealing with difficult issues, the only result will be an invitation for someone to take advantage of you while you're in a very prone position (not to mention having a head full of dirt). You need to face these unpleasant issues head on, which is much better than not at all. They typically don't solve themselves, you know.

HEADLIGHTS

It's always best to avoid the temptation to look straight into oncoming headlights. (Yes, those headlights too.)

HEAD NODDER

Some people think it's polite to mindlessly and incessantly agree with everybody. It's not. So when you nod your head, make sure you really agree with them (see *Mixed Signals*).

HEADS UP

Why do people shout "heads up" when something's coming down from above? Like you'd rather get conked in the face instead of your hard head by looking up?

HEALING

Of course we're all not doctors, but every one of us has the opportunity to help heal. There is so much suffering on our planet, so it's the job of all of us to do our best to heal the world (see *Charity*). Healing usually takes five ingredients; just mix these together and poof! You're healed (or almost healed):

Attitude
Commitment
Desire
Strength
Time

HEALTHY

Your health is the second most important thing in your life (your children being your first). So given the choice, being healthy sure beats the alternative. And be happy while you're at it. They tend to go hand in hand.

HEARING

Your hearing is a precious sense you can easily protect. Blasting window-shattering noise through your speakers or headphones will almost certainly result in irreparable damage to your hearing. That's permanent. Don't be stupid.

HEART

The heart is the most important organ in your body. Most people don't know this, but it's not only your mouth that speaks. Your heart speaks volumes, and it often has a lot to say; you just have to listen. Oh, and it always speaks the truth.

HEART ATTACK

If you're overweight, out of shape, lazy, don't watch what you eat (except when you take a bite) and don't care, you're a wonderful candidate for a heart attack. You may not care, but if you're really lucky, someone else does. Take care of yourself, for God's sake (see *Exercise*).

HEART OF GOLD

One way or another, you'll have a lot of friends if there's gold in your heart.

HEAT OF BATTLE

Sometimes, when we are caught up in the heat of battle, we all say things we wish we hadn't. No, you can't put them back in your mouth, but the words "I'm sorry" may help.

HEAT vs. HUMIDITY

It's not the heat, it's the humidity? Bullshit, it's the heat.

HEAVEN AND HELL

The image of heaven seems to be a place where angels fly around playing harps. And hell is portrayed as a hot place where the bad ones are wearing red costumes and carrying nasty looking pitchforks. I have some different images.

Heaven:

> Dogs don't bite or need to be walked.
> Everyone has 20/20 vision and no one needs glasses.
> Everyone looks hot naked.
> No one has bad breath or hygiene issues.
> You can eat sloppy desserts without gaining weight.
> You can lie out in the warm sun with no bugs to bother you.
> You can sit and watch sports on TV all day long.
> You can spend lots of time watching the Beatles create music.
> You have nice bright white teeth and don't have to brush or floss.
> You really do eat all you can eat at the buffet.
> Your team always wins.

Hell:

> All the joints in your body are on fire.
> Everyone is packed together like sardines.
> Everything smells like shit.
> You are constantly hungry and don't have food.
> You can't find the bathroom and have constant diarrhea.
> You're free falling.
> You're in class unprepared for a big test and naked, no less.
> You're wearing wet clothes in ten degree weather.
> Your team always loses on the last play in triple overtime.

HECK

What the heck is heck? And where the heck is heck? I know it's not hell, because hell is hell, and war is hell. I guess heck is heck.

HELL ON EARTH

Unfortunately, there is such a thing as hell on earth (see *Holocaust* and *War*).

HELPING

Help somebody—anybody. We all could use a hand. You really want to be a helper, not a hinderer, as there are way too many hinderers around these days. They say that God helps those who help themselves (I think this excludes third helpings of dessert, though). So before you ask for help, make sure you really need it.

HELPLESS

Only babies are helpless. The rest of us can do whatever we set our minds to.

HEMORRHOIDS

Hemorrhoids—boy, talk about a real pain in the ass. Why, oh why must we suffer the humiliation and embarrassment of such a nasty ailment? I'm sure this is God's punishment for something. If I ever figure it out, I'll let you know.

HERE AND NOW

If you spend too much time worrying about what-if's and why-not's, you will have completely missed the here and now.

HEREDITY

There's not much you can do about your lineage. You are pretty much stuck with the cards you've been dealt (see *Relatives*). Girls, just remember: the apple doesn't fall far from the tree. You will grow up to be just like your mother. Why? Because that's the behavior you were always exposed to, so that's what you know. Don't believe me? Start listening to yourself after you turn 25. Guess who you sound like? Boys, not to worry—this never happens to us (see *Sexism*).

HERITAGE

It's important to know where you came from. It's even more important to be proud of it.

HERNIA

Because a hernia mostly affects men, shouldn't they call it a him-ia (see *Hitting Below The Belt*)?

HEROES/HEROINES (MINE)

Heroes don't have to wear capes and leap tall buildings. And they come in all shapes and sizes (see *Doctors, Teachers, Nurses, Rabbis, Priests, Soldiers*; again, don't see *Lawyers*).

You can have your heroes, but here are mine:

> Albert Einstein (it's all relative)
> All U.S. Armed Forces (they protect all of us)
> Astronauts (especially the Original Seven)
> Ben Glantz (nothing stops him)
> Bill Cosby (he used to be a very funny fellow)
> Bugs Bunny (my favorite smart-ass)
> Cal Ripken, Jr. (talk about loving your work)
> Cowardly Lion (he helped save Dorothy before he knew he already
>   had the courage)
> Daniel Boone (the TV show was great)
> Detective Andy Sipowitz (tough guy, warm heart)
> Dexter Manley (overcame everything)
> Dr. Jonas Salk (saved a generation)
> Eleanor Roosevelt (I'm partial to anyone named Eleanor)
> Ellen Burns (tougher than she ever knew)
> Fire and rescue personnel (often unsung heroes)
> General George S. Patton (defined both blood and guts)
> Glinda the Good Witch (we need more good witches)
> Golda Meir (what a tough lady)
> Grandma (mine)
> Harry Truman (watch out for those little guys)
> Hayda Nussman (I miss her all the time)
> Homer Simpson (he's fat and stupid, but happy and honest)

Hoss Cartwright (gentle giant)

Howard Stern (not even close to being a shock jock)

Isiah "Ike" Leggett (a very accomplished man who literally started
with nothing)

Johnnie Appleseed (he got to leave his seeds everywhere and didn't
get in trouble for it; see *Sex*)

Lady Gaga (she's her own person)

Lenny Skutnik (look him up)

Louie Armstrong (quite the Satchmo)

Mark Twain (or Samuel Clemens; they were both pretty good)

Mel Blanc ("What's up, Doc?")

Moses (I like those guys with one name)

Mothers (we'd be lost without them)

Mr. Peabody (a very smart dog)

Police personnel (even the chubby ones)

Rudy Giuliani (class act after 9/11)

Steve "the Bear" Sheppard (what a basketball player)

Stevie Wonder (great name)

Superman (now this guy is always wearing his strong suit—Truth,
Justice and the American way)

Thomas Edison (we'd still be in the dark)

Winston Churchill (talk about rising to the occasion)

Wives (not husbands; we're just along for the ride)

Zorro (always left his mark)

HETERONYMS

No, heteronyms have nothing to do with sexual preference. Another fine
example of why people from other countries have so much trouble learning
English. Great, two words spelled exactly the same and pronounced differently,
with two different meanings, no less. You know, Polish and polish; read and
read; wind and wind. I'd love to meet the genius that thought this up. You
would think that somebody would have tried to fix this by now. What exactly
does Congress do anyway?

HEY IS FOR HORSES

Wrong. Hay is for horses. Hey is perfectly OK (see *Homophones*).

HIATUS

Hi, Atus, how you doin'? I'm fine, thanks. Who comes up with these stupid words?

HICCUPS

One question here: Why? What's the point of hiccups? To be embarrassed by yet another bodily function you can't control (see *Diarrhea*)?

HIDING IN PLAIN SIGHT

Sometimes the things you drive yourself crazy looking for are right in front of your nose. Just open your eyes and sniff.

HIGH ROAD

Even for those who are directionally challenged, you can't go wrong by always taking the high road. When it really comes down to it, that's the only road to take. You also stay out of those nasty floods that way.

HIGHS AND LOWS

We sure do enjoy the highs, but also have to endure the lows in life (see *Balance*). You really want to learn from the lows, though, and try to minimize them if you can.

HIGH SCHOOL

Yes, high school is still school and requires learning, studying, taking tests and writing reports. But usually it is also a special time to grow up with people you've known most of your life. Unfortunately, after graduation you will never see many of them again. That's why it is very important to stay in touch with those you want to remain close (see *Friends*).

HILLS

Overcoming hills isn't too difficult; it's the mountains you have to watch out for. It's always best to build up your speed going down to give you a boost and gain some momentum for going up. It doesn't have to be too complicated.

HIPPOPOTAMUS

Yes, God really does have a sense of humor.

HISTORY

The more we study the past, the better prepared we are for the future. History has a tendency to repeat itself, which isn't always good, so it's best not to ignore it.

HITCHHIKING

Don't hitchhike; there are way too many nuts out there.

HITTING BELOW THE BELT

No wonder this is cheating—it really hurts to get hit below the belt, especially for us boys. However, use whatever means necessary (including unfair hitting) to get out of a very perilous situation. There are no rules when it comes to self-preservation. You might also want to wear your belt very, very high.

HITTING BOTTOM

There are times when all seems to be lost and everything is going wrong. We all go through that. Just when you think it can't get any worse, it does. When you realize that you've really hit bottom, stop and think. At that point you only have one direction to go—and that's up (see *Hope*).

HITTING THE NAIL ON THE HEAD

This is the only time hitting is really allowed. And hitting it square on the head happens to be the best way to drive in a nail. Watch your fingers though, as missing those nails is the best way to hurt them.

HOBBIES

Get a hobby, preferably a productive one. It will keep your idle time occupied and help you stay out of trouble.

HOCKEY

No, hockey isn't a passion of mine, and I think most people like it for the fights (see *Morbid*). I'm not too keen on the violence, and that puck moves way too fast for me to follow. Actually, I think it moves too fast for most to follow, except in slow-motion replays (with highlighted graphics). So those spectators are really like me and don't know what's going on.

HOLDING GRUDGES

So you're really holding onto that grudge for years? How's that working out for you? Actually, holding big grudges all your life can be very bad for your health and can even destroy you (see *Forgive and Forget*). Now don't go by me, as I hold grudges with the best of 'em. So imagine all that wasted effort spent on carrying those bad feelings, not to mention the paralyzing effect of having that albatross around your neck. Just let it go. However, if you want to immerse yourself in anger and hatred the rest of your life, go ahead and be my guest (see *Baggage*). Who am I to stand in your way to drown in your pointless and unnecessary emotions? After a while you even tend to forget what that issue was all about. Now as for small grudges, by all means hold onto those. They're not as heavy, and we're only human, right?

HOLD ON

You're talking to someone on the phone and they tell you to hold on. What exactly should you be holding onto?

HOLD YOUR GROUND

Don't let them push you around. If you're right, you're right.

HOLD YOUR TONGUE

Your tongue is rather slippery, so holding it is quite a hard thing to do. But while you're trying, it will at least keep you from saying something you may regret.

HOLIDAY SPIRIT

Why is it that people try to be so nice around the holidays? The homeless get lots of help, charities get lots of money, we all wish everybody a happy whatever. So is there a law against doing this all year round? If there is, let's get that law changed (see *Rules*).

HOLOCAUST

How could an otherwise civilized society in the twentieth century systematically, savagely and almost completely eliminate an entire race of people? Causing all of that suffering is incomprehensible, inconceivable inexcusable and unconscionable. The horrible and unspeakable atrocities that were committed are things none of us will ever understand (thank God). The whole world should never forget this despicable time in history. Anyone who doesn't believe this actually happened (they call themselves deniers) is unquestionably one of the biggest morons on the planet. I get violently ill just thinking about it. I hope it does the same to you. Never again (see *History*).

HOME

Yes, Dorothy, there's no place like home. Anyway, home is where the heart is, you know, and a house is not always a home (it's just a building). Home is wherever you feel very comfortable, welcome and safe. It can be a place of worship, your workplace or someone else's house. Anyway, those warm feelings and memories are really in your heart, not in your house, so they travel with you. It doesn't matter where your home is physically located, as long as you have the feeling inside of you.

HOMEBODY

So what's wrong with being a homebody? It doesn't necessarily make you a recluse (unless you are one). You tend to spend a lot of time in your home, so you might as well enjoy it.

HOMELESSNESS

For there to be homelessness in the most prosperous country in the world is a tragic national disgrace. Everyone, and I mean *everyone,* deserves a home. It doesn't have to be a castle, just a place to live.

HOMEMADE

Who are they kidding? Do you really think they make all those homemade cookies cakes, soups, etc., at someone's house? Handmade maybe, but homemade? Come on.

HOME OWNERSHIP

Home ownership is not all that it's cracked up to be, what with all of that lawn mowing, leaf raking, tree pruning, house painting, garage cleaning, bulb changing—just to name a few. The list of chores is never ending, and there is always some other task lurking around the corner. Tax benefits and building equity aside, there sure is a good case to be made for renting and letting all those pesky jobs be someone else's problem.

HOME RUN

Home runs are hard to hit and don't happen very often. If you spend all of your energy always swinging for the fences, the odds are usually against you. Stick with the singles and doubles to advance your life. Those are way more doable, and the percentages for success are much better.

HOMESICKNESS

There's no real cure for homesickness, and God knows, scientists have searched for one for years. No pill either, although a well-timed hug can often help. Those empty and isolated feelings are very real and difficult to overcome. You've just got to gut it out, and it usually goes away after a while. Staying very busy and remembering what's in your heart helps (see *Home*).

HOMOPHONES

As if this language isn't already hard enough! Why can't you spell words that are pronounced identically the same way? You mean to tell me that if I said that I was going to take a plane, you would think I was going to take a plain? Sheesh!

HONESTLY

Honestly? Quite honestly? In all honesty? To be honest with you? Do you want me to be perfectly honest? Truthfully? To tell you the truth? What do all these expressions imply—and why would you want to qualify what you are saying with any of these phrases? Are you simply not telling the truth the rest of the time?

HONESTY

Honesty really is the best policy—at least 99 percent of the time. And it's the honest ones who represent the pillars of society. Sad to say that this is no longer an automatic character trait. If this is a foreign concept to you, start by being honest with yourself.

HONEY

Why do you suppose it is that at some point during a long-term relationship we simply lose our ability to call each other by our given names? All of a sudden we begin to Honey and Dearie each other to death. Not sure whether that's a good or bad sign.

HONEYMOON PERIOD

There is a point in a budding relationship when the honeymoon period ends and reality sets in. The beginning is often punctuated by lots of hearts and flowers and goo-goo eyes, when we're on our best behavior (see *Farting*). It's after all of the newness wears off that you'll actually know if you have something healthy and sustaining going on.

HONOR AMONG THIEVES

Do you really think there is honor among thieves? Oh, you're killing me. Let's just say that criminals are not the most trustworthy folks, OK?

HOPE

You know those little rays of sunshine that find their way to you from time to time? Well those are rays of hope. So always remember that no matter what you are or what you do, there is always hope. Always. And if that's all you have, hope can take you pretty far. Now if for some reason you're moving too fast and pass it by, just stop and back up. It will be there waiting for you; at least, I hope so. And for those in really dire straits, don't forget that HOPE stands for Hold On; Pain Eases. So no matter what, never, ever, ever lose hope (see *Giving Up*). And as for false hope, there's no such thing; because hope is hope.

HOPELESS ROMANTIC

Yes, some of us are hopeless romantics—so what? It's OK to dream that true romance will get you somewhere. Just know when it's really getting you nowhere.

HORNET'S NEST

Never stir up a hornet's nest, unless you're prepared to be stung.

HOROSCOPES

Don't be so dismissive about horoscopes. There may be something to it, especially if your moon aligns with Uranus (or Myanus).

HORSES

In the old days, horses were beasts of burden and a mode of transportation. That was before bicycles, cars and motorcycles were invented. Guess what? We don't need horses for that anymore. Has it occurred to you that maybe those graceful horsies don't like to run around with your fat ass on their backs? If I were a horse, I'd tell you to take a bus, for God's sake. Or I'd tell you something else that was not so polite. Wild horses seem to roam just fine without carting around lazy human beings. Imagine being a fast horse. Do you think they know if they are really fast, they get to be a stud and spend the rest of their lives screwing their brains out? That would be all of the incentive I would need to run like the wind. Maybe next time for me (see *Afterlife*).

HORSESHIT

For some reason, saying "horseshit" doesn't seem to have the same impact or punctuate speech as well as other descriptive curse words (see *Bullshit*).

HOSPICE

Could you imagine working at a facility where your job is to take care of people who are dying? Neither can I. Those patients are usually there for one reason, with no chance of recovering. Hospice workers are real caregivers with an exceptional level of compassion. Thank God they do what they do (see *Angels*).

HOSPITALS

Hospitals are a place where miracles happen. I just don't like to visit them too often. I'm always afraid that they'll take one look at me and strongly suggest that I stay for a while.

HOST/HOSTESS

Being a good host or hostess is an admirable quality to have. You can really join an elite group here, without taking special courses or possessing obscure inherited skills. All it takes is the ability to be thoughtful, polite and considerate to your guests. It's not always so easy, as you typically have the responsibility and pressure to make sure they have a good time. But it's not rocket science. Just don't forget they're *your* guests, and should be treated that way. They get served first, you know.

HOT AND COLD

So you're running hot and cold about someone or something? You need to make up your mind already (see *Mixed Signals*). The clock is ticking.

HOWARD STERN

Yes, I've heard it all. How can you listen to that guy? He's so disgusting, nasty and, well, even more disgusting? I have to admit, there are some times when I really do have to turn him off, as he can be, well, very obnoxious and disgusting. (I can also find myself being obnoxious and disgusting, but I can't turn myself off.) The good news is that, like many of us, he's mellowing with the years. However, I normally find him quite entertaining, innovative and brave. Yes, brave. He tends to say things that many of us think, but are reluctant to say out loud. And he is an excellent interviewer, who gets people to talk about the most personal, obscure and sensitive subjects. Those who know him well swear that he is a really nice guy; they likely tend to swear a lot too. I give Howard Stern plenty of credit for doing the things he has done (with plenty of repercussions) and being one of those who inspired me to write this book (even though I don't know him). So if you hate my book, it gives you another reason to hate him.

HOW YOU SAY IT

Very often, it's not what you say, but how you say it. It's all in the delivery, so watch yourself. Or at least listen to yourself.

HUGGING

Hugging is one of the most important physical contacts there is. The warmth and calming sense of security of having someone wrap their arms around you is indescribable. Nothing comforts better than a hug, and some of us hugoholics (it's a medical term) can never get enough. It's so nice to be known as somebody who gives good hugs (see *Touching*). And hugs are perfectly OK for men to exchange. We need much more hugging in this world. If you don't get an incredible rush from a hug, go straight to your doctor right away and have a complete physical. Make sure they especially check your feelings; they're usually next to your heart. Oh, and those one-armed hugs are about as sincere as group e-mails. Everybody needs a hug. Everybody.

HUMILIATE

Humiliation is such a horrible feeling. Does anyone like to be humiliated? Precisely, and that's why there is never a good reason to humiliate anyone, even if they deserve it.

HUMILITY

Yes, we can all likely stand more humility. It's good to be humble.

HUMOR

Everything in life isn't funny. Sometimes you have to look real hard, but you can usually find humor in most things. Now it's not a good idea to yuck it up at a funeral. But adding a little levity here and there is usually good, as people tend to take things way too seriously. And of course, laughter really is the best medicine.

HUNTING

Will somebody please tell me why they call hunting a sport (see *Golf*)? I don't get it. Call me stupid (you'll have to stand in line), but most Americans are civilized to the point of not having to hunt for their own food, right? What's the sport in lying in wait, having all of these high-powered rifles and bows and arrows, and shooting at ducks and deer? Now give the little duckies and bambies the same weapons—then it's a sport, with a level playing field. You'll see how much fun hunting is when they can shoot back at you. Anyway, how do you know that one of those little birdies isn't your great-grandmother reincarnated (see *Afterlife*)*? Try shooting skeet or targets for sport; they don't shoot back either and nobody gets hurt.

HURT

Yes, you sometimes hurt the one(s) you love. And this isn't the kind of boo-boo a Band-Aid can help. Sometimes it's about being at the wrong place at the wrong time. Just tell them you didn't mean to (see *I'm Sorry*).

HYGIENE

Bad hygiene is like bird poop: you know it when it hits you. And you don't want to be the hitter or hittee. Bad hygiene will not only keep your friends away, but could result in all types of nasty ailments. So you better take the time every day to brush your teeth, change your underwear, take a shower and put on deodorant. And for God's sake, keep those ears clean. We will all thank you.

HYPHENATED-AMERICANS

We have no caste or class system in this country, as most of our ancestors came from other countries. Lots of other countries (see *Melting Pot*). Remember that in the old days, we were the New World. Not anymore. Therefore, there are no such things as Chinese-Americans, African-Americans and Greek-Americans. After all, you don't hear about Chinese-Germans, or African-Greeks, do you? We're all Americans—just plain Americans. And that's a good thing.

HYPOCRITES

Way too often it's those sanctimonious, holier-than-thou types who are the biggest transgressors against the very things they rail about. Saying one thing and doing something else doesn't say much about your character. It's not always so easy though. Don't I know that.

HYSTERECTOMY

Pardon my ignorance, but I know that when you have an appendectomy, they remove your appendix; a lumpectomy is when they take out a lump; and a tonsillectomy is when they remove your tonsils. So when they do a hysterectomy, do they take out your hysters? All I know is that it's a girlie thing and is very painful. Now when they make a girl into a guy, it's called an addadicktomy.

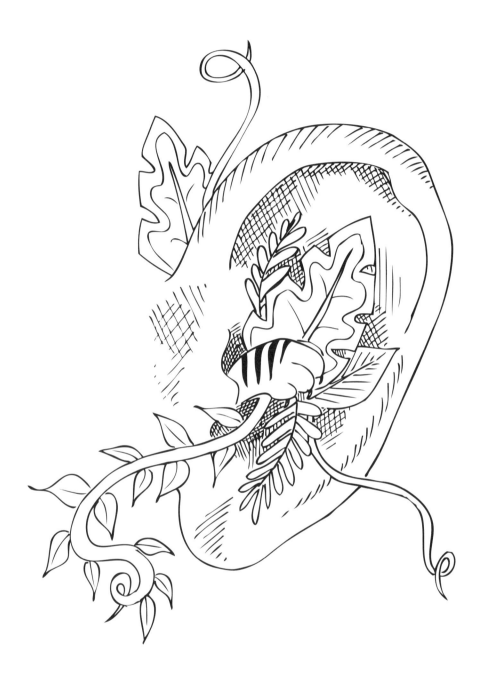

Hygiene

I

I is a very small word, and sometimes takes plenty of credit (often without much justification) when it comes to success. We is a small word too, but there's usually lots of we involved when good things happen. Don't forget all those we's; we're everywhere.

I CAN'T

Oh sure you can (see *Giving Up*). The words "I can't" tend to come out of our lips way too easily. Remember: can't is a four-letter word too, and it's unacceptable. So try figuring out ways that you can. Try this:

> I hope I can.
> I think I can.
> I know I can.
> Of course you can.
> I'm glad I'm not a can.

See? I told you.

ICE CREAM

Ice cream really is a magical food, capable of curing all kinds of problems in life. It has so many fantastic properties designed to bring your mind and body to an elevated level of happiness. Of course, it also elevates our blood sugar and tonnage, but it sure is hard to resist (see *Moderation*).

IDEAS

We all have that creative spark, which sometimes evolves into brilliant ideas. However, what we think is brilliant, others may view as stupid. It's best to ignore them and keep those juices flowing. They're probably just jealous that it wasn't their idea in the first place.

IDOLIZING

No one is larger than life. Idolizing is not fair to them, as they'll never live up to your image, and it's not fair to you either, as you will likely be disappointed. Maybe that's why they put that idol business in the Ten Commandments; it's a no-no there too.

I DON'T KNOW

You shouldn't be afraid to admit that you don't know something. Sometimes people don't hear you when you say "I don't know," so they keep asking (especially the little ones). Therefore, you may want to practice some alternate ways of conveying this message by saying:

Are you deaf?	Go ask someone else.
Beats me.	How would I know?
Do I look like I know everything? (Don't answer that).	I don't have the slightest idea. What are you asking me for?
Don't ask me.	Who knows?
Don't you understand English?	You got me.

Body language also works. Here's how:

Shrug your shoulders.	Roll your eyes.
Stare up at the ceiling.	Pretend you're asleep.
Throw up your hands (but don't throw up).	Walk away.

I DON'T WANT TO

There are plenty of things we don't want to do in life. But sometimes we just have to. Sorry (see *Responsibility*).

IF AT FIRST YOU DON'T SUCCEED

If at first you don't succeed, try, try again. These are good words to live by. So if you didn't make it this time, just give it another shot. You'll get there.

IF I KNEW THEN

Sure, if you knew then what you know now, life would be very different. Who cares? You didn't and you can't, so give it up and waste your idle time thinking about something else.

IGNORANCE

Ignorance really isn't bliss; it's just an excuse to be stupid. What you don't know may really hurt you. The price of education can be expensive at times, but the cost of ignorance is immeasurable. You definitely pay for it, one way or another.

IGNORING

Ignoring a problem (or a person) doesn't normally make it go away, and sometimes makes it worse. It's usually best just to deal with it (see *Pragmatic*).

I KNOW YOU'RE BUSY, BUT

If they know you're busy, then they shouldn't be bothering you, right? Either they don't know what busy is, or they just don't care. So here's the problem for you when you're the busy bee (see *Damned If You Do*): If you say yes, it may put you under; and if you say no, that would cause you not to be busy, which might spoil your whole reason to live. They call that a quandary.

I LOVE YOU

These are the best three words that have ever been strung together. Such a strong and emphatic declaration becomes the foundation of any serious relationship. That is, unless it is one-sided (see *Unrequited Love*).

IMAGE

To some, it's all about image: the look, the glamour, the glitz, the glitter. However, it's best to keep in mind that things aren't always as they appear (see *Beauty*).

IMAGINATION

Your imagination can be limitless. Open your mind and just imagine the possibilities. Open it real wide.

IMITATION

Is imitation the sincerest form of flattery? I've studied this for many years and have come to this conclusion: No. Flattery is the sincerest form of flattery.

IMMATURE

Act your age, not your shoe size. Of course, this mostly applies to adults. Little children usually have low shoe sizes, so that's OK.

IMMIGRATION

Our country was founded by people from other parts of the world and we are a nation of immigrants. Where else in the world can you find such a melting pot of ethnicities and cultures? We just need to find a better way to make sure all those who decide to settle in America do it legally.

IMMORTAL

Yes, even Superman ages (but very slowly), as no one is immortal. Some may not act like it, but none of us will live forever. Oftentimes it's our youth who live their lives as if nothing will ever kill them (see *Risk*). That's not a good thing.

IMPATIENT

Relax. You can tap your fingers and squirm all you want, but whatever is going to happen will happen, regardless of whether or not you're driving yourself crazy about it.

IMPERFECTIONS

Get used to it, because the world is full of imperfections, and they're what make each of us unique. Fortunately, we tend to notice many more of our own imperfections than anyone else does. Remember that the next time a nasty zit pops out.

IMPOLITE

It's not polite to:

> Bug anyone while they're on the phone.
> Burp or fart in any way that can be detected by others.
> Discipline anyone in public.
> Interrupt someone when they're speaking (unless they never stop).
> Leer or stare at any member of the opposite sex (or any particular body part) while in the company of your sweetie.
> Let anyone see what's in your mouth.
> Pull off anyone's bathing suit while swimming.
> Show up an hour late.
> Sit on someone's lap without permission.
> Speak or utter any other sounds while chewing (unless it's gum—then by all means, snap away).
> Stab someone in the back (or front).
> Talk at the urinal.
> Underdress at a black-tie event

IMPORTANT

If you constantly have to tell people how important you are, you aren't.

IMPOSITION

Who decides whether or not you're imposing on someone? My guess is that it's them, not you. So you are not imposing unless they say you are. Release the guilt; go ahead and enjoy their hospitality.

IMPOSSIBLE

Nothing is impossible. Improbable maybe, but not impossible (see *Giving Up*). Anyway, "I'm possible" makes everything possible.

IMPRESS

Opulence, and all the trappings of wealth, impress some people. Not me. It just means that someone who either made or inherited a lot of money spent it on themselves. How hard is that? What really impresses me are people who volunteer at homeless shelters and hospices, help the disabled and give their time and effort to worthwhile causes. I'm impressed, as they are the real stars (*see Heroes*).

IMPRESSIONABLE

Little children (and plenty of the big ones too) are so impressionable. They don't miss much, and often try to mimic your behavior, both good and bad. The problem is that they often don't know the difference. It's best to be careful and watch yourself.

I'M SORRY

"I'm sorry" can sometimes be the toughest words to say. Here, practice with me: I'm sorry; I'm really sorry; I'm really, really sorry. There, that wasn't so hard, was it? Now try saying it when you have to (see *Admit You're Wrong*). These can be two of the most soothing words there are. (Well, maybe it's three words.) So soothe away.

IN

These in's are in:

In a pinch	Inform
Inclusive	Infuse
Incognito	Ingenious
Incredible	Ingest
In crowd	Initiation
Indicative	In jest
Indiscrete	In love
Individuality	Innovative
Indestructible	Inoculate
Indescribably delicious	Input
Indispensable	Inquisitive
Indoctrination (see *Doctors*)	Inseam
Inexact	Insightful
Infinity	Inspire
Influential	Instinct

Insulate
Insure
In sync
Integrate
Interface
Internet
Intimate

Initiate
Intuition
In touch
Invaluable
Investigate
Inviting
Invoke

These in's are out:

Inaccurate
Inaction
In a fix
In a pickle
Inappropriate
In a rut
Inattentive
Incapable
Incessant
Inclement
Incomprehensible
Inconclusive
Inconceivable
Inconsequential
Inconsiderate
Inconsistent
Incorrigible
Incredulous
Indecent
Indecisive
Indefensible
Indifferent
Indignant
Indiscreet
Indiscriminate
Ineffective
Inefficient
Inept
Inequality
Inescapable
Inexcusable
Infamous
Infatuate (see *Dieting*)
Infidelity

Infiltrate
Inflexible
Infuriate
Ingratiate
Inhospitable
Inhuman
Injure
Injustice
Innocuous (I guess)
Inoperable
Insanity
Insatiable
Insecure
Insensitive
Insincere
Insipid
Insistent
Insolent
Instigate
Insubordinate
Insufferable
Insulting
Insurmountable
Intimidating
Intoxicate
Intractable
Intransient
Intransigent
Intrusive
Interrupt
Intimidate
Inundate
Invincible

INCONSOLABLE

Sometimes, no matter how hard you try, you can't really comfort them. Just do the best you can.

INCREDIBLE

We're all incredible. Every single one of us (see *Unique*).

IN DENIAL

Sometimes it's very difficult to ignore the obvious, especially when it's staring you in the face (see *Rationalization*). Try stepping back and objectively seeing the big picture. It's likely that you simply have to accept it. Sorry. The truth never lies.

INDEPENDENCE DAY

July 4th is a real holiday with something important to celebrate (see *Freedom*), so go ahead and party away. But leave the fireworks to the professionals. I guess fire has to work on this holiday; maybe it gets time and a half.

INDEPENDENT

It's great to be on your own, but it's really hard not to depend on anybody. You can't do everything all by yourself (nor should you want to). People need people, you know.

INDULGE

Go ahead and indulge yourself once in a while; after all, we're only human. You deserve to indulge sometimes; just don't make a habit of it (see *Balance*). Overindulging, of course, is not a good thing.

INEVITABLE

Some things are just going to happen whether you like it or not. There is always that impending prostate check or mammogram, meeting with the boss or final exam. You might be able to put off the inevitable for a while, but you can't stop it. If you ever figure out how, please let me know. Quickly.

INFATUATION

Some confuse love with infatuation (see *Lust*). It's very different, as infatuation is not very healthy. No one is that special. Try getting a life.

INFLAMMATORY

Try to diffuse a fight, not inflame it. Adding fuel to the fire, as they say, just makes it worse.

INFLUENCE

Don't allow anyone to have undue influence over you. It's OK to ask for advice, but we all need to have a mind of our own, and not be so easily influenced by others (see *Intimidation*).

INFORMALITY

Our society is much less formal than in past eras. It's a good thing that most of us are on a first-name basis. This has nothing to do with intimacy; it's just that first names are easier to remember than last names (see *Name Tags*).

INFORMATION OVERLOAD

We are constantly being bombarded with information on top of information. It's a wonder we have any idea what's really going on. It gets kind of crowded in our brains sometimes, as there's only so much that will fit in there.

INFORMED

Be informed and stay informed. That way you'll never feel left out. And if the world is ending, you'll know about it.

INHIBITIONS

Yes, we can all afford to lighten up and lose some inhibitions. But not all (see *Exhibitionism*).

INITIAL REACTION

Your initial reaction is often your worst reaction. Step back, take a few breaths and then decide how to deal with the issue or situation, especially if it's a bad one.

INITIALS

It's best to understand our world of abbreviations and acronyms. Here are some commonly used shorthand initials we all should know:

AARP	Old Farts
ACLU	American Civil Liberties Union
AED	Automated External Defibrillator
AFL-CIO	American Federation Of Labor (I don't know the rest)
AKA	What's His Name?
ALF	Alien Life Form
AMF	Adios, Mother Fucker
AOK	Very OK
AOL	Ancient Internet Company
APB	Find the Bad Guys
ASAP	Will You Hurry Up Already?
ATF	Boozers, Smokers and Gun Guys
ATM	Green Machine
AWOL	No Forwarding Address
BFD	Big Fucking Deal
BFF	Unnatural Friendship
BHMF	Bald-Headed Mother Fucker
BM	Do You Have To Ask (see *Shit*)
BMF	Big Mother Fucker
BMOC	Important Guy
BMW	Bavarian Motor Works
BO	PU
BOLO	Be On The Lookout
BPOE	Best People On Earth
BVDs	Underwear (some people can't spell)
BYOB	Bring Your Own Alcohol
CD	Compact Disk/Certificate Of Deposit
CEO	Top Dog
C/O	In Care Of
COB	Close of Business
COD	Pay Up
CPI	Inflation
CPR	Cardiopulmonary Resuscitation
CPU	Computer Guts
CRT	Cathode Ray Tube

CSI	Crime Scene Investigation
CT	(see *Cock Teasing*)
CU	Bye-Bye
CYA	Cover Your Anatomy (ass)
D & C	Dusting & Cleaning
DA	Duck Ass
DDT	Bad Bug Spray
DIY	Don't Get Any Help
DJ	Disc Jockey
DMV	Department of Waiting And Waiting
DNA	Deoxyribonucleic Acid (go ahead, impress your friends)
DOA	Very Dead
DUI	Driving Under The Influence
DWI	Driving When You Really Shouldn't
EKG	Electrocardiogram
EMT	Emergency Medical Technician
ENT	Snot Doctor
ET	Extraterrestrial
ETA	Are We There Yet?
FAQ	Annoying Stupid Questions
FBI	Federal Bureau of Investigation
FEMA	Disaster Relief People
FLOTUS	First Lady Of The United States
FUBAR	Fucked Up Beyond All Recognition
FYI	For Your Information
GED	Other High School Diploma
GI	Government Issue
GPS	Where Am I?
GVW	Grand Vehicle Weight
HEW	Health, Education And Welfare
IBS	Gotta Go To The Bathroom A Lot
ICBM	Big Bad Bomb
ICU	Intensive Care Unit (I see you too)
IED	Cowardly Terrorist Bomb
IOU	Pay Up Already
IPO	Initial Public Offering
IRA	Save Your Money
ISP	Computer Address
IUD	No Baby Device
KISS	Keep It Simple Stupid

KO	Knock Out
LED	Light-Emitting Diode
LEM	Lunar Exploration Module
LOL	Lots Of Love (no, it doesn't stand for Laugh Out Loud)
LOTGLW	Last Of The Great Letter Writers
LOTRHL	Last Of The Red Hot Lovers
LSD	Very Bad Drug
LSMFT	Lucky Strike Means Fine Tobacco; or Loose Strap Means Flabby Breasts (I'm being polite)
MC	Master of Ceremonies
MIA	Missing In Action
MO	Modus Operandi (method of operation)
MPG	Miles Per Gallon
MPH	How Fast Was I Going?
MRE	Nasty Army Food
MSG	Monosodium Glutamate
NCAA	College Sports
NASA	Blast Off
NATO	North Atlantic Treaty Organization
NIMBY	Not In My Back Yard
NRA	Nutty Gun Owners
OCD	Obsessive-Compulsive Disorder
OD	Way Too Much
OJT	Sink Or Swim
OK	Okay (that's a tough one)
OMG	Jesus Christ!
OO	Hug, Hug
OPEC	The Guys Who Control Our Gas Prices
OR	Operating Room
OTC	Legal Drugs
PAC	Group That Buys Politicians
PDQ	Pretty Darn (or damn) Quick
PC	Politically Correct/Personal Computer
PDA	Lots Of Kisses
PJs	Pajamas
PITA	Pain In The Ass
PMS	Stay The Hell Away
PO'd	Pissed Off
POS	Piece Of Crap
POTUS	President Of The United States

PS	Oh, I Forgot
PSI	Pounds Per Square Inch
PTA	Parent-Teacher Organization
PTSD	Post-traumatic Stress Disorder
PU	Pretty Ugly
R & B	Rhythm And Blues
R & R	Taking It Easy
RFP	Request For Proposal
REM	Rapid Eye Movement
RHIP	Rank Has Its Privileges
RIF	You're Fired
RIP	Rest In Peace (see *Napping*)
RNA	Ribonucleic Acid
ROTC	Generals In Training
ROY G BIV	All The Colors
RPM	Revolutions Per Minute
RSVP	Are You Coming or Not?
RTFM	Read The Fucking Manual
S & L	Savings And Loan
SALY	Same As Last Year
SASE	Stamped Self-Addressed Envelope
SBD	Silent But Deadly (you don't want to know)
SEC	Securities And Exchange Commission
SLR	Single Lens Reflex
SNAFU	Situation Normal, All Fucked Up
SOB	Son Of A Bitch (it's a dog thing)
SOL	Shit Outta Luck
SOP	Standard Operating Procedure
SOS	(Don't worry about what this stands for—just HELP!!)
SPF	How Sunburned You're Gonna Get
SPITA	Supreme Pain In The Ass
SPS	Small-Penis Syndrome (OK, I made that up)
SRO	Way Too Crowded
STD	Playing With Fire
SUTJ	Stinking Up The Joint (I made that up too)
SUV	Sport-Utility Vehicle
SWAK	Sealed With A Kiss
SWAT	Sealed With Lots Of Bullets
SWAWT	Sealed With A Wet Tongue
SYL	See You Later

TGIF	Weekend!
TKO	Kinda Knocked Out
TLC	Lots Of Love And Care (lots)
TMI	Spare Me The Gross Details
TMJ	Temporomandibular Joint Disorder (glad you asked?)
TNT	Really Big Boom
TPIC	Tight Pants In Crack
TTFN	Ta Ta, For Now
TWA	Tushie Wipers Association
UFO	Unidentified Flying Object
UN	Not So United Nations
USDA	Stamp Of Approval
VIP	Big Shot
VPL	Visible Panty Line (go commando)
WMD	Really Nasty Bombs
WTF	Huh?
WYSIWYG	What You See Is What You Get
WWW	World Wide Web
XX	Kiss, Kiss (no, this has nothing to do with dirty movies)
XYZ	Examine Your Zipper
YKW	You Know Who

There, now you know everything.

INITIATIVE

Don't wait for somebody else. Get off your ass and take the bull by the horns, as they say.

INJUSTICE

The world is full of injustice. But don't just stand around and watch. Do something about it. You'd be surprised at the impact one person can have. Real change usually starts with one. Be the one (see *Leaders*).

INNOCENT

Only babies are absolutely and completely innocent. Acting like a baby doesn't qualify. That just shows you're not getting your way.

INNOCENT UNTIL PROVEN GUILTY

Everybody is innocent until proven guilty. Everybody. Rushing to judgment caused many lynchings in this country, and remains a terrible blight on our justice system.

INNOVATION

If you always do what you always did, then you'll always get what you always got. There are lots of ways to improve yourself, the situation or anything else (see *Creative*).

IN/OUT OF THE CLOSET

What's going on in all these closets? In the closet; out of the closet. A closet is usually such a stuffy place, so why would anybody want to spend any time in there at all? We're all much better off staying out of each other's closets, that's for sure (see *Privacy*).

INSANITY

Yes, doing the same thing over and over again and expecting different results is the definition of insanity. (Thank you, Albert Einstein.)

INSECURE

Everyone is insecure from time to time; some more than others. Anyone who says they're not is probably even more insecure than you are.

IN SHAPE

We'll all last a lot longer if we keep our parts well oiled and in tune. Everyone need to get in shape and stay in shape (see *Exercise*).

INSIDE SOMEONE'S HEAD

You may think you know what they're thinking, but you have no way of knowing for sure. So it's very unfair to think anyone knows what's on (or in) someone's mind. There may actually be nothing going on at all. Mind readers don't exist either; they're only in your mind.

INSINCERITY

Do us all a favor and save your breath. Mean what you say, and say what you mean.

INSPIRATION

Be inspired by the ones you look up to. Inspire yourself and inspire others. Get that fire in your belly. Sometimes you may have to dig down real deep to find your own inspiration, but it's there, I promise. There's some saying about inspiration and perspiration, but I forget how it goes. However, I'm sure it's very inspirational.

INSPIRATIONAL SISTERS

When it comes time to pick a name for your daughter, consider naming her after any of the inspirational sisters. These girls will always be there for you and will never let you down: Faith, Hope and Joy. And don't forget their cousins Angel, Grace and Charity, who are pretty cool too.

INSTANT GRATIFICATION

Think about how long that gratification lasts and what it took to get it. Was it really so important to have right away? Some things are worth waiting and working for (see *Patience*).

IN STEP

You're not in lockstep with the rest or the world? So what? There's nothing wrong with walking to the beat of a different drummer. You go, girl (or guy).

INSTIGATE

If you start trouble, you better be prepared to finish it.

INSTINCT

I can't explain it, but sometimes you just know what to do. Animals are pretty good at this, and we've got plenty to learn from them—like licking ourselves in the oddest places.

INSURANCE

Here's my take on this: the more insurance you have, the less chance that you'll ever need it. It's the old inversely proportional rule.

INSURMOUNTABLE ODDS

If you know you're right—I mean really right—don't let anything or anybody stop you. The odds are really meaningless.

INTEGRITY

Having integrity is an integral part of one's personality. You won't go very far without it. If you don't have any, get used to being very lonely.

INTELLECTUAL

When they call someone an intellectual, it's usually a nice way of describing them as smart but different from the rest of us. However, what they often lack is real-world experience, which tends to mute ivory-tower thinking.

INTERACTION

Is it me or, with all of this voice-mail, e-mail and teleconferencing, have we forgotten about the old-fashioned face-to-face conversation? We get so caught up in being efficient and saving time that one wonders if interaction is dead. You know, you get to see facial expressions, body language and other stimuli that tickle the senses. Maybe it is me.

INTERNET DATING

Don't knock Internet dating. Take it from me: successful relationships can begin in the strangest ways. You never know.

INTERRUPTING

Interrupting people while they speak is very impolite. OK, so I'm a big offender. But it's so hard when you know you've got something more important to say than they do, and you want to show how smart you are. It's even harder when you actually know everything (see *Obnoxious*). Welcome to my world.

Internet Dating

IN THE BATHROOM

When someone says that they're in the bathroom, it means they're in the bathroom. They're busy doing something, either on or off the throne, and they don't want to be interrupted. No one wants to have a conversation while they're in there, so leave them alone. Only bother them if the house is on fire or you won the lottery. Nothing worse than "dutis interruptis" (that's the technical term). You probably don't want to know what they're doing in there anyway. That's why the door is closed (see *Privacy*).

IN THE HEAT OF BATTLE

Trying to have a calm, rational conversation with someone in the heat of battle is usually a mistake. For example, asking your mate to kindly use her indoor voice when she is in the throes of labor is not a good idea. It's always best to wait until the crisis passes and calmer heads prevail to discuss the issue (see *Self-Control*).

IN THE MOMENT

It is so easy to get distracted in our very busy and overstimulating world. Try as you might, it sometimes takes a lot to clear out your head and enjoy the moment you're in, as they can be so fleeting (see *Discipline*). This is especially important when interacting with your children, as those special times are rarely repeated. If you seem to be having a problem completely immersing yourself during those important moments, try harder.

INTIMIDATION

Ah, they're never as tough as they think they are. And just remember: neither are you.

IN TOUCH

Keeping in touch with family and friends isn't always so easy, especially if they live far away. Like most things, it's worth the effort. So don't be a stranger. Stay close.

INVENTED HOLIDAYS

Mother's Day, Father's Day—how did they become holidays? Don't they already have their day? We call it their birthday, right? It seems to be a very unfair parental conspiracy. Why do they get two special days to celebrate? Whenever I pointed this out, I was told that every day was children's day. Funny, I don't recall getting presents every day. Looks like Grandparents' Day and Bosses' Day never quite caught on; sorry Hallmark. Well, I'm going to initiate my own holidays:

> Dingleberry Day
> Kiss Your Frog Day
> Left-Handed Lesbian Day
> No Reason Day
> Rugby Player Day (they have balls)
> Short Guy Day (my favorite)
> Wake Up Late Day (maybe make that every day)
> Way Too Suntanned People Day
> What's Up Day

So let's celebrate. And lucky for you, I think today is Fodder's Day. So there.

INVENTIONS WE NEED

The world would be a better place if someone would come up with any of these:

> A condom for a computer to keep it from getting a virus
> A machine that converts fart gas to car fuel
> Animals that can read the "Stay off the Grass" signs (same with weeds—reading, that is)
> A switch to turn off your taste buds when you're on a diet
> Automatic baby-sitters (oh, never mind, they have that already—it's called television)
> Bottled adrenaline sold by the shot (never mind, we have that too; they call it coffee)
> Clocks that have a turning-back-time option
> Children born with instruction manuals
> Children born with money-back guarantees
> Children who don't talk back
> External human hard drives to give us better memories
> Eyeglasses that don't get foggy—ever
> Forwarding addresses for dead people
> Human memory delete button (then we really can have selective memories)
> Reflective clothes for deer to wear

Inventions We Need

Renewable limited marriage terms

Reusable paper plates

Rewind button to correct your mistakes

Root canals that feel like having orgasms (we'd sure have a lot of clean roots that way)

Scrumptious, sloppy, gooey deserts that you can stuff your face with while not gaining an ounce

Self-cleaning bathrooms

Self-cleaning cars

Self-cleaning children

Some productive use for leftover foreskins

Stop watches that actually stop time (good when you need to catch up or need a nap)

Teleporters (beam me up, Scotty)

Unobtrusive automatic nose-pickers

INVESTMENTS

By far the best investment we can ever make is in our children. If done wisely, the dividends are priceless and limitless. It's the gift that keeps on giving.

INVINCIBLE

No one is invincible—or even invisible for that matter. Just ask Superman about Kryptonite. Remember that the next time someone appears to be so intimidating. Only you can make them invincible.

IOTA

Why do they say "not one iota"? You never hear them talk about two or three iotas, do you? I don't have the slightest idea what an iota is. Is it a food ("Do you want fries with that iota")? Maybe it's a car ("For sale: two-door 2007 Iota, low mileage"). Nah, it's probably something you wear (you know, "Doesn't the emperor look gorgeous in his lovely royal iota?"). Who knows? Who cares?

IRONY

I used to think that irony had something to do with an ailment. It's kind of ironic that a lot of things I thought turned out to be wrong. (Well, maybe not ironic, but more like stupid.) Anyway, there's plenty of irony in our world, and it may be ironic that we don't know why (see *Fate*).

IRRATIONAL

Some people have the weirdest reactions and do the strangest things. I can't explain this, as it makes no sense to me. It's just not rational.

IRRESPONSIBLE

It's simply a matter of time until even those who care the most get tired of picking up after you (see *Growing Up*). You only want one person to be in charge of your life—you. So get with it. Are you paying attention here? I'm not doing this for my health, you know.

IRREVERENCE

Irreverence is not always considered antisocial behavior. Not being overly influenced by our society's conventional ways of acting and behaving isn't always a bad thing (see *Moderation*). Be yourself; within limits, of course.

IS

Sometimes you just have to accept things the way they are. It is what it is.

ISH

Ish is a great addition to most words and tends to be helpful when it comes to certain time commitments. "I'll be there six-ish." "She seems a bit feverish." "He's a bit piggish, don't you think?" Ish puts you in the ballpark, but not too boxed in. Which may keep you out of trouble.

IS IT

So, is it:

> All cocked up or all cooped up?
> Alzheimer's disease or Old timer's disease?
> Barb wire or barbed wire?
> Butt naked or buck naked?
> Cardinal rule or carnal rule?
> Close to the chest or close to the vest?
> Coming down the pike or coming down the pipe?
> Couldn't care less or could care less?

Crux of it or cruxt of it?
Cut and dried or cut and dry?
Eentsy weentsy spider or itsy bitsy spider?
Exclamation points or explanation points?
Feed corn or field corn?
First come, first served or first come, first serve?
Flesh out or flush out?
Full speed ahead or full steam ahead?
Go along to get along or vice-versa?
Gun ho or gung ho?
Guy wire or guide wire?
Hand in hand or hand and hand?
Hone in or home in?
Ice tea or iced tea?
In like Flint or in like Flynn?
Jury rigged or Jerry rigged? (Who's Jerry?)
Just assume or just as soon?
Moonlit night or moonless night?
No skin off my nose or no skin off my back? (Either way, ouch!)
Old fashion or old-fashioned?
One tow or one toke over the line, sweet Jesus?
On their airwaves or on their airways?
Powers that be or powers to be?
Road to hoe or row to hoe?
Short-sleeve or short-sleeved?
Slow down or slow up?
Supposed to or suppose to?
Supposedly or supposably?
Toss salad or tossed salad
Unbeknownst or unbeknown?
Vicious cycle or vicious circle?
Way of the future or wave of the future?
Whet your whistle or wet your whistle?
Work in process or work in progress?
Wreak havoc or wreck havoc? (What's havoc, anyway?)
Yellow Jack or yellow jacket?
Yikes or yipes?
You can't see the forest from the trees or for the trees?

I'm never quite sure, so don't ask me.

ISOLATION

Don't isolate yourself, because we all should be people people. And it's a proven fact that people people live much longer. Now some may find it attractive to live out in the middle of nowhere, with plenty of property to take care of and lots of grass to cut (oy!); we call them hermits. But privacy can be taken to an extreme, and comes at a price. For me, I'd much rather know my neighbors aren't too far away, especially if I need them.

ISRAEL

There is only one true democracy in the Middle East: Israel. We strongly support democracies. What's the question?

IS THAT ALL THERE IS

If you're disappointed at the end of your quest, it's best to revisit your expectations. Maybe it wasn't all that important after all.

ITCH

So why is it that these itches come at some of the most embarrassing times, and in the most embarrassing places? And the seven-year itch is one that you shouldn't scratch. Avoid that one at all costs.

IT COULD ALWAYS BE WORSE

No matter the hardship, no matter how bad it gets, it can always be worse (see *Perspective*). You want to remember that the next time you're lamenting your problems (see *Count Your Blessings*).

I TOLD YOU SO

Do you really get a lot of satisfaction saying "I told you so"? Me too. However, these are four words that you never really have to say. They already know it.

IT'S NOT THE PLACE

You could be at a palatial estate and be miserable, or be in a broken down old shack and have the time of your life. It's not the place; it's the people.

IT'S NOT WHAT YOU KNOW

They say it's not what you know; it's who you know. They're wrong. Who you know will help, but what you know is far more important.

IT'S THE THOUGHT THAT COUNTS

It really is the thought that counts, as some of us can be very clumsy in expressing our feelings. So look past that ugly tie, wilted flowers or shirt that doesn't fit. We have the best of intentions (see *Trying*).

IT TAKES TWO

One-sided relationships, friendships or any other kind of ships don't work. It takes two, as both sides have to be on the ship. If it's not there, it's not there; you can't force it. Just know when to move on (see *Knocking Your Head Against The Wall*).

It Takes Two

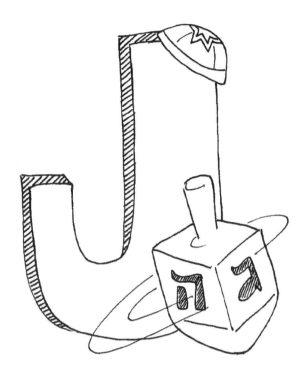

JADED

We all get jaded as we get older. It becomes a rite of passage (see *Elderly*).

JAYWALKING

Poor Jay. Why do we blame him for those idiots that dart into traffic? It should be called stupidwalking. And the punishment should be an order to wash and wax the cars that almost hit them. Of course, they would get an exemption for the ones that do hit them (see *Fairness*).

JAZZ

Jazz is one of the best American musical art forms. It embodies (I always wanted to use that word) great, lively, expressive and distinctive sounds. So jazzy.

JEALOUSY

Jea<u>lousy</u> can be one of the most worthless feelings we have, as it stems from insecurity and self-doubt. Sometimes it's hard to avoid, but trust me: don't waste your time. It makes you feel <u>lousy,</u> and nothing good comes from it. In the end, there's likely nothing to be jealous about.

JESUS CHRIST

You know how they'll (me'll) say "Jesus Christ, that hurt"? Or "Jesus Christ, are you stupid?" How come you never hear someone say "Allah, it's cold outside" or "Buddha, it's so noisy here"? Anyway, you probably shouldn't say that. You are taking someone's Lord's name in vain. If he is your Lord and you keep calling him for no reason, he'll probably stop answering you.

JEWISH HOLIDAYS

For those less enlightened, Jewish people follow the lunar calendar. That means that our holidays don't fall on the same days of the secular calendar each year. For instance, Chanukah has been made to correspond with Christmas, but can be as early as Thanksgiving, or as late as the end of December. Which is why you often hear people talk about the Jewish holidays being either early or late each year. No idea when are they on time.

JINX

I don't believe in jinxes, and neither should you (see *Superstitions*). So blame an unfortunate occurrence on something else.

JOB

You always want to be employed, as it's way easier to afford things that way. That assumes, of course, that the Brinks truck hasn't backed into your driveway. But make sure you work to live, not live to work (see *Balance*). After all, it's just a job.

JOURNEY

Sometimes it's not so much where you go, but how you get there. That's why it's usually about the journey, not the destination. Enjoy the ride.

JOY

How cool would it be to have a name like Joy? You couldn't help but be happy all of the time, right? It would give a whole new meaning to the term spreading joy (don't be fresh). Now if you were a boy named Joy, you'd probably have a tough time with that.

JUDGING A BOOK BY ITS COVER

Of course you can't judge a book by its cover. It's only packaging. That's why you're supposed to read the book, silly.

JUDGMENT

Our judicial system is built on the concept that all are innocent until proven guilty. That concept should guide us in our interpersonal relationships as well. A rush to judgment is very unfair and very unwise, so knock it off.

JUDGMENTAL

Sad to say, but we all get rather judgmental in our old age; sometimes at any age. We shouldn't be particularly proud of this. However, in my case, as this is my book, I have to be judgmental (see *Rationalizing*). Remember: you're no better than they are.

JUMPING TO CONCLUSIONS

Jumping to conclusions isn't fair to anyone—although jumping is good exercise (see *Digress*). Give them the benefit of the doubt, and listen, listen, listen. Stop talking and listen. Are you listening?

JURY DUTY

Stop with the excuses already and fulfill your civic responsibility. In most states jury duty is required and you have no choice anyway. (Yet another thing that makes our country great.) Life and death decisions are literally made by juries, so you want to take this obligation very, very seriously.

JUST BETWEEN YOU AND ME

If someone says "just between you and me," don't believe them; they'll probably tell the whole world (see *Secrets*).

JUSTICE

Justice and vengeance are not the same thing, and are easily confused by those seeking quick resolutions. It may not seem like it sometimes, but ultimately justice does prevail. Well, at least most of the time (see *They Always Get Theirs*).

JUSTIFY

There is only one person to whom you have to justify your actions. That's you, silly. After all, you're not going to believe your own lies anyway.

K

How can one letter have such diverse meanings as one thousand and a strikeout? Geez, there are 25 other letters to choose from. Can't they just use another one?

KEEP 'EM GUESSING

Your life doesn't always have to be an open book, you know. There is some allure to the unknown, so you don't need to let people know everything about you. Otherwise you'll become boring and predictable. The undiscovered mystery will keep them guessing and make you more attractive.

KEEPING UP

In this age of information overload, it's hard to keep up with the latest technology. It changes every minute (more like every second). But you can't afford to let the world pass you by. You just can't, or you'll be left in the dust like yesterday's news. And you don't want to be yesterday's news, do you?

KEEPING UP WITH THE JONESES

Now what makes the Joneses so important, and who cares what they have? I have what I need, thank you. I'm guessing that they also have headaches that I don't want either.

KEEPING YOUR HANDS TO YOURSELF

Do you really want to get your face slapped or, worse yet, punched in your mouth? Then by all means, keep your hands wandering in uninvited places. And knock off that smacking or punching when you're mad. If you're so inclined and can't control yourself, just sit on your hands. You'll tend to stay out of trouble that way.

KEEPING YOUR OWN COUNSEL

Sometimes you have to ask if consulting only with yourself is the best way to come to conclusions. Yes, ultimately the buck stops with you (see *Accountability*), but it doesn't hurt to get outside opinions from those you respect before the big decisions are made.

KEEP YOUR EYES OPEN

The best way to know what's going on is to keep your eyes open. Therefore, the only time your eyes should be closed is while you're sleeping, kissing or playing hide-and-seek.

KICKING 'EM WHEN THEY'RE DOWN

If you kick them when they're down, it doesn't really prove anything. Oh yeah, it does prove something: It proves that you're a jerk.

KICKING THE CAN DOWN THE ROAD

You can make the tough decision now, or you can put it off until later (see *Procrastination*). However, delay tends to compound the problem, which is not a good thing. You've been warned.

KICK IN THE ASS

Sure, we all need a kick in the ass once in a while. It's sometimes referred to as a wake-up call.

KICKSTANDS

When did it become uncool to have a kickstand attached to your bike? I must have been napping when that happened. Come to think of it, I must nap a lot, as I seem to be missing lots of things. But I digress. Yes, I understand that they add weight to the bike, but not 50 pounds, right? The purists claim it throws off your balance. That's really not an issue for me, as I'm rather unbalanced anyway. And since I'm not an Olympic athlete, I'll take the extra weight to keep my bike from being banged up by laying it on the ground or leaning it up against a tree. Or better yet, leaning it against a bike with a kickstand.

KIDNEY STONES

Kidney stones are very nasty, and if you've ever had them, you know what I mean. You certainly don't want to get them again, and there's only one sure-fire way to prevent them. Hydrate, hydrate, hydrate (see *Drink Lots Of Water*). Keep flushing.

KIDS

A kid is a baby goat. We call our offspring children. It's so demeaning to refer to them as goats. They are a very different kind of animal.

KILLING

If you watch too much TV, play violent video games and see way too many action movies, you could easily get caught up in the glorified (not to mention gory-fied) way killing is often portrayed. However, there's a good reason killing is usually frowned upon: that's because it's usually wrong (see *Ten Commandments*). Think about it. If you kill something (spider, mouse, person), it's rather final. You have ended its very existence. There are second chances and no turning back.

KINDNESS

Go ahead and kill them with kindness; gosh, what a way to go. And nobody OD's on kindness. According to the very latest scientific research available, very few people have actually died from kindness. This is the only time killing is allowed.

Kids

KINKY SEX

Anything between two (or more) consenting adults that doesn't involve pain, risk to life and limb (especially limb) and is not illegal is perfectly OK. As long as there is no harm done, knock yourself out (*see Freedom*). Whatever turns you on.

KISSING

Sorry Sam (Bogey's piano player, I think), a kiss is not just a kiss. It typically says a lot. As a public service and for future reference, I'm listing the five levels of kissing:

> Your obligatory cheek meeting, where you really just kiss the air, (hence, air kiss) and don't actually get kissed (probably doesn't count as a kiss, so maybe there are only four levels)
> The non-threatening peck on the cheek
> Kiss on the keppie (forehead), which is a sign of endearment
> Lip kissing, which is for honeys, family and close friends
> And finally, the passionate jamming of the tongue down someone's throat, spreading lots of germs (see *Lust*).

By the way, boys, nothing wrong with kissing your dad, brother, uncle, etc. But you want to make sure to keep your tongue in your mouth during those, as it can prove to be very embarrassing. Kissing ass is not recommended; unless that's your thing, in which case it should be kept in the privacy of your own home (see *Sex*).

KNEE-JERK REACTION

Take your time before you react, and use your head. The jerk in this term wasn't put there by accident.

KNOCK FIRST

When you encounter a door that's closed, it's best to knock and wait for a response before entering. That's one way to avoid unnecessary embarrassment (see *Masturbation*).

KNOCKING IT

Don't knock it till you try it? That goes for lots of things, like eating cauliflower (I don't like it), being in bed by ten-thirty (I like that) and camping out (I'm not sure). But you don't have to try skydiving, swallow golf balls or shoot yourself in the foot to know you won't like it. Use your head, you nut.

KNOCKING YOUR HEAD AGAINST THE WALL

I wouldn't recommend knocking your head against the wall, as it will accomplish nothing except to give you a headache. Talk about a classic example of an exercise in futility. As with most self-inflicted pain, it tends to feel much better when you stop. So stop already.

KNOT

It's _not_ hard to make a k_not_ (get it?), but it takes a very special skill to be a good knot-taker-outer. They call that stick-to-itiveness (see _Patience_).

KNOWLEDGE

Knowledge really is power (also priceless, by the way), and the more you have, the better off you are. You learn something new every day, whether you know (or like) it or not. No one knows more than they don't know, so there's plenty to learn. Learn, learn, learn—all day, every day. Thrive on an insatiable thirst for knowledge, and your brain cells will never atrophy; they will actually thank you. Feed your head, and expand your mind. Robbers and bad people can surely take things from you, but knowledge is something you'll always have, as no one can ever take it away. In most of life's contests, knowledge usually wins.

KNOWLEDGE vs. WISDOM

Having knowledge is very important. The ability to use that knowledge—now that's called wisdom.

KNOW-IT-ALLS

The only one who knows it all is God. So if you're not God, you don't know it all. Unfortunately, too many people think they're God. Go figure.

KNOW WHAT YOU KNOW

Know what you know (see *Confidence*), but more importantly, know what you don't know. Of course, you can't know everything, but you do know yourself, right? And don't be afraid of the unknown; either learn about it or rely on others for help.

KNOW WHY

So you didn't get the job. So the lady and/or guy never called you back. So they told you that they're not in love with you anymore. Sometimes you will never know why and have no way of ever finding out. It's frustrating and disappointing, but that's the way it is. So what? No point in letting it eat away at you. Just accept it. After all, only the know-it-alls know everything, you know.

KNOW YOURSELF

You may not like to admit this, but no one knows you better than you. If you are at all unsure, simply look in the mirror and get introduced (see *Being Honest With Yourself*).

KVETCH

Sometimes being a kvetch is a good thing. Look it up (see *Pain In The Ass*).

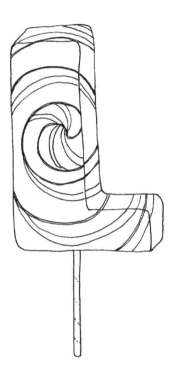

LABOR OF LOVE

A labor of love is one of the most rewarding jobs there is. I'll take twenty years of that kind of hard labor anytime.

LABOR UNIONS

Labor unions continue to be an important force in our country. Without them, who would look out for the welfare of our working men and women? However, their declining membership and loss of influence are actually products of their success. Unions have done so well over the years in securing better benefits and working conditions for their members that those extra costs are the first ones cash-strapped governments and businesses look to cut. A classic example of the price of success.

LADIES' NAMES

Now listen, boys, if you call or refer to a woman by any of these names, you'll either be ignored or get your face slapped:

Arm candy	Hose bag
Babe	Hot stuff
Bitch	Hun
Broad	Lady (unless she's royalty)
Chick	Ma'am (if she's under
Chickie babe	50? 60? 70? 80?)
Chubby	Madam
Doll	Sweater meat
Doll face	Thunder thighs
Dame	Toots
Gal	Tootsie

Now, if you really want to ingratiate yourself to her, use any of these:

Babe-alicious	Lover
Baby (but not "Hey Baby")	Sugar
Dear	Sweetie
Honey	Sweetheart
Honey Bunch	Your Loveliness
Honey-Snookums	

LAND OF OPPORTUNITY

Land of the free, home of the brave. (No, not the Atlanta Braves.) Is this country great or what? Most all of us really do have unlimited opportunities. All we have to do is get up off our respective asses (I'm very respective of asses, by the way). It's no wonder America is the best country in the world.

LANE CHANGING

So they want to come into your lane. Oh, go ahead and let them in, what's the big deal. It's not some sort of contest, is it (see *Road Rage*)? Maybe for some it is, but you'll still get there. Just be a courteous driver; those two seconds won't make a difference. And make sure you use your turn signal when *you* change lanes.

LANES

No, men never ask for directions, but at least we'll read a map as a last resort. However, try as we might, we'll never find these Lane's:

Jack La Lane
Lois Lane
Lover's Lane (well, maybe you'll find that one)
Memory Lane
Penny Lane

LANGUAGES

I don't know about you, but I marvel at people who can speak a second or even a third language. I find it amazing, as I have enough trouble with English. So the next time you're making fun of someone's broken English, see how good you are at speaking their language; then you'll really see how smart you are (and especially how smart they are).

LAP DANCING

If I were a woman, I think I would find public lap dancing to be a rather demoralizing, degrading and exploitive act. Then again, I'm not a woman. Now, in the privacy of your own home—knock yourself out (see *Kinky Sex*).

LAST LAUGH

Sure, they can laugh at you; just make sure you have the last laugh. Ha-ha.

LAST MILE

If you ever run a race, you'll agree with me. I swear that the last mile is way longer than the first mile (see *Conspiracy Theories*).

LAST MINUTE

Waiting for the last minute to get things done will rarely allow you to display your best work (see *Half-Assed*). Start early and you'll be done early. Duh!

LAST NAMES

How come they never gave these people last names? Maybe their parents couldn't afford them.

Aaron Rogers	Benjamin Harrison
Abe Lincoln	Bernie Mac
Adam	Bernie Williams
Admiral Matthew Perry	Bernadette Peters
Agatha Christie	Betsy Ross
Alexander Hamilton	Bette Davis
Alexander Scott	Beyonce
Allan Sherman	Big Ben
Alsace-Lorraine	Big John
Amazing Grace	Bill Bailey
Amy Irving	Bill Clinton
Andrew Jackson	Bill Curtis
Andy Taylor	Bill Murray
Andy Williams	Bill Russell
Ann B. Davis	Billy Dee Williams
Ann Margaret	Billy Joel
Anne Frank	Billy Martin
Anne Murray	Billy Preston
Anson Williams	Billy Ray Cyrus
Archimedes	Billy Reuben
Ariel Sharon	B. J. Thomas
Arlene Francis	Black Bart
Arm Candy	Blake Edwards
Artemus Gordon	Bloody Mary
Arthur Murray	Blue Jay
Aston Martin	Bluto
Aunt Bea	Bobby Darin
Auntie Em	Bob Dylan
Average Joe	Bob Evans
Axl Rose	Bono
Babe Ruth	Boy George
Baby Ruth	Branch Rickey
Barbara Ann	Brian Keith
Barbara Hale	Brian Williams
Barbie	Bronco Billy
Barney Frank	Brown Betty
Bazooka Joe	Bruce Lee
Bea Arthur	Bruce Wayne
Bear Bryant	Bruce Willis
Benedict Arnold	Buck Henry
Ben Franklin	Buck Owens

Buck Rogers
Bud Abbott
Buddy Guy
Buddy Holly
Buffalo Bill
Buffalo Bob
Bungalow Bill
Byron Allen
Caesar
Caesar Augustus
Calamity Jane
Captain Richard Phillips
Carl Albert
Carly Simon
Carrie Ann
Carroll O'Connor
Cary Grant
Cash Flo
Cat Stevens
Charlie Daniels
Charlie Parker
Charlie Rich
Charlie Rose
Chatty Cathy
Checkpoint Charlie
Cher
Chester A. Arthur
Chip Douglas
Christopher Lloyd
Chuck Connors
Chuck Robb
Cindy Williams
Clarence Thomas
Clarence Williams III
Clark Clifford
Clark Kent
Cleopatra
Clifford Irving
Cokie Roberts
Commissioner Gordon
Connie Francis

Connie Stevens
Corbett Monica
Cracker Jack
Craig T. Nelson
Crazy Eddie
Crepe Suzette
Cross-Eyed Mary
Curious George
Dale Evans
Danica Patrick
Daniel Craig
Dan Martin
Danny Kaye
Danny Thomas
Dan Patrick
Dave Barry
David Clayton Thomas
Dean Cain
Dean Martin
Dear John
Deborah Harry
Della Reese
Del Shannon
Delta Dawn
Denise Richards
Dennis James
Dennis (the Menace) Mitchell
Dennis Wilson
Dexter Gordon
Diahann Carroll
Diamond Jim
Dick Clark
Dick Gregory
Dick Martin
Dick Tracy
Dina Merrill
Dion
Dirty Harry
Diver Dan
Dizzy Dean
Doc Adams

Dollar Bill	Fabian
Don Adams	Famous Amos
Don Cornelius	Fannie Mae
Don Juan	Fast Eddie
Donna Douglas	Fay Vincent
Donna Reed	Fay Wray
Donovan	Fess Parker
Don't Know Jack	Flip Wilson
Doubting Thomas	Foster Brooks
Dred Scott	Frank Lee
Dr. John	Frank Howard
Dr. No	Frank Thomas
Dr. Oz	Fred Allen
Dr. Phil	Frederick Douglass
Dr. Ruth	Full Nelson
Duke of Earl	Galileo
Dumb Dora	Garth Brooks
Duran Duran	Garrett Morris
Dylan Thomas	Gary Lewis
Earl (the Pearl) Monroe	Geez Louise
Earl Warren	Gene Barry
Ed Harris	Gene Kelly
Eddie Albert	General William T. Sherman
Edie Adams	Gentleman Jim
Edward Bennett Williams	George Allen
El Al	George C. Scott
Eli Lilly	George Harrison
Elizabeth Taylor	George Michael
Elmore Leonard	George Marshall
Elton John	George Wallace
Emo Philips	George Will
Ernie Douglas	Geronimo
Esther Williams	Gilligan
Et Al	Gina Davis
Ethan Allen	Ginger Rodgers
Etta James	Glen Campbell
Eubie Blake	God
Euclid	Goliath
Evan Thomas	Good Night Irene
Eve	Good Old Mr. Wilson
Even Steven	Good Time Charlie

Grace Kelly
Grandma Moses
Great Scott
Greg Morris
Gulliver
Guy Williams
Hail Mary
Hal David
Half Nelson
Hamilton Jordan
Hamlet
Hannibal
Hank Aaron
Hank Williams
Hanna Barbera
Hanukkah Harry
Harold Lloyd
Harold Melvin
Harriet Nelson
Harry James
Harry Morgan
Helen Thomas
Help Me Rhonda
Hillary Clinton
Hill Billy
Holy Joe
Homer
Honest Abe
Hootin Annie
Horatio Nelson
Hot Rod
Howard Dean
Hubert Humphrey
Huey Lewis
Hugh Grant
Hugh Laurie
Inger Stevens
Jack Benny
Jack Daniels
Jack Edwards
Jack Nicklaus

Jack Ruby
Jack Russell
Jack Ryan
James A. Garfield
James Dean
James Earl Ray
James Joyce
James Madison
James Monroe
James Taylor
James T. Kirk
Jamie Leigh Curtis
Janet Leigh
Jane Pauley
Jane Russell
Jan Michael Vincent
Jasmine Guy
Jason Alexander
Jay Thomas
Jeb Stuart
Jefferson Davis
Jennifer Tilly
Jenny Craig
Jerry Lewis
Jesse Jackson
Jesse James
Jesse Owens
Jill St. John
Jim Dandy
Jimmy Carter
Jimmy Dean
Jimmy Mack
Jimmy Stewart
Jodie Foster
Joe Clark
Joe Frazier
Joe Louis
John Adams
John Alden
John Candy
John Dean

John Edwards	Laurence Olivier
John Glenn	Lazy Susan
John Henry	L'Bron James
John Lucas	Lee Marvin
John Mitchell	Lenny Bruce
John Roberts	Leon Harris
Johnny Carson	Leon Russell
John Quincy Adams	Leslie Ann Warren
John Paul Stevens	Les Paul
John Roberts	Lex Luthor
John Tyler	Liberace
John Wayne	Lil Abner
John Williams	Linda Carter
Jolly Roger	Linda Evans
Joni Mitchell	Lionel Ritchie
Joltin Joe	Little Eva
Jon Stewart	Little John
Judd Nelson	Little Orphan Annie
Judy Collins	Little Richard
Jules Verne	Lloyd Bentsen
Julia Roberts	Long John
Julius Irving	Loretta Lynn
Jumping Jack	Lorne Michaels
Jungle Jim	Lou Christie
Karen Allen	Lou Diamond Phillips
Karl Marx	Lt. Dan
Katy Perry	Luke Perry
Keith Richards	Lulu
Kelly Robinson	Lumber Jack
Ken	Mac Beth
Ken Curtis	Mackenzie Phillips
Ken Howard	Madonna
Kirk Douglas	Mama Cass Elliot
Kit Carson	Manta Ray
Kitty Russell	Marie Antoinette
Kobe Bryant	Marion Barry
Kurt Russell	Marion Ross
Lamar Alexander	Mark Anthony
Lanny Davis	Mark Down
Larry David	Mark Lindsay
Laura Nero	Marky Mark

Marlo Thomas	Mr. Livingston
Marshal Dillon	Mr. Roberts
Marsha Mason	Mr. Rogers
Martha Rae	Murray the K
Martha Stewart	Mustang Sally
Martin Lawrence	Nancy Drew
Mary Kay	Nancy Wilson
Mary Martin	Nasty Nelly
Mary Richards	Nathan Hale
Mason Reese	Nat King Cole
Mason Williams	Neil Patrick Harris
Mata Hari	Nelson Eddie
Matthew Perry	Nero
Matt Damon	Nervous Nellie
Matt Dillon	Nick Charles
Maureen Vincent	Nipsey Russell
Maya Rudolph	Noah Webster
Meg Ryan	Nolan Ryan
Meg Tilly	No, No, Nanette
Mel Allen	Nora Charles
Melanie	Nora Roberts
Mel _____	Norma Rae
Michael Douglas	No Siree Bob
Michael Jackson	Nosy Nelly
Michael Jordan	No Way Jose
Michael Richards	Old King Cole
Michelangelo	Oliver
Mike Douglas	Omar Bradley
Mike Todd	Opie Taylor
Miles Davis	Oprah
Miley Cyrus	Oral Roberts
Milt Jackson	Orange Julius
Minnie Pearl	Oscar Madison
Miss Kitty	Ossie Davis
Moby Dick	Overdue Bill
Moe Howard	Owen Wilson
Mona Lisa	Ozzie Nelson
Montel Williams	Paladin
Moses	Pal Joey
Moshe Dayan	Papa John
Mr. Ed	Papa John Phillips

Patch Adams
Pat Garrett
Patrick Henry
Pat St. John
Paula Abdul
Paula Deen
Paul Harvey
Paul Ryan
Paul Simon
Paul Williams
Pecos Bill
Peeping Tom
Pee Wee Herman
Pee Wee Reese
Peggy Lee
Penny Marshall
Peppermint Patty
Perfectly Frank
Perry Mason
Peter Max
Pete Rose
Phyllis George
Pinocchio
Plain Jane
Plato
Pollyanna
Polly Esther
Ponce De Leon
Poor Richard
Pop Art
Popeye
Port-a-John
Prima Donna
Prince
Private Benjamin
Quiche Lorraine
Rachael Ray
Raggedy Andy
Raggedy Ann
Ramsey Lewis
Randy Travis

Randolph Scott
Raul Julia
Ray Charles
Ray Lewis
Ready Freddy
Reggie Jackson
Rex Harrison
Richard Burton
Richard Harris
Richard Lewis
Richard Rodgers
Richard Wagner
Rick James
Rick Nelson
Robert Conrad
Robert E. Lee
Robert Perry
Robert Vaughan
Robin Roberts
Robin Williams
Rob Roy
Rod Stewart
Roger Williams
Ron Jeremy
Ron Howard
Ron Paul
Roseanne
Rose Marie
Rosie
Round Robin
Roy Rodgers
Ruby Dee
Rumpelstiltskin
Runaround Sue
RuPaul
Ruth's Chris
Ryan Phillips
Sally Jesse Raphael
Salt Peter
Samuel Adams
Sandra Dee

Sandy Duncan
Samantha Stevens
Sammy Davis
Samuel L. Jackson
Sara Gilbert
Sarah Lawrence
Sarah Vaughan
Sara Lee
Satan
Sean Taylor
Serena Williams
Shane
Shari Lewis
Sheldon Leonard
Sherwin Williams
Simple Simon
Sinclair Lewis
Skip Jack
Sloppy Joe
Smart Alec
Smokin Joe
Sneaky Pete
Socrates
Sophia Loren
Sorry Charlie
Spencer Davis
Spencer Tracy
Spike Lee
Steady Eddy
Steak Diane
Steely Dan
Stephen Douglas
Steve Allen
Steve Harvey
Steve Lawrence
Steve Martin
Steven Tyler
Stevie Ray Vaughan
Sting
Stonewall Jackson
Stubby Kaye

Sugar Ray Leonard
Susan B. Anthony
Susan St. James
Tara
Tarzan
Ted Williams
The Donald
Thingama Bob
Thomas Dewey
Thomas Jefferson
Thurgood Marshall
Tiger Lilly
Tim Allen
Tim Robbins
Tina Louise
Toby Keith
Toby Tyler
Tom Arnold
Tom Brady
Tom Foolery
Tom Hanks
Tommy James
Tommy John
Tom Paxton
Tony Bennett
Tony Stewart
Tracy Morgan
Treat Williams
T. S. Eliot
Two Ton Tessie
Typhoid Mary
Ulysses
Ulysses S. Grant
Uncle Ben
Uncle Sam
Unpaid Bill
Up Chuck
Upton Sinclair
Vanessa Williams
Venus Williams
Vera Miles

Vernon Davis
Vicki Lawrence
Vivien Leigh
Wayne Newton
Wayne Rogers
Wesley Clark
Wes Paul
Wet Willie
Whoa Nellie
Whoopsie Daisy
Willard Scott
William Bennett

William Conrad
William Holden
William Jennings Bryan
William Perry
Wilson Phillips
Woodrow Wilson
Woody Allen
Wolfman Jack
Yanni
Yoda
Zorro

LAST ONE

If you take or use the last one, be good to your fellow man (or woman) and restock. Don't wait for someone else to do it. That goes for toilet paper, toothpaste and cookies, to name a few. Oh, and if you're the last to leave, always remember to turn out the lights (see *Conservation*).

LAST TO KNOW

Ever get the feeling that you're the last one to know? Well, guess what? If it happens a lot, it's probably you and not a coincidence. Either you're not paying close enough attention or you're being ignored. Find out which one it is, and fix it.

LAST WILL AND TESTAMENT

Yes, it's not only the rich who need a will. Everyone does. It's very important for your loved ones to know all about your final wishes as they relate to the disposition of your cherished (and not so cherished) belongings. Spell it out for them so they don't have to guess. Either that or leave a forwarding number after you're gone so they can ask.

LATCHKEY CHILDREN

What's the matter with you? Are your children such an inconvenience, that you can't be around when they come home from school? What do you do? Just leave a bowl on the floor for them in case they're hungry? Time to readjust some things in your life; maybe a lot of things (see *Priorities*). Now if you're a single mother or single father—never mind. This does not apply to you.

LATE

Oh yeah, late is way better than never. Being punctual does have its pluses, but it's not always so simple. Just remember that no matter what it is, it's never, ever too late. Never.

LATE BLOOMERS

Well, some of us do take longer than others; however, we eventually get there (see *Patience*). Some things are worth waiting for, you know. Sorry, fellas, but this is mostly true with boys. There's always hope.

LAUGHINGSTOCK

Do you want to know what to invest in? For me, it's that laughingstock. I can't get enough. And the price is right too—very affordable.

LAUGHTER

Laughter is absolutely the best medicine, even when you're not sick. It's not just the comedians who get us to chuckle, you know. Do something especially goofy or embarrassing, and you'll get a laugh out of people—whether you want to or not. You might prefer them to laugh with you rather than at you, but sometimes you don't have a choice. Laugh a lot and you'll live longer. And we don't stop laughing because we get old; we get old because we stop laughing.

LAW

If you take the law into your own hands, you may wind up losing an appendage. Just leave it to the enforcers to carry out the law (see *Police*).

LAWYERS

Kill all of the lawyers? Nah, just some of them. As with most things, unfortunately, a few unscrupulous ones tend to give a profession a bad name (see *Bad Apples*). Most attorneys help protect our rights and keep our documents straight. Yes, of course we need lawyers. Just don't swim with the sharks; they bite, you know.

LAZY

Who isn't lazy from time to time? We all indulge ourselves when the spirit is having trouble moving us. Just don't make a career out of it (see *Moderation*).

LAZY MAN'S STUDYING

There is an ancient art to proper studying, which I have proudly perfected through years and years of practice. You simply get into a nice, comfortable reclining chair (a bed will also do), lay back, put your book on your chest, close your eyes and in a few hours you have completely digested all that is in the book. We call this osmosis.

LEAD, FOLLOW

Lead, follow or get out of the way. Pick one—quick. Decide already; we don't have all day.

LEADERS

Being a real leader is something to aspire to. After all, there's a reason people follow the leader. The reason is that leaders are decisive and tend to lead by example. Lead on.

LEAP OF FAITH

If the only thing that's left requires a leap of faith, go with it, as sometimes there's no other choice. You just need to close your eyes and believe (see *Hope*).

LEAP YEAR

Why do they call it leap year? Who's doing all that jumping around anyway? They should just call it what it is: extra-day year. No wonder people have so much trouble with the English language. And whose idea was it to add it to February? Hello—it's cold in the winter. Couldn't we use another day during the summer? They never listen to me.

LEARNING

Learning is a pathway to growth, knowledge and success. Every day we learn lots of things, whether we know it or not. If learning doesn't outpace change, you fall behind; and who wants to fall on their behind? Remember: the more you learn, the more you earn. That's just one side benefit. Learning makes you smart, and you want to be smart, right? Never stop learning.

LEARNING THE HARD WAY

When you learn something the hard way, you'll likely never forget it. That's why they call it the school of hard knocks. It's often not the best way to learn, but it sure is an effective way to keep things in your noggin.

LEAVE WHEN YOU'RE ON TOP

How many times have you seen formerly great athletes, now well past their prime, still in the game? Or worse yet, trying to make a comeback? It's hard to admit that your career is waning or even over, but it's better to move on when you're on top, rather than when you're embarrassingly at the bottom (see *Quit While You're Ahead*). It's best to retire from the business; don't let the business retire you. (That's exactly what Jim Brown did in his football career.) This way, you get to stop on your own terms, not someone else's (see *Dignity*).

LEAVING WELL ENOUGH ALONE

We perfectionists have lots of trouble leaving well enough alone. You shouldn't, as well enough is fine enough.

LEFT-HAND TURNS

Left-hand turn, left-hand side, left-handed compliments, left field, lefty—talk about discrimination. Why is it that we ignore left feet—except with bad dancers?

LEFT LANE

If you can't at least drive the speed limit, stay out of the left lane. Remember: slowpokes and Communists: stay to the right.

LEFT OUT

No, left out is not a baseball position in the outfield. It's that lonely feeling of not being included with the rest of the crowd. If you've ever felt left out, that alone should prompt you not to let anyone else ever feel that way.

LEGACY

There's always something to pass on (as opposed to pass out or pass over) to future generations. Sure, your legacy can be a building, street, endowment, etc. But whatever you do, you want to leave this world a better place than you found it. And your children often can be the best legacy you can leave. So put your stamp on whatever you do, and you'll never be forgotten.

LESSONS

Whatever happens to you (good or bad), there's always a lesson in it. Life is full of instructions; you just have to pay attention. The lesson may not be so obvious, but trust me, it's there (see *Mistakes*).

LET BYGONES BE BYGONES

I say let them be whatever they want to be: bi, straight or otherwise.

LET SOMEBODY ELSE DO IT

You know when you pass a car on the side of the road with a flat tire and figure that someone else will help them? Or you read about a fund drive for flood victims and assume someone else will donate. Or you see some trash on the ground and decide that someone else will pick it up? Here's a radical idea. Once in a while, try being that someone else. The best way to keep from being a nobody is to be that somebody. And do it for a very important reason: it's the right thing to do (see *Selfish*).

LETTER CLOSINGS

Now here is where you can differentiate the personal feelings in letters from the impersonal ones (see *Sincerity*). By reading between the lines, this is what these letter closings actually mean:

> All my love (all? really?)
> Best (too lazy to add wishes)
> Best regards (see *Regards*)
> Best wishes (wish you were here? probably not)
> Don't forget to write (a reminder)
> Fondly (you don't know if you're liked or not)
> Get lost (probably best not to write back any time soon)
> Good riddance (same)

Hugs and kisses (cute and semi-serious)

Keep smiling (cheer up)

Kind regards (kinda noncommittal)

Love (typically genuine)

Love and kisses (semi-romantic)

No letter closing (they can't stand you)

Regards (noncommittal)

Sealed with a kiss (corny)

Sealed with a wet tongue (accurate)

See you soon (kind of serious)

Sincerely (my favorite—genuine, yet tastefully simple)

Take care (usually sincere)

Take good care (even more sincere)

Talk to you soon (last letter you'll get—I'll call instead)

Thanks for the memories/mammaries (you'll never hear from them again)

Warmest regards (very noncommittal)

Warmly (a little less warm)

Yours truly (oh please, who are you kidding—it's never really meant, especially when you see it in a form letter that began with "Dear Sir/Madam")

When in doubt, you can always close your letters with LOTGLW (last of the great letter writers). On second thought, no you can't; because that's what I use.

LETTER SHORTAGE

Are we running out of letters? Is that why everyone insists on abbreviating the words in their messages? Does it really take that much more time to spell out "see you" instead of "cu"? OMG.

LETTING GO

Unfortunately, there are no hard and fast rules on this, but you've just got to know when to let your children fly away. You can't be with them forever, so it's really best for you—and for them—to let them go free (see *Parenting*).

LETTING YOURSELF GO

So now that you've got your life mate, it's OK to turn into a fat slob, right? Think again. Many get way too comfortable and let things go—really let things go. That's not only a bad reflection on you (see *False Advertising*), but it's also a bad reflection on them (see *Respect*). Fear the spread.

LIAR

Lying once doesn't make you a liar; it just makes you human (see *Perfection*). If you lie a bunch of times, then you're stuck with that label. And who wants that (see *Reputation*)?

LICORICE

Licorice is a great source of fat free junk food. Of course, too much of a good thing is bad for you (see *Moderation*). This may not be politically correct, but I never liked black licorice. Cherry is OK, but strawberry is better.

LIFE

If you think about it, life is really temporary, so it's best to add lots of meaning and significance to yours. Yes, it can be very complicated at times, but it sure beats the alternative—I think (see *Afterlife*). Actually, I think life is really practice for something later; kind of like a test or a dry run. Life is always ahead of you, not behind you; yet another reason to look to the future and not focus on the past. So don't look back, and live life to the fullest. Go on and enjoy it. What are you waiting for? Go already.

LIFEMATE

If you haven't found your lifemate yet, he or she is probably out there somewhere. It may seem like it can take an eternity to find them, but they are looking for you too. Just remember: there is someone for everyone. It just may be a while before you discover each other (see *Patience*). It's a big world, you know, but it's even possible that they're actually hiding right in front of you.

LIFE OR DEATH

Sometimes things may feel rather critical, but rarely are you in a true life or death situation. Think about it (see *Perspective*).

LIFE'S TOO SHORT

Life is way too short (see *Time*). Keep that in mind the next time you're driving yourself crazy over nonsense.

LIGHT AT THE END OF THE TUNNEL

If something has a beginning, it usually has an ending. So when you feel like you'll never get to the finish line, remember that there is typically a light at the end of the tunnel. It's not always readily apparent, but it's there. You just have to keep an eye out for it. And maybe take those sunglasses off.

LIGHTEN UP

Don't take everything or yourself too seriously; no one else likely does. The world isn't ending, so have some fun, for God's sake (and for your sake).

LIGHTS

Always turn off the lights when you leave the room. That goes for all unused electrical applications too (see *Waste Not*).

LIKE

"And, like, I like went to, like, the mall today, and, like, I bought some clothes, and like, like, like…." Do you know how torturous it is to listen to that? It's like, she's like, he's like. How many likes do you need? New rule: one like to a sentence. Make that every other sentence. That's what I'd like.

LIKE YOU

Yes, we all want to be liked and accepted, but not everyone is going to like you. Big deal! Are you in a popularity contest? Sometimes there's simply no accounting for taste, so why worry about it? It's entirely their loss. Just make sure you like you.

LIMBO

What if you end up in limbo (you know, that place between heaven and hell) when you die, and don't know how to do the Limbo Rock? Is that the determining factor in deciding whether you descend into hell? If so, I've got some practicing to do. A lot of practicing. How low can you go?

LIMITATIONS

Yes, Dirty Harry was right, as every man (or woman) should know their own limitations. Actually, you're in a better position to know them than anybody else. Now I never did understand the "do you feel lucky today?" question he asked (see *Sex)*.

LIMITS

The sky's the limit? Actually, in most situations there are no limits; that is, unless you set them.

LINES

The shortest distance between two points is a straight line. (I learned that in seventh grade.) Sometimes it's not any more complicated than that. Now as for the lines we have to stand in, they are truly endless, which makes waiting in them often insufferable.

LIP SERVICE

Giving lip service is really an insult, as you're not doing anyone any favors. Don't say things just to appease, placate or accommodate someone. Mean what you say, and say what you mean.

LIP SYNC

I have two words for you lip syncers: cop out. This is ridiculous. Why would anyone pay good money (as opposed to bad money) to see a performer simply mouth the words on stage? Would you like to see the symphony pretending to play their instruments while the music is actually played on tape? Or maybe someone will give a speech without really talking. I want my money back.

LIQUID COURAGE

If you need to get all wasted to stand up for yourself, you'd better just sit down.

LISP

So you want to make fun of someone with a lisp, stutter or any other speech impediment? That would make you the one with the bigger disability (see *Idiot)*.

LISTENING vs. HEARING

The best way to learn is to close your mouth and open your ears. That's the reason we have two ears and only one tongue. It's typically difficult to hear when you're blabbing away, as most of us can't do two things at once. Of course, there's a big difference between hearing and listening. Listening requires processing, while hearing can allow important information to go in one ear and out the other. By the way, hearing what you want to hear is also a problem (see *Selective Memory*). Please show people some common courtesy when they speak, and let them finish (see *Interrupting*); I've really got to work on that. And once in a while you might want to listen to yourself. You'd be amazed to hear some of the things you say.

LISTEN TO YOUR BODY

There you are, in the middle of your intensive workout, and your body starts screaming at you, telling you all about this nasty pain that keeps getting worse. Can't you hear it? Well stop already, especially if you see blood. What are you trying to prove anyway (see *Martyr*)? No one knows your body as well as you. Sometimes it's best to close your mouth and listen to what it your body says.

LISTS

Do you want to be organized and get things done on time? Then you definitely want to make a list. It's best to keep it kind of short, or you'll take one look and walk away (see *Overwhelming*). You can always add to it as you triumphantly cross things off (see *Accomplishment*).

LITERAL

Some of us take others way too literally. Oftentimes they don't actually mean everything they say. The key is to try to understand what they really mean.

LITTERING

What possesses anyone to simply toss their trash out the window? How irresponsible can you be? If you're a transgressor, shame on you. Nobody wants to clean up your mess, so don't be lazy, and learn to dispose of your trash properly. Anyway, if you see garbage lying around, go ahead, bend down and pick it up. Who cares if it's not yours (see *Good Deed*)? Just don't forget to wash your hands.

LITTLE BIT

Every little bit helps. When you add up a bunch of little bits, you end up with a whole lot of bits. And that's a good thing.

LITTLE GIRLS

Little girls are way cuter than little boys (sorry, guys). Must be the sugar and spice.

LITTLE PACKAGES

Yes, good things do come in little packages. Just ask the recipient of those little diamond earrings, or the lover of that less than greatly endowed guy. It's all about quality, not quantity.

LITTLE THINGS

It's typically not the bears in life that get to you; it's those damn bugs. But it's best to ignore the gnats, as those little things can morph into really big problems if you let them (see *Avalanche*).

LIVE AND LEARN

The longer you live, the more you learn. That's kinda what this whole life business is about, you know (see *Experience*).

LIVE FOR TODAY

You want to live your life to the fullest, but don't just live for today. Do yourself a favor and live for tomorrow too. Otherwise, you use up all of your todays and have nothing left (see *Saving*).

LIVE TO TELL ABOUT IT

Oh, you adventurous souls who like to live on the edge. If you go too far, you won't be able to share your wild stories with anyone. Maybe you should step away from that cliff just a little bit.

LIVING IN THE PAST

We often embellish the past, both in good and bad ways. However, it's the future that we can somewhat control, and should look forward to.

LIVING LONGER

Want to live longer? Then watch what you eat and get up off your ass (see *Exercise*). It's usually not much more complicated than that.

LIVING ROOM

Why do they call it the living room? Does anybody actually live there? It should be called "the wasted space that we pass all the time but aren't allowed to use because it's really for company" room.

LIVING THEIR LIVES

Help is one thing; completely running their lives is absolutely something else. Remember: They will end up completely relying on you, and you won't always be there. But more importantly, in the long run you're really not doing them any favors. You can really paralyze them by stymieing their growth and keeping them from developing (see *Wiping*). Do you want 35-year-old children living with you? Let them live their lives already.

LIVING WITHIN YOUR MEANS

If you consistently spend more than you have, you'll always be behind. Sounds simple, right? However, for most of us, this is a very difficult proposition. Following this deficit-spending path, we heap lots of additional pressure on ourselves to make ends meet. It's impossible to make a dollar pay for something that costs two, so it's best not to even try.

LOCKS

Locks are a great security measure to safeguard your assets. However, they won't do you much good if you don't use them. Guess what? More unlocked cars are broken into and stolen than the ones that are locked up. So keep your doors locked, drawers locked, bikes locked and lips locked (that's only if you have a willing partner). Now as for having your jaws locked—that hurts.

LOLLIPOPS

A lollipop serves two very important purposes. First, it's something sweet to suck on (oh grow up!). And second, it lets you look and act like a child (see *Fun*).

LONELINESS

Sure, we all get lonely and feel empty now and then. Sometimes you can be literally surrounded by people, yet feel terribly alone. If that's the case, look to the ones who are close to you to help find a way to get rid of that nasty feeling. A simple phone call can do wonders. And don't be afraid to ask for some attention, because staying lonely can be very unhealthy and cause lots of problems.

LONELY AT THE TOP

Yes, you don't typically have much company when you're the boss or have reached the pinnacle of your career. And that can be the price of success. However, the more you let it go to your head, the lonelier it can become (see *Power Corrupts*).

LONG SENTENCES

"The dooholly and the sneezinfrazin malfunctioned during their upward trajectory, causing the failure of the related component to perform its intended function, resulting in a reconsideration of the options available and concluding it best to engage the self-destruct mode." Try saying: "The damn thing just didn't work right"? Or instead of "at this particular point in time," how about just saying "now"? Long sentences waste lots of time; and most of us don't have lots of time, do we?

LOOK AHEAD

You can't do a whole lot about the past, but you probably can impact the future. There's a reason you don't have eyes in the back of your head, you know. Just keep your eyes looking forward (see *Tomorrow*).

LOOK BOTH WAYS

It's best to look both ways before (not after) you cross the street. In fact, you probably want to look both ways before you do lots of things.

LOOK 'EM IN THE EYE

Don't stare at the ground when you're speaking with someone. Make eye contact. It shows your strength and confidence. Now look at me when I'm talking to you, and stand up straight while you're at it. Excessive blinking will give away your fear, so be careful. And when you're chatting, don't be looking all around for someone else more important to talk to. They can see that too, you know (see *Rudeness*).

LOOKING BUSY

There's an art to looking busy, especially when you are very busy being lazy and doing nothing. If you're walking around, carry a tool, a book or your lunchbox; people will think you're either going somewhere or coming from someplace. Walking quickly is also a good way to fool them. If instead you're sitting still, furrow your brow or mumble to yourself; they'll think you're deep in thought and will likely leave you alone. It's all about appearances.

LOOKING FOR APPROVAL

We waste so much time in our lives looking to someone else to approve of the way we are, what we wear or what we're doing. You really don't have to go much further than your mirror when looking for approval.

LOOKING GOOD

You always want to look your best, as you never know who you'll run into. Most of us care about our looks, although some care way too much (see *Vain*). But the best way to look good is to feel good, and vice versa.

LOOKING OVER YOUR SHOULDER

If you spend a lot of time looking over your shoulder, your neck will hurt. Focus on what's ahead, not behind. You shouldn't be staring at people's behinds anyway.

LOSER

Not winning doesn't make you a loser. It just means that you didn't win. So what? Giving up on yourself—now that makes you a loser. Oh yeah, and a user is a loser (see *Drugs*).

LOSING FAITH

It doesn't really matter what you believe in; just never lose faith. Think about it: If you lose faith, what else do you have (see *Hope*)?

LOSING WEIGHT

I have a theory: There's a constant amount of aggregate weight in the world (sort of like a weight bank). If someone loses weight, someone else finds it. Like a giant balloon, if you clamp down on one part, the air goes into another area. Makes sense, right? My problem is it often seems to find me, and I'm not even looking for it. I guess it's finding plenty of others too.

LOSING WHAT YOU NEVER HAD

How often do we lament losing that great job opportunity, can't miss investment or chance to date Mr. or Ms. Perfect? Time to get over yourself and shake it off. You can't lose something you never had, silly.

LOST

Well Toto, I don't think we're in Kansas anymore. Being absolutely and completely lost is such a lousy feeling—and it's not just related to driving issues. (Don't I know!) Us guys have a real problem with this, but as a last resort, try asking for help (see *Directions*).

LOTTERY SUBSCRIPTIONS

For years I thought it was so much more convenient to buy an annual lottery subscription, rather than buy a ticket every week. It finally dawned on me that the reason I'm not showered with millions is because those bastards probably know I never check the winning numbers and expect them to notify me. They probably yuck it up in their office while splitting up my winnings. I'm guessing I've actually won five or six times by now (see *Conspiracy Theories*). It's my only explanation.

LOUD

I don't like loud, and I know I'm not alone; it's way too loud. So please tone it down if they (or I) ask you to (see *Manners*).

LOVE

Love is a spectacular four-letter word, and a very intense emotion. Deeply caring for someone and longing to be in their company is especially gratifying when reciprocated. Sometimes it can really hurt, but overall a loving experience is well worth it. Now when you say you love someone, just make sure you mean it—really mean it—because unfortunately love has become a rather trivialized and overused term. Some people throw this word around way too freely, as in "I love your sweater/haircut/house/perfume." Do you think they really love all those inanimate objects? Probably not. Save the word for important things like people, chocolate or naps. And love isn't something that can be forced or hurried. If it's not there, it's not there. It shouldn't be confused with infatuation, lust or adulation either. Those are way different, which is why you want to stay away from that love-at-first-sight business (which is absolutely not possible, although lust at first sight happens all of the time). And there are those who are simply in love with being in love, and just get attached to the next schlub or schlubette who happens by when they're in the mood. That's not love. Falling in love is a wonderful, indescribable feeling; that's the easy part. Staying in love—now that's what takes a lot of work. Just make sure you don't look for love in all the wrong places. Does love really conquer all? No, but it's sure hard to fight when there's a lot of love around. Remember: it is definitely better to have loved and lost than never to have loved at all. (Nice guy, that Shakespeare; see *Name-Droppers*).

LOVE CHILD

If you wanna play, you gotta pay (see *Parenting*). Having a love child rarely has anything to do with love (see *Lust*). Children have enough trouble growing up in this world. With unattached parents or, worse yet, parents who don't even know each other, baby will have at least one strike against them before they're even born. So what does that do to their odds of making it in life? It doesn't enhance them, that's for sure. Luckily, scientists have discovered the cause of love children, and have even invented a way to prevent them (see *Condoms*).

LOVE 'EM AND LEAVE 'EM

One night stands? Can you be any more shallow and insincere? Going through those of the opposite sex like going through toilet paper is a strong reflection of your true self. Not a very nice image (see *Reputation*).

LOVE IS

Love is never having to say you're sorry? Hardly. What a ridiculous concept. Of course you've got to say you're sorry; usually pretty often. What do you think you' do if you step on your loved one's foot by accident? Tell them you don't have to apologize because you're in love? How stupid is that? And by the way, love is also saying thank you—lots and lots of times (see *Taking It For Granted*).

285

LOVE IS BLIND

Yes, sometimes love is blind and causes us to do some really stupid things. (Maybe more than sometimes). It also can make us rationalize and overlook the obvious; yet another reason to keep your eyes open. However, lust is way blinder (see *Cheating*).

LOWLIFES

You can't get much lower than lowlifes, so you want to stay away from them, as some of their behaviors might rub off. And make sure those people are always lower than you.

LOYALTY

If you're not going to be loyal to your friends, family and country, do me a favor: Lock yourself in your room, turn off the lights and quit the human race. You see, to be in the people club, you have to be loyal. So never give up on your friends, because real friends don't ever give up on you. The only reason not to stay fiercely loyal is if they don't deserve it and intentionally hurt you (see *Forgive and Forget*).

LUCK

Is it begtter to be lucky than good? Probably not. Luck is where opportunity meets preparation. You actually make your own luck. You really do.

LUCK OF THE DRAW

So why is it that we were born in this country, and don't have to live in mud huts with no running water or electricity? Why don't we (most of us, anyway) have to beg for food and clothes? It's the luck of the draw. Think about that the next time you feel you've got something to complain about.

LULL

Don't let people you don't know lull you into a false sense of security. It can't hurt to keep your eyes open, as lulling isn't always such a good thing.

LUNATICS

Yes, I'm convinced we're all nuts—every one of us. It's just a matter of degree (see *Normal*).

LUST

Lust is one thing, but true love is really tested when the lights go on.

LYING

Sometimes telling a lie is unavoidable, but you shouldn't make a habit of it (especially since you don't want your nose to grow). Like most things, there are grades of lies. Big ones are really bad. Little ones tend to add up and can total more than the big ones. Often one lie leads to another, which just compounds, and before you know it, you're in big trouble (see *Avalanche*). So it's best not to even start, as they do tend to catch up with you. You see, lying is often the easy part; recanting can be very, very hard. And you don't want to be one of those who lies like a rug either (see *Silly Phrases*).

LYME DISEASE

Lyme disease is one of the most misdiagnosed maladies to face our society. It tends to have very bizarre and seemingly disconnected symptoms and is often mistaken for lots of other ailments. If you have something wrong with you and they can't diagnose the problem, make sure you get tested for Lyme. And stay away from simple two-week treatments, as it usually takes much longer to kill this disease. Untreated, an individual can experience very debilitating and life-threatening consequences. Trust me, it's very bad stuff.

MACHO

Acting macho went out with the last century (see *Evolution*).

MADE IN AMERICA

I know this revelation comes as a terrible blow to the global economy, but given the choice, I'll buy our country's goods first. Call me a homey.

MAGIC

Do you believe in magic? You should. Magic isn't just practiced by magicians, you know. Here, watch me put a smile on your face. Poof! That's magic.

MAGIC WORDS

To refresh your memory, "please" and "thank you" do wonders. "You're welcome" will also get you far. Using these words will magically open plenty of doors for you. It will also put smiles on people's faces (and you sure want to put smiles on their faces). That's what makes it magic.

MAIDEN NAMES

There should be a rule that after a divorce everyone goes back to their maiden names. That goes for boys too.

MAINTENANCE PEOPLE

Those people who pick up after you aren't invisible, you know. Offices don't get cleaned by themselves. Everybody likes to feel appreciated, so would it kill you to smile and say hi to them once in a while (see *Manners*)? And that name tag on their shirt is not just decoration, as it typically means something too.

MAKE TIME

We can always find time to do the things that are important to us. You control your life, so there's really no such thing as not having enough time (see *Priorities*).

MAKEUP

Makeup can only seem to make you look better. But it really just covers up and doesn't change what's important—and that's what's underneath (far underneath). No amount of makeup can cover up a rotten personality; their horrible nature will bubble up through it. Remember: what's skin deep is only packaging (see *Beauty*).

MAKING A FOOL OF YOURSELF

Sometimes they do try to make a fool out of you, and it may not be so easy to prevent. But you can certainly keep from making a fool of yourself (see *Alcohol*).

MAKING ENDS MEET

Want to make ends meet? Then don't spend money you don't have (see *Living Within Your Means*).

MAKING EXCUSES

Who likes being the kind of person who has very little credibility? It's rather hard to believe that "your dog ate your homework," "your alarm clock didn't go off" and "your car broke down"—all at the same time. The real fault may not be too hard to find (see *Responsibility*).

MAKING FUN

Sure, most of us can stand a little teasing here and there, with little being the operative word. It's always better to make fun of those who are already making fun of themselves, as they typically laugh with you. There are some rules though. You don't want to make fun of anyone's:

Complexion
Cup size (that goes for boys
   and girls)
Facial features (e.g., enhanced
   proboscis area)
Hair (or lack thereof)

Height (or lack thereof)
House (cars are OK)
Limp
Paycheck
Weight

MAKING IT UP TO THEM

Face it. You can't undo what you did. But if you're wrong, you can at least try to make it up to them.

MAKING LOVE

Making love is what sex is supposed to be all about. That's why it was invented.

MAKING MONEY

Wouldn't it be nice if we could just print money when we need a few bucks? Sorry, no can do. However, some people are completely obsessed with making money. But once they've amassed their fortune, they might have to spend the rest of their lives making up for all of the time they lost getting there (see *Priorities*).

MAKING OUT

I don't know why they call it making out. What are they making? It's really just a lot of kissing (tonguing) and hugging, with some wandering hands thrown in, right?

MAKING THEIR DAY

It is so much fun to make someone's day, and usually doesn't take a whole lot of effort. Give them flowers, call them up, send them a card, stop by and visit, take them to dinner—get the picture?

MAKING UP

Making up is usually much better than breaking up, and it's the fun part of having an argument. Oh, and it's not always so hard to do.

MAKING UP FOR LOST TIME

Because it's not possible to change the past, you really can't make up for lost time. You can mend your ways and impact the future, but time can't be rerun or replaced. That's usually a good thing.

MAKING YOUR BED

They say that if you make your bed, you've got to sleep in it. No, you don't. Some of us can sleep anywhere, even in an unmade bed. Anyway, we don't really make our beds, since they're already built. So that's a big misnomer (or misternomer), as it should really be called "smoothing out the covers on your bed, and making it look neater."

MANATEE

Enough said (see *Hippopotamus*).

MANIPULATION

You can use the phone, you can use the bathroom and you can even use a tissue (see *Nose Picking*). But don't ever use someone else. Not only doesn't it say much for them, but it says even less about you.

MANNERS

It's not very hard to have good manners. Here are some bad ones to avoid:

Burping at the table
Burping under the table

Coughing without covering your mouth
Having your fingers visible anywhere near your nostrils
Interrupting (that's a tough one for a lot of us)
Not saying thank you
Putting your elbows on the table (that one is hard for me to avoid; see *Lazy*)
Speaking with food in your mouth
Talking on your cell phone while at the urinal
Talking on your cell phone while on the toilet
Texting or talking on your cell phone at the dinner table

MARRIAGE

Getting married is easy. Staying married—to the same person, that is—now that's the hard part. It's supposed to be a lifelong commitment. Think about it: "till death do you part" could be a very long time. Unfortunately, our society makes it far too easy to walk away (or run away) from that sacred vow. Just imagine, living with the same person year after year. People today get tired of everything, so how can it last? Like everything else that's worth it, marriage takes work—lots of hard work every day. And lots and lots of love and understanding. A good marriage epitomizes the very definition of compromise. The number one reason marriages fall apart is lack of good communication (see *Listening*). Here's my idea: There should be a law preventing anyone from marrying before they're 30 (and having children before then, for that matter). And there should be mandated three-year renewable marriage terms. That would probably keep everybody on their toes (see *Letting Yourself Go*). And you know that "for better or for worse" part? When you're old and shriveled up, who do you think will still want to be around you? Your spouse, that's who. So if you can find someone willing to put up with you for the rest of your life, you might want to take a very hard look. Maybe they're really great or maybe they're just nuts. Sometimes it's hard to tell—although ultimately it may not matter.

MARRIED COUPLES

Research tells us that the average married couple has sex two to three times a week. As far as I'm concerned, the average married couple seems to lie a lot (see *Average*).

MARTYR

They bury martyrs because they are dead. Is that really something you aspire to be? I didn't think so. Therefore, it's probably best to knock off the dramatics. If you're not dead and still act like a martyr, you've got a problem. Likely more than one.

MASTICATION

Always chew your food slowly. The longer it takes you to eat, the less you end up eating. Your brain gets satisfied more slowly than you can shovel the food into your mouth, so take your time. Once your brain gets bored, you stop eating—eventually. Yes, you can get bored eating. It wouldn't hurt to try smaller portions also.

MASTURBATION

Everyone masturbates. If someone tells you that they don't, they're either lying, oversexed or very confused, as the biggest deniers tend to be the biggest practitioners. Because they (you should pardon the expression) come with a lifetime warranty and are built to take a beating (so to speak), your goodies won't break or wear out. Just give them a rest once in a while (see *Moderation*). Self-gratification isn't always so bad. We indulge ourselves in good food, fast food, nice clothes and expensive entertainment. How is masturbation any different? Please don't try to explain it to me. It's OK. Just keep your door closed, thank you.

MATCHING

Yes, you probably want to make sure the carpet matches the drapes (see *False Advertising*). It's also best to have your belt match your shoes.

MAYBE

Sorry, maybe is not an answer (see *Decisive*). It's either yes or no.

MEALS

Five or six small meals sure beat the hell out of two or three big ones each day. It's so much easier to digest, get full and lose weight that way.

MEAL TICKET

If your sweetie just becomes your meal ticket, you'll likely end up with indigestion. Eventually you both will.

MEANT TO BE

Not to say that most things in life are preordained, but some are just meant to be. And no matter how hard you try, some things are simply not meant to be. Either way, you just have to accept it (see *Fate*).

MEDIA

Our media, especially the nonprint kind, have gotten rather carried away with themselves. It used to be that they just reported the news, and we were left to draw our own conclusions. But we have turned our newscasters into TV personalities and larger-than-life people. They no longer just give us facts; now we also get to hear their opinions. After they have crossed that line, one wonders how they can ever be objective in their reporting. Why do I care what they think? Don't they pretty much just read the news? Please just let me know what's going on and I'll form my own opinions, thank you. Call me naïve, but I prefer to read the paper. At least those opinions are mostly on the editorial page. (OK, so I'm naïve.)

MEETINGS

Holding one-hour meetings is the rule. If you can't get your business completed within that period of time, either your agenda is too long or people are flapping their gums too much—usually the latter. Yes, it's important to reach consensus on issues, but you typically find more individuals expressing the same opinions, rather than simply voting on the issue and moving on. Time is a terrible thing to waste.

MELODRAMATIC

Don't bother being melodramatic to get attention. Leave this to the professionals (see *Acting*). They can do it a whole lot better than you.

MELTING POT

We are a nation of immigrants and most of us can trace our roots back to other countries. No other nation can make that same claim. OK, maybe the Pitcairn Islands can (that's a country—I looked it up). I think that's one reason for our almost 250-year success in nation building. The diverse backgrounds, cultures and traditions brought here during our history make us stronger and continue to add to our positive accomplishments (see *Synergy*).

MEMORIES

Here's something no one can ever take from you: memories. Now that can be both good and bad. The bad ones are hard to erase, as you can't un-see something you saw and those visuals can end up haunting you for a very long time. However, the good memories can be relived in your mind anytime; it's like video on demand (without the cost). Sure, you can misplace or lose valuable photographs and mementos, but the cherished memories will always be there. Enjoy them.

MEMORY

I, of course, have my own explanation for memory problems. Like computers, our noggins have only a finite amount of memory available. Once it's full and other information comes in, something has to drop out. We call that forgetfulness. I think it works in LIFO order (Last In, First Out), so we usually can't remember what we had for breakfast, but that time we got yelled at for staying out too late is a vivid memory. (I actually think that memories from our earliest years stay in there forever.) Maybe we should all be equipped with external hard drives to give us more disk space, as information overload will probably kill us. I'll recommend that to the engineer working on the next model (see *God*).

MENDING FENCES

If you really want to mend some fences, you don't have to be very handy, and you don't even have to have any tools. All you need is some motivation and a little compassion, mixed in with some humility. No sweat. Mend away.

MENDING YOUR WAYS

It's never, ever too late to change and mend your ways. It may not be very easy, but you're not dead yet; so give it a try. (You might want to write that down.)

MENOPAUSE

Menopause is another one of those cruel twists of fate inflicted on the human race. You see, it's the stage of life where women go through complete changes in their hormonal makeup (among other things). Their emotional and physical lives are literally turned upside down. However, there is a very plausible explanation for the derivation of this term. You see, it is in <u>men</u>'s self-interest to give plenty of <u>pause</u> when dealing with menopausal women, as even the slightest wrong glance at an affected lady can actually lead to a life-threatening situation and have the most dire consequences. Although menopause is clearly a women's issue, I believe whoever coined this term really understood the resulting punishment for men (see *Conspiracy Theories*). And there is such a thing as male menopause (see *Midlife Crisis*).

MENSTRUATION

According to legend, menstruation was God's way to punish Eve for giving Adam the apple (Adam's apple). Actually, it's payback for that stupid Adam and all future Adams, who are subjected to the resulting mood swings. That's what the men part is for.

MENT

You can take these mints to the bank (get it—they make money at the mint… stay with me here):

Accomplishment	Enjoyment	Peppermint
Accoutrement	Enlightenment	Refreshment
Astonishment	Enrollment	Refurbishment
Commitment	Establishment	Sacrament
Compliment	Implement	Sentiment
Contentment	Improvement	Spearmint
Document	Liniment	Supplement
Encouragement	Management	Temperament
Endearment	Merriment	Testament
Engagement	Parchment	

These mints aren't so good for you (see *Bad Breath*):

Abandonment	Harassment	Temperament
Argument	Mismanagement	Unemployment
Detachment	Mistreatment	Vehement
Entanglement	Predicament	
Entrapment	Punishment	

MENTAL BLOCKS

Everybody has mental blocks; you know, when you're stuck and just can't get it out (see *Constipation*). The trick is to find a way around them. Sometimes it's best to walk away from it for a while (figuratively or physically) and come back later.

MESSES

Most of us love to make messes, but we sure don't like to clean them up—way too much work. The best way to avoid that is not to make the mess in the first place. Duh! (This just in: the sky is blue.)

ME TIME

There is nothing selfish about taking some time for you (see *Recharging Your Batteries*). We all need to indulge ourselves here and there, and do things just for us and no one else. It's even better to actually schedule some fun and rewarding time each day. However, as with most things, there are limits (see *Moderation*). It's not a good idea for everything to always be about you.

ME TOO

Those of us who crave undue attention suffer from the "me too" syndrome. You know, the ones who keep jumping up in the back of the room, not wanting to be forgotten. Making grand entrances is also a sign of this. And if your name is Mr. or Ms. Meetoo, that's also a dead giveaway. Remember: you'll get your turn too (see *Patience*).

MICROMANAGING

Why, oh why do some of us insist on tending to every single detail of our home or work world? Just because you believe you know the right way to do things (see *Your Way*) doesn't mean that others don't. Time is such a precious commodity, so leverage yours. Allow others to do their jobs; stay out of their way. You will not only empower and encourage them, but you will take self-imposed and unnecessary pressure off yourself. Don't be stupid.

MIDDLE-CHILD SYNDROME

Yes, there is such a thing as middle-child syndrome (see *Sibling Rivalry*). It all has to do with being passed over, ignored and forgotten. It's typically not intentional or the parents' fault. It's just a fact of life. I'm an expert.

MIDDLE CLASS

I sometimes think a lot of middle-class people have more class and better values than the upper crust (see *Stereotypes*). However, first class in a plane sure beats the hell out of coach. Or so they say, as I wouldn't know (see *Travelitis*).

MIDDLE NAMES

Why do they use the full names of the bad guys but usually not the good guys?

Bad Guys:

> Attila The Hun
> Baby Face Nelson
> Big Bad Wolf
> Bruno Richard Hauptmann
> Ivan the Terrible
> Jack the Ripper
> James Earl Ray
> John Wilkes Booth
> Lee Harvey Oswald
> Mark David Chapman
> Sirhan Bishara Sirhan
> Son of Sam

Good Guys:

> Albert Einstein
> Abraham Lincoln
> Captain Kangaroo
> Dudley Do-Right
> Hanukkah Harry
> Indiana Jones
> Lone Ranger
> Moses (I guess the really good guys can't afford
>   a last name)
> Santa Claus
> Underdog
> Uncle Sam

MIDLIFE CRISIS

I used to think a midlife crisis was just an excuse for people to have affairs or buy expensive cars. It may be for some, but for most it's very real and not much fun. For me, I wrote a book. Indulging yourself with a fancy new car may not seem cheaper than an extramarital relationship, but it is. Way cheaper.

MIDWIFE

Yes, childbirth is a very natural process. But with today's technology, why in the world would someone take any risks with a baby? If you want to keep your midwife around, fine—but take her with you to the hospital.

MIGHT MAKES RIGHT

Might doesn't make right. Right makes right (and left makes left). Might has nothing to do with it.

MILITARY

It's unfortunate that during the Sixties it was fashionable to hate the military, what with the Vietnam War and such. Times have changed, and so have they (see *Gulf War I*). Now we're all big fans, which is the way it should be (see *Count Your Blessings*). For our military I have two words: thank you.

MIND

It's one thing to have a big head, but there really are no limits to expanding your mind. You can keep your hat size the same and still fill your mind with all kinds of cool stuff. And talk about the benefits of having an active mind. It's the best way to stay young, for one. So keep your noggin cooking.

MINDING YOUR OWN BUSINESS

Here's what I think. Unless someone tells you to mind your own business, don't. Everybody needs well-intended advice, or a view from a different perspective. Too many things are left unsaid in life.

MIND OVER MATTER

If you don't mind, it doesn't matter, right? Well maybe, but you never want to underestimate its ability. Your mind can be the most powerful implement in your proverbial tool belt. Use it or lose it.

MINTS

If someone offers you a mint, always graciously accept it. Take a hint and take the mint, as you don't want to be stupid—or smelly.

300

MIRACLE METS

I love the underdog. Midway through the 1969 season, the Mets were going nowhere. Then they started their meteoric rise to success. Up until then, the Mets had been the worst team in baseball. They were pathetic. They were laughable. But they believed in themselves, worked as a team, beat all of the odds and became World Series Champions. It's a great story—very inspiring. You gotta believe.

MIRACLES

Yes, miracles really do happen every day. And you don't have to look much further than the hospital delivery room (we call that the miracle of birth). Try to keep your eye out for miracles, as you'll know them when you see them (see *Children*).

MIRRORS

Mirrors aren't only used to see if you're pretty (you are) or if you have a booger sticking out of your nose (you don't). When you look in the mirror, the truth stares back at you. There is no escaping it—sorry. If being really truthful with yourself is a problem, you might want to think about keeping your mirrors covered.

MISERY

You're damn right—misery loves company. Some people thrive on sharing their unhappiness with everybody else (we don't care for them). Just don't go out of your way to cause misery (unless of course, they're bastards), as it will usually come back to bite you. Ouch!

MISPLACED ANGER

Always direct your anger to the source of your problem. It's very unfair to punish the rest of the world just because you're pissed off at something or someone else. There's a clear fairness issue here. Let them pay, not us.

MISPRONOUNCED WORDS

It's so cute to hear the little ones getting their words all mixed up. For instance:

Incorrect	Correct
Ambilance	Ambulance
Aminal	Animal
Babin suit	Bathing suit
Balentimes Day	Valentine's Day
Bedgtable	Vegetable
Belcro	Velcro
Brang/brung	Brought
Bunked into	Bumped into
Diarear (how appropriate)	Diarrhea
Drownding	Drowning
Excape	Escape
Expecially	Especially
Explanation points	Exclamation points
Grosheries	Groceries
Incept	Except (my personal favorite)
Jamamas	Pajamas
Lyberry	Library
Love-a-bye	Lullaby (I think they should just change this word, as love-a-bye sounds so much better)
Make-a-believe	Make believe
Memember	Remember
Mongster	Monster
Opposed to	Supposed to
Pacific	Specific
Pisgetti	Spaghetti
Picshure	Picture
Poison ivory	Poison ivy
Prolly	Probably
Remory	Memory
Sammich	Sandwich
Susplain	Explain
Thamiliar	Familiar
Widdle waddle	Widdle waddle

MISSED OPPORTUNITIES

So you think you missed the boat? Don't worry, you'll get it the next time. There's always a next time. It's not a missed opportunity; it's just that the timing wasn't right. Trust your judgment, make your decisions and move on (see *Coulda, Woulda, Shoulda*). You'll have lots of opportunities tomorrow.

MISSING

It's such an empty feeling when you miss somebody. But just think: they probably miss you too. And if they're in your thoughts, it's almost like they're here, right? Nice try, huh? Well, phones work, you know, as do visits, e-mail and snail mail. So take your pick.

MISTAKES

Everybody makes a mistake now and then (see *Accountability*). Admit it, get over it and move on. Otherwise what would we do with all of those erasers? Sure, we often end up paying for our mistakes, but the trick is not to keep making the same ones and learn from the ones we made. And whatever you do, don't ever take advantage of someone else's mistake.

MISTER

How old do you have to be to be called Mister? My rule is that you must be older than me. When people call me Mister, I think they're talking to my father, not me. There's a certain comfort level being on a first-name basis with others, even with people you don't know. Now calling someone Miss doesn't seem to have the same connotation (especially if you're talking to a guy). It just sounds polite.

MISUNDERSTANDINGS

Why isn't this misterunderstanding or missesunderstanding? Actually, I think the politically correct term is msunderstanding. Anyway, huge battles have been fought over misunderstandings, which is very unfortunate. Misunderstandings are usually unintentional, no matter which side you're on, so go ahead and get it fixed (see *Communication*).

MIXED SIGNALS

Make sure that your yes means yes, and your no means no. If you're sending mixed signals, you'll get yourself into trouble. You can't have it both ways, you know.

MODELS

No one really looks like a model (see *Normal*), and I don't know who would want to emulate them. Their job is just to sell clothes, makeup and stuff. Therefore you only want to try to look like them if your job is to sell clothes, makeup and stuff.

MODERATION

Too much is too much. Not enough is not enough (see *Balance*). That's why we need moderation. I'm way too much, by the way.

MODESTY

It's usually a good idea to keep your privates private. Sure, there are those who like to flaunt themselves (see *Cleavage*), but most of us could do the world a favor by covering up. Modesty is often the best policy.

MOMENTUM

Boy, once you finally get going, you don't want anything to slow you down, do you? There sure is nothing like being on a roll. You just have to avoid those obstacles in your way (see *Bumps In The Road*). Keep going.

MONDAYS

Don't we love Mondays: the beginning of the week, a way to make a fresh start? You get up in the morning, all bright-eyed and bushy-tailed (who has a bushy tail?) and ready to go. Really? Mondays are usually a drag, and Tuesdays aren't much better, if you ask me. Are you asking me? Fridays—now we're talking. Let's change every day to Friday.

MONEY

Ca-ching! Is money the root of all evil? No, evil is the root of all evil; money is just a means to an end. It does make the world go around, although nobody ever seems to have enough. There are even those who can't afford to pay attention. But I digress (yet again). Certainly some people go crazy over money. Just don't spend money you don't have and you won't go wrong. Now rarely do you ever hear anyone complain that they have too much money (or too much sex either), right?

MONEY TALKS

It's only money, but yes, money does talk. And unfortunately, it sometimes has a lot to say. Mine, of course, doesn't say a damn thing. I want my money back.

MORALS

Just like tools, you always want to keep a good set of morals handy. It's your ethics and morals that help define you. If you want to sleep well at night, keep the moral meter set to high (see *Conscience*).

MORAL VICTORY

A victory is a victory, moral or otherwise.

MORE THAN YOU CAN TAKE

They say that God gives the hardest battles to his strongest soldiers. I think that's true. The man (or woman) upstairs typically knows your limits, even if you don't, and doesn't pile on more than you can take. Yet another reason why you shouldn't give up. It may not seem like it sometimes, but you can handle it.

MORNING

The morning is the best part of the day. It's brand new and gives you a fresh start every single day. Look at it this way: If you wake up, it's already starting out great. See?

MORTALITY

Don't forget, everyone is mortal. This is bad news for some, and good news for others.

MOST

If you can't have the most of what you want, it's best to make the most of what you have. That works for me.

MOTHER NATURE

Ever hear of Father Nature? No, just Mother Nature (see *Sexist*). As an unwed mother, what does that say for her offspring? Does that make all of those flowers and trees bastards? Who knows? Maybe it has something to do with that immaculate deception thing.

MOVIES

Just remember: movies aren't real either (see *TV*).

MOVING

You want to always keep moving, so those joints can stay properly lubed (see *Couch Potato*).

MOVING AWAY

Sometimes it can't be helped, but if the reason for moving away is solely to make more money, carefully consider the needs, feelings and effects it will have on others, like your family and friends (see *Selfish*). Ultimately, it may not be worth it.

MOWING THE LAWN

How stupid are we? (Speak for yourself.) We spend lots of money to keep our lawns nice and green, so our grass can grow and grow. Why? So we can work all afternoon in the hot sun mowing it. We've really outsmarted ourselves here. Now don't pay someone else to cut it; do it yourself (see *Exercise*). And you never want to cut your lawn the same way each time. Alternate between these methods: back and forth, up and down, and concentric circles. Also mulch the cuttings (don't bag), as it's much better for the environment. And while we're at it, why does grass (and hair) tend to grow where you don't want it? Weeds too, although I don't know where you would want weeds to grow. Another one of life's unsolved mysteries.

MULTITASKER

It takes a special talent to be able to juggle more than one thing at a time. Most of us can't. Only the best can multitask efficiently and effectively. Yet another thing to strive for. Oh well.

MUMBLE-ITIS

Mumble-itis is a disease you don't want to catch. Speak clearly, and get those marbles out of your mouth. How good can they taste, anyway? Enunciate, for goodness' sake. Your friends will thank you.

MUSIC

The creative genius that it takes to make or play music is something that amazes me. I just don't know how they do it. Someone figures out the order and speed of the notes to play and conjures up all of the instruments necessary to make the sounds. Creating music and arranging it takes an unbelievable amount of imagination. It brings you to special places by touching your heart, mind and soul. If you really want to be moved, listen to the music with your eyes closed, especially classical music. You too will marvel at its awesome beauty. Music soothes the savage beast (whatever that is), you know. So what if you fall asleep—that's the soothing part.

MUST WIN

In most "must win" situations, you "will lose." When you put that much pressure on yourself by making it a life or death issue, the odds are against you. That goes for getting that special job, wooing that potential lover or winning that impossible game. It's typically when you have something else to fall back on—and a take-it-or-leave-it attitude relieves some pressure—that you end up winning. Lighten up, already; the world's not ending.

MYTHS

By definition, myths are not true (which is why they are myths, silly). So you can dispel or debunk (how would one bunk in the first place?) most of these:

> All good things must come to an end (oh, they can go on forever).
> Big feet, big hands, big… (don't count on it).
> Epileptics (or anyone) swallow their tongues (a tongue can block one's air passage, but you can't swallow it).

Mumble-itis

Excessive masturbation will make your goodies fall off (your goodies
    stay with you; you just get tired).

Expect the unexpected (then it wouldn't be unexpected, would it).

Get your head out of your ass (it's probably rather difficult getting it
    there in the first place, so getting it out shouldn't be a problem).

If you sit on a toilet seat, you can get pregnant (you're confused; see *Sex*).

Just killing time (not possible; now, wasting time—there's plenty of
    that around).

Men lose their strength after getting a haircut (ask Samson).

Overnight success (that would be more like overnight luck; success
    usually takes a lot of hard work).

Phone rang off the hook (this can only happen when it's on vibrate).

Telling someone to go fuck themselves (most of us don't have enough
    parts to do that).

Time stood still (somebody's clock is always ticking).

Women lie about their age (everyone lies about their age).

You can't fight city hall (oh sure you can).

You can't put Humpty Dumpty back together again (I've seen it done in
    cartoons plenty of times).

You can't put the genie back in the bottle (so what—the genie is much
    more valuable outside the bottle anyway; three wishes, you know).

You can't put the toothpaste back into the tube (maybe, but why would
    you want to, what with all the mess and all).

You can't take it with you (dead people usually have nothing in their
    pockets, so to speak; but they can't come after you to get it either).

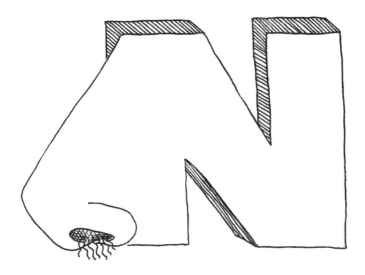

NAGGING

Nobody likes a nag. Some people really do like to nag, though. If you do things the first (or even second) time you're asked, you can avoid their incessant nagging. And who really needs to listen to that?

NAME BRANDS

Go ahead and buy generic. It's usually the same stuff, only with different packaging (see *Saving*).

NAME-DROPPERS

You shouldn't be impressed by name-droppers (see *Substance*); I'm not. Simply knowing or meeting allegedly important people doesn't make them important. It just makes them think they're important.

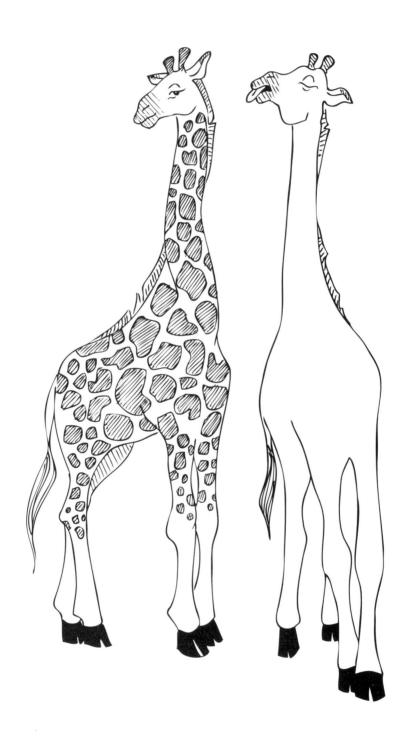

Name Brands

NAMES

I really admire those who can remember the names of people they've just met. It's so hard for me (see *Impossible*). I've tried everything. I'll repeat their names when we're introduced. I'll look at them and look for something to help me remember. No luck. How does anybody do it? Of course, there are some names which have—what's a polite way of saying—lost their luster. Why anyone would saddle children with these antiquated names these days is beyond me. They tend to stay with them for a while (thank God for nicknames):

Abbott
Abby
Abel
Abner
Ace
Addison
Adele
Adlai
Adolph
Adrian
Agatha
Aggie
Agnes
Albert
Alden
Alexander
Alf
Alfred (two names)
Alice
Alistair
Alma
Aloysius
Alva
Alvin (or his Chipmunks)
Alvira
Amelia
Amos
Anderson (that's a last name)
Angie
Angus
Annabelle

Annette
Ansel
Anson
April (why not October?)
Ara
Archibald (with or without
    hair)
Archie (same thing)
Arlen
Arlene
Arlo
Arnold
Arsenio
Artemis
Arthur
Arva
Ashton
Astrid
Audie
Augie
Avery
Bailey
Barnett
Barney
Barack
Bart
Bartholomew
Barton
Bat
Beatrice
Beaver

Bela
Belle (ding-ding)
Benedict
Bennett
Benson
Bernadette
Bernadine
Bernard
Bernice
Bert
Bertha (or Big Bertha)
Beryl
Bess
Bessie
Betsy
Biff
Bing
Blaine
Blake
Blanche
Blondie
Booker
Boris
Bradley
Brandon
Brandy (or Booze)
Brant
Brendan
Brent
Brooks (or Streams)
Brunella
Bruno
Bryant
Bryce
Bubbles
Buck
Bucky
Bud
Buddy
Buford
Burl

Burton
Buster
Butch
Buzz
Byron
Cain
Caleb
Calhoun
Callista
Calvin
Cameron
Camille
Campbell
Candy
Carlton
Carmela
Carson
Carter
Cary
Casper
Cassidy
Cecil
Cecilia
Ceil (why name your child
   after an animal?)
Chad
Champ (dog's name)
Charlotte
Chase
Chatsworth (for what it's worth)
Chauncey
Chester
Chet
Cheyenne
Chip
Christian (name him Buddhist)
Cissy
Claire
Clara
Clarabelle
Clarence

Clarissa
Clark
Claude
Claudia
Clay (or Playdough)
Clayton
Clem
Clementine
Cleo
Cletus
Clifford
Clifton (that's a place)
Clint
Clinton
Clive
Cloris (or Clorox)
Clyde
Coco
Cokie
Cole
Colin (or any other body part)
Colleen (Collie for short?)
Conan
Condoleezza
Conrad
Cora
Corbett
Corey
Cornelius (if he had children,
    he'd be Popcorn)
Cosmo
Cousin It
Cubby
Cullen
Curt
Curtis
Cyrus
D'Artagnan
Dabney
Dagwood (or Dogwood)
Daisy (too fresh)

Dakota (North or South)
Dalbert
Dallas
Damian
Damon
Dandy
Daphne
Darby
Darian
Darius
Darla
Darlene
Darrell
Darren
Darth
Darwin
Daryl
Deacon
Dean (that's a last name)
Deke
Del
Delbert
Delores
Delta
Demi
Derrick
Desi
Desmond
Dewey (or Don't We)
Dexter
Dick (no need to explain this)
Dilbert
Dirk
Dixie
Dobie
Dolf
Dolly
Doobie (Joint?)
Dora
Dorian
Doris

Dorothy
Dot
Dottie
Drake
Duane
Dudley (nickname Dud?)
Duke
Duncan
Dustin
Dusty
Dwight
Dylan
Earl
Ebenezer (or any other Ezer)
Edgar
Edith
Edna
Edwin
Effie
Elaine
Eli
Elias
Elijah
Elke
Ellie
Elliott
Ellis
Ellsworth
Elmer
Elmo
Eloise
Elroy
Elsa
Elsie
Elvira
Elvis
Elwood
Elyse
Emile
Emmitt
Emory (Board?)

Endora
Engelbert
Enid
Enoch
Enola
Enos
Erma
Ernest
Ernestine
Ernie
Erroll
Ertha
Esmeralda
Essie
Ethel
Etta
Eubie
Eunice
Evelyn (nickname Evil?)
Everett
Ezra
Fanny (or Tushie)
Farrah
Felix
Ferdinand
Ferguson
Ferris
Fess
Fester
Fifi
Flip
Flo (To's cousin)
Flora
Florence
Fontella
Foster
Franklin
Frasier
Fred
Frieda
Fritz

Gabby
Gabe
Galen
Garfield
Garrett
Garrick
Garth
Gavin
Gaylord (Gay for short)
Georgia (who wants to be
    named after a state?)
Gerard
Gertrude
Gia (it's a pet's name)
Gideon
Gil
Gilbert
Gilda
Gilligan
Ginger
Gino
Gladys (or not so Gladys)
Gloria
Godfrey (nickname God,
    for short?)
Goldie
Gomer
Gomez
Goober
Graham (that's a cracker)
Grant
Greer
Greta
Gretchen
Gulliver
Gus
Guy
Gwedolyn
Gwen
Hale
Halle

Hamilton
Hamlet
Hank
Hannibal
Harold
Harriet
Harris
Harrison
Harvey
Hazel
Heath (bar)
Heather
Hector (Heck for short)
Hedda
Hedy
Heidi
Helen
Helga
Heloise (oh Hell)
Hennie
Henrietta
Henry
Herbert (want some sherbet
    with that?)
Hermione
Hilda
Hilde
Hiram
Hoah
Holden
Hollis
Homer
Honey
Honus
Horace
Horatio (don't use math terms)
Hortense (or Pretense)
Horton
Howard
Hoyt
Hubert

Huck
Huckleberry
Huey
Hugh
Hugo
Humphrey
Hunter (go get 'em)
Hyman (see *Sex*)
Ian
Ichabod (nickname is Icky?)
Ida
Igor
Ilsa
Imogene
Ingrid
Irene
Irma
Irving
Irwin
Isadora
Isadore
Ishcabibble
Jackson
Jada
Jade
Jake
Janice
Janis
Jasper
Jeb
Jed
Jeeves
Jehosaphat
Jerome
Jessie
Jethro
Jezabel
Joan
Joni
Josiah
Joyce

Judd
Julius
June (or July)
Keanu
Kermit
Khyler
Kimba
Kirk
Knute
Kurt
Lamar
Lana
Lance
Laurel
Laverne
Lawrence (or Laurence)
Leland
Leona
Leonard
Leroy
Les (More or Less)
Lester
Levi
Lex
Lilith
Lillian
Lincoln
Linus
Lionel
Liv
Livingston
Liza
Lloyd (do they really need
    two Ls?)
Logan
Lois
Lola
Lon
Lonnie
Lorna
Lorne

Lorraine
Luann
Lucas
Lucifer
Lucille
Lucinda
Lucretia
Ludwig
Luella
Luke
Lulu
Lulubelle
Luther
Lydia
Lyle
Lyman
Lyndon
Mabel
Mac
Mack
Madeline (she's always Mad)
Madge
Madison
Mae
Maggie
Malcolm
Margaret
Margie
Maria
Marie
Marilyn
Marlon
Marsha (or Marcia)
Marshall
Martha
Marvin
Mason
Matilda
Maude
Mauna
Maureen

Maurie
Mavis
Max
Maximillian (thanks a million)
Maxine
Maxwell
Maynard
Melvin
Meredith
Merle
Merlin
Merv
Midge
Mildred (or Dread)
Miles
Millard
Millicent
Millie
Milton
Mimi
Minnie (or Maxi)
Miranda
Mitzi (or Ditzi)
Mona
Monroe
Montel
Montgomery
Morris
Morticia (or Lessticia)
Mortimer
Murgatroyd
Muriel
Murray
Myrna
Myron
Myrtle (or Turtle)
Nanette (no, no)
Nell
Nelly (or Nellie)
Nelson
Nero

Newt
Newton
Nigel
Niles
Nils
Noah
Nolan
Nora
Norma
Norman
Norton
Norv
Norville
Octavia
Odie
Ogden
Oglethorpe
Oleg
Olga
Olive
Oliver
Olivia
Omar
Ophelia (or I don't feel ya)
Opie
Orel
Orson
Orville
Oscar
Ossie
Oswald
Otis
Otto
Owen
Ozzie
Paige (or Book)
Paris
Parker
Paxton
Pearl
Penelope

Percy
Pernell
Perry
Peyton
Phineas
Phoebe
Pia
Pinky
Pippi
Poindexter
Polly
Preston
Priscilla
Prudence
Quimby
Quincy
Quinn
Quint (or Quaint)
Quintin
Raleigh
Ralph
Rand
Randolph
Reese
Regina
Regis
Reid
Reuben (that's a sandwich)
Rex (or Wrecks)
Rhea (as in dia)
Rhett
Rhoda
Rhonda
Riley
Rita (she's so lovely)
Robinson
Rocco
Rocky
Rod
Rodney
Roland

Rollo
Roone
Roscoe
Rosie
Roxie
Roy
Rudolph
Rudy
Rue
Rufus
Rumpelstiltskin
Rupert
Rusty
Sada
Sadie
Sally
Sanford
Scooter
Sebastian
Selma
Seymour (or Seeless)
Shelby
Sheldon
Sherlock
Sherman
Sherwin
Shirley (don't call me Surely)
Siegfried
Sigourney
Simon (unless he has
    something to say)
Sinclair
Sissy (Wimpy)
Skeeter (or Miskeeter)
Skip
Skippy
Slim
Smedley
Snidely
Snoop
Sophie

Spencer
Stanley (Stan is OK)
Stella
Stillwell
Strom
Stymie (what a rascal)
Sybil
Sylvan
Sylvester
Sylvia
Tab
Tabitha
Taffy
Tag (he's it)
Talia
Tallulah
Tanner
Tanya
Tara (that's a place, right?)
Taylor
Thaddeus
Thelma
Theodora
Theodore
Tilly
Tip
Tippi
Tish
Tito
Tobias
Trent
Trevor
Tripp (whoops)
Tristan (or Tristen)
Trixie
Troy
Tucker
Tuesday
Twig (or Branch)
Ty
Tyler

Tyne	Wiley
Upton	Wilford
Uriah	Wilhelm
Ursula	Wilhelmina
Van	Wilkes
Vanna	Willard
Vaughn	Willis
Velma	Wilma
Vera	Wilson
Vernon	Winifred
Veronica	Winston
Victor	Winthrop
Viola	Wolf
Violet	Woodrow
Virgil	Woody (just call him Penis)
Virginia (enough with the states, already)	Wyatt
	Wydell
Vivian	Wynonna (why not?)
Wagner	Yale
Walden	Yogi
Waldo (where is he anyway?)	Yoko
Wallace	Yul
Wally	Zachariah
Walter	Zachary
Wanda (like magic wanda)	Zane
Ward	Zasu
Warren	Zeb
Webster	Zebulon
Wendell	Zeke
Wendy	Zelda
Wesley	Zoe
Wilbur	Zola

NAME TAGS

Requiring everyone to wear name tags would solve most people's problem (including mine) with remembering names. They should be permanently affixed to an unobtrusive yet visible part of the body—the forehead, for instance. Now if this goes anywhere, don't forget it was my suggestion, as you heard it here first; so I get all the credit. Great, you've probably already forgotten my name, haven't you?

Name Tags

NAPPING

Whoever invented naps had the right idea (see *Recharging Your Batteries*). Naps are nice, but napping more than once a day is a problem. Napping here and there definitely has its benefits. Although taking a nap while driving, operating heavy machinery or having sex is definitely frowned upon.

NARCISSISM

I don't know what this is either, but it sounds so cool. Hmm, maybe not so much.

NASAL

Don't talk through your nose; it's horrible to listen to. Use your diaphragm when you speak (not that diaphragm, you nut).

NATIONAL DEBT

What a lovely legacy we leave to our children. Don't they have enough problems without us saddling them with our spending excesses? What lessons are we trying to impart to them anyway (see *Living Within Your Means*)?

NATURAL GAS

Here's my idea to save both our energy and global warming problems: find a way to harness the vast power of the world's unlimited supply of tushie gas. Think of the possibilities. No more paying those huge energy conglomerates just to drive our cars or heat our homes. Imagine a world where we value our farts and put all of that gas we emit to good use. Our country is chock full of cutting-edge technology scientists—and natural gas. Someone should be able to find a way to bottle it and sell it, right (see *Capitalism*)?

NAUGAHYDE

So how many little naugas do you suppose they have to kill to make a Naugahyde jacket?

NAVAL ACADEMY

Imagine a school devoted entirely to the study of the belly button. Well who'd of thought?

Naval Academy

NAYSAYERS

Naysayers have nothing to say, so don't bother listening to them.

NAZIS

What would possess anyone to jump at the opportunity to join what began as a political club founded by a psychopath, whose sole purpose was complete destruction? Then to morph into a bloodthirsty nation bent on the annihilation of its enemies—this is entirely beyond my comprehension. It was only fitting that such an unfathomable, venom-filled, hate-mongering society was destroyed by the good guys. A classic example of good triumphing over evil; but the ultimate cost was staggering and impossible to calculate. If I were alive then, I would have hated them—and that would be OK.

NEATNESS

Yes, neatness usually counts. Sometimes you even get extra credit.

NEATNICKS

Neatnicks are nudniks (see *Moderation*).

NECESSARY EVIL

Evil is never necessary. Never, ever. Ever. Did you get that? Are you taking this down?

NECESSITY

Necessity is the mother of invention. Whoever thought this up really knew what they were talking about. But who's the father?

NECKTIES

Why do we wear neckties (see *Peer Pressure*)? They're uncomfortable as hell, impossible to clean and always get in the way. Must be some primal fascination with nooses around our necks or something. Maybe this is where the term hanging around comes from. And have you ever seen those guys who toss their ties over their shoulder while they're eating? How weird is that look? (By the way, go with the Windsor knot; the other one make you look rather wimpy.)

NEGATIVE CAMPAIGNS

If you read some of the campaign mail you get or watch political commercials, you are led to believe that most opponents are child molesters, murderers and rapists (see *Politicians*). Do they really think we believe that nonsense? It's an insult to our intelligence and causes us to support the other candidate. Stupid and demeaning, and an insane waste of money.

NEGATIVITY

Allowing negativity into your life will turn you into a nasty and miserable person. Who would want to be around you, with all of your complaining and rotten attitudes? Negativity is like a disease, and other people would be afraid they might catch it from you. Be positive. I'm absolutely positive about that.

NEGLECT

Never neglect:

> Those you care about.
> Those who care about you.
> Yourself.
> Your zipper.

NEIGHBORS

Don't forget: you buy a neighborhood, not just a house. You really have a vested interest in maintaining and improving your surroundings, so be a part of your community and get to know your neighbors. Good ones always take care of each other, because you end up having a lot in common. Your neighbors often become lifelong friends. They say that fences make good neighbors, but I don't know what that means.

NERVOUS

Oh, don't get so excited. We all get nervous; every last one of us. Just take a deep breath and try to relax.

NEVER

Never is a very long time. Never say never, as it may someday come back to bite you in the tush. Ouch!

NEVER STOP

Never stop:

Believing
Caring
Creating
Cuddling
Dieting
Dreaming
Eating
Giggling
Hoping
Hugging
Laughing

Learning
Living
Loving
Playing
Questioning
Reading
Singing
Smiling
Snuggling
Striving
Succeeding

Sweating
Teaching
Thinking
Thriving
Trying
Walking
Wanting
What you start
Wishing

NEW LEASE ON LIFE

You know how anxious you are when anticipating and fearing bad news, especially when it's health related? And you know the relief you feel when, for whatever reason, that bad news doesn't come, and you have that euphoric feeling? It seems like a huge boulder has been removed from your shoulders and an albatross is off your neck. Often at that moment, you promise to be good forever, now knowing that your future is secure. How about harnessing those special feelings and really making some positive changes in your life? Just a suggestion.

NEWS

No news is good news? Not for me. I want plenty of news. Gimme, gimme, gimme. I want to know what's going on in the world and with my friends and family. It's the non-newsers who wonder why the world keeps passing them by.

NEWSPAPERS

Don't expect to be up on things by just watching TV, surfing the Internet or listening to the radio. You've got to read the newspaper. It's the only way you can really keep up with what's going on out there. The best part is that you can digest the news at your own pace, instead of just trying to catch snippets. Too bad newspapers will soon be extinct, only available as an online reading vehicle.

NEW YEAR'S

Will someone please tell me why people make such a big deal about New Year's? It's marking the passage of time, for gosh sakes. Do we celebrate the beginning of the week (no, we dread that), the beginning of the month or the beginning of a new season? Of course not. It's not some famous somebody's birthday; it's just another day. The only change is that we have to write a different year on our checks, and that usually takes a couple of weeks to get it right. And celebrating New Year's Eve is more of an expensive entertainment obligation anyway—when normal prices skyrocket (by coincidence I'm sure). Plenty would rather stay home, but won't admit it. I like to boycott New Year's, but it still seems to come and go, whether or not I celebrate.

NEW YEAR'S RESOLUTIONS

Why torture yourself? Why should we go through this annual ritual of making unrealistic pledges to change our lives? It's an exercise in futility. If you still insist on making New Year's resolutions, don't waste any time. Just break them on January 2, to avoid unnecessary drama and pressure. Instead of all that nonsense, we should be constantly attempting to improve ourselves; but the key is a little at a time (see *Change*).

NEW YORKERS

New Yorkers are a tough bunch; they don't take shit from anybody. That's why it's always best to have them on your side in sporting events and wars—which are sometimes the same thing.

NICE

Do something nice for people every day, and you'll live longer. You'll also be a happier person—and so will they. It doesn't take much time or effort and is often incredibly appreciated. Here are some suggestions:

Bring fresh baked cookies to the firehouse.
Call an old pal, just like that.
Contribute to a charity.
Drop off some food or clean clothes to a homeless person living on the street.
Give a gift to someone close to you.
Kiss your best friend.
Pay the parking fee or toll for the person behind you.

Pop in for a visit.
Put a card in the mail to someone special.
Send flowers to a friend.
Send a card or gift to a soldier serving our country overseas.
Smile at the oncoming person walking by.
Take some flowers to a complete stranger at a nursing home.
Write a letter or email to the special one you care about.

NICE GUYS

Do nice guys finish last? No, that's just an excuse to be a jerk (see *Assholes*). Nice guys are always tops in this world. If no one else recognizes this, at least you will.

NICE TO MEET YOU

Nice to meet you? Better to say "nice to see you." That way if you're too stupid to realize you've already met them, they'll never know.

NICKNAMES

I'm all for shortening names; the fewer syllables the better for me. And I understand that Al is short for Albert, and Sin is short for Cindy, and Lou is short for Loser. But I sure don't know how they got these:

Barney for Bernard
Beaver for Theodore
Betty, Betsy and Bess for Elizabeth
Bill for William
Bob for Robert (Bobert?)
Chip for I don't know what
Chuck for Charles
Dick for Richard (Dick is also for Dickface or Dickless)
Fritz for Walter
Hal for Harold
Hal, Harry and Hank for Henry
Hank for Harry (way too confusing!)
Ike for Dwight
Irv for Irwin
Jack for John (John isn't short enough?)
Larry for Lawrence (I really don't get that)

Meg, Maggie, Peggy and Peg for Margaret
Sasha for Alexander
Ted for Edward
Ted and Teddy for Theodore
Tess for Theresa

Go figure.

NIGHT-LIGHTS

They require smoke detectors in houses; they should also require night-lights. It would help some people keep from stumbling around during the night (see *Coordination*). Plenty are always in the dark (even during the day), so it probably won't help them (nothing usually does). But lots of stubbed toes would be eternally grateful. I'd go with the clownie or duckie night-lights.

NIPPLES

Why do boys have nipples? Besides confusing little babies, what useful purpose do they serve? On second thought, we would probably look kind of silly without them.

NO

For such a small and simple statement, no is often one of the most misunderstood words in the English language. Just remember that if you keep saying no to others' requests, at least there's a possibility they'll stop asking (it's remote, but possible). Some people never know when or even how to say no (serious character flaw). Would-be Romeos think that even though she says no, she really means yes. Well guess what, idiots? She really means no; NO means NO. Also that sales gimmick of never taking no for an answer is quite ridiculous (see *Obnoxious*). And don't be afraid to say no, especially if you're asked to do something that makes you feel very, very uncomfortable. It can be very empowering to just say no, you know. You have lots of choices in life, and no is usually a choice. Don't worry about offending people; worry about them offending you. There shouldn't be any mixed messages here. If you say no, you better mean it (see *Mixed Signals*). Children sometimes think no means that they should ask 40 more times to wear you down, which is often not a bad strategy. Now maybe is a very different word—but it usually means no too.

Night-Lights

NOBODY

Are you really nobody until somebody loves you? Of course not. You're nobody unless *you* love you. And plenty of people love you too. Just look around.

NODDING OFF

If you find yourself nodding off, especially while driving, pull over for God's sake. Do you really want to endanger yourself or, worse yet, hurt someone else? I didn't think so.

NOISE

I'm not a big fan of noise. It can often be too distracting, polluting and, well, noisy. Silence is golden, you know.

NONCONFORMIST

Must we always be like everyone else and do things the conventional way? Of course not. Never be afraid to be yourself. I'm not.

NONSENSE

No matter how hard you try, you'll never be able to make sense out of nonsense. (Thanks, Debra.) Don't even try.

NOODGE

We noodges play a very important role in our society (see *Pain In The Ass*). Think about it. Life would be so boring and uneventful without us.

NO ONE TELLS ME ANYTHING

How can you always be left out? Some worldwide conspiracy? You can't always be excluded. Maybe you're just not listening. (Never mind the maybe.)

NORMAL

Since we're all crazy, I think it's very normal to be nuts.

333

NOSE HAIR

Cut that unsightly nose hair, for God's sake, as nobody wants to see it. That goes for boys—and you girls too. Unsightly means it should be out of sight. And do something about that ear hair too, while you're at it (see *Hygiene*).

NOSE PICKING

Yup, everybody picks their nose (see *Farting* and *Masturbation*). And some people think their car windows are made of one-way glass. News flash: they're not. We sure can see you, and it's rather nauseating, especially when you're up to your second knuckle. Either do it in private (not just by rolling up the window, that is) or be discreet and use a tissue. Please spare us. Oh, and as the saying goes, you can pick your friends and you can pick your nose, but you can't price your friend's nose.

NOSEY

Your nose is for smelling and for blowing. Keep it out of places where it doesn't belong (see *Brownnosing*), and try to mind your own business.

NO STRINGS ATTACHED

Always beware of any sales gimmick claiming there are no strings attached. They're attached alright, just not so clearly spelled out (see *Fine Print*).

NOTE TAKING

Who can recall all that stuff we're supposed to remember. There's only so much room in the old noggin, you know (see *Memory*). Write it down and take copious notes, as there are lots of lessons to learn in life.

NOTHING TO DO

How many times have you heard a child complain that there is nothing to do? There's no such thing, as there's always something to do. Tell them to wash your car, clean their room or take out the trash. Then they'll find something (else) to do real quick. It works every time.

NOTHING TO LOSE

Even if you feel very desperate—no matter what, you've always got something to lose (see *Dignity*).

NOTHING'S EASY

When it comes right down to it, nothing really is easy. That's why they call it work. Easy come, easy go (see *Appreciation*).

NOTICED

We all want to be noticed, but you don't want to make a spectacle out of yourself. Or do you?

NO TIME LIKE THE PRESENT

There's no time like the present, so get it done already. That's the spirit. Tomorrow may be too late (see *Procrastination*).

NOT-ME SYNDROME

Some think rules and regulations apply to everyone but them. They're very wrong. Our society does not exempt even the most important from basic rules.

NOT TO WORRY

When they tell you not to worry, it's time to worry.

NO WAY

No way? There's always a way. Always. Especially if there's a will. Now where is Will when you really need him?

NO WAY OUT

Even in the deepest and darkest times, when you feel completely closed in, there's always a way out. Just keep looking. The only way out is often just to get through it.

NUCLEAR FAMILY

I think the end of the Cold War also ushered in the demise of the nuclear family. Coincidence? I think not. Unfortunately, gone are the days when families would eat all of their meals together, enjoy vacations together and go to the movies or ball games together. Today either Mom or Dad do their own thing while the children go in a hundred different directions. Smart phones, TV, e-mail, Internet and video games have become our family (see *Socialization*).

NUDITY

Nudists claim that being naked gives them a sense of freedom. As for me, it gives a sense of embarrassment (and that windchill could be nasty too). However, our sex-obsessed society makes such a big deal about nudity. Most of us were born naked and it didn't bother us then. Other cultures don't pay as much attention to being unclothed, so maybe we can learn something from them. Maybe a lot of somethings.

NUDNIK

Nudnick is a semi-endearing term. You know it if you are it.

NURSES

Nurses get an automatic direct pass to heaven. They work in the most honorable and worthy profession there is, and you can never pay them enough. Nurses not only take care of you, but they often clean you up in very disgusting circumstances. They're the best people in the world. Angels of mercy, I say. How do they do it (see *Compassion*)?

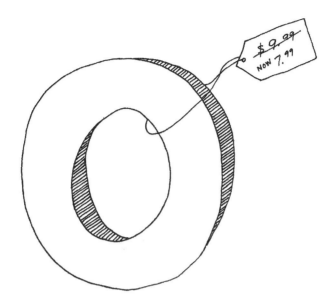

OBESITY

You like to make fun of obese people? Think it's funny? Shame on you, and don't be an idiot. It's a disease, so treat it and them that way. Sometimes it's not what you eat that gets you into trouble, it's what's eating you.

OBJECTIVE

Sometimes your objective may seem like a moving target, but keep after it (see *Eye On The Ball*). You'll get there—trust me. Don't walk away from it.

OBLIVIOUS

If you're oblivious to everything, you'll miss all that's going on. But at least you won't get ulcers, so maybe that's not so bad after all.

OBNOXIOUS

One example of being obnoxious is using too many parentheses (see *Overkill*).

OBSCURE

Now here's a word you want to weave into your conversation. You don't hear it very often, because it's way too obscure.

OBSERVANT

Some people possess a unique ability to never miss a trick. At least they appear not to. Paying attention can surely have its benefits.

OBSESSION

When there is something you're especially worried about (awaiting serious lab results, an uncomfortable discussion with your boss, expecting your boyfriend/girlfriend to give you the boot), it takes so much strength and discipline to get it out of your mind. It's just so hard to shake. Try to focus your mind on something else (see *Sex*). Now if you can't stop obsessing and fixating no matter how hard you try, you've got a problem (see *Psychotherapy*). Do something about it. Don't wait.

OBSTACLES

Don't let those obstacles in life stop you; just find a way to go around them. However, you want to careful near police barriers and things like that. They really don't like you going around those.

OCCUPY YOUR MIND

A busy and challenged mind will often keep you out of trouble. Stay occupied.

OEDIPUS COMPLEX

This Oedipus complex is way too weird for me. Freud must have really had his own share of issues. Maybe too much cocaine. Or too much Mommy.

OFFBEAT

If we all walked to the beat of the same drummer, the world would be a real boring place. Follow your own beat.

OFF-COLOR REMARK

We all say stupid things. And we all say stupid things we don't mean. Making an off-color remark or repeating a bad joke doesn't necessarily make someone a bigot. It makes them stupid and insensitive. Now if they do this on any kind of recurring basis, they can easily fall into the racist category (see *Assholes*).

OFFENSE

In football, the best offense is a good defense? No, the best offense is a good offense. The offense normally has the advantage, as the defense doesn't really know what they're going to do. They can only anticipate so much.

OFFENSIVE

If you don't want to be offensive, then be defensive. Wash your hands, brush your teeth, shower daily and put on some deodorant. You only want to smell from your nose, you know.

Other tips to keep from being offensive:

> Change your socks once in a while.
> Do a mirror check before you go out.
> Don't be afraid to bathe.
> Eliminate whining and all other high-pitched speaking.
> Have breath mints handy.
> Keep your mouth closed while eating.
> Think before you talk.

OFFICE SUPPLIES

When you're working for someone, their office supplies are designed to stay in their office. They don't go home with you (see *Stealing*).

OFF THE RECORD

Off the record? Don't believe them, as nothing's ever off the record. They can't forget they didn't hear what you said, can they (see *Selective Memory*)?

OH MY GOD

OMG? What makes you think it's just your God (see *Self-Absorbed*)?

OIL

Our quest continues to be to get more and more energy from resources stored in the inner reaches of our planet. I wonder what will happen once they suck all of this oil and natural gas out of the earth. Will it collapse and shrink up like a prune? Maybe we all should worry about that. I know I do.

OIL AND WATER

It seems that no matter what you do, some things (and some people) just don't mix. End of story.

OLD

My definition of old is someone older than me. It's the best way to stay young, so it will probably work for you too (see *Rationalizing*). You only get old if you let yourself get old.

OLD CLOTHES

No, old clothes are not going to come back in style. And no, you are not going to fit back into them. So stop dreaming and get rid of them already (see *Pack Rat*).

OLDER AND WISER

The older you get, the wiser you get. It's a plain fact (see *Experience*); that is, unless you've never learned anything in life.

OLD MOVIES

Why do people run around so fast in those old black-and-white silent movies? Must be because they never seemed to have bathrooms in those movies; so when they had to go, they had to go. You'd think that someone would have figured out a way to slow them down by now.

OLD PEOPLE

Yeah, their ears and noses droop with age, and all kinds of other things sag as well. They get shorter and start to walk funny. Some even seem to drive their cars by holding their arms up over their heads. It's been proven that the older you get, the more stupid things you say (something else to look forward to; see *Silly*). And older folks can be completely intolerant of even the slightest change in their daily routines (which is then amplified to a larger-than-life issue), as they tend to be very set in their ways. This of course requires more patience on their parts, but especially on our parts. As far as I'm concerned, old people really are allowed to be cranky and ornery sometimes, as they've kinda earned it. We simply have to tolerate it (see *Respect Your Elders*). Remember that if you're really lucky, you'll be just like them someday.

OLD SONGS

It's so cool how hearing an obscure old song can really take you back. Don't ask me why, but as you close your eyes (not while driving) you can literally visualize where you were and what you were doing when that song was popular. Certain odors can sometimes do that as well, but there doesn't seem to be much else that can have that effect on you, as it is such a random occurrence. Hopefully it all brings back good (and not bad) memories.

OLD WIVES' TALES

Now who would really want to see old wives' tails? Perverts, I guess.

ONE

How come there are so many ones? Shouldn't there be only one one? Another reason we're all so confused:

Anyone	No one	That one
Each one	Only one	Which one
Everyone	Right one	Wrong one
Last one	Someone	

Old People

ONE BITE AT THE APPLE

Who says you only get one bite at the apple? No, it takes lots of bites to finish it, right? That is, unless you have a very large mouth. You usually have more than one chance at everything.

ONE DAY AT A TIME

Don't get ahead of yourself; just take things one day at a time. Unless you're Rip Van Winkle or in a coma, you really don't have a choice now, do you?

ONE HAND WASHES THE OTHER

You scratch my back and I'll scratch yours? No, it doesn't always work that way. You should do a favor for someone because you want to, not because you get something in return.

ONE SIZE FITS ALL

How can one size fit all? Not a chance. I think it's just a ploy to make everyone feel fat. The ploy works.

ONE THAT GOT AWAY

So you want to haunt yourself forever, because the alleged love of your life seemed to slip by at some point. You just want to pine away and make yourself miserable, don't you? Well, wake up! If it didn't work, it didn't work. It wasn't right then and it's not right now, so move on (see *Meant To Be*).

ONE THING AT A TIME

If you try to do too much at once, you likely won't get a lot done. Then you may piss off people counting on you and end up being thoroughly frustrated. Knocking things off one at a time will give you a better sense of accomplishment. These tasks may not look quite as daunting when you write them down (see *World Coming To An End*). Or maybe they might; so just write small.

ONLY THE STRONG SURVIVE

Darwin was mostly right about natural selection. But many of the weak survive too, and typically need plenty of help. That's why we all have to give them special attention, or they surely won't make it (see *Kindness*).

ON SALE

Some really overdo it when they find a sale. But even if an item is on sale, you still have to pay something for it, right? Rationalization only goes so far (see *Debt*).

ON YOUR OWN

Being on your own can be a rather daunting experience, but it really does mark your passage into adulthood. Don't be afraid—we all go through it. Well, the successful ones do, anyway.

OPEN CASKETS

I don't mean to insult anyone's religion, and pardon my insincerity, but what are open caskets all about? You hear mourners say "Doesn't Aunt Gladys look wonderful?" Seriously? No, she looks dead. At a funeral, I once saw an undertaker take off a dead guy's glasses and put them in his suit pocket before closing the casket. How weird is that? I'm thinking that the dead guy probably didn't need them anymore, and maybe someone else could still find a use for them. Geez, donate them to the Lion's Club or something (see *Recycling*). But I digress. So please close the casket, as it may smell and attract bugs. Nobody really wants to see dead people anyway.

OPENING DOORS

You want to help your family and friends if you have good leads or contacts for new opportunities. By all means, open the door for them by giving an introduction. However, leave it to them to consummate the deal (see *Living Their Life*). They'll feel better knowing they accomplished this themselves, as you just gave them a little nudge.

OPEN MIND

It's one thing to stick to your guns, but it's another to have a closed mind. Believe it or not, others may have better ideas than you, so it's best to at least listen (see *Stubbornness*).

OPEN THE DOOR

By all means, open the door, as in "ladies first." Boys, nothing wrong with being a gentleman once in a while; and girls, nothing wrong with letting them. And guys, it wouldn't kill you to always walk closest to the curb when you're out strolling with your sweetheart. It's a Sir Walter Raleigh thing. Chivalry doesn't have to be dead, does it?

OPINIONS

One of the great benefits of democracy is that everyone is entitled to their own opinion—even you. No matter how nutty or outrageous, we're all allowed to have them. Now this may come as a shock to you, but I have quite a few (see *Sure Dad, You Know Everything*). However, if you find yourself constantly shopping for others' opinions, you need to put away those credit cards and generate your own.

OPPORTUNITY KNOCKS

You don't have to jump at every opportunity that comes by, but at least open the door and see what it's all about (especially if the knocking gets pretty loud). If you want to just use the peephole, that's OK too.

OPTIMIST'S CREED

Optimists have it right. The best is yet to come, and tomorrow will be a better day. We all need this or we'll never get to tomorrow. Believe me, there are always brighter days ahead.

OR

Life is so full of choices, and it's sometimes rather easy to be overwhelmed by them. Here are a few:

All or nothing
Bad or good
Beg, borrow or steal
Be there or be square
Boom or bust (see *Breasts*)
Boxers or briefs
By hook or by crook
Chicken or egg
Coming or going
Dead or alive
Do or die (I'd go with do)

Fight or flight (flight would be my choice; see *Fear*)
Fish or cut bait
For better or for worse
For or against
Friend or foe
Give or take
Heads or tails
Hell or high water (go with high water)
Help or hindrance
Here or there

Hit or miss
Ifs, ands or buts
In or out
Kill or be killed
Life or death
Life or limb
Little or no
Live free or die
Make or break
More or less
Naughty or nice
Now or never
Paper or plastic
Pick or chose
Pro or con
Put up or shut up
Rain or shine
Ready or not
Rhyme or reason
Right or wrong (can't go
   wrong with right)
Right, wrong or indifferent (I'd
   still go with right)

Safe or sorry
Shape up or ship out
Shit or get off the pot
Shit or go blind (shit would
   be less permanent)
Sink or swim
Slim or none
Stag or drag
Take it or leave it
This or that
This, that or the other thing
Time or place
Trick or treat
True or false
Truth or consequences
Truth or dare
Us or them
Way, shape or form
Whether or not
Winds or knot
Win, lose or draw
Yes or no
You or me

ORDER

There's something about the natural order of things. You know, the leaves turn brown and fall off, then come back each year. It's best not to disturb things like that, as Mother Nature will likely get upset (see *Global Warming*). You also want to bring a sense of order to your life, because deep down we really crave it (whether we admit it or not).

ORGAN DONORS

Being an organ donor puts you in the "maybe going directly to heaven" category. There is no better present to give, as it really is the gift of life. And listen, you probably don't need most of your parts after you're gone anyway (see *Recycling*). Even if you did, you'd be wearing a sheet, running around spooking everybody; so who would know what's underneath. Go ahead and check that box on your driver's license that says "By all means, take my guts after I'm dead."

ORGANIZED

Oh ye of the organizationally challenged variety—you've got to find a way to get it together. Trust me, it will make your life so much easier. Start with the simple things. If you can't do it yourself, have someone get you organized. Pay them if you have to; it's worth it.

ORGASMS

Some people confuse orgasm with organism. They are entirely different orgs. An organism is some ugly microscopic creature, and an orgasm is an indescribable feeling of ultimate ecstasy (however short lived). That is some wild feeling our Maker(s) invented. Could you imagine if there was some way to bottle that up and bestow it on your most feared enemy? They'd be your friend forever. Kinda brings a whole new meaning to the term bosom buddy, doesn't it? What a charming way to avoid all kinds of nasty conflicts (see *War*). So instead of wasting time, money and energy inventing the next super-annihilistic weapon, let's try to figure out a way to mass-produce the chemical orgasm. The only problem is that the resulting afterglow would likely be a boon to that nasty tobacco industry (see *Smoking*).

OTHER SIDE

There are two sides to every issue; sometimes three or four. It can be very difficult to view a situation through someone else's eyes. However, the best way to win an argument or reach a decision is to really try.

OUTLIVING THEIR USEFULNESS

I'm sure these had a purpose once upon a time, but we clearly don't need them anymore:

Bad breath commercials	Cemeteries
Badly behaved children	Constipation
Badly behaved adults	Disappearing ink
Belly buttons	Double chins
Belly button lint	Ear hair
Big toes	Ear wax (purpose?)
Boogers	Electoral College
Brussels sprouts	Enemies
Cauliflower	Excessive nose hair

Foreskins (or fiveskins)
Goose bumps
Headaches
Hemorrhoids (when were they
    ever useful?)
Hiccups
Landlines
Maps
Nipples on men
Pennies
Phone books
Rectal thermometers
Snot (who needs that?)

Spare tires (big guts)
Squirrels
Spiders
Tartar
Underarm hair
Wars
Weeds
Wisdom teeth (unless you're
    kinda short in the smarts
    department)
Yawning

While they're at it, they can get rid of diarrhea and vomiting. Oh yeah, and pain. That can go too.

OUT OF SIGHT

Out of sight, out of mind? That doesn't say much for your relationship now, does it? Some use that as an excuse to fool around (see *Cheating*). Love shouldn't depend on face time alone. Can you get any more shallow than that?

OUT OF YOUR ELEMENT

Know when you are out of your element, and learn how to deal with it, as that can be rather uncomfortable. Getting back into your comfort zone is the path you want to take (see *Directions*).

OUT OF YOUR WAY

Sometimes we are the biggest impediments to our own progress. Therefore it's best to try to stay out of your own way. This tends to keep you from tripping all over yourself (see *Embarrassment*).

OUTSIDE

I'm afraid we are raising a generation of house puppies. Too much Internet, TV, video games, etc. Go outside, play outside, walk outside—the fresh air will do you good. Just don't be on the outside looking in; they call that being a Peeping Tom, you know.

OVER A BARREL

Yup, they've got you over a barrel. Boy, talk about a prone position (see *Doctors*); they've clearly got the advantage. Another reason you always want to be careful when you bend over.

OVERDOING IT

Some of us never really know when to stop. That's why you should always know your limits—and theirs too.

OVERDRESSED

It's way better to be overdressed than underdressed. You see, shedding that jacket and tie at an informal event is easy, but if you come in tattered jeans and everyone else is dressed up, you look like a real schlump and your options are severely limited. Therefore, when in doubt, go with the fancier wardrobe; can't go wrong. You may even class up the crowd.

OVEREATING

This may come as a shock to you, but if you eat excessively, you get fat. It's not any more complicated than that.

OVEREXTENDED

None of us are supermen (or superwomen), and we simply can't do everything. That's an indisputable fact. We may think we can, but we can't. Therefore, it's OK to decline once in a while (see *Limitations*).

OVERKILL

Too much is usually better than not enough. Overkill "R" us (see *Sure Dad, You Know Everything*).

OVERPROTECTIVE

At some point you've got to let go. It's one thing to make sure your friends and family are safe. It's another to inhibit their growth. Unless you plan on living with them in their college dorm room or going with them on their honeymoon, cut some of those apron strings earlier rather than later.

OVERSTAYING YOUR WELCOME

Know when it's time to leave, literally and figuratively. You don't want to wear out your welcome mat.

OVER-THE-HILL

If someone tells you that you are over-the-hill, tell them to go to hell (or go to hill). Only you can decide that the years are catching up to you (see *Age*).

OVERTHINKING

Sometimes it's best to take things at face value. Thinking about it too much could definitely drive you crazy. We don't need any more reasons, as we're crazy enough already.

OVERTIME

Instead of volunteering to work overtime to make that extra buck, try spending more time with your loved ones. You (and they) may really like it.

OVERWEIGHT

Most of us gain an average of one pound a year after we graduate from high school. Think about it: by age 38 you've probably gained 20 extra pounds. And if you're in a very comfy relationship, you may gain weight even faster. Not good. If you don't have a medical condition that causes excessive weight, lose it. Period. End of story (see *Discipline*).

OVERWHELMING

Why do we get so overwhelmed? I'm glad you asked. Sometimes when lots of things happen at once, or when we get into high-pressure situations, we can really fall apart. And it can feel like everything is collapsing on top of us and our world is closing in. We panic, get all caught up in what's happening, lose focus, tend to shut down and actually end up doing nothing. It's very easy to get sucked down the drain by all of this. So what should you do? Compartmentalize. What does that mean? I'm glad you asked about that too. That means to break down all of the issues into different components and smaller pieces, and deal with one thing at a time, chipping away at the big project or issue. You take one step at first; it's OK even to start with baby steps. Life isn't so intimidating when you handle things that way (see *Lighten Up*).

OVERWROUGHT

Overwrought is not a word I use. Sorry, can't help you here. Overcooked—now that I understand. Anyway, enough of these overs already. I think I'm finally over it.

OWING

Given the choice in this world of keeping score, I'd rather owe less and have others owe more. And we're not just talking about money here (see *Helping*). The ones who end up being owed the most tend to go to heaven, you know.

OWN COMPANY

Because you end up spending so much time with yourself, it's best to enjoy your own company. This can be accomplished by simply taking yourself out to get an ice cream cone, going for a walk or going to the movies. The really happy ones have perfected this to an art form (see *Contentment*).

OWNERSHIP

Ownership isn't just about having material things. You also own the decisions you make, both good and bad. The good ones will help you have pride in ownership.

OXYMORON

Doesn't the word bittersweet seem just a tad contradictory? It kind of cancels itself out, as bitter and sweet are mutually exclusive, right? How about jumbo shrimp? Near miss? Awfully good? Small fortune? Military intelligence used to be an oxymoron, but it's no longer cool to make fun of our Armed Forces. But Internal Revenue <u>Service</u>? I guess that accounts for the moron part of this word. No wonder we're so confused.

351

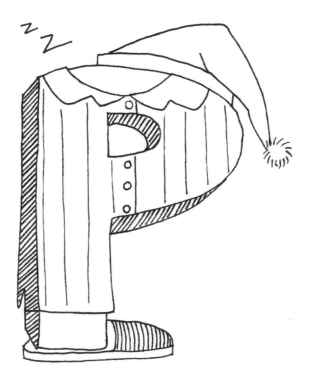

PACE YOURSELF

It's always best to pace yourself. If you blow your wad in the beginning, you'll have nothing left for the end. That goes for money, energy and love (see *Sex*). Don't wear yourself out.

PACKAGES

Why do you suppose the product, food or clothes never look the same as the picture, once you take it out of the package? That especially applies to do-it-yourself projects (see *Conspiracy Theories*). Bastards. And good luck trying to get the item back in the package if you want to return it.

PACK RAT

Here's the rule: If you haven't used it, worn it, sat on it, read it, eaten it or looked at it in the last twelve months, you probably don't need it. A better way of putting it is: if in doubt, throw it out. Junk sure has a way of propagating and growing exponentially.

PAIN

At times emotional pain can feel worse than physical pain; it really can. They're both bad, although physical pain is easier to treat. Unfortunately, no amount of comforting words, reassurance and rational thinking can seem to make it go away. It just sucks. The good news is that you can't recreate the pain in your mind; you just remember the hurt. And I don't believe in that "no pain, no gain" stuff either. Just sayin'.

PAIN IN THE ASS

It's not really a pain in your tush you know; that's just an expression (PITA). However, if your bottom really hurts, go get some help (see *Doctors*). But I digress. I don't know what's worse: a pain in the ass or a pain in the neck. Both are a problem, I suppose. Now if you insist on being one, at least make sure you're a royal PITA or a supreme pain in the ass (SPITA). Something to be very proud of.

PAIRS

Some things just go together, like peanut butter and jelly. Here are a few examples (only a few):

A and P	Alive and kicking
Abercrombie and Fitch	Alive and well
Abbott and Costello	Allen and Rossi
Above and beyond	Alm and joy
Abra and cadabra	Alsace and Lorraine
Abuse and neglect	Alvin and the Chipmunks
AC and DC	Always and forever
Accidents and incidents	Amos and Andy
Aches and pains	Antony and Cleopatra
Adam and Eve	Anything and everything
Ad and finitem	Apples and honey
Advise and consent	Apples and oranges
Agony and ecstasy	Arbitrary and capricious
Aid and abet	Architects and engineers
Aid and comfort	Ark and Dove
Air and space	Arm and arm
Ali Baba and the Forty Thieves	Arm and leg

Arm and Hammer
Armed and dangerous
Around and about
Arts and crafts
Arts and entertainment
Arts and humanities
Arts and industries
Arts and letters
Arts and sciences
Ass and nine
Assault and battery
Asti and Spumante
Atlantic and Pacific
Back and forth
Back and gammon
Bacon and eggs
Bagels and lox
Bait and switch
Bait and tackle
Ball and chain
B and B
Bar and grille
Barbie and Ken
Barnes and Noble
Barnum and Bailey
Bartles and James
Bask and Robbins
Bat and ball
Bat and cage
Bathe and beauty
Batman and Robin
Bausch and Lomb
Beak and Hill
Be all and end all
Beans and rice
Beany and Cecil
Beavis and Butt-head
Beck and call
Bed and breakfast
Bell and Howell
Bells and whistles

Belt and suspenders (they
    should match)
Ben and Jerry's
Benny and the Jets
Benson and Hedges
Bert and Ernie
Best and brightest
Betwixt and between
Bewildered and befuddled
Big and strong
Big and tall
Big and tough
Big Brother and the Holding
    Company
Bigger and better
Bill and Hillary
Bill Haley and the Comets
Bitch and moan
Bits and bytes
Bits and pieces
Black and blue
Black and Decker
Black and white
Block and tackle
Blood and guts
Blood and Thunder
Blue and gray
Bob and Ray
Bob and weave
Body and soul
Bonnie and Clyde
Boo and hiss
Books and records
Born and raised
Bottle it and sell it
Bought and sold
Bound and determined
Bound and gagged
Bow and arrow
Boys and berry
Boys and girls

Bra and panties
Brains and brawn
Bread and butter
Bread and water
Breaking and entering
Brenda and Eddie
Brick and block
Bricks and mortar
Bride and groom
Briggs and Stratton
Bright and airy
Bright and cheery
Bright and early
Bright and sunny
Brothers and sisters
Bump and grind
Bump and run
Bumps and bruises
Burger and fries
Burgundy and gold
Burn and love
Burns and Allen
Bushel and peck
Business and industry
Butch Cassidy and the
    Sundance Kid
By and by
By and far
By and large
Cab and fever
Cain and Abel
Cake and ice cream
Came and went
Can and can (get it—cancan?)
Can and should
Cap and gown
Captain and Tennille
Car and driver
Cards and letters
Care and feeding
Care and welfare

Carpet and drapes (they
    should match too)
Carrot and stick
Cash and carry
Cat and mouse
Cats and back (she was a
    Senator, you know)
Cats and dogs
Cats and kittens
Cause and effect
Cease and desist
Chad and Jeremy
Chase and Sanborn
Charts and graphs
Checks and balances
Cheech and Chong
Cheese and crackers
Chicken and egg
Chico and the Man
Chief cook and bottle washer
Chip and Dale
Chip and dales
Chip and dip
Chit and chat
Chocolate and vanilla
Church and state
Chutes and Ladders
Circles and arrows
Clear and calm
Clear and present danger
Clean and sober
Click and clack
Cloak and dagger
Coat and hat
Coat and tie
Cock and bull (story)
Coffee and cake
Cold and damp
Cole and oscopy
Cole and Powell
Command and control

Commander and chief
Come and go
Come and gone
Comes and goes
Coming and going (go already)
Comfy and cozy
Compare and contrast
Cookies and cream
Cooking and cleaning
Cops and robbers
Copy and paste
Country and Western
Cowboys and Indians
Crash and burn
Crate and Barrel
Crime and Punishment
Crimes and misdemeanors
Crimson and Clover
Cruel and unusual
Cup and saucer
Curds and whey (which way?)
Cut and dried
Cut and paste
Cut and run
Cuts and bruises
Danny and the Juniors
Dark and dusty
David and Goliath
Day and age
Day in and day out
Day late and a dollar short
    (double trouble)
Day and night
Dead and buried
Dead and dying
Dead and gone
Death and destruction
Death and dismemberment
Death and taxes
Dead and dying
Death and dying

Debits and credits
Derek and the Dominos
Devil and the deep blue sea
Ding and dong
Dick and Jane
Dilly and dally
Dining and dancing
Dis and dat
Dish and out
Divide and conquer
Dog and pony (show)
Dos and don'ts
Dollars and cents
Donny and Marie
Doom and gloom
Down and dirty
Down and out
Down and the dumps
Drawn and quartered (ouch)
Dribs and drabs (what's a drib?)
Drive and ambition
Dr. Jekyll and Mr. Hyde
Drum and bugle
Drunk and disorderly
Duck and cover
Dues and subscriptions
Dull and dirty
Dumb and dumber
Dungeons and Dragons
Dunk and Donuts
Dunn and Bradstreet
Dust and Hoffman
Dusting and cleaning
Dusty and dirty
Each and every
Early and often
East and West
Eat and run
Ebb and flow
Ebony and ivory
Effer and vescence

Efficient and effective
Em and em
Erlichman and Haldeman
Ernest and Julio
Everybody and their brother
Eyes and ears
Facts and circumstances
Fair and balanced
Fair and honest
Fair and square
Fame and fortune
Fame and glory
Far and above
Far and away
Far and wide
Fast and dirty
Fast and furious
Fast and loose
Fat and happy
Fat and lazy
Father and son
Feed and grain
Few and far between
Field and Stream
Fife and drum
Fine and dandy
Fire and brimstone
Fire and ice
Fire and rain
Fire and rescue
First and berg
First and foremost
First and goal
First and line
First and ten
Fish and chips
Fish and fowl
Fit and trim
Fits and starts
Five and dime
Fixed and dilated

Flatt and Scruggs
Flesh and blood
Flesh and bones
Flora and fauna
Flotsam and jetsam (George Jetsam)
Food and drink
Food and friends
Food and water
Footloose and fancy-free (rarely free)
Forever and a day
Forever and ever
Forgive and forget
Fortune and fame
Fortune and glory
Frank and berries
Frank and Stein
Franks and beans
Fred and Ethel
Fred and Ginger
Fred and Wilma
Freddie and the Dreamers
Free and clear
Free and easy
French and fries
French and Indian (War)
Fresh and clean
Frick and Frack
Friend and need
Friends and family
Friends and lovers
Friends and neighbors
Friends and relatives
Front and back
Front and center
Fruits and nuts
Fruits and vegetables
Full faith and credit
Fun and frolic
Fun and games

Funk and Wagnalls
Gary Lewis and the Playboys
Gary Puckett and the Union Gap
Gas and go
Gas and oil
Gay and lesbian
Gentleman and scholar
Gerry and the Pacemakers
Get up and go
Ghosts and goblins
Gifted and talented
Gin and tonic
Girls and boys
Give and go
Give and take
Gladys Knight and the Pips
Glitz and glamor
Glitz and glitter
Gloom and doom
Go and out
Goals and objectives
Gold and brown
Gold and silver
Goldilocks and the Three Bears
Gold and rule
Good and bad
Good and evil
Good and good for you
Good and plenty
Good and ready
Good and tired
Good and welfare
Good news and bad news
Goods and services
Government and politics
Grab and go
Grab and hold
Grace and dignity
Grease and grime
Green Eggs and Ham
Grin and bear it (or bare it)

Grit and grime
Guard and hose
Guns and ammo
Guns and Roses
Guts and glory
Guys and Dolls
Guys and gals
Hag and daz
Half and half (equals a whole,
  right?)
Hall and Oates
Ham and cheese
Ham and eggs
Hammer and sickle
Hand and foot
Hand and glove
Hand and hand
Hands and knees
Hans and Franz
Hansel and Gretel
Happy and healthy
Hard and fast (rule)
Hare and hounds
Harold and Maude
Hat and gloves
Hatfields and McCoys
Haves and have-nots
Have and hold
Head and shoulders
Health and happiness
Health and Human Services
Health and well-being
Health and welfare
Heart and soul
Hearts and flowers
Hearts and minds
Heat and humidity
Heaven and earth
Heaven and hell
Heckel and Jeckel
Hee and haw

Hell and back
Hell and damnation
Hell and Redding
Hell and wheels
Hemming and hawing (I don't
    know how to haw)
Herb Alpert and the Tijuana Brass
Here and there
Here and now
Hi and Lois
Hide and seek
High and dry
High and low
High and mighty
Highways and byways
Hill and dale
Hip and hop
Hiroshima and Nagasaki
His and hers
Hit and miss
Hit and run
Hither and yon (say hi to Yon for me)
Hoity and toity
Hole and one
Home and away
Honey and dearie
Honest and true
Honor and respect
Hoof and mouth
Hook and eye
Hook and ladder
Hoot and Annie
Hoot and holler
Hope and pray
Hopes and dreams
Hopes and prayers
Horse and buggy
Horse and carriage
Horse and radish
Hoss and feffer
Hot and bothered

Hot and cold
Hot and heavy
Hot and humid
Hot and spicy
Hot and steamy
Hot and sweaty
Hotdogs and hamburgers
House and home
How and why
Huck and Fin
Huff and puff
Hugs and kisses
Hum and dinger
Humpty and Dumpty
Hunky and dory
Hunt and peck
Hunters and gatherers
Hunting and fishing
Huntley and Brinkley
Husband and wife
Hustle and bustle (bustle?)
Ice and snow
Ice and tea
If and only if
If and when
Ike and Mike
Iliad and Odyssey
Immigration and
    Naturalization
In and of (itself)
In and out
Incidents and accidents
Intents and purposes
Interest and penalties
Ins and outs
Itchy and scratchy
Jack and Diane
Jack and Jill
Jacket and tie
Jacob and Esau
Jan and Dean

Jay and the Americans
John and Yoko
Johnson and Johnson
Josh and jibe
Joy and laughter
Joy and rapture
Judge and jury
Just and time
Kate and Allie
KC and the Sunshine Band
Ketchup and mustard
Kibbles and Bits
Kicking and screaming
Kiss and hug
Kiss and make up
Kiss and Ride (do)
Kiss and tell (don't)
Kinder and gentler
Kings and queens
Kit and caboodle (where did I
    leave my caboodle?)
Kit and Kat
Knees and toes
Knife and fork
L and M
L and R
Lach and Simkins
Ladies and gentlemen
Lady and the Tramp
Lady and waiting
Large and small
Last will and testament
Latest and greatest
Laurel and Hardy
Law and forcement
Law and order
Lean and mean
Leaps and bounds
Leather and lace
Left and right
Lennon and McCartney

Leopold and Loeb
Lerner and Loewe
Lewd and crude
Lewd and lascivious
Lewis and Clark
Lexington and Concord
Liberty and justice (for all)
Lie and eyes
Lie and wait
Life and death
Life and limb
Life and times
Light and airy
Light and fluffy
Light and lively
Lilo and Stitch
Linc and Center
Linc and Logs
Lions and tigers
Little Anthony and the
    Imperials
Live and be well
Live and breathe
Live and die
Live and large
Live and learn
Live and let die
Live and let live
Liver and onions
Lo and behold
Lock and key
Lock and load
Loggins and Messina
Lond and bridges
Long ago and far away
Long and hard (don't see *Sex*)
Long and short (of it)
Look and good
Look and see
Lord and master
Lost and alone

Lost and found
Loud and clear
Love and affection
Love and care
Love and devotion
Love and hate
Love and kisses
Love and marriage
Love and money
Love and peace
Love and understanding
Love and war
Love 'em and leave 'em
Lovers and Other Strangers
Lovers and sinners
Luck and cup
Luke and Laura
Lulav and etrog
Mace and Williams
Macaroni and cheese
Make and bacon
Make and love
Make and model
Make and out
Male and female
M and M
Mamas and Papas
Man and wife
Man and woman
Marco and Polo
Marsh and mallow
Martha and the Vandellas
   (what's a Vandella?)
Martin and Lewis
Martini and Rossi
Mashed potatoes and gravy
Mason and Dixon
Masters and Johnson
Math and science
May and September
Me and My Shadow

Me and you
Mean and nasty
Meat and potatoes
Meek and mild
Meet and greet
Men and jitis
Men and women
Mice and men
Mike and Ike
Milk and cookies
Milk and honey
Milt and Bradley
Miscellaneous and sundry
Mix and match
Mix and mingle
Moan and groan
Mold and mildew
Mom and dad
Mom and pop
Mop and Glo
Mop and pail
Morg and Stanley
Mork and Mindy
More and more
Mortar and pestle
Mother and child
Mother and daughter
Motherhood and apple pie
Mortise and tenon
Mount and due
Mount and men
Mover and shaker
Muff and man
Murder and mayhem
Muck and mire
Multiply and divide
Music and dance
Mutt and chops
Mutt and Jeff
Nasty and rotten
Near and dear

Near and far
Neat and clean
Neck and neck
Needles and pins
Needles and thread
Nervous and jerky
New and exciting
New and improved
News and notes
Nice and dry
Nice and easy
Nice and neat
Nice and nice
Nice and tidy
Nick and Nora
Nickel and diming
Night and day
Nip and tuck
Nooks and crannies (it may be crooks and nannies—not sure)
Normal and customary
Norm and Schwartzkoff
North and South
Now and again
Now and forever
Now and then
Null and void
Nut and doing
Nut and honey
Nuts and bolts
Oats and barley
Odds and ends
Odds and evens
Off and running
Officer and gentleman
Oil and gas
Oil and lube
Oil and vinegar
Oil and water
Old and crotchety (they must like crotchety)
Old and decrepit

Old and gray
Older and wiser
On and off
On and on
Once and for all
One and all
One and done
One and one
One and only
Oohs and ahs
Onward and upward
Open and fair
Open and honest
Open and shut (case)
Ordinary and necessary
Otis Day and the Nights
Out and about
Over and above
Over and done (with)
Over and out
Over and over
Over and under
Ozzie and Harriett
Pain and pleasure
Pain and sorrow
Pain and suffering
Parent and child
Park and lot
Park and place
Park and Ride
Parks and Recreation
Part and parcel
Parts and labor
Pat Garrett and Billy the Kid
Paul Revere and the Raiders
Paul Winchell and Jerry Mahoney
Peace and harmony
Peace and love
Peace and prosperity
Peace and quiet

Peace and tranquility
Peaches and cream
Peaches and Herb
Peaks and valleys
Peanut butter and jelly
Peas and carrots
Peck and paw (Sam)
Pen and ink
Pen and pencil
Penn and Teller
Pens and pads
Peter and Gordon
Peter and the Wolf
Phil and Don
Pig and a poke
Pick and choose
Pick and shovel
Pickles and ice cream
Picks and pans
Pidge and toed
Pig and poke
Pins and needles
Pipe and drum
Piss and moan (bladder infection)
Piss and vinegar (not on my salad)
Pistil and stamen
Pit and pendulum
Pitch and catch
Pizza and beer
Plain and fancy
Plain and simple
Please and thank you
Plotting and scheming
Plug and play
Plusses and minuses
Poise and ivory
Point and click
Point and time
Policies and procedures
Polly and Esther

Pomp and Circumstance
    (I get the pomp part, but
    circumstance?)
Porgy and Bess
Pork and beans
Pots and pans
Pratt and Whitney
Precious and few
Present and accounted for
President and CEO
Pretty and please
Pretzels and beer
Pride and joy
Prim and proper
Primping and preening
Proctor and Gamble
Products and services
Profit and loss
Pros and cons
Protect and defend
Ps and Qs (best to mind them)
Puff and Stuff
Pulling and tugging
Punch and Judy
Pure and simple
Push and pull
Pushing and shoving
Puss and Boots
Q and A
Question Mark and the
    Mysterians
Questions and answers
Quick and dirty
R and B
R and R
R2 and D2
Rack and pinion
Radio and TV
Rain and cats (and dogs)
Rain and snow
Ralph and Alf
Rank and file

Ranting and raving
Rape and pillage
Reading and writing (and
    'rithmetic too)
Real and imagined
Really and truly
Reap and sow
Relief and recovery
Ren and Stimpy
Repairs and maintenance
Research and development
Rest and relaxation
Rice and Roni
Rich and famous
Rig and mortis (I kill me)
Right and left
Right and wrong
Rich and famous
Rise and shine
Rob and Hood
Rob and redbreast
Rob and Williams
Robin Hood and His Merry Men
Rock and chair
Rock and roll
Rocking and reeling
Rocking and rolling
Rocky and Bullwinkle
Rocky and Friends
Rod and reel
Rodgers and Hammerstein
Rodgers and Hart
Rods and cones
Rolls and Royce
Rome and candle
Rome and hands
Rome and holiday
Romeo and Juliet
Romulus and Remus
Room and board
Root and tootin'

Roped and tied
Rose and bloom
Roto and Rooter
Rough and ready
Rough and tough
Rough and tumble
Rowan and Martin
Roy Rogers and Dale Evans
Ruby and the Romantics
Rude and crude
Rules and regulations
Rules and responsibilities
Rum and coke
Run and gun
Run and hide
Run and muck
Run and place
Run and shoot
Rhythm and blues
S and P
Sacco and Vanzetti
Sackcloth and ashes
Sad and blue
Sad and dismayed (or
    datmayed)
Sad and lonely
Safe and secure
Safe and sound
Safe and warm
Said and done
Salsa and chips
Salt and pepper
Salt and Peter
Sam and Dave
Sam the Sham and the
    Pharaohs
Samson and Delilah
Sanford and Son
Satin and lace
Savings and loan
Science and technology

Scotch and soda
Scratch and sniff
Scrimp and save (scrimp?)
Seals and Crofts
Search and destroy
Search and rescue
Search and seizure
Sears and Roebuck
Securities and Exchange
    Commission
Seek and destroy
Send and receive
Separate and apart
Separate and distinct
Seven and Seven
Shake and Bake
Shape and size
Shipping and handling
Shirts and skins
Shits and grins
Shock and awe
Shock and horror
Shocked and dismayed
Shoes and socks
Short and sweet
Shot and killed
Show and tell
Shower and shave
Shuck and jive
Shy and inhibited
Shy and lonely
Shy and retiring
Shy and unassuming
Sick and tired
Sickness and health
Siegfried and Roy
Sights and sounds
Simon and Garfunkel
Simon and Shuster
Sinners and Saints
Siskel and Ebert

Sit and pretty
Skill and grace
Skin and bones
Skull and Bones
Skull and crossbones
Slash and burn
Slice and dice
Slip and fall
Slip and slide
Slow and steady
Smash and grab
Smith and Wesson
Smoke and gun
Smoke and hot
Smoke and mirrors
Smokey and the Bandit
Smokey Robinson and the
    Miracles
Snatch and run
Soap and water
Sodom and Gomorrah
Song and dance
So and so
Soft and Dri
Sons and daughters
So on and so forth
So on and so on
Song and dance
Sonny and Cher
Soul and inspiration
Soup and salad
Snatch and grab
Snow and sleet
Spaghetti and meatballs
Spanky and Our Gang
Speech and hearing
Spic and span (how does one
    spic, or even span—unless
    you're a bridge)
Spit and polish
Spoke and word

Stacked and packed
Standard and Poors
Stars and Stripes
Starsky and Hutch
State and local
Steak and ale
Steak and eggs
Step and Fetchit
Step and out
Step and stone
Step and time
Steve Lawrence and Eydie Gormé
Sticks and stones
Stitch and time
Stocks and bonds
Stop and go
Stop and shop
Stop and think
Straight and narrow
Stuffed and mounted
Style and grace
Such and such
Sugar and spice (see *Little Girls*)
Suit and tie
Sum and substance
Sunny and pleasant
Sunshine and rainbows
Supply and demand
Surf and turf
Surf and web
Sweet and sour
Swing and a miss
T and A
Tax and spend
Tea and crumpets
Tender and juicy
Tar and feather
Tea and sympathy
Tea and tea
Terms and conditions (see *Fine Print*)
Thelma and Louise

Then and now
Then and there
The Young and the Restless
Thick and rich
Thick and thin
This and that
Thoughts and prayers
Thrust and parry
Thunder and lighting
Thus and so
Tick and foot
Tigris and Euphrates
Time and again
Time and effect
Time and effort
Time and energy
Time and money
Time and motion study
Time and place
Time and space
Time and time
Time and time again
Tits and ass
To and fro (how far can
    you fro?)
Today and tomorrow
To have and to hold
Tom and Jerry
Tom and Ray
Tommy James and the
    Shondells (what's a
    Shondell?)
Tom Petty and the
    Heartbreakers
Tone and deaf
Tongue and cheek
Tongue and groove
Tony Orlando and Dawn
Tool and die
Toot and common
Tooth and nail

Topsy and turvy
Tortoise and hare
Toss and turn
Touch and go
Touchy and feely
Track and field
Tractor and trailer
Travel and entertainment
Trial and error
Trials and tribulations
Tried and true
Trip and out
Truth and lending
Tweedle Dee and Tweedle Dum
Twist and shout
Twist and turn
Twists and turns
Unique and interesting
Until and unless
Up and at 'em
Up and arms
Up and away
Up close and personal
Up and coming
Up and down
Up and over
Up and running
Up and up
Ups and downs
Usual and customary
Various and sundry
Vice and versa
Vim and vigor
Vim and vinegar
Vitamins and minerals
Vodka and tonic
Wage and hour
Wait and see
Wally and the Beaver
Wants and desires
War and peace

Warm and cozy
Warm and dry
Warm and fuzzies
Warm and fuzzy
Warm and tender
Warm and toasty
Wash and dry
Wash and wax
Wash and wear
Washer and dryer
Watch and chain
Ways and means
Wear and tear
Weather and traffic
Weights and measures
Well and good
Wet and wild
Wheeling and dealing
Whine and complain
Whips and chains
Widows and orphans
Wild and crazy
Wild and wacky
Wild and wooly
Wife and child
Will and Grace
William and Mary
Willing and able
Windows and doors
Windy and cold
Wine and cheese
Wine and dine
Wine and roses
Wing and a prayer
Winners and losers
Wishing and hoping
Wise and himer
Wit and wisdom
Women and children
Woodward and Bernstein
Woofers and tweeters

Work and play
Work and process
Work and progress
Xs and Os
Yelling and screaming
Yes and no

Yesterday and today
Yin and yang
You and I
Young and old (alike)
Zager and Evans
Zig and zag

PANDERING

Don't you just hate it when someone lavishes you with a stream of insincere, syrupy compliments? We call that the Eddie Haskell approach to socialization. News flash: most of us see through that kiss-up communication style. The rest of us need to pay closer attention.

PARALLEL PARKING

Speaking of a pain in the ass, parallel parking can really be a challenge sometimes, especially if there's traffic behind you. It seems that whatever you do, you could either use a little more space or a little less car.

PARANOID

No, the whole world isn't out to get you. You're not that important.

PARANORMAL

Paranormal? Got me (See *Normal*).

PARENTING

No, unfortunately children are not born with an instruction manual; therefore parenting is the hardest job there is. It's an awesome responsibility to have someone depend on you for so much. It can be demanding, frustrating, thankless—and exceptionally rewarding. It's also a job for which we are usually the least prepared. Being a parent is not like a profession where we have supervisors or evaluations (except, of course, from our own parents). We really don't know if we're doing a good job until our children are older and we see the results. And if they grow up to be bad, you likely didn't do too well. Even if you think you know what you are doing, you don't know what you're doing. Parenting is also the most important duty you can ever perform in your life. Maybe there should be some licensing requirement before you can have children. That's what we need: more government interference in our lives. Well, maybe that's not such a good idea. Children deserve, and often demand, our attention; but we really can't spend enough time raising and nurturing them. It doesn't matter if they are perfect (fat chance), physically or emotionally challenged, in trouble, not in trouble, cute, ugly, happy or unhappy—you must love them unconditionally. Forever. This is a "have to"—no opting out here. If you make your bed, you've got to sleep in it; so if you have a whoopsie (see *Love Child*), get married and get serious. Raising a happy and healthy child is the biggest contribution you can ever make to society, you see, as good parenting makes all the difference in the world. Ultimately, it's the parents who have the largest impact on whether a child succeeds or fails in life. Now as for our own parents, they are always with us, because we'll never get their annoying voices out of our heads. This is especially true when we're doing something wrong—so that might not be so bad after all. If you don't have children of your own, find some to fall in love with and help raise them (see *Village*).

PARTNERS

There was a time when business partners were real friends and did almost anything for each other. Those days are gone, as it is more of a convenient business arrangement than anything else today. The loyalty lasts as long as the money is coming in. Sad, but true.

PARTY'S-OVER SYNDROME

After all of the planning and anticipation, it's usually a letdown when the party's over. And it often goes by so fast. This is especially true on Sunday nights (see *Mondays*). But remember: there will always be other parties, events and Sunday nights to look forward to.

PASSING THE BUCK

The buck stops here. President Harry Truman had that sign on his desk and it was quite effective. In today's world we call that taking responsibility. Taking is perfectly acceptable here.

PASSION

Passion drives success, and it's the foundation of accomplishment. Sometimes it's hidden, but we've all got it. You may have to reach way down to find your passion, but it's absolutely there. It's that little spark you can fan into a flame to make life worthwhile. That's why you want to be passionate—especially compassionate. Remember that someone else's passion doesn't have to be yours; it's a free country, you know. So find your own passion, and let it drive you (see *Directions*). It will keep you from being a boring nobody.

PASSIVE-AGGRESSIVE

I have no idea how to be passive-aggressive. It's either one or the other for me. You're probably better off looking that one up yourself.

PAST

You can't do anything about the past, because it has already passed (get it?), so look to the future. Living in the past is a waste of time, as is spending a great deal of time revisiting it. And remember: your past shouldn't matter to someone you intend to spend your future with.

PASTA

Pasta is good, and good for you (see *Moderation*), especially if you load up on the tomato sauce. There's lots of cancer-killing stuff in that red sauce, you know.

PATH OF LEAST RESISTANCE

The path of least resistance is not always the road you want to take. The easy way out isn't necessarily the right or best way out.

PATIENCE

Patience is a virtue; one that I don't have, but a virtue nonetheless. Doctors—now they have lots of patients, and the best have plenty of patience as well.

PATRIOTISM

Like so many other things, some people go way overboard in their displays of patriotism. And there's nothing wrong with that. Never be afraid to show the level of pride and love you have for your country (see *America The Beautiful*).

PATRONIZING

Of course you can patronize without being patronizing. But only saying things that people want to hear will get you nowhere in life. It's one thing to be delicate in giving someone unpleasant news; it's another to completely lie to them. "No dear, your huge fat ass doesn't look big in those jeans." That might get you some action, but you're not doing her any favors when others point and laugh.

PAY ATTENTION

Don't let life simply pass you by. Keep your eyes and ears open to make sure you know what's going on. Think about what would happen if they changed the words to "Tequila" or the Batman TV theme song and you missed it? Boy, would you be embarrassed.

PAYBACKS

Yes, paybacks can be hell. But don't forget: what goes around, comes around (see *Getting Even*). Just be patient.

PAYING DUES

You've got to pay lots of dues in life, and sometimes it doesn't ever seem to be enough. The good news is that as you get older, most of those dues have been paid in full (see *Experience*).

PEACE

Do you know that in the last several hundred years, there has been a total of only a few days that some country was *not* at war in the world? I read that somewhere, so it must be true. Anyway, my point is this war business doesn't seem to be working too well, so maybe we should be more innovative and find other ways to resolve conflicts (see *Orgasms*). Give peace a chance. John Lennon was on to something. I think he was on to a lot of somethings.

PECKING ORDER

Pecking order is for the birds.

PEDIGREE

Where you came from and how you got here are not nearly as important as what you do with what you have.

PEDOPHILES

Pedophiles are very sick people, and should be banished from the planet. Taking advantage of innocent children is one of the most disgusting and heinous crimes there is. They better get some help before society cuts off their weenies.

PEEING IN THE SHOWER

So you think you're the only one who pees in the shower? Nah, everybody does. Anyway, it all goes down the drain and saves a flush, right? However, I wouldn't suggest peeing while you're taking a bath (see *Germs*). Now as for pooping in the shower, that's not at all recommended.

PEELING SKIN

Why does our skin peel? Are we snakes or what? It's not very appealing to be peeling, so I guess it's someone's (or something's) way of telling us we got too much sun (or too much skin). A gentle reminder would be enough for me.

PEER PRESSURE

Either you let others talk you into doing something you don't want to or shouldn't do, or you stick to your convictions and do what's right. You decide. (Hint: Giving in is rarely worth it).

PEN

Oh yeah, the pen is way mightier than the sword. It can be quite powerful, by both building up and tearing down (ambidextrous pens). Using that pen can really cut down on wars that's for sure—and can turn all those leftover swords into plowshares (whatever they are).

PENIS

So who is responsible for naming this very important male appendage? I'm big on naming things related to their uses. It should have been called pee-er, not penis. It pees; it doesn't nis, right? Another one of life's baffling mysteries.

PENIS ENVY

Listen ladies, there's not a whole lot to get very envious about with penises. When you think about it, it's a rather odd body part. So it serves a couple of good purposes, but otherwise it's very painful when hurt and often gets in the way. That being a larger problem for some than others, if you know what I mean. See how much you like it when you get kicked in the nutskies. If you notice, we gents never talk about vagina envy now, do we? Anyway girls, penises would look funny on you, so find something else to be envious about. Look at it this way: at least you'll never suffer from "Limpus Dickus" (that's a medical term). Now boys, penis envy shouldn't be an issue for you. If it is, you've got some real problems (see *Psychotherapy*).

PENMANSHIP

Good penmanship is way overrated. Especially since we of the penmanship-challenged persuasion have computers to make our handwriting look so much better.

PENNIES

A penny is a classic example of something that is no longer needed. (Nickels aren't far behind either.) Pennies smell, they tend to weigh you down and they are a complete waste of copper (or whatever the hell they make them with). We use the decimal system, so how about rounding to the nearest ten? Then we would only have to carry around dimes. However, I guess we'd have to turn quarters into 20-cent pieces. Oh well.

PEOPLE DON'T CHANGE

People don't change? Nonsense, of course they do. We all change every day. Our bodies change, our needs change and even our underwear changes (for most of us, that is). Sometimes the change is for the better (attitude), and sometimes it's for the worse (attitude). But no one always stays the same.

PEOPLE, NOT PLACE

The place is really secondary, as it's always the people, not the place. The place is less important and can be anywhere, as long as you have the right people.

PEP TALK

Everyone can use a pep talk now and then (see *Advocate*). If you run out of people who need pepping, give one to yourself.

PERCEPTION

Sorry, but perception often is reality. It may be unintended, but it can be very difficult to convince someone that their perception is wrong. However, don't let that stop you from trying.

PERCEPTIVE

You don't have to be able to predict the future to learn how to draw your own conclusions (see *Keep Your Eyes Open*). And you don't have to be an artist either. (Get it—drawing? Please pay attention. Do you think I'm doing this for my health?)

PERCOLATE

Often it's a good idea to let your thoughts percolate for a while, especially when you're really angry. Take a deep breath. Thinking can never be a bad thing to do. You might even come up with some useful ideas.

PERFECT GENTLEMEN

Boys should always be perfect gentlemen (see *Open The Door*). This is the exception to the *Perfection* rule.

PERFECTION

We should always strive to be better, but seeking perfection is not something I would ever aspire to. You shouldn't either. If we were all perfect, what would we have to complain about? Maybe we'd whine about ending sentences with prepositions.

PERFUME

It's nice to smell good, but you don't have to take a bath in it, for gosh sake (see *Moderation*). Same for cologne.

PERKY

Perky is OK, but some people can be way too perky. I bet if you cut off their caffeine, they'd be like the rest of us. I'm not a big fan of perky.

Perky

PERMISSION

When in doubt, it usually can't hurt to ask permission. This applies to taking the last cookie and lots of other things (see *Sex*).

PERSEVERANCE

Perseverance is a good thing (see *Giving Up*). You may be quite surprised at what you can accomplish when you really try. Never underestimate yourself.

PERSISTENCE

A closed door should just inspire you to find an open one—or at least to look for an open window nearby. Keep at it and you'll get there, as persistence usually does pay off (see *Trying*).

PERSON

Yes, one person can make a difference in this world. Even you can make lots of difference. Just try.

PERSONAL GAIN

If you compromise a transaction for personal gain, it's the same as stealing (see *Rationalizing*).

PERSONAL TOUCH

Nothing beats the personal touch, as it shows a special side of you: the caring side, which tends to distinguish you from everyone else. Better to be distinguished than extinguished, I always like to say. (Well actually, not really always; more like sometimes.)

PERSPECTIVE

One of the hardest things to do in life is to put things in perspective. It isn't always easy, but it's best to keep little things little and big things from getting too big. Step back, and you'll find that most of your issues and problems aren't of the life or death variety. The world isn't coming to an end either, so you want to take that into consideration too.

PERSPIRATION

Never let them see you sweat? That's not my motto. Seeing the sweat on your brow shows them you're working hard; so sweat away. You might want to load up on the deodorant though (see *Hygiene*).

PERSUADE

The art of persuasion is not easily mastered. It takes a lot of P's (patience, perseverance and persistence) to be successful in getting your point across logically and convincingly. Try to keep the emotions down; and give a little wink here and there to win them over (see *Charm*).

PET PEEVES

Is it just me, or do these things just drive you crazy (hell, it's probably is just me):

> Advertisers who repeat the same commercial several times during the same program. I know they think we're all stupid and need to hear that irritating jingle plenty of times so it will sink in. That doesn't mean I have to like it.
>
> Air guitars. Really?
>
> Air kisses (see *Sincerity*).
>
> Air quotes. Why do some people insist on using their fingers as quotation marks? We get the idea without all of the dramatics.
>
> Answering machine messages that say things like: "This is the desk of" or "This is the office of." You can't fool me; desks and offices can't talk.
>
> "At this particular point in time." How about just saying now?
>
> "Back in the day." Exactly what day are they talking about—yesterday?
>
> Billboards. What a blight on our environment. Talk about visual pollution.
>
> Blinkers that stay on after you change lanes. Maybe you really enjoy that annoying clicking.
>
> Children telling their parents what to do. Especially in public. Not cool.
>
> Companies that use letters instead of numbers for their phone numbers. 1-800-EAT-ME.
>
> Dress shirts with removable collar stays. Don't we always want our collars to stay straight? Hello—can't they all be permanent?
>
> Exclamation points. Way overused. Know what I mean?!!!!!
>
> Fancy and expensive watches. Don't they tell the same time as the cheap ones?

"Fixing" lunch, hair, drinks. Are they all broken?

"Holy crap!" There's no such thing.

Hotels without fans in the bathrooms. Who enjoys those nasty smells escaping into their sleeping and living quarters? And how are you supposed to shave using those foggy mirrors after a shower?

"How are you doing?" It's not a genuine question, as few really want to know the actual answer.

"If a tree falls in the forest and no one is there, will it make a sound?" Who cares?

"If I don't say so myself." Who else is talking to me? A ventriloquist?

"I know that area like the back of my hand." Hell, I don't even know which side of my hand is the back and which is the front.

"I know what you're thinking." If you could really read minds, you would not be wasting your time talking to me now, would you?

"In other words." Were the words they already used not good enough? Why didn't they use the right words the first time? Why waste my time! Another reason to choose your words carefully.

It's end quote, not unquote.

It's not white knight. It's a knight on a white horse.

It's oriented, not orientated.

It's used to, not use to.

Jumping up and down. How do you jump down?

"Just touch base." Keep your hands off my base.

Knocking on wood. How about knocking on bricks, or paper, or your friend's head for good luck?

Leaving crumbs in the butter after you spread it on your toast. Is it so hard to scrape them off?

"Let me ax you a question." No, you use an ax to cut down a tree. If there is no one else around, see if it makes any noise while you're at it.

Locks on trash cans. Would someone really want to steal your trash?

Loud music at parties, restaurants, bars and receptions. How are you supposed to have a conversation (see *Socialization*)?

Mimicking a phone call while making your hand appear to be a phone. Can you hear me now?

Mixed nuts. Sorry, I hate to be labeled a segregationist (see *Politically Correct*), but mixed nuts get so confused that they all tend to taste the same. They can't like it either, so split 'em up, already.

Paying for air at the gas station. Air is free everywhere else, right? At least for now anyway.

People who ask you to give them your phone number. What they really want is for you to tell them your phone number. Because if you give them yours, then you won't have one.

People who blow their noses in restaurant napkins. And then leave them on their laps or, worse yet, on the table to use to wipe their mouths later. Yech!

People who don't know the difference between your and you're, whose and who's, there and their (and they're) in their writing. Time for a basic grammar review.

People who don't use their turn signals when changing lanes. Do they think we have ESP and can read their minds?

People insist on taking their glasses off when their picture is being taken. Why wouldn't they want to look like themselves? Maybe they should shave their heads while they are at it, or lose thirty pounds and really look like someone else. Or just wear a mask.

People who inspect their hankies after they blow their noses. What do they expect to find in there—car keys?

One-armed hugs (see *Sincerity*). Is a full embrace such an extra effort?

Replaying the highlights when you're listening to a football game on the radio. Do you see it better the second time?

Ringing the bell and clapping when the stock market closes for the day. Is everyone that happy when their stock portfolio won't plunge any lower until tomorrow?

"See what I'm saying"? No, I can only hear what you are saying.

"Setting" the table. You don't set the table, as it's already set up. You put dishes and silverware on the table.

"She's got more money than God." How silly! Everybody has more money than God. When would God ever need to have pocket change, right?

Songs that don't end. You know, those songs that go on and on at the end, and then just stop.

Starting a request with "I know you're busy." If you know I'm busy, then just leave me alone.

"Till I'm blue in the face." Only the Royals get blue in the face. Come to think of it, everything about them is blue, especially their blood.

TVs in the bedroom. It's either the sleep room or the play room (see *Sex*); it's not the entertainment room. Unless that's your idea of a good time.

Two glass doors at an entrance when only one opens. The locked door is never labeled, and it's rarely consistently locked or unlocked. How about putting a window there instead?

Voicemail messages when the caller rattles off their phone number. Like everybody can write that fast. Why don't they just say their number slowly and then repeat it?

Voice prompts when you call a company. Have we run out of people to answer the phone?

Wearing shoes with no socks. How smelly is that? I'd also put wearing socks with sandals on the list—really?

Wearing sport jackets without ties. You look rather incomplete. Either you're dressed up or you're not dressed up; no halfway here. Anyway, without a tie those collars look stupid under the jacket no matter what you do.

"Well personally, I think." Very redundant. Who else's thinking would you be talking about?

"We need to sit down and discuss this." So why can't we discuss things standing up?

"We're pregnant." Who are you kidding? We're not pregnant—she's pregnant, you nut. Which "we" does all of the screaming, grunting and moaning when that baby pops out? No, gentlemen, the ladies do all the work during pregnancy. We just stick around to get yelled at.

"When all is said and done." What does that mean?

When people speak in the third person. We know they are talking about themselves, right?

When the receptionist asks you to "give her your name." If you comply, then she has two and you have none, right?

When the sales clerk says "if you need my help, my name is Esmeralda." What's your name if I don't need any help?

"You're more than welcome to." How can you be more than welcome? Welcome is welcome, right? That also goes for "more than happy to" too.

PHOBIAS

We all have things that we're afraid of; however, some fears are really weird. Very weird. There are over 500 types of phobias; yes, something for everyone. There's even phobophobia, which (silly me) I thought was the fear of phobos, but is actually the fear of phobias (I'm scared to death of that one). My favorite is allodoxaphobia, which is the fear of opinions. That's one I don't have.

PHONE COMPANY

You'd think at least the phone company would allow you to talk to a human when you call them, right? No. Instead, we get voice prompts. And we pay every month for that privilege. Why do we put up with that?

PHYSICAL ACTIVITY

Move around or your body will turn to mush. And nobody wants a mushy tushie. Buns of steel aren't the way to go either. That can't be too comfortable to sit on.

PICKING UP THE PIECES

When disaster strikes (and disaster has lots of different meanings), it's very difficult to pick up the pieces in the aftermath. You really have no choice, as forward is the only direction left to go. Best to get some help (see *Friends*).

PICKING YOUR BATTLES

Some things are just not worth arguing over. Anyway, if they think they won an argument and you really don't care, you win, right? Save your energy and the real battles for issues that are really important to you. They can't all be important (see *Self-Absorbed*).

PICKUP LINES

Here are some pickup lines you probably want to avoid, as I'm told they don't work:

> Are those space pants you're wearing, 'cause you're out of this world?
> Come here often?
> Don't I know you?
> New in town?
> Nice eyes.
> Nice tits.
> That's a very nice dress you have on, Mrs. Cleaver.
> Wasn't I married to you once?
> What's your sign?
> Wow, you look just like (insincerely insert name of any famous person here).
> You sure look familiar.
> Your children are so beautiful, and I love children.

Try this; it'll probably work:

Hi, I'm so-and-so (very common name).

PICK YOURSELF UP

Go ahead and dust yourself off, and start all over while you're at it. Tomorrow's another day.

PICNICS

Real picnics have too many bugs. Aren't we civilized enough to eat inside and play outside? The bugs aren't nearly so bad when you're playing.

PICTURES

Take lots of pictures, as it's an excellent way to help preserve memories. However, they can sometimes be painful: "Gee, I guess I really was that thin/young/sexy/tall/tan." Anyway, a good picture is worth a thousand words. (Don't ask me what you can buy with a thousand words.)

PIPELINE

In life, it's often advisable to have lots of things on deck, so to speak. That goes for places to visit, potential job opportunities and alternative date choices, to name a few. We call that your pipeline.

PISSED ON

They say it's better to be pissed off, than pissed on. I don't have any firsthand experience here, but I'm guessing they're probably right.

PISSING IN THE WIND

Pissing in the wind sounds like a rather futile act to me. But if this is your idea of a good time, go ahead and enjoy yourself. Girls, I think you may have trouble attempting this (see *Penis Envy*).

PISSING PEOPLE OFF

Some of us relish the possibility of pissing selective people off (see *Pain In The Ass*). We even delight in irritating the real jerks in our world. I, of course, see nothing wrong with that, as it tends to keep them on their toes. However, you may want to be careful of who you piss off, especially if they're bigger than you.

PISTACHIOS

You know how you sometimes get one of those hard-to-open pistachio nuts? Those are the ones that are mostly closed up, with a very small opening. Before you sacrifice a fingernail or take a hammer to them, here's a helpful hint: Take a leftover half shell and jam it into the small slit. Wiggle it around until you get the shell to budge. Then just crack it open like the others. Voilà! If only every problem could be so simple to solve.

PITCHING A FIT

It's not a good idea to pitch a fit, as it usually won't get you anywhere. Try pitching a tent or a ball instead; you'll get much better results.

PJs

Well boys, pajamas are for little ones, old men and fashionable women. Real guys wear their undies (boxers, please) to bed.

PLAN

You can have a master plan, or you can fly by the seat of your pants. It's always best to have a plan and a backup plan. However, you want to be flexible and be prepared for unanticipated situations, as even the best laid plans can go awry. Failing to plan is planning to fail, you know.

PLAN B

That's your backup plan.

PLANTS

Who made this verb (planting) into a noun (plant)? Do you ever hear of someone driving their drive (car) or picking their pick (nose)? Nope. I think there was a conspiracy when all of this was invented (see *English Language*), and my guess is that there were drugs involved. Likely mind-altering drugs.

PLAYING

Just because you work hard doesn't mean you have to play hard. Play nice. They call it a game, you know, so ease up, already. Remember: if you gotta play, you usually gotta pay, as everything comes with a price. And that's not so bad.

PLAYING FAVORITES

Sure, everyone has their likes and dislikes. That's one of the things that makes us, well, us. However, when you're in a situation when all should be treated equally (for example, your children, parents, students, marshmallows), it's best not to single one out for special treatment. That behavior can be very unfair to them, especially the marshmallows.

PLAYING GOD

Sorry, that part's been taken.

PLAYING HOOKY

So who doesn't develop that mysterious life-threatening illness, which is so debilitating that it tends to keep you out of work or school? Of course, the fact that this happens on the nicest day of the year is a mere coincidence. And by some strange occurrence or quirk of fate, you quickly recover by the next day (see *Miracles*). It's a good idea not to make a habit of playing hooky, as they'll soon be on to you. And you don't want that, do you?

PLAYING HOUSE

Like most things, playing house looks much easier than it is. Being a real mommy and daddy and running a household isn't always fun and takes lots of hard work. Lots.

PLAYING WITH FIRE

Play games, play with your friends, play dress-up, play ball (see *Masturbation*). But you're just asking for trouble if you play with fire. It doesn't play fair, and you can really get burned.

Playing With Fire

PLAYTIME

As busy as we often get, it's best to try to make some time for play (see *Balance*). Your brain will thank you.

PLEASE

For a small word, please can sure open lots and lots of doors. Some windows too (see *Manners*).

PLEASING

If you run your life trying to please the rest of the world, they'll be thrilled, but you won't be very happy. Unfortunately, some are on a lifelong quest to please their parents, which is not always the way to go (see *Exercise in Futility*). Like Rick Nelson said, you can't please everyone, so you've got to please yourself. That's not being selfish; it's simply experiencing the joys that life has to offer.

POCKET POOL

Boys, find another sport. Girls, you shouldn't be playing this.

POETIC JUSTICE

Poetic justice doesn't rhyme and usually isn't recited. But it's still my favorite kind of poetry.

POKING THE BEAR

Are you crazy? Are you really looking for trouble (see *Death Wish*)? When you know you're going to get the nastiest of reactions, why in God's name would you antagonize someone you know will hurt you? Don't be an idiot.

POLICE

Sure, nobody likes to get a ticket. But a police officer's main job is to help and protect you (and me). I think that's such a comforting concept. So if you're ever in trouble, call them. Don't ever, ever hesitate.

POLISHED SHOES

A polished shoe is a sign (shine) of good upbringing. Keep buffing.

POLISH JOKES

Do you really want to display your ignorance? Then by all means tell a few Polish jokes, or any other jokes that make fun of people. Telling racist or ethnic jokes isn't at all funny; it just shows how stupid you are.

POLITICALLY CORRECT

Being politically correct is way overrated (see *Form Over Substance*). The worst racists can painstakingly use the currently proper terms for everything. Yet the most well-intended of us can unknowingly stumble over the latest and greatest words to use. Remember: it's the intention that really counts.

POLITICIANS

It's great to dedicate part of your life to public service. In its purest form, vying for elective office is the ultimate way to be helpful and participate in democracy. However, many get so carried away with themselves that it's a wonder anyone can tolerate their very existence (see *Power Corrupts*). And sometimes it seems that the thickness of politicians' skin is inversely proportional to their ability and effectiveness; some really can display the ultimate in pettiness. If you have the desire, make sure you enter politics for the right reasons; it can be a very honorable aspiration.

POLITICS

Sorry, politics is a necessary evil (see *Democracy*). And yes, most everything in our society has some political influence. That can be good or bad.

POLLING

Pollsters attempt to gauge the opinions of the masses. But plenty of people lie and just tell them what they think they want to hear (they did a poll on this). What do I care if 47 percent of adult white males think Mickey Mouse is a child molester (he's not)? Why should I be concerned that 93 percent think the earth is burning up (it is)? My opinions are not influenced by what the majority or minority thinks. I draw my own conclusions, and so should you.

POLLUTION

Pollution is a horrible problem that shouldn't be dumped on our children (see *Legacy*). There's plenty that can be done to stop it and to clean up the current messes we've made. Like many things, it just takes time, money and effort—and a dash of commitment.

PONDER

If reading this book doesn't cause you to sit back and ponder once in a while, you're not doing your job. Or maybe I'm not doing mine.

PORES

Oh, you gotta keep those pores open and let 'em breathe. A clean pore is a happy pore (see *Hygiene*).

PORN

Yes, it's a fact of life that most of us get stimulated looking at pictures or videos of naked people (especially of the opposite sex). And yes, some take things to an extreme and actually get addicted to porn, which is bad. We all have our fantasies and ways to get excited. As long as it's not illegal, demeaning or disgusting, porn is not such a horrible thing. Just don't go crazy over it (see *Moderation*).

PORTION CONTROL

If you don't control your portions, they will control you (see *Overeating*).

POSITIVE REINFORCEMENT

Who doesn't like positive reinforcement? It's by far the best way to motivate anyone. If you lay off that negative approach, you'll likely have much better results in influencing others' behavior. That's why you should accentuate the positive. Are you paying attention here?

POSSESSIVE

Being protective of the ones you care about is one thing; being overly possessive is another. You don't own them, you know. Even with the best of intentions, you can inadvertently stifle someone's growth by trying to keep them too close. Let the birdies fly. If you did a good job, they'll fly back.

POSSIBLE

When you think about it, anything is possible. It really is.

POSTURE

Didn't you listen to your mother? Stop slouching and sit up straight. One shouldn't underestimate the value of good posture. Your back will thank you, and you won't shrink down to four feet tall when you're 70. Now go ahead and tuck your shirt in while you're at it.

POTBELLY

It's a free country, so you're entitled to look like a slob if you want to. However, when your health is endangered, just know how stupid and selfish you are (see *Consequences*). If you don't mind taking ten years off your life, then by all means, potbelly away.

POWER CORRUPTS

Good thing the U.S. of A. has so many institutional checks and balances, not to mention elections (see *Democracy*). Unchecked power is bad news, and once some people have the kind of clout that goes to their heads, it is very difficult to give it up. They can develop this unnatural sense of entitlement, which is very bad. Power can corrupt. And yes, absolute power corrupts absolutely.

POWER OF POSITIVE THINKING

Positive thinking can literally change your life and change the world. A bright and cheery disposition will bring you plenty of health and happiness. Imagine the possibilities of a veritable epidemic of positive thinking that catches fire and sweeps the world. It could happen. Start with you (see *Miracles*).

PRACTICE MAKES PERFECT

Does practice make you perfect? Of course not (see *Perfection*). Practice makes you better, but nothing makes you perfect. Haven't I made this clear already? I can't stand repeating myself, so pay closer attention, will you?

PRAGMATIC

When all else fails, be pragmatic. It's usually the best option.

PRAYER

It's neat to have a rather one-way conversation with whoever it is upstairs. At least you get to collect and focus your thoughts—and maybe someone or something is out there listening. Praying silently can be a most intimate way of communicating your thoughts; your heart is speaking directly to the Higher Power, which makes it exceptionally personal. However, simply going through the motions of reading written prayers and reciting someone else's words likely accomplishes very little. Prayers have to come from your soul to be effective. And you'll really never know if praying doesn't work, right?

PRAYER IN SCHOOLS

Even though the really desperate students pray a lot ("please let them forget to give us that test today"), prayers have no place in schools. Talk about jamming your religious values down someone else's throat. Since when is your way the only way? Why stop there? How about a prayer before TV shows, at the movie theaters or after making left turns? There's a reason for a separation between church and state (see *Constitution*). Let's keep it that way. How, when, where or if you pray is no one's business, much less a school's.

PRAYING

Some people think praying is like asking the genie for three wishes. It's not. Don't pray to win the lottery or anything like that; it won't work (believe me, I've tried—plenty of times). You should limit it to health, ending world hunger and wars, and other truly important requests. Remember: God helps the needy, not the greedy. And don't assume that whoever you're praying to has nothing better to do than rescue you from your latest tragedy. Best to try to straighten it out yourself before you seek a Higher Power.

PRECIOUS

Lots of things are precious, but life is the most precious. Don't ever forget that. (This is where a note to self is an excellent idea.)

PREDICTABLE

Ah, you shouldn't always be so predictable. Keep 'em guessing and on their toes once in a while. That tends to make life more interesting—for them and for you.

PREJUDICE

I feel so sorry for prejudiced people. They are afflicted with the worst handicap there is: being blinded by hate. And this isn't a malady we are born with. It is a learned trait, which is often passed down from generation to generation. Breaking that cycle is one way to stop it. Opening your heart is another way (see *Tolerance*).

PREOCCUPIED

They say that being preoccupied is a sign of intelligence (see *Rationalizing*). However, you don't want to get so wrapped up in what's on your mind that you start walking into doors and talking to yourself and stuff, as that could really get you into trouble. Now, what were you saying?

PREQUELS

Prequels make no sense to me. I much prefer things to be in order, so I don't get too confused (see *Sequels*).

PRESENTABLE

If you go out of the house looking like a slob, you are a slob. Any questions?

PRICE OF FORGIVENESS

Sometimes the price of forgiveness is less than the price of permission. If you're afraid to ask first and you screw up, at least make sure you apologize after.

PRICE TAGS

If you have to ask how much it costs, you probably can't afford it. Remember: everything ultimately has a price tag on it, even though it may not be obvious (see *Fine Print*).

PRIDE

You should have lots of pride in the kind of person you are and the things you do, especially the good ones (see *Accomplishment*). Just make sure you don't let your pride stand in the way of doing the right (or smart) thing.

PRIESTS, MINISTERS AND NUNS

I admire people who devote their lives to their religion and helping people, as long as they are not fanatics. Most religious leaders don't do it for the money or perks. They chose this field because they really feel a calling to serve, which is a wonderful quality. One that I don't have, but wonderful nonetheless. God love them.

PRIORITIES

Always try to keep your priorities straight and in good order. Sounds easy, but sometimes it's very difficult. Start with number one. Please don't ask me what that is; you should have one. I can't tell you everything.

PRIVACY

If you inadvertently see something you're not supposed to (like someone's privates), you might want to tell them that their goodies are hanging out, to spare them further embarrassment. In those situations you should politely avert your eyes (see *Cleavage*).

PROACTIVE

You can be proactive or reactive. Being reactive will likely keep you behind, while being proactive will tend to get you ahead. It's up to you (see *Choices*).

PROBLEMS

You think you have problems? Take a look the next time you see someone in a wheelchair—or missing an arm or a leg—or who can't speak, or see, or hear. Now, do you still think you still have problems?

PROBLEM SOLVER

It's much better to be a problem solver than a problem maker, as the best problem solver focuses on the solution, not the problem. If we had more solvers than makers, our world would be a better place. We'd have fewer problems, that's for sure.

PROCRASTINATION

Some people think that tomorrow was invented for procrastinators. They follow the procrastinator's creed: "Why do today what you can put off till tomorrow?" Why? Because you may run out of tomorrows, that's why, silly. You can't do everything at the last minute, you know. Go ahead and try to do some of it today; you'll feel better (see *Accomplishment*). Tomorrow is another day though.

PRODUCTIVE

Try to do something positive each day, as it makes your life worthwhile. Don't forget that being productive is much better than being destructive. Duh. Think of that the next time you're being critical of anyone.

PROFESSIONAL ATHLETES

I have a theory here. Pay professional athletes for all of their accomplishments *after* their careers are over. Also, by then they're older and wiser, and won't tend to piss all of their money away. When you're young and making millions, it's too easy to get distracted (like I know, right?). Invariably, they get a big raise after a good year and can rarely repeat those feats. Hey, anybody ever hear of incentives? You tend to do better when you're striving for something and reach certain goals. And how about letting them stay on the same team for more than two years in a row. Hello! What does that teach our children about team spirit, anyway?

PROLIFIC

Be fruitful and multiply. That's what God said to somebody in the Bible. I can multiply just fine, but I've never been real fruitful. I don't even know how to be fruitful. Fruity—now that I know. Color me fruity.

PROMISCUOUS

Alluring is OK. Even sexy is OK. Promiscuous is not OK, as you probably don't want to be too well known for that (see *Reputation*).

PROMISES

If you're going to make promises, make attainable ones and don't break them. Stay away from the empty kind too. You never want to make promises you can't keep (reneging is bad). And remember that your word is your bond (see *Reputation,* again). Therefore it's best to keep your promises, and hold others to theirs.

PROSTATE vs. PROSTRATE

It's prostate, silly. Don't be stupid by displaying your ignorance and mixing these words up. They mean very different things.

PROUD

Always keep your head up, no matter what. That's why you don't want to put yourself in a position to be ashamed of who you are, what you are or what you do. It's a great feeling to be proud of someone, and even greater to be proud of yourself.

PROVE YOURSELF

In the final analysis, the only one you have to prove yourself to is you. And don't let anybody tell you otherwise.

PRO WRESTLING

Get real. Pro wrestling is as fake as a three-dollar bill. It's nothing but scripted theater, which I guess is some form of entertainment. I think they call it comedy.

PSYCHOTHERAPY

You go to your regular doctor for your annual (or as long as you can put it off) physical, don't you? You get all of your insides checked out, right? You go to the dentist each year? Eye doctor? So how about taking care of what's upstairs? You don't want to neglect your noggin, you know. We call it a checkup from the neck up. Go see a mental health professional, especially when you're not in a crisis mode; that's called preventive medicine. The more you learn about yourself, the better off you'll be. No one's head is screwed on so well that they can't use a tune up now and then (see *Normal*). Think about it: you can have your own personal independent advocate. Talking to a trained professional

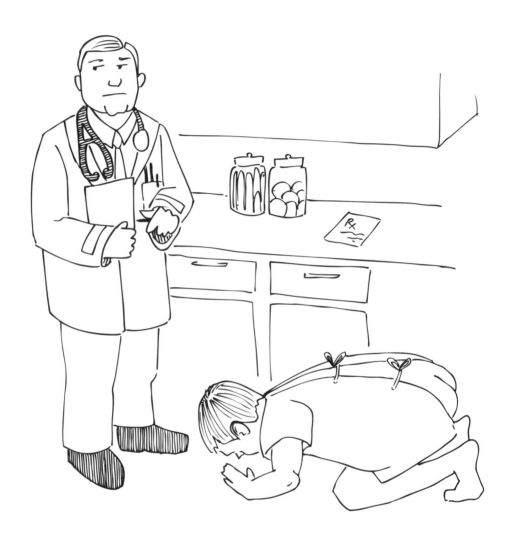

Prostate vs. Prostrate

can be very therapeutic; that's why they call it therapy, you nut. Oh, stigma, shmigma. It's your business and no one else's.

PUKING

Do you know that some people throw up on purpose? What's up with that? This is clearly the worst feeling known to man or woman. It sure isn't something I enjoy doing. For me, food tastes way better going down, rather than coming back up.

PULLING STRINGS

You may think you're helping, but you're not always doing someone a favor by pulling strings for them. People rarely appreciate things that are just given to them and not earned (see *Spoiled*).

PULLING THE PLUG

Sad but true, but when it's time to go, it's time to go. If that's the case, let them die in peace (see *Dignity*), as it's hard to forestall the inevitable.

PUN

Yeah, well, most puns are intentional. They sure are here anyway.

PURPOSE OF LIFE

For centuries people a whole lot smarter than me have pondered the purpose of life. I don't think anyone really knows the answer, so I've got no great ideas here. But I do know that you can certainly add plenty of purpose to your own life. Plenty.

PUSH

Everybody needs a gentle push now and then—with gentle being the operative word (see *Encouragement*). However, it's always best to know how close someone is to the edge of that cliff. That's not the time to give them a push.

PUSHING BUTTONS

When someone knows how to get under your skin, they can really take advantage of you. They often get pleasure out of driving you crazy. Therefore, it's always best to keep those buttons hidden (see *Modesty*).

PUSHING THE ENVELOPE

There are those who insist on going as far as they can, and then tend to go even further. Trust me, it's just not the way you want to run your life (see *Risk*).

PUSHING YOUR LUCK

Luck is clearly not something you can ever count on, so you can only push it so far (see *Temptation*).

PUSH YOURSELF

There is only one way to test your limits, and that's by pushing yourself. The result will likely surprise you (see *Strength*). And of course, after a while, push comes to shove. (I don't know what that means). Just remember that pushing is usually easier than pulling. Well, maybe not.

PUTTING IT BACK

Always put things back where you found them. That goes for tools, hairdryers, toothbrushes, penises—everything. Otherwise, you'll piss a lot of people off; especially if you don't put that penis away.

PUTTING ON A PEDESTAL

Sure, your sweetheart is the best, and you're so lucky to have him or her in your life. So what do you do sometimes? You put them on a pedestal and make them larger than life, transforming them into this image of a person that doesn't exist and that no one can possibly live up to (see *Disappointment*). Well get a grip, as you are not doing them, or you, any favors. It's not fair to either one of you. Stick with reality. They are just as human as you. No better.

PUTTING WORDS IN YOUR MOUTH

Accusing someone of putting words in your mouth is a popular excuse. But when you think about it, that's really not possible, as only you can control your words. Of course, there are other things they can put into your mouth, but I'm not talking about that (see *Hygiene*).

PUTTING YOUR BEST FOOT FORWARD

Well, you have a 50-50 chance of getting this right. Not that it really matters. Which would be your worst foot anyway?

PUTTING YOUR MIND TO IT

If you really put your mind to it, your body will follow (see *Exercise*). It just doesn't have a choice.

PUT UP OR SHUT UP

At some point, words become less effective, and acting on those words becomes much more important. Do what you say you'll do. Put up or shut up.

PUZZLES

Puzzles are great, especially jigsaws and crosswords. Finishing a jigsaw puzzle gives you a nice feeling (see *Accomplishment*). It's something you can start easily, is not very hard on the noggin and you can finish without too much trouble. However, it's not as mindless as you may think; some people have very organized strategies when putting a jigsaw puzzle together. On the other hand, crossword puzzles are often tough and difficult to complete—unless you find a shortcut (see *Cheating*). They are challenging and keep your smarts smart. The only person I knew who could usually finish a crossword puzzle—in pen, no less—was my grandmother. And she lived, really lived, well into her 90s. So what does that tell you?

QUALITY OF LIFE

Modern medicine is always trying to prolong life. That's usually a good thing. However, sometimes I think we lose sight of what people are living with. If the cure is worse than the disease, maybe it's not always worth it, and we should let nature take its course. We have to decide if extending someone's life is really for us or for them. And while we hate to see them go, we have to ask if extending their agony is worth it or allows for a higher quality of life. Oftentimes it doesn't.

QUALITY TIME

Quality isn't a function of the amount of time you spend; it's how you spend it. You know—uninterrupted, focused individual attention. Qualitative, not quantitative (yes, I like big words).

QUARTERBACK

The quarterback is probably the most pivotal position in all of sports. Even more important than the pitcher. So much depends on the quarterback that it's hard to win a football game with a bad one. They tend to have the most leadership (or losership) skills on the team.

QUEASY

Nothing _easy_ about feeling qu_easy_. I think this nasty feeling was invented to punish us for drinking too much (see _Alcohol_). And the only way you feel better is by throwing up. Go figure. Somewhat counterintuitive (look it up) if you ask me.

QUESTION

Don't answer a question with a question, as that's rather annoying. Repeating a question, or telling the questioner "that's a good question," is an obvious stall tactic, which is very transparent. So you want to be suspicious of those kinds of responses. If you don't know, you don't know. Now if you have a question, it rarely hurts to ask; so ask away.

QUESTIONS

Do yourself a favor and try not to ask these questions (see _Diplomatic_), as you might not like the answers. Either that or you'll get smacked.

Are those real?
Are we there yet?
Are you in yet?
Are you married?
Are you pregnant?
Did I do that?
Does my ass look big? (If you have to ask, the answer is yes.)
Do I look fat in this?
Do you know where you're going?
Do you love me?
Do you remember me?
Do you want to know the truth?
Hello, are you there?
How much do you weigh?
How old did you say you were?
Wanna fuck?
Was I married to you?
Was that you or me?

However, these questions are fine to ask:

> Are you feeling better?
> Can I help?
> Have you lost weight? (Make that sound like a real question; see *Sincerity*.)
> Is the Pope Catholic? (Never mind; you probably know the answer already.)
> Is there anything I can do?
> Wanna dance?

Now if the answer to any of these questions is yes, someone's in trouble:

> Are you out of your mind?
> Did somebody pee in your cornflakes this morning?
> You got a bug up your ass or something?

QUIPS

Being quick on the quip is a mark of intelligence. Just be careful you aren't too quick (see *Taking It Back*).

QUIRKY

Oh, it's cute to be quirky, as we all have our idiosyncrasies. Otherwise you'd be like everyone else, and who wants that (see *Normal*)? Want to know what a quirk of fate is? Ask someone else.

QUITTING

It's way too easy to quit; it's the ones who tough it out that really make it in this world. Quitters never win, and winners never quit (see *Giving Up*). And remember: quitters make bad lovers (a proven fact), and nobody likes a quitter. Unless, of course, you're the one who quit smoking. If so, everybody likes and admires you. If they don't, they should.

QUIT WHILE YOU'RE AHEAD

Some people sure have a knack for snatching defeat from the jaws of victory. Know when you've gotten what you were looking for, and stop. Leave well enough alone.

RABBI

The definition of rabbi is actually "teacher." Of course, I'm a big fan of teachers (see *Teachers*). A rabbi is a spiritual leader who teaches their congregants about life. We need lots of people to teach us about life; especially those who know something about it.

RACE

There is no such thing as a white or black race. We are all members of the human race. Except for those of us in the rat race. It's hard to win that race though.

RACEHORSE NAMES

Who names these horses, anyway? What if racehorses really knew what their names meant? How would they introduce themselves to other horses? "Hi, my name is Uncle Ralph's Sister." "Nice to meet you, my name is "Kiss My Ass." Does anyone consider that it could be very embarrassing for the horses? If it were me, I would be very nice to them (see *Paybacks*).

RADIATE

It's not just the sun that radiates, you know. We can all radiate. So radiate happiness, sweetness, gentleness and all the other goodnesses. Throw in some confidence and caring while you're at it.

RAGE

By far, the biggest cause of blindness is rage.

RAINY DAY

Rainy days were invented to give you an excuse to lie around and be worthless all day. It's a little bit like snow days (without having to shovel the snow or develop cabin fever). Some people want to save things for a rainy day. Not me. I don't want anything to get in the way of being lazy. All day long.

RAISING YOUR VOICE

If you constantly have to raise your voice to get your point across, you might want to rethink the effectiveness of your communication skills. In this case, they are severely lacking, as less is more.

RANDOM ACTS OF KINDNESS

Anonymously doing special things for complete strangers is the purest form of giving there is. It's such an easy way to put a smile on their faces—and on yours too.

RAPE

Words can't possibly describe the outrageous and despicable atrocity of rape. What would possess anybody to commit such a horrible, humiliating and violent act? To brutally take advantage of someone like that is unconscionable. And date rape? Listen guys, NO means NO! I don't care what the circumstances are. De-nutting (technical term for castration) these worthless bastards is too good for them.

RAP MUSIC

I mean no disrespect here (see *Politically Correct*), but why do they call this music? And please pardon my ignorance, but is there really a melody? It's just drum beats, right? At best, it's poetry—maybe. Anybody ever hear of articulation, by the way?

RATIONALIZING

The human mind can be very innovative and inventive. When we put our minds to it, we can actually rationalize almost anything: borrowing (stealing) cupcakes, starting wars, cheating, you name it. You can find excuses to do lots of things. But the only one you can't ever fool is yourself.

REACH OUT

Extending your hand to someone who needs it speaks volumes about your character. You want volumes.

REACTION

There is a principle in physics that says "For every action, there is an equal and opposite reaction. "If someone's reaction to your action is unnatural or particularly nasty (or overreaction, as we say), you've got to assume other things are going on. It could be their pent up anger relating to another issue entirely. Or they could just be nuts. It may pay to ask—that is, if you're not afraid of getting your head bitten off—as it's always possible the reaction has nothing to do with you (see *Misplaced Anger*).

READ BETWEEN THE LINES

You'll never know what you'll find reading between the lines (especially these lines) unless you look very closely (see *Subtle*). This is one of the beauties of the English language. We slow readers have a clear advantage with this one.

READING

Reading opens up all kinds of exciting new worlds. Using your imagination to visualize the written word can be magical and limitless. So be a voracious (I don't know what that means, but it sounds so cool) reader, and read all you can, when you can. Remember: reading is <u>fun</u>damental, so go ahead and read—and read—and read some more. You might even learn something.

READING IN THE CAR

There are two kinds of people in this world: those who can read in the car, and those who can't. I can't, as I'll throw up. How others can do it is beyond me. Now reading while driving is probably not such a good idea.

READING MINDS

We can't read other people's minds, although we often think we can. I for one have no desire to know what's going on inside someone else's head; I have enough trouble knowing what's going on inside mine. We'd clearly know what others thought of us—and that might not be a good thing.

READY

Even when you think you're really prepared, surprises come along. You can't be ready for everything.

REALITY

Reality sucks? Well maybe, but I'll take a good dose of reality any day. You may not like it, but knowing is much better than not knowing.

REALITY CHECK

Sure, it's a good idea to check occasionally to see if you're on the right planet. Imagination can only take you so far.

REALITY SHOWS

There's nothing real about reality TV. They should call it voyeuristic TV—or unreality TV. How real can anyone be when there are cameras following their every move? Some people get off watching others humiliate and embarrass themselves in the most unrealistic situations. In fact, many people enjoy it. I don't; it's a stupid waste of time.

REAL MEN

Of course real men don't eat quiche; and real men don't wear tights. But oh yes, real men surely do cry (see *Feelings*).

REAL THING

Ain't nothing like the real thing. There really isn't. After all, fake is so fake.

REASON vs. EXCUSE

Reasons and excuses are often confused. Examples of valid reasons are as follows:

> I didn't call (or come over) because:
>
>> I didn't want to.
>> I got into a car accident.
>> I was too busy.
>> My house burned down.
>> My dog died.

Excuses are these:

> I didn't call (or come over) because:
>
>> I ran out of time.
>> I won the lottery.
>> My alarm didn't go off.
>> My dog ate my homework.
>> My cat died.

REASONS

There's a reason for everything (or almost everything). We're just not always smart enough to figure it out, since the reason may not be so obvious. It often reveals itself and becomes apparent in very interesting ways. So stay tuned.

REASSURING

Be the reassuring type. If people come to you to be reassured, you're definitely on the right track in the life department (see *Character*).

REBOUND GIRL OR GUY

Yes, after the breakup of a serious relationship, the rebound person gives you all of the things you allegedly missed the last time: attention, attention and, of course, more attention. But the things you didn't have before and crave the most do not necessarily make for a happily ever after. Rebound relationships definitely fill a void and serve a purpose, but rarely last forever. A starving person doesn't solve all of their problems with a slice of bread. Therefore, marrying the rebound girl or guy is usually a huge mistake. Give yourself plenty of time to recover and better understand yourself before you settle down again, so you won't repeat your mistakes. You don't buy the first new pair of shoes or new dress you see, do you? Well, maybe you do.

RECHARGING YOUR BATTERIES

A little catnap here and there is a good way to recharge your batteries. Nap away.

RECIPE FOR DISASTER

Sometimes you really can predict the future. You can look at something and just see that it's a recipe for disaster. If you see it coming, you ought to do something about it. Fortunately, those of us who are of the cooking-challenged variety don't have to worry about these or any other recipes. (God knows what kinds of consequences would result.) Which is another reason to stay out of the kitchen.

RECOGNITION

It's human nature to enjoy being recognized for your accomplishments Just make sure that is not your primary motivation for doing good (see *Self-Serving*).

RECYCLING

We live in a very wasteful society. If we're tired of something or it doesn't work right, we just throw it away. Well, the world doesn't have enough room for all of our trash, as even landfills have their limits. There's only so much garbage we can bury. When you take the time to sort your trash and separate the junk that can be recycled, you help to solve that problem. You also help provide raw materials to the industries that can use your leftover crap. Recycle away.

RED LIGHT

Yes, there are way too many red lights in this world; but that doesn't excuse you from stopping at them anyway. Same with stop signs.

RED MEAT

Oh, go on and admit it: you like red meat. It tastes good and it really won't kill you (see *Moderation*). After all, we are carnivores, you know. Otherwise you have to get your protein and iron from something else, like that nasty tofu. Yech.

REENACTORS

You know those people who think they're Robert E. Lee, all dressed up, hanging around Civil War sites? Well, they really scare me. Because Robert E. Lee is dead, right?

REFLECTING

Mirrors only reflect an image. What's inside is sometimes very hard to see. It's usually good to sit back (or stand up) and reflect on things. The fancy term for this is self-evaluation.

REFRIGERATE

If in doubt, put it in the fridge. You can't go wrong. That is, unless it's already rotten.

REGRETS

Regrets—we all have a few; but then again, some have too few to mention (thanks Frank). However, others have a lot more than a few. We tend to regret the things we haven't done, not the things we have, which is another reason to always try. Not much you can do about it, except to learn from your mistakes (see *Look Ahead*). Now as for me, I've always regretted not being five inches taller and born into royalty. Both have been a lifelong problem for me.

REINVENTING THE WHEEL

Sorry, too late. It's been done already. Lots of times.

REJECTION

Rejection is one of the hardest emotions to deal with. Being unwanted is such a miserable feeling. But their loss is someone else's gain. Remember that the next time someone slams a door in your face.

REJUVENATE

To rejuvenate is fine, but wouldn't you be better off if you just juvenated it right in the first place? I can't stand redoing things.

RELATIONSHIPS

Relationships don't just happen. Successful ones are built and usually require plenty of work and nurturing to maintain. Once you forsake them, they will forsake you.

RELIABLE

Unfortunately, you can't always rely on people. Be the exception.

RELIEF

Relief is another one of those feelings that's completely beyond description (see *Gotta Go*). The feeling you get when you find out the test is negative (or positive, if that's what you're looking for), or when that police car with the siren blaring goes after someone else, is indescribable. Indescribable—but a wonderful feeling.

RELIGION

I strongly believe that organized religion serves a useful purpose. There are many ways you can choose to practice your religion, as long as you believe in something. However, there are those who go overboard with religious teachings, customs and traditions (see *Hypocrites*). Better to treat those precepts as guidelines and examples for living a wholesome life. Taking religious principles to their literal extremes and out of context can blind you to the general meaning of the very philosophies you are trying to follow. Keep it simple and balanced.

RELIGIOUS CONVERSION

Only change your religion when you're moved by strong beliefs, not just to please someone else. If you're simply trying to appease them and make them happy, it's not worth it. Stay where you are instead.

REMARKABLE

If you think about it—I mean really think about it—the way the world works is truly remarkable. Flowers bloom, trees grow, birds fly, winds blow, dead skin falls off. It's all rather cool, if you ask me. And I know you're asking.

REMEMBERING

Am I the only one who has trouble here? I can remember every useless fact and insignificant detail about some of the most ridiculous things. But don't ask me what I did yesterday. When I'm trying to remember something, I go through the alphabet to help jog my memory; fortunately, I can still remember my ABCs. You can try that too. Or when you forget something, you can just sit down, and it will likely come back to you (see *Patience*).

REPETITION

Repetition is my middle name (that's what the N stands for). Sometimes you've got to say the same thing lots of different ways to get your point across (see *Sure Dad, You Know Everything*).

REPLACEABLE

Sorry to say, but in the grand scheme of things, we're all replaceable. Everyone is special, but none of us are all that important. The earth will continue to spin and most activities will go on just fine without us—or without them.

REPRIMAND

Reprimand your children all you want. Just don't do it in front of anyone else, especially their friends. Talk about lasting scars. If you can reprimand without screaming, you'll really get somewhere (see *Parenting*).

REPUTATION

Your reputation is one of your most important assets. (I said assets, not asses—grow up, will you?) And it's usually something you can influence. Everybody in this world isn't going to like you; so what! Remember: it mostly matters what you think about you, not what others think. So if you're a dirty rotten bastard and are proud of it and everybody knows it, then live and be well. But if people think you're a dirty rotten bastard and you're not, straighten them out. It's worth it.

RESILIENT

It's the ones who can take the constant pounding in life that tend to last the longest. Grow a thick skin and be resilient.

RESOURCEFUL

Those resourceful people really have it over everyone else. So go ahead and use your special abilities to impress the hell out of people. Do the most with what you have. The more innovative you are, the more points you score in the game of life.

RESPECT

Respect should be automatic for older people. All others should have to earn it, as nobody has it just coming to them. Sadly, respect is something which seems to be in rather short supply in our society today. Too bad. You can't control others' feelings, but you certainly can respect people in general—older and younger.

RESPECTING PRIVACY

Sure, you want to help your friends and family when you think they need you. But sometimes they decide it's important to keep things to themselves. Some topics are simply off limits, and you need to accept that. You'll show them lots of respect if you let their private issues stay private. It goes both ways, as you want them to respect your privacy too.

RESPONSIBILITY

Boy, sometimes responsibility sucks. It's usually kind of an adult thing, but after a while, you really have to be responsible. Shirking isn't generally allowed; shucking either. If things are always someone else's fault, it's likely your issue, not theirs. The earlier you learn to take responsibility, the better, because as you get older, you have more and more things to be responsible for. If you're lucky, you'll have family, job, coworkers, friends, house, spouse, children, you name it, to deal with. Unfortunately, responsibility is not a subject they teach in school; you've got to learn it on the job.

REST

Is there no rest for the weary? Of course there is. Go take a nap when you're tired. It's always best to pace yourself, because if you go a hundred percent all of the time, you'll burn yourself out (see *Cremation*).

RESTING ON YOUR LAURELS

Unfortunately, we live in a "what have you done for me lately" world. Too many people tend to have short memories, which can force us to have to prove ourselves again and again. That may not necessarily be so bad, as we'll tend to stay helpful and productive that way. But there are times when your good reputation should count for something.

RESTRAINT

It's often a lot harder to hold yourself back, rather than immediately reacting to something or someone that's irritating you. If you show some restraint, you will really display your strength. No sweat is typically involved.

RETIREMENT

You've worked all of your life, and it gets to be time to hang it up. So now what do you do? You find something to do, that's what. Put your life experiences to good use, as there are plenty of people and organizations that can benefit from your expertise and wisdom. The last thing you want to do is sit around in your jammies and watch TV all the time. Everyone needs a place to go each day (see *Routine*). If you don't have a sense of purpose in life, you'll just shrivel up and die. And who wants to do that?

RETURNING PHONE CALLS

Returning phone calls within 24 hours is the rule of thumb here. If you don't want to talk to someone, call them back at lunchtime. Or tell them you died.

REVERSE PSYCHOLOGY

Reverse psychology doesn't work anymore. People, especially the little ones, are way too smart to fall for that. It's the end of an era.

RIGHT

Just thinking you're right doesn't make you right. You have to convince others that you are right.

RIGHTY TIGHTY, LEFTY LOOSEY

Righty tighty, lefty loosey is my motto. You want to keep this in mind whenever you're in the Harry or Harriet Homeowner mode; it'll save you lots of trouble. But for the real stubborn ones, just take a sledgehammer to them.

RIGHT-OF-WAY

You can only give someone else the right-of-way, as you can't take it (I learned that in driver's ed class). It's just a fancy way of saying you should let them go first.

RIGHT vs. WRONG

Unfortunately, some people seem to have trouble knowing the difference between right and wrong. If you really have doubts, it's probably the wrong thing to do. And simply getting away with something doesn't make it right.

RIGHT WAY

Not only is the right way usually the best way, but it's most often the only way.

RISE AND SHINE

Is waking up fun or what? Definitely what. Who really likes to rise and shine? Just leave us alone and let us sleep.

RISING TO THE OCCASION

Until you're challenged, you'll never know what you can do when you put your mind to it (see *Strength*). We humans are remarkably capable, especially in the worst of circumstances and situations, so you may surprise yourself.

RISK

Yes, life is full of risks, many of which you can't control. But life without any risk can be rather dull. When you have a choice, it's not wise to risk what you can't afford to lose—including yourself (see *Reputation*); that's called a calculated risk. And if you insist on engaging in very risky behaviors, you may just wake up dead one day. Here's how it works. If you have nothing, then you have nothing to lose. But if you've got something, you have something to lose. (Hint: we all have at least something.) The potential gain should be more valuable than the potential loss. So keep that in mind the next time you are thinking about going for broke.

ROAD RAGE

What's all this road rage about? So someone cut you off—BFD (see *Initials*). There are lots more important things in life to get upset about. Get over it. Now if you are the victim of this absurd behavior, keep your windows up and don't engage the idiot. Just quietly drive away (see *Risk*).

ROLE MODELS

Like it or not, we're all role models (both good and bad) for children. They tend to mimic what they see and look up to all adults, even the jerks. Since children are typically very observant, our behavior often leaves a lasting impression on them. So watch what you do when they are nearby. Always.

ROMAN NUMERALS

I get so confused with Roman numerals. We don't use Chinese or Hebrew numerals, do we? Why can't we just use regular numbers?

ROMANTIC

Being romantic is a nice way to fulfill your dreams of the ultimate loving relationship. The beneficiary of this attention might like it as well. Go for it.

ROOTS

Always remember where you came from. We all have roots, and they stay with us forever. Some we have to overcome and others we embrace. Keep this in mind when assembling your guide to life (see *Perspective*).

ROUND TUIT

Ah, the ever elusive round tuits. They are indigenous to most Western civilizations and aren't as hard to find as one might expect. Procrastinators, for instance, are always looking to get a round tuit. Get it?

ROUTINES

We all need routines and function much better with them. It's about having order in your life. If you don't have some scheduled activity most days, you will likely find it unsettling and unproductive (see *Couch Potato*). Now sometimes we fall into bad routines, so be careful of obsessive-compulsive stuff; that's nuts.

RUBBERNECKING

Really? Can't you keep your eyes off that accident or the car that just got pulled over? These situations are often on the other side of the median, for God's sake. Must you slow down and look? Sure is a nice way to contribute to traffic jams and other problems.

RUBBING IT IN

OK, great. So this time you were right. One hundred percent right. You know it, and they know it too. Be a big person and just leave it at that (see *Paybacks*).

RUDENESS

Rudeness is a nasty quality, and one you shouldn't possess. Not liking or not respecting someone doesn't excuse you from having proper manners (see *Impolite*).

RULES

Rules are made to be broken? Hardly. They are made for a reason and need to be followed. Now that's not to say you can't bend them a little, but if some rules seem unfair and really bother you, go get them changed (see *Democracy*). You'll likely stay out of trouble that way.

RUMORS

Spreading rumors is an exercise in stupidity. Rumors are rarely true, and some can be quite nasty and vicious. Mindlessly passing them on is a very heartless and hurtful thing to do to someone. It's therefore wise to confirm your facts before talking about people.

RUN AND HIDE

You can usually run, but you can't always hide (see *Accountability*). You will probably find you.

RUNNING

Running is a good but not great exercise, as it's tough on your body in the long run (get it—long run?). A good run tends to clear your head though. Ever notice that most runners don't smile when they pass you? Probably because it's so much like work (or maybe it's the chafing). In any case, never run alone; especially you ladies. And those headphones may take your mind off the monotony, but they keep you from hearing what's going on around you, and that can be rather dangerous too; so lose them. Who wants to be run over by a tractor trailer before you can hear it coming? You'd rather be run over after you hear it, right?

RUNNING AWAY

Even if you're very, very fast, you likely can't escape whatever it is that you're trying to run away from. Especially if it's in your head.

RUNNING INTERFERENCE

If you're a bit on the timid side and want to know if the object of your affection likes you, it's perfectly OK to use an intermediary to find out. It's always nice to have someone do your advance work, at least to get you started. This strategy may also cut down on awkward situations, especially when you can't read the other person's signals—or lack thereof (see *Embarrassing Moments*).

RUNNING UP THE SCORE

So you won. Does it really matter by how much (see *Rubbing It In*)?

RUTHLESS

If being ruthless is bad, does that mean ruthmore is good? How do you get more ruth, anyway? I'm so perplexed by these unanswered questions.

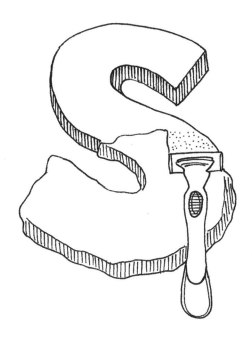

S

Too bad we can't find a way to eliminate these S's:

> Sadness
> Sickness
> Sorrow
> Suffering

SACRIFICE

There are times when you have to sacrifice some of what you have so others can have something. That's just the way it is, so get used to it (see *Charity*).

SADNESS

Yes, sadness is part of life, and our world has way too much unhappiness in it. When you can, work to keep the teary things to a minimum, and try to turn the sadness into gladness.

SAFETY

It sure is better to be safe than sorry. And you can never be too safe, you know (see *Accidents Waiting To Happen*). Well, maybe you can. You don't want to be too sorry though. Now remember: there really is safety and strength in numbers. Another reason to keep your friends and family close.

SAGGING

Yeah, as we get older, lots of our body parts start to sag. Blame it on gravity.

SALIVA

Saliva was invented to aid in the digestive process. So keep it in your mouth at all times (see *Spitting*).

SAME OLD

If you always do what you always did, then you'll always get what you always got. You might want to write that down. (I just did.)

SAMSON EFFECT

I ascribe to the proven theory that haircuts sap your strength. Just ask Samson. As luck would have it, ladies, this only happens to the guys.

SANCTIMONIOUS

Watch out for sanctimonious people, as they're probably the biggest hypocrites you'll ever meet.

SANDMAN

You'd think that Sandman guy would have better things to do than run around and put all that gook in our eyes at night. Maybe he could do something more productive, like do our laundry while we're sleeping.

SANITY

Who is really sane? You define it—then we'll both know (see *Normal*). Be my guest.

Sandman

SANTA CLAUS

Of course there's a Santa Claus. Probably even more than one. It's a big world, you know; way too big for one person to handle. I sure do like that twinkle in his eye; it seems is so genuine. But I think he's in semi-retirement now, hanging out with the Tooth Fairy and the Sandman, and having those elves do most of the work. The elves get very little credit, but they're the ones who run around doing all of those wonderful things. And you'd be very surprised to know who these elves are, as they wear very clever disguises. They mostly look just like you and me, mixing in with the general population. Of course, Santa only comes out during Christmastime, checking those lists and all. (This is absolutely true, so be good, for goodness sake.) And oh yeah Virginia, there is certainly a Virginia.

SARCASM

Sarcasm usually masks truthful thoughts and comments, and some of us would be completely lost without it. You don't have to read very far to find plenty of it here. Sorry, I can't help it. You wouldn't want me to be lost now, would you (see *Sense Of Direction*)?

SATISFACTION

We often live our lives trying to satisfy everybody else. But the only one you really have to satisfy is yourself.

SAVING

You don't just save for a rainy day. You should be saving for every day. It's not too hard: just make an automatic deduction from your paycheck into your savings account. You won't miss it or spend it; and one day you'll wake up and have a pile of money lying around. Now I don't know why you would save for posterity, because I have no idea who that is.

SAYINGS/QUOTES

I don't know who said these, but I like 'em:

> Absolute power corrupts absolutely.
> A life of passion will keep you alive.
> An exercise in futility is an exercise in stupidity.
> A place for everything, and everything all over the place.

Building character is doing right when no one else is watching (too bad General Petraeus didn't listen to himself).

Do what you say, and say what you do.

Don't eat the yellow snow (see *Urinating*).

Don't open a door you can't close.

Don't sweat the small stuff (it's all small stuff—except the big stuff).

Don't talk about it—be about it.

Even if you're on the right track, you'll be run over if you just sit there (had to be Will Rogers).

Everyone gets theirs (it may take some longer than others, but they all get theirs, since what goes around comes around—just stick around and watch).

Failing to plan is planning to fail.

Failure is not falling down; failure is falling down and not trying to get back up.

Finish what you start.

From your mouth to God's ears.

Get on the train or be run over by it.

Giving is good for the soul.

God helps the needy, not the greedy.

Good friends are family you choose.

I'd rather fail at something I love, than succeed at something I hate (actually, George Burns said it, but he may have stolen it from someone else).

If fate hands you a lemon, open up a lemonade stand (you have to go through a lot of lemons to make lemonade though).

If in doubt, throw it out.

If it ain't broke, don't fix it (please forgive the poor English).

If this van's a-rockin', don't come a knockin'.

If you always do what you always did, then you'll always get what you always got (I've said that before, but it bears repeating).

If you can't have the most of what you want, it's best to make the most of what you have.

If you can't stand the heat, get out of the kitchen (no problem for me— I'm lost in the kitchen).

If you can't take it, don't dish it out.

If you can't tell your mother or your children about it, then you probably shouldn't be doing it.

If you don't ask, the answer is always no.

If you don't have something nice to say, don't say it (good advice, but I've really got to work on that one).

If you don't like the answers, don't ask the questions.

If you don't stand for something, you stand for nothing.

If you don't stand for something, you'll fall for everything.

If you lie down with dogs, you wake up with fleas.

If you live in the past, you die in the past (Mike Ditka was on to something).

If you love what you do, you'll always do what you love.

If you're not moving forward, you're falling behind.

If you're not part of the problem, be part of the solution.

If you're swimming in unfamiliar areas, turn around; don't drown.

If you see something, say something (advice from the police).

It's never the place; it's always the people.

It's not what you gather in life, but what you scatter to the world.

Keep your eyes on the prize.

Knowledge is power.

Luck is where opportunity meets preparation.

Measure twice, cut once.

Never let the facts get in the way of a good argument.

Never make a promise you can't keep.

Nice and easy does it every time.

No guard in the stand—keep your feet in the sand (at the beach).

No matter what, hold your head up high.

No one can make you feel inferior without your consent (OK, so I found out that Eleanor Roosevelt said this).

Once you get rid of the crap in your life, windows and doors open wide.

One man's ceiling is another man's floor (oops, that's Paul Simon).

People don't care how much you know until they know how much you care.

Put things back where you found them.

Quitters never win, and winners never quit.

Retire from the business; don't let the business retire you.

Teachers don't teach for the income; they teach for the outcome.

The arc of history is long and bends toward justice (MLK really had a way with words).

The better it tastes, the worse it is for you.

The difference between stupidity and genius is that genius has its limits (and who understood this better than Albert Einstein).

The man upstairs gives the hardest battles to his strongest soldiers (same goes for the woman upstairs).

The mind can only absorb as much as the tush can tolerate.

There is no shame in failure; the only shame is in not trying.

Time is a terrible thing to waste.

Tough situations don't last; tough people do.

Treat people as you would like to be treated.

Verify before you vilify.

Vision without execution is hallucination.

We are not responsible for the sins of our fathers.

We can't solve problems by using the same thinking we used to create them (more words of genius from my hero Mr. Einstein).

We don't stop laughing because we get old; we get old because we stop laughing.

Whatever doesn't kill you makes you stronger.

When you're deep in a hole, stop digging (duh).

Women/Men! You can't live with them, and you can't live without them (see *Choices*).

Work to live; don't live to work.

You can't make sense out of nonsense (thank you, Debra).

Your children will someday become who you are, so be who you want them to be.

SAY IT

No one can read your mind; so if you've got something cooking in there, just say so. Speak your mind, and exercise your First Amendment rights. However, be sure to say it; don't spray it. We want the news, not the weather, you know (see *Enunciate*).

SCARY MOVIES

Do you really enjoy "entertainment" that causes you to pee in your pants and have bad dreams? Some enjoy having the shit scared out of them; I don't. I'd much prefer to see some mindless, silly movie, as that's entertainment to me. Especially if it has a happy ending. Call me simple.

SCHMALTZ

There's way too much schmaltz in TV sports reporting, especially during important events like the Olympics. Up close and personal, my ass. Just let me watch the game, race or match already. Save it for the real dramas.

SCHOOL CLOTHES

Whatever happened to school clothes? There used to be a difference between play clothes and school clothes. I guess we now play at school too.

SCHOOL'S OUT

After another long, insufferable year, school's out. Oh, what a feeling! Just remember that your newfound freedom may be rather short-lived, as summer doesn't last forever (see *Good Things*). But then again, neither does summer school.

SCHOOL SPIRIT

Be true to your school, especially your high school, as you will spend some of your most formative years there and make lasting memories. Once you graduate, you won't ever see most of your classmates again. Too bad (or maybe that's not so bad).

SCRATCHING

Ah, the age-old question: to scratch or not to scratch. Oh, go ahead and scratch (see *Itch*). You'll feel better. And who cares who's watching or what you look like. Like they never had to scratch in those nasty places either?

SCREAMING COACHES

Please tell me why a coach thinks that players will respond well to yelling and screaming? Is fear a better motivator than supportive instruction? Sure, in the heat of battle, emotions typically can run wild, and it likely gets very frustrating when the players aren't performing up to the expectations of their coaches. But hollering at the players, especially publicly, can be very demoralizing and unproductive. There are better ways to achieve success. Try a little tenderness, will ya?

SCREWING UP

It's bad enough to screw up, but lying about it just makes it worse. If you own up, they'll go easier on you. Well, at least they say they will.

SEAT BELTS

Seat belts are not in your car for decoration. If you don't use them *every time you're in a car*, you're pretty stupid. THEY SAVE LIVES. PERIOD. (Am I clear here?). Don't be an idiot—use your seat belt.

SECOND CHANCE

Everybody deserves a second chance. Sometimes they even deserve a third chance. Just don't let that be an excuse to be used and stepped on (see *Doormat*). Now if someone is good enough to give *you* another chance, don't waste it.

SECOND-GENERATION LEADERS

Ever wonder why you don't hear much about George Washington's offspring? Or Abe Lincoln's, or FDR's or other great leaders'? That's because the famous guys drained most of the family brain trust, which didn't leave much to pass on. Good thing that works for dictators too.

SECOND-GUESSING

What's the point of second-guessing? There isn't any way to undo something that has already happened. And you can end up undermining an important decision by questioning your judgment after the fact. Hindsight gives you an unfair advantage, so it's best to simply save your breath (see *Coulda, Woulda, Shoulda*).

SECOND OPINION

No, doctors don't know everything. Sometimes they are even wrong, and it's not necessarily their fault. However, if they give you bad news—I mean really bad news—get a second opinion. That's not being in denial or shopping for better news. It's making absolutely sure.

SECRET

Secrets are often hard to keep, but sometimes really fun to tell (see *Temptation*). However, you want to be a trusted soul for your friends and family, and not reveal confidential information. We all have our own secrets that we really don't have to share with anyone. Oh, and an open secret is *not* a secret.

SECRET OF LIFE

What is the secret of life? I can't tell you—it's a secret. Aren't you learning anything here?

SECURITY

Sure, burglar alarms are fine, but the best way to keep the bad guys away is to have lots of outside lights. And it really helps to turn them on at night. However, you don't want to have your house all lit up like a Christmas tree (see *Moderation*). But it seems that burglars, vampires and the Wolf Man have plenty in common: being afraid of the light is one of them.

SEEING IS BELIEVING

Seeing isn't always believing, as sometimes the hand is quicker than the eye. So seeing can be very deceiving. Another reason to pay close attention.

SEEING THE LIGHT

Go ahead and follow the light, and mend your ways. It's never too late, you know.

SEEKING A MATE

Before making final decisions on your choice of a lifemate, make sure you witness them in full-raging anger mode. If you can handle that behavior, it's a match made in heaven.

SELECTIVE MEMORY

We tend to remember things we want to remember, and the way we want to remember them. Unfortunately, the truth usually gets in the way. Reality sucks sometimes.

SELF

When you have a little spare time (and some courage), take a good hard look in the mirror. If you're not madly in love with yourself, find out why and fix it (see *Psychotherapy*). God knows, if you don't love yourself, who will?

Security

SELF-ABSORBED

A sign of being self-absorbed is writing a book consisting entirely of your own incessant ramblings (see *Ego*).

SELF-APPOINTED LEADERS

Self-appointed leaders are not always the best ones to have in charge. It's one thing to step up and help out, but you really want to get a consensus from the rank and file before you crown yourself emperor (see *Democracy*).

SELF-CENTERED

It's always about you, isn't it? I hate to burst your bubble, but you're not the center of the universe—or of your own little world either. Look around. There are plenty of other people on this planet, and the world does not revolve around you. Not even a little bit.

SELF-CONSCIOUS

Chances are, the thing you're most self-conscious about, nobody else even notices. They're too busy worrying about their own imperfections.

SELF-CONTROL

Sad but true that it's way too easy to give in to life's impulses and distractions. So if you can't control yourself, who do you expect will? It's all up to you.

SELF-DEPRECATING

If you can't laugh at yourself, you're taking things way too seriously. Go ahead and celebrate your self-inflicted funny moments. I obviously do.

SELF-DOUBT

Of course we all have doubts about ourselves. It's safe to say that you're not the only one who's not so sure about everything. Welcome to the human race.

SELF-FULFILLING PROPHECY

It seems that if you are absolutely determined to fail, you will. That's a self-fulfilling prophecy.

SELF-HELP

Self-help is the best help there is.

SELF-IMAGE

Why, oh why don't we ever sound or look like we think we do? Looking in the mirror or hearing a recording of ourselves is typically a real letdown. Self-image is usually way different from those reflections. (Blame bad lighting and malfunctioning audio equipment.) I prefer not to see or hear how others view me and live in my own fantasy world, believing that I'm tall and handsome, with a deep resonant voice (see *Reality*).

SELF-IMPORTANCE

Some people have a really bad case of self-importance—and go to great lengths to make sure everyone knows it. Don't be fooled. They are no more important than you.

SELFISH

Me, me, me. Consider others once in a while. Now this is a kind of fish I wouldn't mind seeing extinct.

SELFLESS

To be selfless is to be a hero in many people's eyes. Even your own.

SELF-MEDICATING

Are you a doctor? If not, leave prescribing medication to the professionals. They usually know way more than you do.

SELF-PITY

So you think if you feel sorry for yourself, everyone else will join you—and somehow that will solve your problems? All you'll accomplish is to make them worse (see *Do Something*).

SELF-PRESERVATION

Take care of your body, and your body will take care of you.

SELF-PROMOTION

You want to stay away from those who insist on telling you how great they are. They are mostly trying to convince themselves.

SELF-RELIANT

Who can you rely on if you can't rely on yourself?

SELF-RESPECT

If you don't respect yourself, what makes you think someone else will?

SELF-RIGHTEOUS

Often the ones who preach the most and the loudest about the evils of wayward living tend to be the biggest waywarders (see *Hypocrites*).

SELF-SACRIFICE

There's sacrifice, and then there's self-sacrifice. Either way, there's plenty of blood involved. Unfortunately, these rituals are not as outdated as you might think (see *Shaving*).

SELF-SERVING

How insincere can you get? If your only motivation to do something good, nice or right is to raise your perceived stature in the eyes of others, you've really missed the boat. You've actually missed a lot of boats.

SELF-SOOTHING

We all have our own ways to calm ourselves down. Some sing, some hum, some rock back and forth, and some bang their heads against the wall (I'm an expert at that). It's kind of an individual thing, so go with whatever works for you. Just make sure your soothing ways don't disgust others who might be watching (see *Nose Picking*).

SELF-SUFFICIENT

No one can be totally self-sufficient in this world. You still have to depend on somebody. That's a good thing.

SENSATIONALIST JOURNALISM

Does an impending snowstorm have to mean the end of the world? Do all news events have to be laced with insinuations of scandal? Does every good intention have to suggest a hidden agenda? Instead of the exaggerated and often spectacular reporting of the news, unbiased and unemotional journalism would be much more effective and productive. (One can dream, can't one?)

SENSE OF DIRECTION

There are those who were born with a sense of direction, and those who were not. Unfortunately, it appears that I was busy talking to my neighbor when they were handing this out. So those of us who are directionally challenged can either ask for directions (against the law for men), look at a map or never stray very far from a GPS. The last seems to be the smartest choice—if you can stand that lady constantly telling you that you are going the wrong way. Some of us just get used to her.

SENSE OF HUMOR

If you have a sense of humor, consider yourself lucky, as it's a very valuable quality to possess. If you don't—sorry, you can't fake it, so it's best not to try. Stay home, lock your door, draw your shades and live like a hermit. Others will simply find the humor in that.

SENSES

Most people think we have only five senses, but they're wrong. There are actually 20:

Abandonment	Pride
Accomplishment	Relief
Belonging	Right and Wrong
Calm	Security (it's usually false)
Common	Sight
Direction	Smell
Extra-sensory perception (or ESPN)	Sound
Fairness	Taste
Honor	Touch
Humor	Urgency (see *Gotta Go*)

Sense of entitlement doesn't count. Oh, sorry, there are really 21. I forgot nonsense.

SENSITIVITY

We'd all be better off if we showed more sensitivity. Everyone is human, and it's nice to display that sometimes.

SEPARATING THE MEN FROM THE BOYS

I don't make a distinction between men and boys. Real men have lots of boy in them. Otherwise, they're just old men (see *Age*).

SEQUELS

Why try to improve on a masterpiece? If the original was that good, what makes you think the next one will be better? Still waiting for the Mona Lisa II or Whistler's Father? The sequels are rarely as good as the first, and hardly ever better. Anyway, the wild hype around the sequel is usually a bad sign (see *Disappointment*). Of course, I take all of this back (and then some) if this book becomes popular. Capitalism is alive and well with this boy. Ready for Volume II?

SERIOUSLY

Lighten up, and don't take everything so seriously—especially yourself. That's one way to get old fast. Adding a little levity helps in most situations. However, you may want to go easy on the jokes during an earthquake or other disaster.

SETTLING

When you settle for something, keep in mind that you are likely lowering your standards. If it's something you can control, it may not be worth it. So don't settle unless you really have to.

SEX

Don't get me wrong: sex is great, but it's way overemphasized in every aspect of our society. Sex can be wonderful (acrobatic sex can be dangerous—or dangerously wonderful), especially when it's with someone you love, but some people are very casual and cavalier about it. Like there are no consequences resulting from this intimacy. Right? Don't they call it making love for a reason? We spend way too much time and effort obsessing and worrying about sex (see *Lust*). If we put all of that emphasis and attention toward something else (like curing cancer), just think how much better off we all would be. Oh, and yes, oral sex is sex (sorry, Mr. Clinton).

SEXIST

In our politically correct world, it's no longer appropriate to be gender specific in our conversations. There is now no such thing as an actress, stewardess or waitress. In my humble quest to keep up with the times and recognize equality between the sexes, I've deleted the following references to our male-dominated society from my daily word usage (see *Extremes* and *Obnoxious*). You should too; that is, if you're an idiot like me:

Abdomen
Acumen
Admen
Advance man
Airmail
Airman
Alan Ladd
Al Jolson
All man
Almanac
Altar boy
All the King's Men
Amana
Amanda
A Man for All Seasons
A man of few words
Amen
Amend
Amman
Anchorman
Animal husbandry
Antihistamine
Ape man
Army man
Artillery man
Assemblymen
Ass man
Astro Boy
Atta boy

Ax Men
Backstreet Boys
Bad boy
Bad guys
Bag man
Baha Men
Bail bondsman
Ball boy
Barry Manilow
Bass man
Batboy
Batman
Batsman
Beach Boys
Bedfellows (especially the
    strange ones)
Bellboy
Bellman
Best boy
Best man
Better man
Betting man
Big Boy
Big Brother
Big Daddy
Big man
Big Sur
Birdman
Blackmail

Blood brother
Boatman
Boisie, Idaho
Boisterous
Bondsman
Boogie Man
Bowery Boys
Boycott
Boyfriend
Boy George
Boyhood
Boyhood home
Boy oh boy
Boys and girls
Boy Scout
Boysenberry
Boys in blue
Boys in the Band
Boys of Summer
Boys room
Boystown
Boys will be boys
Boy toy
Boyz II Men
Boyz n the Hood
Brakeman
Breast man
Brethren
Brinkmanship
Brotherhood
Brotherly love
Bub
Bud
Buddy
Buddy boy
Bugle boy
Buoyant
Busboy
Bushman
Businessmen
Cabana boy

Cable guy
Camera man
Candyman
Carmen
Cash man
Catmandoo
Cattle man
Cavalryman
Caveman
Certificate (think about it)
Chairman
Changed man
Chapstick
Charles Mann
Chef Boyardee
Chico and the Man
Choir boy
City boy
Command
Common man
Company man
Congressmen
Con man
Consummate gentleman
Copy boy
Corpsman
Councilman
Counterman
Countermanded
Country boy
Countrymen
Cowboy
Coxman (see *Sex*)
Craftsmen
Crawdad
Crazy man
Crewman
Culligan Man
Cutoff man
Dad
Daddy

Daddy longlegs
Dairyman
Danny Boy
David Letterman
Dead man
Dear old Dad
Delivery boy
Delivery man
Demand
Dexter Manley
Dirty boy
Dirty old man
Dismantle
Doggie Daddy
Doodad
Doorman
Doughboy
Down boy
Draftsman
Dude
Ed McMahon
Eggman
Elephant Man
E-mail
Emanate
Emancipate
Emanuel
Enlisted man
Everybody and their brother
Everyman
Every man for himself
Express Mail
Fair-haired boy
Fairy godfather
Fall guy
Family Guy
Family man
Fan mail
Farm boy
Father
Father and daughter

Father and son
Father Christmas
Father figure
Fatherhoodw
Fatherland
Father's Day
Father, Son and Holy
    Ghost/Spirit
Father Time
Fat man
Favorite son
Fella
Fellow man (two-fer)
Fellowship
Fellow woman
Female
Firemen
First baseman
Fishermen
Flamboyant
Flyboy
Flyman
Forefathers
Foreman
Fraternity brother
Freemen
Freshmen
Frogman
Frontiersman
Front man
Funny guy
Funnyman
Gal Friday (just making sure
    you're paying attention)
Gambling man
Game Boy
Gamesmanship
Garbage man
Gas man
Gay guy
Gent

Genteel

Gentile

Gentle

Gentlemen

Gentlemen's agreement

German

Gingerbread man

G-Men

Godfather

Good boy

Good fellow

Good guys

Good man

Good old boy

Go-to man

Grandfather

Grandfathered

Grandpa

Great man

Groomsmen

Guitar man

Gunman

Guy

Guy Lombardo

Guys and Dolls

Guy Smiley

Guy thing (see *Penis Envy*)

Guy Williams

Guy wire

Handyman

Hangman

Harry Truman

Hatchet man

Heisman Trophy

Helmsman

He-man

Henchman

Henny Youngman

Henry Wadsworth Longfellow

Herbie Mann

Herman (both male and female)

Hey man

Him

Himalayas

His

His and hers

History

Hit man

Homeboy

Homer Simpson

Horace Mann

Horseman

Houseboy

Househusband

Houseman

Human

Humane

Humanely

Humanity

Human nature

Huntsman

Hymen (see *Irony*)

Hymn

Hysterectomy (see *Irony* again)

Ice cream man

Iceman (he cometh)

Idea man

Iggy Pop

I'm a man

In demand

Infantryman

Inhuman

Insurance man

Intake manifold

Investment guy

Invisible Man

Irishman

Ironman

Isle of Mann

Jaywalk

Jasmine Guy

Jazzman

John Boy
John Houseman
Jolly good fellow
Journeyman
Jungle boy
Kathmandu
Key man
King
Kingmaker
King me
King of the hill
King of the jungle
King's ransom
Kingston Trio
King Tut
Knights of the Round Table
Lad
Laddie
Lady's man
Lance man
Landsman
Last man standing
Lawman
Laymen
Lazy Boy
Leading man
Left-hand man (see *Politically Correct*)
Lineman
Linesman
Linksmen
Little Big Man
Little boy
Little Boy Blue
Little green men
Little guy
Little man
Little Sir Echo
Lobsterman
Lollipop
Longshoremen (and shortshoremen)

Lord and master
Lost Boys
Lot boy
Lover boy
Low man on the totem pole
Lucky guy
Lumen
Lyman
Madman
Mad Men
Maintenance guy
Maintenance man
Mailbox (see *Penis Envy* again)
Mail call
Mailman (another two-fer)
Mamma's boy
Man
Man about town
Manage
Management
Manager
Manatee
Manchester
Manchuria
Man cub
Mandarin
Mandate (see *Gay*)
Mandatory
Mandible
Mandingo
Mandolin
Mandy
Man-eater
Man-eating lion
Man-eating monster
Manfred
Manfred Mann (yet another two-fer)
Man from U.N.C.L.E.
Mangle

Mango

Manhandle (see *Masturbation*)

Manhattan

Manhole (see *Asses*)

Manhole covers (see *Modesty*)

Manhood (see *Condoms*)

Man-hours

Manhunt

Man hunter

Mania

Maniac

Manic

Manicotti

Manicure

Manifold

Manifold gasket

Man in the Moon

Manipulate

Mankind

Manliness (next to godliness)

Manly

Manly man

Manly woman

Manmade

Manna from heaven

Manned

Mannequin

Manners

Mano a mano

Man of La Mancha

Man of leisure

Man of Steel

Man of the hour

Man of the house

Man of the Year

Man-of-war

Man oh man

Man-oh-Manishewitz

Man on the street

Man overboard

Manpower

Man's best friend

Manservant

Manslaughter

Man's world

Man-to-man

Mantra

Manual

Manuel

Manufacture

Man up

Manwich

Marksman

Marksmanship

Masculine

Mason

Master

Master of Ceremonies

Master of the Universe

Masterpiece

Masturbator

Medicine man

Menial

Meningitis

Men in Tights

Menlo Park

Menopause (see *Irony*, yet again)

Mensa

Men's room

Menstruation (more *Irony*)

Mental

Mental blocks

Mention

Men Working

Merry Men

Michelin Man

Middleman

Midshipman

Military man

Militiaman

Milkman

Minuteman

Mister Rogers
Modern man
Momma's boy
Moneyman
Monkey's Uncle
Moon Man
Mother Nature (still paying
    attention?)
Motorman
Mountain man
Mr. America
Mr. Big
Mr. Bass Man
Mr. Bubble
Mr. Clean
Mr. Ed
Mr. Know-It-All
Mr. Magoo
Mr. Meaner (think some more)
Mr. Miyagi
Mr. Mom
Mr. Mooney
Mr. Moonlight
Mr. Nice Guy
Mr. Peanut
Mr. Pibb
Mr. Potato Head
Mr. Sandman
Mr. Saturday Night
Mr. Smarty-Pants
Mr. Smith
Mr. Universe
Mr. Wonderful
Mr. X
Muffin Man
Muscleman
Music Man
My Guy
National Guardsmen
Net men
New man

Newsman
Newspaperman
Nice guy
Nice Jewish boy
Night watchman
Noblemen
No-man's-land
Norman
Normandy
No sir
Nowhere man
Nurseryman
Oak Ridge Boys
Oarsman
Odd man out
Of Mice and Men
Oh boy
Oh brother
Oh man
Oilman
Old boys' club
Old man
Old Man River
Old Man Winter
Oman
Omega Man
Omen
On demand
One-man band
One-man operation
One-upmanship
Ottoman
Outdoorsman
Outmanned
Pac-Man
Pageboy
Papa Bear
Paparazzi
Paperboy
Paternal
Patrolman

Paul Newman
Penmanship
Pep Boys
Perfect gentleman
Perth Amboy
Piano Man
Pie man
Pillsbury Doughboy
Pitchman
Pizza guy
Pizza man
Plant mister
Point man
Policeman
Pool boy
Pool man
Poor man
Pop art
Popcorn
Popeye the Sailorman
Pop music
Popover
Pop rivet
Popsicle
Pop-up fly
Poster boy
Postman (he always rings twice)
Prince
Prince Charming
Princely sum
Puff Daddy
Pullman
Ragman
Rail man
Rain Man
Ramen noodles
Real men
Regimen
Remainder man
Renaissance man
Repairman

Repo man
Rich man
Rifleman
Right-hand man
Right man
Rocket man
Roman
Sailorman
Salamander
Salesman
Samson
Sandman
Sanford and Son
Seamen
Second baseman
Semen
Serenity
Serviceman
Sex maniac
Shemale (see *Confusing*)
Sherman
Showman
Showmanship
Sir Duke
Sir Galahad
Snail mail
Snowman
Soda pop
Solitary Man
Son
Song and dance man
Sonny
Sonny Boy (two-fer)
Son of a bitch
Son of a gun
Son of Sam
Soul Man
Soundman
Spaceman
Spiderman
Spokesman

Sportsman

Sportsmanship

Stable boy

Stamen

Stand-up guy

Statesman

Stepdad

Stepfather

Stepson

Stock boy

Straight man

Straw man

Strongman

Stuntman

Sugar Daddy

Sunbathing

Sunburn

Sundance Kid

Sunday

Sunday drive

Sunday driver

Sundown

Sunlight

Sunny day

Sunrise

Sunscreen

Sunset

Sunshine

Sun shower

Suntan

Sunup

Superman

Super Mario Brothers

Surname

Surprise

Surtax

Survey

Surveyor

Swingman

Swordsman

Taxman

Tenth Man

The Man

The Man Upstairs

Thin Man

Third baseman

Thomas Mann

Tiananmen Square

Tin Man

Tin Woodsman

TMEN

To a man

Tradesmen

Trash man

Tribesmen

Triggerman

Twelfth Man

Two-man bobsled

Two-man job

Uncle Sam

Underclassmen

Undermanned

Unmanly

Unmanned

Upmanship

Upperclassmen

Utility man

Walkman

Wanted man

Watchman

Water boy

Waterman

Weatherman

Whipping boy

Who's your daddy?

Wildman

Willie Loman

Wingman

Wise guy

Wise Men

Wolf Man

Woman (talk about *Irony*)

Womanly	X-Men
Women	Yemen
Woodsman	Yeoman
Working man	Yes-men
Workman's comp	Yes sir
Workmanship	Young buck
Workmen	Young man

SEX MANIAC

If you only think about sex during every waking moment of your life and can never get enough, you've got a problem (see *Psychotherapy*). Find a hobby.

SEX SCENES

You mean to tell me that they're really acting during those love scenes, and they don't get truly aroused? How can that be? Either they lie, are very good at their trade or are simply repulsed by each other. Anyway, in movies I find that, less is more. When things are left to your imagination, it is much more provocative, erotic and interesting. However, I'm like any other red-blooded, all-American boy and watch those sex scenes very closely (only to learn new techniques, of course). Convincingly portraying extremely intimate moments while still clothed—now that's acting. That's real acting.

SHALOM

One word meaning hello, good-bye and peace. Very cool. That can really cut down on long conversations, can't it?

SHAME

Having no shame isn't always such a bad thing (see *Humor*).

SHARE

Remember what your mother taught you: always share. It doesn't stop with your toys either. Share your thoughts, memories, sadness, good times, lunch, clothes—most things. You'd be amazed to find out how many people really want to share with you. There are, of course, some things you don't want to share: secrets, showers (well maybe that's OK), colds, boyfriends, to name a few.

446

SHAVING

Men, don't go out of the house without shaving, because you look like a slob. Especially you older guys; that gray stubble is not a good look (unless you want to look homeless). Remember when women used to go out with rollers in their hair, and how ridiculous that looked? Well, you guys don't look much better. I know it's an insane idea to mercilessly scrape your face with a very sharp implement every morning, but that's the price we pay to live in a civilized society. Something that sharp should not be put into your hands when you're still half asleep. One slip-up and you're very wide awake though. Ladies, who cares what they do in Europe; hairy legs and pits are a real turnoff. And whatever you do, don't shave your pubes. Your mate shouldn't want you to look like a little boy or girl. Anyway, if you paid attention in biology class, you'd know that we were designed to have hair grow down there. Kind of cuts down on the friction, if you know what I mean. Now don't ask me why some guys insist on removing the hair from their chests. I guess they think it's a better way to show off their muscles. But I think they just want to look like girls.

SHIP

So what's with all these ships that can't even float?

Companionship	Leadership	Showmanship
Fellowship	Marksmanship	Sponsorship
Friendship	Ownership	Sportsmanship
Gamesmanship	Penmanship	Statesmanship
Hardship	Relationship	Workmanship
Internship	Scholarship	

SHIPPING AND HANDLING

Shipping and handling rarely represent additional costs incurred by the seller. It's usually just an excuse to charge more.

SHIT

Shit is a word that is so often misused. Here are some prime examples:

> Are you're shitting me (best to grab the raincoat and hat)?
> Beats the shit out of me (there's gotta be a better way to get rid of it; use your imagination).

447

Come on, get your shit together (see *Diarrhea*).

Cut the shit, will you (use an old knife)?

Damn, they just gave me a shitload of work to do (I'd give it to someone else).

Don't be such a shit (sorry, I don't have the slightest idea here).

Don't get shitty with me (you can, of course, get shitty with someone else).

Don't give me a raft of shit (does it float?).

Don't go apeshit on me (didn't we evolve from apes?).

Don't take any shit from them (like you need that advice).

Duty calls (OK, technically that's not shit, but it's close enough; this is my book, remember).

Eat shit and die (yes, *that* may kill you).

Geez, you scared the shit out of me (that should cure you; see *Constipation*).

Give me all the poop (by all means, you can have the poop—and it's still my book).

He doesn't know whether to shit or go blind (given the choice, I would go with shit).

He's just like a pig in shit (the inference here is that pigs love to be in shit; so how would anybody actually know what pigs like?).

He's on the shit list (is that some bathroom checkout form?).

He's so full of shit his eyes are brown (so that's how that happens).

He was wearing his shit-kicking shoes (new Olympic sport, I guess).

He went to take a shit (I hope he didn't take it where I'm going).

Hey, shit for brains (I'm guessing there are some serious neurological problems here; brings a whole new meaning to the term gray matter).

Holy shit (maybe their shit really doesn't stink; because it's the purest of poop).

I don't give a shit (so would someone really want it if you gave it?).

I don't have to take this shit from you (re-gifter).

I feel so shitty today (I guess that's part of that touchy-feely stuff).

If you throw enough shit against the wall, something's bound to stick (I'd find something better to do with my time).

I guess you're just shit outta luck (I don't know what shit and luck have to do with each other).

I just shit my brains out (that would make for a pretty low IQ).

I'm all pooped out (again, technically not shit, but this is still my book).

I'm so happy I could just shit (I find better things to do when I'm happy).

I'm tired of taking your shit (it's a stinking job).

I'm up shit's creek (that's no place to go for a swim).

I sure as shit don't know (how sure is shit?).

It's cold as shit outside (now how cold do you suppose that is?).

I've got to go take a shit (me, I'd leave it alone; but if you must, at least take it away from me).

I was scared shitless (no shit?).

Jack Shit (I don't know him—and what a silly name to have; maybe Ralph Shit is better)

Like flies on shit (who likes flies on shit?).

Man, I just shit a brick (so that's where they come from).

No shit (see *Constipation,* again).

No shit, Sherlock (that must be why he had all that extra time to solve mysteries).

Oh fuck that shit (probably not too pleasant an activity).

Oh, she's in deep shit (like being in shallow shit is so much better?).

Oh shit (I think it's a racial slur to the Irish—O'Shit—get it?).

Oh, we were just hanging around, shooting the shit (target practice).

Oh, you think you're such a big shit, don't you (I wouldn't be so proud)?

Oh, you're so full of shit (that surely doesn't leave much room for anything else; and don't call me Shirley).

She's built like a brick shithouse (I sure wouldn't want to live there).

She's in deep shit (never get in over your head).

She walks around like her shit doesn't stink (if she's figured out how to do that, she ought to patent it and sell it; she'd make a fortune).

Shit happens (oh yeah, it does).

Shit or get off the pot (maybe go to drug rehab instead).

Shit rolls downhill (no idea what that means either).

So you think you're hot shit, huh (not something I'd want to be).

That causes a real shit storm (another reason to keep that umbrella handy).

That's a bunch of shit (it comes in bunches?).

They don't know shit (I don't think I'd want to know it either).

They don't know shit from Shinola (I must confess, neither do I, as I don't have the slightest idea what a Shinola is; I've heard of the USS Shinola, though).

They kicked the living shit out of me (boy, I bet that hurt; at least they left the dead shit).

They live in a real shit hole (didn't know people can actually live there; see *Butt*).

They're as close as stink on shit (way too close for me).

They scared the living shit out of me (it's alive?).

They went batshit (hanging upside down).

Uh-oh, the shit's going to hit the fan (don't forget your umbrella—and wear that hat again).

What a chicken shit operation this is (what do you think they remove
 during *that* surgery?).
What the shit is going on here (do you really have to ask)?
Wipe that shit-eating grin off your face (I'd wipe the shit off first).
Wow, they were so shit-faced last night (they've got to be pretty drunk
 to have shit all over their faces, right?).
Yeah, same shit, different day (try a new diet).
You are a lazy sack of shit (worse than a hard-working sack of shit?).
You are a worthless sack of shit (I think they sell those at the feed store,
 next to the sack of oats).
You better know your shit (better than knowing someone else's shit).
You don't like it? Well tough shit (see *Constipation,* yet again).
You're a real shithead (probably better than being a fake shithead; and I
 sure don't want your hat).

I need to take a shower now. Way too much shit around here.

SHOE ON THE OTHER FOOT

Now how comfortable can it be to have a shoe on the other foot? Everybody
should know their right from their left, right? Left. The grass isn't always so
green on the other side, is it?

SHOOT FIRST

Shoot first and ask questions later? Not me. I'm going to ask the questions first.
Way less dangerous.

SHOPPING

Shopping is the act of looking for and buying something you need or want. It's
not an event, social or otherwise. If some had their way, it would become an
Olympic sport. And I know plenty who could take the gold.

SHORT

Short, tall, big, little—who cares about the exterior? It's what's on the inside
that matters, you know. However, good things do come in small packages. And
the more compact tend to be better and more efficient. Anyway, that's my take
on "short" (see *Rationalizing*).

SHORTCUTS

Taking shortcuts often saves time and aggravation, which is a good thing. You just want to be careful not to cut across someone's front lawn or living room, or step on anyone's toes, to get to your destination.

SHORT SHRIFT

Nope, you sure don't want to give people short shrift, do you? Curiously, you never hear about a long shrift. What's a shrift anyway? Probably some fashion accessory.

SHOTGUN APPROACH

The theory of the shotgun approach is that if you scatter your firepower at a target, you're more likely to hit something. Or, in more colloquial terms, if you throw enough shit against the wall, something's bound to stick (haven't we been through enough shit already?). Yes, this can work, but I favor a more focused approach. Remember: scatter less, focus more (see *Conservation*).

SHOTS

Does anybody like getting shots? Of course not; and that's because they hurt. However, it stings a whole lot less if you don't watch. If you really don't want to feel the pinch, watch someone else getting one instead. And don't be such a baby.

SHOWER

Shower every day, and wash your hair while you're at it (assuming you have some; see *Baldness*). You know, it's best to only smell with your nose.

SHOW-OFF

Great, so you can do something others can't. Wonderful—but nobody likes a show-off (see *Bragging*). Well, maybe their mothers do, but that's all.

SHUN

Here are some of the shuns you should embrace:

Action	Inspiration	Perception
Ambition	Instruction	Procreation
Animation	Integration	Reception
Appreciation	Investigation	Recreation
Articulation	Invitation	Relaxation
Attention	Libation	Salutation
Carnation	Locomotion	Salvation
Concentration	Mastication	Simplification
Conservation	Migration	Solution
Conversation	Moderation	Sophistication
Discussion	Motion	Succession
Emotion	Motivation	Synchronization
Expectation	Multiplication	Transition
Fascination	Ovation	Transportation
Imagination	Ovulation	Vacation
Innovation	Participation	Vaccination

And these are the ones you really want to shun:

Aggravation	Indignation	Perspiration
Aggression	Inhibition	Procrastination
Constipation	Intimidation	Rejection
Desperation	Machination	Ruination
Disintegration	Malnutrition	Saturation
Distraction	Mutation	Starvation
Humiliation	Mutilation	Tarnation
Indigestion	Operation	Temptation

SHUT UP

Shut up is a very abrupt and confining thing to say. It carries so much finality to it. How about saying "be quiet" instead (see *Impolite*)?

SHYNESS

Some people grow out of their shyness, but there's nothing wrong with being a little bashful at times (see *Modesty*). Just don't let it run your life.

SIDES

Everybody has sides. Here are the ones you want to be on:

Bright side
Good side
Left side (in the U.K. and a few
    other countries)

Right side
Strong side
Upside
Winning side

You don't want to be on these:

Back side (unless that's your
    thing)
Blind side
Dark side
Flip side
Losing side
Sideways (makes you way too dizzy)

Weak side (unless you're a weak
    side linebacker,
    whatever that is)
Wayside (things keep falling
    by there)
Wrong side

SILENT

Silent and listen have the same letters. Coincidence? I think not. Is silence really golden? Yes, it can be, and sometimes it actually speaks volumes. Silence also gives you plenty of quality time to spend with someone special—even yourself.

SILLY PHRASES

These phrases, words, expressions, clichés and metaphors sound pretty silly and outdated to me. Using them shows you don't really express yourself properly. I know I don't.

A babe in the woods (oh babe).
A bird in the hand (better to wear gloves).
Ace in the hole (I'd rather have an ace in my hand).
Across the board (or down the plank).
Adding fuel to the fire (otherwise no fire, right?).
Adding insult to injury (equals what?).
Adding their two cents (see *Pennies*).
A dime a dozen (good price though).
Ad nauseam (see *Puking*).
A drop in the bucket (drug testing?).

After a while crocodile (or sooner for all alligators).
Aftermath (recess is usually after math).
Ain't we got fun (I got it)?
Alas (I used to think that was how you spelled Alice).
A legend in your own time (who owns time?).
A little birdie told me (little birdies can't talk—Big Bird can though).
All balled up (see *Sex*).
All choked up (better than all coked up).
All cooped up (it's a chicken thing).
All decked out (you don't want to be all decked in).
All dolled up (see *Blow-up Dolls*).
All dressed up and nowhere to go (then go clothes shopping).
All fucked up (at least it's not fucked down).
All gussied up (oh that Gus).
All hands on deck (both hands).
All hell's breaking loose (see *Big Bang Theory*).
All hot and bothered (see *Menopause*).
All in a day's work (six to create the universe).
All in the same boat (gotta be a big boat).
All keyed up (find the right lock).
All on the same page (that could get crowded).
All over creation (see *God*).
All over God's green earth (ditto).
All over the map (see *Directions*).
All that jazz (love that jazz; see *Music*).
All thumbs (what a funny-looking hand).
All told (who told?).
All wound up (wrapped too tight).
All's fair in love and war (see *Rules*).
All spruced up (that's a tree thing).
All's well that ends well (it's always about the ends).
A long road to hoe (why would anyone hoe a road?).
Alrighty dighty (clean diaper, I think).
A man after my own heart (I'll keep my heart to myself).
A month of Sundays (at least you always know what day it is).
And twice on Sunday (Sundays are so special).
Another day, another dollar (live long and prosper).
Any port in a storm (depends on the size of the ship).
A-OK (what, just OK isn't good enough?).
Apple of your eye (part of the iris, I think).
Arch enemy (poor Archie).

A real Donnybrook (small creek).

Are we having fun yet (don't you know?)?

Armed to the teeth (confused anatomy).

Around Robin Hood's barn (he was not a farmer, so he didn't have a barn).

Ask for her hand in marriage (sorry, it's all or nothing).

As far as the eye can see (with or without glasses?).

As healthy as a horse (they don't get sick?).

As happy as a clam (is that good?).

A shot in the arm (better than in the tush).

A shot in the dark (duck).

Asking for the moon (I'd ask for something else).

Asleep at the wheel (see *Distracted Driving*).

As luck would have it (I'll take it).

As old as the hills (Benny Hill's family?).

As plain as the nose on your face (who has a plain nose?).

As serious as a heart attack (now that's serious).

As sharp as a tack (very tacky).

A sight for sore eyes (use eye drops).

As sure as I'm standing here (I'm sitting, and I'm not so sure).

Attaboy (what a boy).

Attagirl (probably nothing like atta gas).

At breakneck speed (way too fast).

At each other's throats (a passionate embrace?).

At the boiling point (hot stuff).

At the end of my rope (see *Neckties*).

At the end of the day (nighttime, right?).

At the drop of a hat (whoops).

At their wits' end (where is the beginning?).

At the top of their game (batter up).

At the top of their lungs (I would think the bottom works as well).

At this stage of the game (innings, quarters, halves, periods, sets—no stages, right?).

Avoiding it like the plague (hide).

Back at the ranch (old standby salad dressing).

Backbiting (hungry?).

Backbreaking (that can hurt).

Back in the day (which day?).

Back in the saddle (that's how you get saddle sores, silly).

Back talk (you're better off front talking).

Back to basics (probably square one).

Back to square one (how about round two?).

Back to the drawing board (or the coloring book).
Bad apple (it just takes one).
Bad to the bone (now that's a bad apple).
Bah, humbug (must be a nasty, resilient illness)!
Ballyhoo (bally how?).
Baloney (salami!)!
Baptism by fire (I thought they used water for that).
Barking up the wrong tree (is there a right tree?).
Basket case (wouldn't that be a case of baskets?).
Basking in the limelight (better use sunscreen).
Bats in the belfry (is that like the dugout?).
Batten down the hatches (don't leave your hatches up).
Be all and end all (that's all).
Beaten within an inch of your life (do they use a ruler for that?).
Beating a dead horse (if that's your idea of a good time).
Beating a path to your door (oh just ring the bell).
Beating around the bush (see *Sex*).
Beating it into the ground (it's all about the beat).
Beating them off with a stick (see *Masturbation*).
Beating them to the punch (stay away from the punch).
Beauty sleep (some clearly need this).
Bed of roses (not real comfortable, what with all of those thorns).
Beddy-bye (lost your bed?).
Been living under a rock (yes, and I'm very happy there)?
Been there, done that (world traveler).
Been around the block a few times (see *Exercise*).
Beg off (begging is so unbecoming).
Behind the eight ball (I see you hiding).
Being a guinea pig (I want to be the walrus).
Being hip (I'd rather be a toe).
Being remiss (don't be).
Being taken to the cleaners (must really smell).
Being their whipping boy (see *Sex,* again).
Being well-grounded (and well-groomed).
Being well-rounded (see *Dieting*).
Believe you me (isn't it one or the other?).
Belle of the ball (what sport is that?).
Belly up to the bar (get your belly off the bar; see *Manners*).
Bellyaching (or body aching).
Bend over backwards (contortionist trick).
Bending your ear (it's all cartilage).

Bending the rules (this often takes great strength).

Best-case scenario (Oscar winner).

Best idea since sliced bread (was that such a great idea?).

Be still my heart (not me—keep it beating).

Best of both worlds (I'd be satisfied with the best of just one—how many are there anyway?).

Best thing that ever came down the pike (or up the street).

Be that as it may (or June or July).

Between a rock and a hard place (no good choices).

Between the devil and the deep blue sea (just between them).

Bet your bottom dollar (rather than your top dollar).

Biding my time (I don't know how to bide).

Big cheese (for Green Bay Cheeseheads).

Big deal (I guess they use large playing cards).

Bigger fish to fry (whale shark fries?).

Bigger than a breadbox (large loafers?).

Big man on campus (see *Sexist*).

Big shoes to fill (big feet, big hands, big…?).

Big to-do (make a list).

Bill of goods (or bads).

Bimbo (relative of Dumbo).

Bing, bang, boom (and fee-fi-fo-fum).

Bippy (my bippy hurts).

Birds of a feather flock together (as long as they don't flock over me).

Bite the bullet (what an aftertaste).

Bite your tongue (that'll keep you quiet).

Biting off more than you can chew (see *Dieting*).

Biting the hand that feeds you (cannibal).

Black sheep of the family (no sheep in my family).

Bleeding 'em dry (see *Giving Blood*).

Bless her heart (why not the rest of her?).

Blew their lid (hats off to them).

Blew their stack (use red instead).

Blew their top (what's with all the blowing?).

Bloodbath (can't get very clean bathing that way).

Blowing a gasket (blowing in the wind).

Blowing smoke up your ass (ah, the hazards of second-hand smoke).

Blowing their doors off (can't they just open them?).

Blown away (see *Sex*).

Blown to smithereens (smithereens?).

Blow your mind (boom!).

Boilerplate (it's all about the warmth).
Bold-faced lie (I prefer faceless lies).
Bone-chilling cold (put some meat on those bones).
Book 'em, Danno (and check his library card).
Boondoggle (likely something to do with Daniel Boone).
Bone dry (you want those bones to be wet).
Bone of contention (next to the femur, I think).
Bone to pick (see *Nose Picking*).
Boobirds (can't please them).
Boo-hoo (who?).
Bored to death (what a way to go).
Bored to tears (find something else to cry about).
Born with a silver spoon in your mouth (that must have been an
    interesting delivery).
Bottle it and sell it (see *Capitalism*).
Bottom of the barrel (always best to drink from the top).
Bottoms up (I'd get dizzy; see *Amusement Rides*).
Boys will be boys (like they'd be something else).
Bragging rights (don't brag about your wrongs).
Brand spanking new (ouch!).
Breaking bad (see *Habits*).
Breaking bread (how do you fix it?).
Breaking the bank (sperm bank?).
Breaking the ice (let it melt instead).
Breaking their balls (ouch, ouch, ouch!).
Breaking their necks (that's a deal killer).
Breaking the logjam (some kind of jelly or preserves).
Breathing down your neck (breathe from your nose).
Bric-a-brac (I want my brick back).
Bright-eyed and bushy-tailed (now who wants a bushy tail—ever hear
    of electrolysis?).
Bringing home the bacon (don't forget the lettuce and tomato).
Bringing up the rear (tushie tuck).
Brouhaha (haha—what's so funny?).
Browbeat (ever been beaten by a brow?).
Brownie points (cool desserts).
Buckle down (best to keep the buckle closed).
Buck up (or down).
Bugaboo (peekaboo).
Bug off (yeah, get that bug off)!
Building up a head of steam (vaporized brains).

Bull's eye (culinary delicacy).
Bullshit artist (do they teach that in art school?).
Bummer (see *Butt*)!
Bump on a log (just ice it).
Bumps in the road (use more ice).
Bunch of Malarkey (it comes in bunches?).
Burning the candle at both ends (a sure way to get burned).
Burning the midnight oil (see *Pollution*).
Bursting at the seams (see *Dieting*).
Bursting with pride (what a way to go).
Bury the hatchet (it will grow into an ax).
Busting your ass (careful, it's already cracked).
Busting your chops (leave my chops alone).
Busy as a bee (how busy do you really think they are?).
Busybody (see *Sex*).
Buttering them up (see *Sex*, again).
Buttonholing (that may hurt).
Buying the farm (get the tools and equipment too).
Buzz off (or just buzz)!
By all means (don't be mean).
By cracky (who's Cracky?)!
By George (always stand by George)!
By Jove (stay away from Jove)!
By the same token (buy plenty of tokens).
By the seat of your pants (what a way to fly.)
Cabbage patch (no, babies aren't born there).
Caddy-corner (that's where the golf helpers stay).
Cakewalk (I never take my cake for a walk).
Calling it a day (what else would you call it?).
Calling off the dogs (unless they're on the cats).
Calling out the National Guard (they don't like being called out).
Calling the shots (hello, Mrs. Shot?).
Can of worms (in the canned food section).
Can only take in small doses (One-A-Day).
Can't beat Mother Nature (bad form).
Can't beat that (it might beat you back?).
Can't believe my ears (do ears lie?)!
Can't fight city hall (bad odds).
Can't make a silk purse out of a sow's ear (good thing).
Can't make heads or tails out of it (better get your eyes checked).
Can't put your finger on it (probably better off).

Cardinal rule (I thought the Pope rules).
Carved in stone/granite/bronze (I don't think you can carve bronze).
Cash on the barrelhead (or in my pocket).
Casting a wide shadow (see *Dieting*).
Catch-22 (there's always a catch).
Catch as catch can (how do you catch a can?).
Catching hell (see *Fishing*).
Catch my drift (only if it's thrown your way).
Catch you later (what am I, a baseball?).
Cat got your tongue (that would hurt)?
Cathouse (meow).
Cat nap (something like catnip).
Caught in red tape (yellow tape is worse).
Caught in the crosshairs (try bikini wax).
Caught red-handed (what color is your hand?).
Caught with your pants down (don't you just hate that?).
Causing a ruckus (classic cause and effect).
Cha-ching (catching)!
Chalking it up to experience (back to the drawing board).
Chances are slim and none (yes, and Slim left town).
Changing horses in midstream (always change your horses when you
    change your underwear).
Changing their tune (see *Singing*).
Cheapskate (skates aren't so cheap).
Cheaper by the dozen (unless you don't need a dozen).
Checking under the hood (ask her first).
Chickens coming home to roost (wouldn't that be roosters?).
Chip off the old block (sculpting).
Chief cook and bottle washer (like Chief Sitting Bull?).
Chitchat (or any kind of chat).
Chock-full (full of chock?).
Chomping at the bit (bad for your teeth).
Chowderhead (soup head?).
Circling the wagons (getting nowhere fast).
Citizen's arrest (arresting citizens?).
Claim to fame (like a baggage claim).
Clean as a whistle (now just how clean do you suppose a whistle is?).
Cleaning their clocks (don't you just hate those dirty clocks?).
Clear as a bell (unimpeded ding dong).
Clear as day (noncloudy day).
Clear as mud (not real clear, right?).

Clear sailing (no waves).
Clear the air (see *Farting*).
Clear the deck (I hate a cluttered deck).
Climbing the walls (go Spiderman).
Clip joint (see *Haircuts*).
Close, but no cigar (see *Smoking*).
Close call (phone call nearby?).
Closemouthed (way quieter that way).
Close enough for government work (probably not too close).
Coast is clear (tell Paul Revere).
Cockamamie (see *Penis Envy*).
Cock-and-bull story (wonder if it has a happy ending?).
Coining a phrase (I thought only the mint could coin).
Cold as hell (you're very confused).
Come and get it (it's yours)!
Come as you are (like there's another way).
Come hell or high water (I'd take my chances with the water).
Comme ci, comme ça (just come already).
Comfy cozy (extra cozy).
Comfy womfy (womfy?).
Coming apart at the seams (see *Exercise*).
Coming down the homestretch (home is where the heart is).
Coming home to roost (another rooster thing, I guess).
Coming on like a freight train (just a come on).
Coming out of your shell (kinda cramped in there anyway).
Coming out of the woodwork (call the exterminators).
Coming-out party (see *Gay*).
Coming through with flying colors (how do colors fly?).
Coming unglued (see *Duct Tape*).
Coming up short (or going down long).
Coming with your hat in hand (belongs on your head, right?).
Command performance (you will perform!).
Conversation piece (does it talk?).
Cooking your own goose (I don't want to cook anyone's goose).
Cool as a cucumber (keep it in the fridge).
Cool beans (they're usually hot; see *Beans*).
Cool your heels (keep them in the fridge too).
Cool your jets (jets are so cool).
Cooties (medical term).
Copacetic (or copathetic).
Costs an arm and a leg (dollars work best for me).

Counting sheep (I'll count my blessings).
Crackpot (I thought they use bongs for that).
Crack the whip (a cracked whip doesn't do much).
Crankpot (get the plug-in kind).
Crapola (not like the crayon).
Crapshoot (see *Shit*).
Cream of the crop (doesn't cream come from cows?).
Crimping their style (that sounds like it hurts).
Crocodile tears (do they cry—I wouldn't suggest checking).
Crown jewels (any kind of jewels is fine with me).
Crushing defeat (that's why you want to keep da feet covered).
Cruisin' for a bruisin' (drive safely).
Crying a blue streak (blue mascara?).
Crying in your beer (see *Waste Not*).
Crying uncle (I hate it when he cries).
Crying wolf (enough with the crying, already).
Crying your eyes out (talk about overdoing it).
Cry me a river (no water shortage).
Cuckoo (special nut).
Curses, foiled again (always reuse the foil)!
Cut and dried (probably something like drawn and quartered).
Cute as a button (seen any cute buttons lately?).
Cut out the middleman (that's gotta hurt).
Cutting a rug (you cut it, you own it).
Cutting corners (that makes it round).
Cutting 'em a break (how do you cut something that's already broken?).
Cutting 'em off at the pass (or passing 'em at the cut).
Cutting 'em some slack (I'll take half a pound of slack).
Cut to the chase (make it a clean cut).
Cutting off your nose to spite your face (now don't you look silly).
Daddy longlegs (to the little ones, dads always have long legs).
Dagnabbit (or any nab it)!
Dame (there's nothing like a dame).
Damnation (foreign country)!
Dang (southern dung)!
Dapper (not to be confused with diaper).
Darn tootin' (car horn)!
Dastardly (bastardly).
Day in and day out (I know what a Day's Inn is, but what's a Day's Out?).
Day late and a dollar short (those damn short dollars).

462

Day of reckoning (that's usually a Monday).
Dead as a doornail (the knob is deader)
Deadbeat (dead and beat seem to go together).
Dead center (middle of the road).
Dead-end (the ultimate end).
Dead giveaway (see *Free Samples*).
Dead heat (now that's hot).
Dead in the water (we call that drowning).
Dead ringer (need a new doorbell).
Dead serious (as opposed to live serious).
Dead to rights (or lefts).
Dead to the world (redundant).
Dead wrong (that's very, very wrong).
Death watch (who wants to watch that?).
Deep six it (seven is better).
Devil's food (see *Dieting*).
Diamond in the rough (smooth out that diamond).
Diamond Jim (such a jewel).
Diddly (I don't know what that is).
Diddly squat (that either).
Different strokes for different folks (see *Masturbation*).
Digging ditches (I can dig it).
Digging in your heels (a shovel works better).
Digging your own grave (not much future in that).
Dillydally (same as sillysally).
Dimwit (better than no wit).
Ding-a-ling (doorbell chime).
Dipsy-doodle (very tipsy).
Discombobulated (or datcombobulated).
Dodging a bullet (something like dodgeball).
Doesn't amount to a hill of beans (see *Farting* again).
Dog ate my homework (hungry dog).
Dog-doo (dog don't).
Dog-eat-dog world (nothing worse than a cannibal dog).
Doggone it (where did that doggie go?)!
Doing their bidding (maybe bidding their doing).
Doing the nasty (and naughty).
Done deal (good deal).
Do not pass go (you can rest at stop).
Don't be a killjoy (sorry, Joy).
Don't be a tattletale (shouldn't have any tail; see *Asses*).

463

Don't bet the ranch on it (who's got a ranch?).

Don't call us, we'll call you (sure we will).

Don't count your chickens before they hatch (that would be counting eggs, right?).

Don't cry over spilt milk (oh come on, it's OK to cry).

Don't give a rat's ass (I'll pass).

Don't give me that song and dance (entertain yourself).

Don't give up the ship (no ship for me).

Don't have a cow (I don't have a cow).

Don't have all day (I still don't have a cow).

Don't hold your breath (you'll turn blue).

Don't knock it till you've tried it (knock yourself out).

Don't know from Adam (or Eve).

Don't know if they're coming or going (see *Directions*).

Don't let the door hit you where the good Lord split you (you don't want that crack to get any worse).

Don't look a gift horse in the mouth (ugh, another horse).

Don't rock the boat (rocks don't float).

Don't spare the horses (I don't have any spare horses).

Don't spend it all in one place (spend it all over the place).

Don't take any wooden nickels (depends on who gives them out).

Don't tread on me (stay off the treads).

Don't upset the applecart (it's very sensitive).

Doodad (don't dad).

Doohickey (see *Sex*).

Do or die (go with do).

Double-edged sword (don't all swords have two edges?).

Down for the count (countdown?).

Down in the dumps (it smells in the dumps).

Down the road (a piece).

Down the hatch (don't eggs hatch?).

Down the line (the line never ends).

Down the tubes (tie those tubes).

Down to earth (where else would we be?).

Down to the short hairs (buzz cut).

Down to the wire (barbed wire?).

Dragging your feet (behind what?).

Drawing a blank (how can you draw a blank?).

Driving a hard bargain (probably some kind of import).

Driving 'em crazy (designated driver).

Driving 'em up a tree (see *Directions*).

Driving 'em up a wall (ditto).
Drop a dime on (moneybags).
Drop everything (then you have nothing).
Drop in the bucket (see *Urinating*).
Drunk as a skunk (I just thought they smelled; I guess they hit the bottle too).
Dry heaves (never heard of wet heaves).
Dry run (stay out of the rain).
Dude (ranch name).
Dudette (ranchette name)
Duking it out (John Wayne thing, I guess).
Dumb-ass (better than a smart-ass).
Dumb blond (can't they talk?).
Dumb bunny (how can you tell?).
Dumber than a doorknob (as dumb as a doornail?).
Dumber than a doornail (what's a doornail?).
Dummy up (don't wake my dummy up).
Duty calls (don't answer).
Dyed in the wool (see *Death*).
Eager beaver (dam it).
Early bird (are they ever late?).
Early bird catches the worm (what does the early worm catch?).
Earning your keep (keep what you earn).
Earning your stripes (can't spend stripes).
Easier said than done (so don't do it).
Easy as pie (eating it is the easy part).
Easy peasy (see *Urinating* again).
Eating bonbons (they grow on trees, I think).
Eating crow (another white meat).
Eating out of the palm of your hand (hope you washed up first).
Eating them out of house and home (love that gingerbread).
Eating your heart out (how heartless).
Eating your words (add salt).
Eenie, meenie, miney, mo (I think they're some of the Seven Dwarfs).
Elbow grease (bottle it and sell it).
Eureka (my reka)!
Even Steven (what a guy).
Everybody and their brother (no sisters?).
Every dog has its day (I think it's Thursday).
Everything but the kitchen sink (oh go ahead and throw that in too).
Everything's coming up roses (even tulips?).
Everything under the sun (that would be pretty much everything).

Exit, stage left (that's the one on the left).
Eyes in the back of your head (that would explain hindsight).
Face the music (and bow to your partner).
Fair to middling (weather forecast).
Fall by the wayside (which side?).
Fall flat on your face (ouch!).
Falling flat (splat).
Fall off the face of the earth (Mr. Columbus figured out that can't happen).
Fall off the wagon (use seat belts).
Fall on deaf ears (silence is golden).
Falling through the cracks (I don't like anything falling through my crack).
Family jewels (every family has them).
Fancy meeting you here (it's a fantasy).
Fancy-pants (black tie optional).
Fanning the flames (don't fans cool you off?).
Far-fetched (see *Dogs*).
Far-out (or far-off).
Feasting your eyes (hungry eyes).
Feast or famine (feast works for me).
Feathering your nest (use the feather duster).
Feather in your cap (leftover from the nest).
Feeding frenzy (food orgy).
Feel free (or is that free feel?).
Feeling the pinch (you better feel it).
Fess up (probably like throw up).
Feverishly working on (you get sick from it).
Few and far between (maybe in those cracks again).
Fighting City Hall (they usually win).
Fighting fire with fire (I think you'd do better with water).
Fighting like cats and dogs (they don't fight fair).
Fighting tooth and nail (I'd use my fists).
Figment of your imagination (aren't figments in light bulbs?).
Filled to the gills (don't you just hate to have your gills filled?).
Fill me in (or fill me up).
Final nail in the coffin (they don't really use nails, do they?).
Finding your bearings (now where did I leave those bearings?).
Fire at will (poor Will).
First and foremost (or fivemost).
First dibs (they can have my dibs).
Fistful of dollars (nothing up my sleeve).
Fits like a glove (what if it's a shoe?).

466

Fit as a fiddle (are fiddles fit?).
Fit to a tee (see *One Size Fits All*).
Fit to be tied (see *Sex*).
Flabbergasted (watch that gasket).
Flash in the pan (Peter Pan?).
Flew the coop (too cooped up, I guess).
Flip-in (or flap-in).
Flip the switch (on or off?).
Fly-by-night operation (it's safer to fly during the day).
Flying in the face of (hate those flies in my face).
Flying off the handle (stay on the handle).
Fly in the ointment (damn houseflies).
Fly on the wall (enough with the flies).
Fold your tent (see *Neatness*).
Food for thought (can't get fat on that).
For all intents and purposes (or porpoises?).
Forbidden fruit (I thought fruit was good for you).
Forcing your hand (or pulling your leg).
For Criminy's sake (who?)!
For crying out loud (beats crying in soft)!
Forever and a day (does that day really add much?).
For heaven's sake (that's different from hell's sake)!
For hours on end (time never ends, right?).
Fork in the road (pick it up before someone gets a flat tire from it).
For Pete's sake (I still use this one)!
For the life of me (that's life).
Forty winks (we call him Blinky).
Four corners of the earth (isn't the earth round?).
Fraidy cat (or Freddy cat).
Freak accident (oh, those freaks).
Freaking out (don't wear your freaking out).
Free as a bird (what's with all the birds?).
Friggin (oh go ahead and say the real F-word, will ya?).
From soup to nuts (no nuts in my soup).
From stem to stern (don't you stir with the stem?).
From the get-go (let go).
Fuddy-duddy (you're so fuddy).
Full-blown (think about it).
Full-court press (it's an ironing thing).
Full-fledged (I'm only half-fledged).
Full of piss and vinegar (probably not too tasty).

Full speed ahead (don't speed).
Full steam ahead (more speed, I guess).
Funny as hell (lotta yucks down there?).
Futzing with things (I hate to futz).
Gadzooks (oh my Gad).
Gainfully employed (redundant).
Gal (almost as bad a ma'am).
Gallivanting (I'm always vanting).
Ganging up on them (try ganging down).
Gee whiz (Cheez Whiz?)!
Gee willikers (shave off those willikers)!
Geez Louise (love that Louise)!
Gentle as a lamb (Gentile?).
Get a grip (see *Masturbation*).
Get crackin' (popcorn instruction).
Get it, got it, good (maybe that's bad).
Get lost (see *Directions*)!
Get off your high horse (use a stepstool).
Get on the stick (how comfortable can that be?).
Get outta here (go somewhere)!
Get outta town (not here)!
Get the show on the road (road show).
Get-up-and-go (mine got up and went).
Get with the program (to the road show).
Getting a fair shake (see *Lap Dancing*).
Getting a handle on it (or off of it).
Getting ahead of yourself (that I'd like to see).
Getting all caught up in it (it's catching).
Getting a pat on the back (be gentle).
Getting a piece of the action (I'll stick with a piece of pie).
Getting a pink slip (don't wear it with a white dress).
Getting a rise out of them (see *Sex*).
Getting a run for your money (must be a racetrack thing).
Getting away with it (love it).
Getting away with murder (you never get away with that).
Getting a word in edgewise (sideways is better).
Getting bawled out (as opposed to getting bawled in?).
Getting blood out of a stone (takes a lot of work).
Getting blood out of a turnip (that takes more work).
Getting called on the carpet (just hang up).
Getting carried away (who wants to walk anyway?).

Getting chewed out (better than getting bawled out).
Getting cold feet (another reason to wear socks).
Getting down to brass tacks (sales tax).
Getting down to business (bad business.)
Getting down to the nitty-gritty (some kind of sandpaper, I think).
Getting fed up (better for the food to go down).
Getting hammered (or screwed).
Getting hot under the collar (take a cold shower).
Getting in on the ground floor (the only way to go is up).
Getting in under the wire (limbo lower now).
Getting into a pissing match (like a tennis match).
Getting it down to a science (if only I understood science).
Getting it off your chest (must be lint or something).
Getting it out of their system (see *Diarrhea*).
Getting lost in the shuffle (card trick).
Getting nowhere fast (at least you're not lost).
Getting off scot-free (leave Scott alone).
Getting off the dime (how do you fit on a dime in the first place?).
Getting off the mark (yeah, leave Mark alone too).
Getting on your soapbox (too slippery).
Getting out from under (or in from over).
Getting out of hand (must be a big hand).
Getting plastered (home improvement).
Getting raked over the coals (another way to get burned).
Getting sandbagged (better than sandblasted).
Getting set up (at least you get something).
Getting sidetracked (see *Directions* again).
Getting squared away (go away).
Getting stabbed in the back (like getting stabbed in the front is any better).
Getting taken to the woodshed (what's a woodshed?).
Getting the ball rolling (downhill is best).
Getting the best bang for your buck (see *Sex*).
Getting the goods on someone (no bads).
Getting the hell out of Dodge (what was hell doing in there anyway?).
Getting their lumps in (none for me, thanks).
Getting the lead out (use a pen instead).
Getting the lowdown (down low).
Getting the monkey off your back (should be in the zoo anyway).
Getting them off your back (get the monkey off first).
Getting the short end of the stick (take the other end, silly).
Getting the skinny (I like to get skinny).

Getting the straight skinny (too skinny).
Getting the wind knocked out of you (see *Farting*).
Getting to the bottom of it (see *Butt*).
Getting whipsawed (I bet that hurt).
Getting with the program (or on the program).
Getting your ass handed to you (rump roast).
Getting your bearings straight (aren't bearings round?).
Getting your bell rung (ding-dong).
Getting your digs in (use a shovel).
Getting your due (I'm overdue).
Getting your fair shake (see *Urinating*—boys only).
Getting your feet wet (I told you to stay with the socks).
Getting your goat (you can have my goat).
Getting your hand caught in the cookie jar (use two hands).
Getting your head handed to you (on a silver platter?).
Getting your Irish up (or your Italian down?).
Getting your just desserts (sure, I'd like to have just dessert).
Getting your marching orders (how about gentle suggestions instead?).
Getting your money's worth (what's your money worth?).
Getting your nose out of joint (try cosmetic surgery).
Getting your second wind (see *Farting*—yet again).
Getting your signals crossed (smoke signals).
Getting your ticket punched (wear body armor).
Getting your wings clipped (it's OK; we can't fly anyway).
Getting your wires crossed (that causes smoke signals).
Get you coming and going (either way).
Giddy up (Hi-yo, Silver)!
Give 'em a dirty look (see *Hygiene*).
Give 'em a gold star (money is better).
Give 'em a thrill (see *Lap Dancing* again).
Give 'em hell (if it's yours to give).
Give 'em the boot (or any shoe is fine).
Give 'em the bum's rush (see *Asses*).
Give 'em the business (naw, let them pay for it).
Give 'em the cold shoulder (or the hot foot).
Give 'em the finger (I don't have any to spare).
Give 'em the green light (go already).
Give 'em the time of day (never enough time).
Give a hoot (leave it to the owls).
Give it a fair shake (vanilla is best).
Give it a rest (rest not, want not).

Give it a shot (see *Guns*).

Give it a whirl (see *Amusement Rides*).

Give me a break (shake it, don't break it)!

Gives me the creeps (I don't like creeps).

Give the devil his due (maybe overdue).

Give them a piece of your mind (don't be so generous—the mind is a terrible thing to waste).

Give them a run for their money (never run from money).

Give you a piece of my mind (some have way less to spare).

Give your eye teeth (just hold onto those wisdom teeth).

Giving away the store (big sale).

Giving it the old college try (or the new college try).

Giving it your best shot (aim high).

Giving them the once-over (maybe twice over).

Gobbledygook (I think they call that oatmeal).

Go blow it out your nose (please use a hankie)!

Godsend (another reason to check your mailbox).

Goes in one ear and out the other (kinda gives a new meaning to being empty-headed).

Go fly a kite (keep your feet firmly planted on the ground)!

Going all out (let it all hang out).

Go play in traffic (at least that's something to do when you're stuck in traffic).

Going back to square one (see *Round Tuit*).

Going back to the well too often (stick with indoor plumbing).

Going batty (at least you're going somewhere).

Going belly up (vs. belly down).

Going bonkers (coming or going).

Going by the wayside (I only know oceanside and bayside).

Going cold turkey (hot turkey is way better).

Going downhill (beats going uphill).

Going down in flames (hot time).

Going down the drain (can't go up the drain).

Going down the primrose path (be sure to smell the roses).

Going down to the wire (don't let it get crossed).

Going down with the ship (better to swim away).

Going for broke (if it ain't broke….).

Going for the brass ring (not ass ring).

Going from bad to worse (that sounds bad).

Going full blast (what a blast).

Going full bore (a mole thing, I think).

Going full tilt (I'd rather go straight up).

Going great guns (guns are not great).
Going hand in hand (keep your hands to yourself).
Going hog wild (I stay away from wild hogs).
Going like gangbusters (go ahead and bust up those gangs).
Going like hotcakes (cake is best served cold).
Going nowhere fast (at least it's somewhere).
Going nuts (eating nuts—now that's for me).
Going off half-cocked (see *Penis Envy*).
Going off into the sunset (those solar flames will kill you).
Going on the straight and narrow (see *Directions*).
Going out on a limb (arm or leg?).
Going overboard (all aboard).
Going over like a lead balloon (they go under).
Going over with a fine-tooth comb (see *Dentist*).
Going places (going crazy).
Going stir-crazy (stay out of the wash cycle).
Going through the motions (causes seasickness).
Going through the roof (heads up!).
Going to bat for (pinch hitter).
Going toe-to-toe (do-si-do).
Going to hell in a handbasket (what's a handbasket?).
Going to pieces (Humpty Dumpty).
Going to pot (see *Drugs*).
Going to the wolves (I steer clear of wolves).
Going to your head (see *Sex*).
Going up in flames (having a hot time).
Going up in smoke (where there's smoke, there's fire).
Going whole hog (hogs again?).
Gold digger (see *Nose Picking* again).
Golly (lolly?)!
Golly gee (golly eff is better)!
Golly gee whiz (see *Urinating*)!
Gone haywire (see *Hey Is For Horses*).
Gone to the dogs (hot dogs).
Good, bad or indifferent (pick one).
Good egg (not a rotten egg).
Good golly (apparently there are no bad gollies)!
Good golly, Miss Molly (enough with the gollies already)!
Good gravy (nothing like real good gravy)!
Good grief (see *Oxymoron*)!
Good heavens (just one heaven, right?)!

Goodness gracious (goodness is next to godliness)!
Good to go (best not to pass a restroom without stopping).
Goody-goody (very goody).
Goody, goody gumdrops (even better goody).
Goody two-shoes (everybody has two shoes).
Goof off (you don't want to goof on).
Goo-goo eyes (too much Sandman).
Goosebumps (do you think geese get these?).
Goose that laid the golden egg (I'm definitely going to visit her).
Go pick on somebody your own size (size matters).
Gosh (at least it's not another golly)!
Got a plane to catch (so you'd be good to go).
Got 'em dead to rights (no idea).
Got 'em in their sights (what a sight to see).
Got game (no cheating).
Got the hots for him/her (better than the colds).
Got time on your hands (maybe you should wash it off).
Got time to kill (too violent).
Got your hands full (likely with too much time).
Grand Pooh-Bah (how about just President Pooh-Bah?).
Grapevine (I know I heard it somewhere).
Grasping at straws (wouldn't you rather suck on straws?).
Greased lightning (does it really need the grease?).
Greasing the skids (gotta have slippery skids).
Great balls of fire (thrown by the best pitchers)!
Great Scott (what makes him so great?)!
Green with envy (it's no fun being green).
Grin and bear it (see *Exhibitionism*).
Grody to the max (don't ask me)!
Groovy (very bumpy)!
Gross out (cross out?).
Grudge match (light my fire).
Guilty as sin (sorry, sin is always guilty).
Gung-ho (Don Ho's brother).
Gun-shy (damn right, I'm shy around guns).
Guru (way too gooey).
Half-baked ideas (watch out for E. coli).
Hand-me-downs (pick-me-ups?).
Hanging by a thread (I'd prefer a rope).
Hang in there (no hanging for me).
Hanky-panky (weird handkerchief).

Happy as a clam (how do you know when they smile).
Happy as a lark (are they really happy?).
Happy-go-lucky (that's backwards—if you're lucky, you get real happy).
Happy trails (I'll stick with paved paths)!
Hardy har har (very har)!
Has what it takes (give it back).
Hatchet job (is that how they make a totem pole?).
Haven't seen hide nor hair of them (who would hide their hair?).
Having a conniption fit (my conniption never fits).
Having a cross to bear (sorry, never seen bears wear them).
Having a crush on someone (that may hurt).
Having a devil of a time (he made me do it).
Having a falling out (see *Embarrassment*).
Having a field day (farmer talk).
Having a fit (see *One Size Fits All*).
Having a hell of a time (that would be bad—because hell is bad, right?).
Having a leg up (see *Urinating,* again).
Having an ax to grind (organ grinder).
Having a shining moment (dressed in silver).
Having a short fuse (see *Penis Envy*).
Having big shoes to fill (try wearing lots of socks).
Having egg on your face (must be a fashion statement).
Having no skin in the game (I'll keep my skin on, thank you).
Having one foot in the grave (you want to keep both feet out).
Having the gift of gab (silence is golden).
Having their way with you (my way).
Having their work cut out for them (please cut out my work).
Having the upper hand (basketball advantage).
Having the world on a string (very long string).
Having to spoon-feed them (let them use a fork instead).
Having your finger on the pulse (where are the other fingers?).
Having your hands tied (better to use Velcro).
Having your heart in the right place (where else would it be?).
Having your shit together (see *Diarrhea*).
Head for the hills (I have a head for hills).
Head over heels (yes, my head is way over my heels).
Heads will roll (bad hair day).
Healthy as a horse (horses never get sick?).
Heaven forbid (I think it forbids hell).
Heavens to Betsy (direct line, I think).
Heavy hitter (lightweight).

Hell's bells (whose bells?).
Helter-skelter (shelter?).
Hemmed and hawed (sewing terms, I think).
Henpecked (go lay an egg).
He really laid an egg (silly, only she can lay an egg).
Here comes the Cavalry (and there goes the neighborhood).
Here comes the judge (and there goes the Cavalry).
Here for the duration (tarnation).
Here's mud in your eye (don't look now).
Here's the scoop (see *Ice Cream*).
Here's to you (Mrs. Robinson).
Here's your hat, what's your hurry (see *Gotta Go*)?
Heyday (heynight).
Hey is for horses (what's this thing with horses?).
Hiding in plain sight (then it wouldn't be hiding, would it?).
Highfalutin (as opposed to lowfalutin).
High as a kite (always need that strong wind).
Highbrow (see *Unibrow*).
High-handed (basketball term).
High jinks (oh, hi there, Jinks).
High noon (I'm fine, how are you?).
High stakes (must be very tall steers).
Hightailing it (vs. lowtailing it).
Highway robbery (they call that carjacking).
Hillbilly (Uncle Jed).
Hip hip hooray (you want to put your hips into it)!
Hissy fit (my hissy doesn't fit either).
Hit the ceiling (very tall).
Hit the ground running (splat!).
Hit the road (it can hit back, you know).
Hit the roof (very, very tall).
Hitting below the belt (another reason to go beltless).
Hitting pay dirt (you have to pay for dirt?).
Hitting the bottle (bad bottle).
Hitting the mark (poor Mark).
Hitting the nail on the head (best place).
Hodgepodge (I never podge—or hodge either).
Hog calling (can you hear me now?).
Hogwash (I'm not washing hogs).
Hog-wild (when are they ever tame?).
Ho-hum (now how does that go?).

Hold at bay (bay window?).
Holding court (here comes that judge again).
Holding down the fort (it may fly away).
Holding their feet to the fire (there's an easier way to tell if it's hot).
Hold that thought (too slippery).
Hold your horses (more horses?).
Holier than thou (is thou holy?).
Holy cow (they make Swiss cheese)!
Holy mackerel (it's very blessed)!
Holy moly (or moldy)!
Holy Moses (he's so transparent)!
Holy smokes (special cigarettes)!
Holy Toledo (you're killing me already)!
Home free (living with parents).
Home, James (he knows the way).
Honest to goodness (goodness is close to godliness).
Honk if you think he's guilty (he is).
Hoochie coochie (see *Sex*).
Hook, line and sinker (stinker).
Hoopla (basketball).
Hootenanny (for those important childcare needs).
Hop in the sack (has to do with sack races, I think).
Horse of a different color (equal opportunity horse).
Horse-trading (what do you trade them for?).
Horsing around (enough with the horses already).
Hot diggity dog (love the diggity)!
Hot off the press (must be just ironed).
Hotsy-totsy (everyone likes Totsy).
Hot to trot (more horses?).
Hot under the collar (that's why you want to wear collarless shirts).
Housecoat (if you can fit a house in there, you're really in trouble).
Housedress (same thing).
Household names (mixer, oven or fridge?).
Hoity-toity (very toity).
How do you do (do what?)?
Howdy (I don't know how).
Howdy doody (see *Shit*).
Howdy, pardner (pardon me).
How's it hanging (mostly a boy question)?
Hubba hubba (lots of hubba).
Humdinger (big-time home run, I think).

Humdrum (like a snare drum?).

Hung like a horse (see *Penis Envy* again).

Hunker down (down in front).

Hunky-dory (love that dory).

Hustle and bustle (how do they go together?).

I can't hear myself think (you must not be listening).

Icing on the cake (we all want that).

I'd like to be a fly on the wall (I'd rather be the king of England).

I don't know them from a hole in the wall (I'd know it if I saw it).

If push comes to shove (aren't they the same?).

If the mountain will not come to Muhammad (oh he can probably get
    there on his own).

If the shoe fits, wear it (what else would you do with it?).

If you can't find 'em, grind 'em (get a mouth guard).

If you can't stand the heat, get out of the kitchen (I try to stay out of
    the kitchen anyway).

If you play your cards right (isn't that the object of the game?).

Ignorance is bliss (bliss is bliss).

I have a bone to pick with you (see *Nose Picking*).

I have to go winky tink (does that necessitate an announcement?).

I know you are, but what am I (don't you know?)?

I'll drink to that (just don't drive).

I'll fix your wagon (those damn wagons always break).

I lost my head (check the lost and found).

I'm all ears (you must look very silly).

I'm game (they eat game, you know; see *Hunting*).

In a bind (see *Kinky Sex*).

In a dither (dither?).

In a fix (just fix it).

In a funk (fix that too).

In a jam (bring the peanut butter).

In a jiffy (that's the peanut butter).

In a lather (soap up).

In and of itself (what can that possibly mean?).

In a New York minute (probable only 59 seconds).

In another world (see *Aliens*).

In a nutshell (that's where you'll likely find a nut).

In any case (suitcase?).

In any event (the main event).

In a pickle (see *You Are What You Eat*).

In a pig's ear (you want to stay out of their ears).

In a pig's eye (eyes too).
In a pinch (ouch!).
In a rut (groovy).
In a tizzy (get out already).
In crowd (better than the out crowd).
In deep doo-doo (don't-don't).
In for the long haul (love those truckers).
In harm's way (get out of the way, silly).
In hog heaven (that's gotta smell).
In hot water (cook 'em, Danno).
In like flint (what's like flint?).
In no way, shape or form (that's rather limiting).
In one ear and out the other (clears out cobwebs).
In one fell swoop (I hate those birds).
In other words (what's the matter with the first set of words?).
In over your head (use a snorkel).
In rare form (really watch out for E. coli).
In seventh heaven (I thought there was only one).
In spades (diamonds are better).
In the back of your mind (talk about knowing yourself).
In the ballpark (oh go ahead and hit one out).
In the cards (nothing up my sleeve).
In the catbird seat (catbird?).
In the crosshairs (down to the short hairs).
In the dark (put a light on).
In the doghouse (it's a dog's life).
In the driver's seat (can't drive from the back).
In the driver's seat (backseat driver).
In the hopper (kangaroo house).
In the hot seat (that's one way to get a red tush).
In the lap of luxury (see *Lap Dancing*).
In the loony bin (laundry receptacle).
In the loop (think lasso).
In the middle of nowhere (now you're really lost).
In the nick of time (or nicotine).
In the public eye (as opposed to private eye).
In the swing of things (strike one).
In the thick of it (thin it out).
In the throes of (what?).
In this day and age (or time and place).
In tip-top shape (I think that's good).

In your neck of the woods (I would keep my neck out of the woods).
In your skivvies (skivvies?).
Ipsy-pipsy (the pipsiest).
I smell a rat (how do rats smell?).
It all comes out in the wash (use that extra stain remover).
It gives me the heebie-jeebies (give it back).
It gives me the willies (I've got way too many willies).
It goes without saying (so why say it?).
It hit me right between the eyes (hit it back).
It just dawned on them (it was the crack of dawn).
It'll make your head spin (and the rest of your body too).
It pays for itself (I'll buy that).
It's a crying shame (no shame in crying).
It's a dog-eat-dog world (dog food?).
It's a doozy (what's a doozy).
It's a small world (not to an ant).
It's a waiting game (how do you know if you win?).
It's in the bag (what's in the bag?).
It's Greek to me (or French to them).
It's none of your beeswax (it's my beeswax).
It's not my bailiwick (some candle thing, I guess).
It's now or never (go with now).
It's on your nickel (George Washington is on my nickel).
It's written all over your face (wash it off then).
Itsy-bitsy (teeny weeny).
It takes one to know one (I know you).
It takes two to tango (and get tangled).
It went out the window (flew the coop?).
I've got you covered (with what?).
I wasn't born yesterday (good thing—you would have missed my birthday).
I wouldn't touch it with a ten-foot pole (see *Keeping Your Hands To Yourself*).
Jackass (good old Jack).
Jack of all trades (he's great, right?).
Jalopy (probably means gelato).
Jazz up (rock on).
Jeepers creepers (creepy crawlers)!
Jeezy peezy (see *Urinating*)!
Jerry-rigged (crazy Jerry).
Jibber-jabber (no idea what that means).

Jig is up (how can you tell?).
Jim-dandy (or any other dandy).
Jiminy Christmas (Santa's other name?)!
Jockeying for position (underwear thing, i.e., TPIC; see *Initials*).
Johnnie-come-lately (now where did he come from?).
Johnnie-on-the-spot (see *Bathroom*).
Jumping in with both feet (can you jump in with only one foot?).
Jumping Jehosephat (with both feet)!
Jumping Jiminy (oh, that must be jumping with one foot)!
Jumping the gun (must be some child's game).
Jumping through hoops (if that's your idea of a good time?).
Jumping to conclusions (I'm getting tired from all this jumping).
Jump their bones (jumping jacks are easier).
June is busting out all over (we like her; see *Cleavage*).
Jury's still out (lunch break).
Just a coinkidink (coin noise).
Just a hop, skip and a jump from here (Olympic event).
Just as an aside (or astride).
Just a stone's throw away (varies from arm to arm).
Just between us girls (nothing comes between us girls).
Just got off the boat (rocky start).
Just what the doctor ordered (℞).
Kaput (another Olympic sport).
Keep a stiff upper lip (is that a stiffy?).
Keeping a level head (and perfectly square too).
Keeping a lid on it (nothing can escape).
Keeping an ear to the ground (I'd just keep an eye on it).
Keeping both feet on the ground (no jumping).
Keeping mum (where do you keep her?).
Keeping tabs on them (I would remove them—fashion statement).
Keeping them at arm's length (two feet away).
Keeping them at bay (or in the bay).
Keeping them on their toes (ballet move).
Keeping them under your wing (see *Deodorant*).
Keeping up with the Joneses (that's got to be hard—there are a lot of
    Joneses).
Keeping your ducks in a row (smart ducks).
Keeping your head above water (use floaties).
Keeping your nose clean (keep everything clean).
Keeping your nose to the grindstone (that sounds painful).
Keep your pants on (you'll get cold otherwise).

Keeping your powder dry (hate wet powder).
Keeping your wits about you (don't let those get away).
Keep on truckin' (you need a special license, I think).
Keep your shirt on (see *Modesty*).
Kept in the dark (get that flashlight again).
Kept in the loop (ah, that endless loop).
Kept on a short leash (a tall order).
Kept under wraps (all wrapped up).
Kept under your hat (that would be your head).
Kewpie doll (doll face).
Kill two birds with one stone (good aim, big rock or stupid birds).
Kilroy was here (no more killing).
Kinfolk (redundant).
King of the hill (anthill).
Kiss of death (what a way to go).
Kit and caboodle (what's a caboodle?).
Knee-slapper (that's why you should keep your hand off her knee).
Knickknack (paddy whack).
Knock-down, drag-out (hard knocks).
Knock 'em dead (harder knocks)!
Knocking heads (and banging knees).
Knocking your head against the wall (don't knock it until you've tried it).
Knock it off (oh go ahead and leave it on)!
Knock on wood (why is that good luck?).
Knock the daylights out of me (but not the night-lights).
Knock yourself out (that's the hardest knock).
Knock your socks off (no socks, no service).
Know it inside and out (to know it is to love it).
Know it like the back of my hand (which side is the back?).
Know which side your bread is buttered on (hint: it's the slippery side).
Knucklehead (odd body combination).
Knuckle sandwich (you want fries with that?).
Kook (a kind of cook?).
Kooky (not cooking).
Lamebrain (better than no brain).
Land sakes (alive)!
Last of the Mohicans (they save the best for last).
Last roundup (it's a math thing).
Laundry list (keep it clean).
Laughingstock (good investment).
Laughing your head off (now won't you look silly?).

Laying it on the line (or drying it on the line).
Laying your cards on the table (and out of your sleeve).
Lazybones (you want to have energetic bones).
Lazy Susan (maybe lazy is too harsh of a term for her).
Laying down the law (no tickets that day).
Lead-pipe cinch (no cinching pcv pipes?).
Learning the ropes (I've learned not to hang from one).
Leaves something to be desired (isn't something always desired?).
Leaving 'em in the dust (too allergic).
Leaving 'em in the lurch (you want to stay outta the lurch).
Left hanging out to dry (just hanging around).
Left high and dry (better than low and wet).
Left holding the bag (depends on the bag).
Left out in the cold (bring a sweater).
Legwork (see *Exercise*).
Lend a hand (you'll give it back, right?).
Lend an ear (who has one to spare?).
Let bygones be bygones (I don't think I want to be a bygone).
Let it slide (slip and slide?).
Let's blow this popsicle stand (what a waste of popsicles).
Let sleeping dogs lie (how can they lie when they're asleep?).
Let that be a lesson to you (always thinking).
Let the baby have their bottle (better them than me).
Let the chips fall where they may (watch out for cow chips).
Letting grass grow under your feet (better than over your feet).
Letting it all hang out (see *Modesty*).
Letting the cat out of the bag (I say leave the cat in the bag; see *Cats*).
Letting them off the hook (that hook really hurts).
Letting off some steam (leave it anywhere).
Letting the wind out of your sails (or pants).
Letting your hair down (how did it get up?).
Liar, liar, pants on fire (no lie)!
Lickety- split (is that like a banana split?).
Licking your wounds (sounds like an invitation to infection).
Life is just a bowl of cherries (but too many can give you a tummy ache).
Lifting a finger (middle finger?).
Lighting a fire under them (that they would notice).
Like a ball of fire (you don't want to catch it).
Like a bat out of hell (don't they live in caves?).
Like a big dog (big dogs scare me).
Like a bull in a china closet (now how did that bull get in there?).

Like a deer caught in the headlights (we call that entanglement).
Like a duck to water (don't forget to duck).
Like a fish out of water (I like my fish out of water).
Like a fish to water (water, water everywhere).
Like a madhouse (be happy)
Like a pig in shit (dirty bacon).
Like putty in my hands (silly putty).
Like a stuck pig (stuck in shit?).
Like a ton of bricks (you still ducking?).
Like a walk in the park (or a run in the street).
Like a well-oiled machine (Tin Man).
Like every Tom, Dick and Harry (they're all the same).
Like flies on shit (fly away).
Like it or lump it (lump it?).
Like it's going out of style (not to worry—it will come back).
Like night and day (what would that be like?).
Like putty in their hands (wear gloves).
Like pulling teeth (nobody likes that).
Like signing your own death warrant (I'm not signing).
Like taking candy from a baby (shame on you).
Like talking to a wall (imagine being caught doing that).
Like the fox guarding the henhouse (does he wear a uniform?).
Like the pot calling the kettle black (pots and kettles don't talk in my house).
Like the Queen of Sheba (is she like the Queen of Hearts?).
Like there's no tomorrow (who stole tomorrow?).
Like the tail wagging the dog (how funny would that be to watch?).
Like two peas in a pod (IPod?).
Like watching paint dry (don't knock it till you try it).
Like water off a duck's back (just don't be stuck with the duck's bill).
Lily-livered (blue plate special?).
Lion's share of the work (roar).
Listening with half an ear (that would be 25 percent of total audio capacity, right?).
Lit up like a Christmas tree (not really a Jewish thing).
Living high on the hog (hogs get you high?).
Living in the boondocks (that's really living).
Living it up (down boy).
Living large (see *Dieting*).
Loaded for bear (that's really loaded).
Locked and loaded (keep it locked; see *Guns*).
Lollapalooza (special lollipop).

Lollygag (I prefer a lollipop).
Long and short of it (see *Oxymoron*).
Long arm of the law (too obvious for undercover cops).
Long in the tooth (likely long everywhere else too).
Look before you leap (I'll look, but no leaping for me).
Looking through rose-colored glasses (probably not too clear).
Look, Ma, no cavities (save it for Dad)!
Look, no hands (no brains either)!
Look what the cat dragged in (have I mentioned I don't like cats?)!
Look what the wind blew in (dust most likely)!
Loose lips sink ships (no, big holes in ships sink ships).
Loosey-goosey (see *Diarrhea*).
Lordy lordy (do you have to repeat yourself?)!
Losing your cool (and I just saw it—now where the heck did I leave it?).
Losing your shirt (see *Exhibitionism*).
Lost my train of thought (just listen for the choo-choo).
Lots of ground to cover (paint it).
Lovey-dovey (some kind of soap, I think).
Lowbrow (see *Unibrow*).
Lowering the boom (boom!).
Low man/woman on the totem pole (it's lonely at the bottom).
Lovesick schoolboy (love doesn't make you sick).
Lovesick schoolgirl (same thing).
Luck of the draw (I have no luck at drawing).
Lying like a rug (see *Baldness*).
Lying through your teeth (then close your mouth).
Made a beeline to (can't make a bee do much).
Made from scratch (I'd prefer made from food).
Made you look (you may want to avert your eyes).
Make like a tree and leave (make like a dummy and shut up).
Make my day (see *God*).
Making a federal case out of it (keep it in state courts).
Making a fool out of them (they probably do that themselves).
Making a fool out of yourself (do you need help?).
Making a go of it (better pass go).
Making a killing (wouldn't that be more like destroying?).
Making a name for yourself (don't you like the name you already have?).
Making a pass at (pass on the left).
Making a splash (cannonball).
Making hay (hey!).
Making headway (my head is often in the way).

Making mincemeat out of them (can't be too tasty).
Making money hand over fist (bank robbers say this, but they mean hand over the money).
Making my head spin (spinning out of control).
Making out (making babies).
Making out like a bandit (sounds kinda kinky).
Making small talk (pygmy language).
Making up for lost time (kissing and making up?).
Making up ground (I didn't make that up).
Making waves (see *Farting*).
Man after my own heart (keep back—you already have one).
Man-to-man (sorry, girls).
Mark my word (wouldn't that be Mark's word?).
Mexican standoff (all the more reason not to travel).
Mincing words (must be like mincemeat).
Minding your Ps and Qs (I guess the other letters are OK).
Mind like a steel trap (I guess it traps all of the steel).
Mind over matter (if you don't mind, it doesn't matter).
Mishmash (side dish with dinner).
Missed the boat (another one will always come by).
Missed the mark (who misses Mark—and why do they keep picking on him?).
Mixed bag (bag of tricks?).
Moneybags (I never get these).
Money doesn't grow on trees (damn).
Money talks (not mine).
Monkey business (that's my business).
Monkeying around (leave it to the monkeys).
Monkey see, monkey do (we're big on monkeys here).
Monkey's uncle (I guess they know).
Mop-up operation (kitchen duty).
More power to you (turn on the switch).
More than you can shake a stick at (if that's your idea of a good time).
More the merrier (misery likes company).
Morning, noon and night (what's left?).
Mother hen (kinda redundant, right?).
Motherhood and apple pie (either works for me).
Mouthwatering (they call that drooling).
Moving heaven and earth (see *God* again).
Moving into high gear (hi, Gere).
Much obliged (not really so much).
Muckety-muck (clear as mud).

Muddying the waters (more mud).
Mulling it over (lawnmuller?).
Mumbo jumbo (a dance step).
Mum's the word (no, the word's the word).
Music to my ears (direct link to my heart).
My ass is grass (my ass is fat).
My grandmother can do that (not that she'd want to).
My heart bleeds for you (try a big bandage).
My old stomping ground (who stomps?).
My word (does everything have to be yours?)!
Naked as a jaybird (they have feathers, don't they?).
Neato (everything in its place)!
Neato torpedo (torpedoes cause lots of damage; neat—not so much)!
Needle in a haystack (careful where you sit).
Needless to say (then don't say it).
Need that like a hole in the head (another ear, perhaps?).
Neither here nor there (then where?).
Neither hide nor hair (hair it is).
Nest egg (leave it to the hens).
New lease on life (I'll just renew the old one; I'm used to it.)
Nickel-and-dime operation (managed care).
Nifty (swifty).
Nincompoop (see *Shit*).
Nine'll get you ten (I guess you get a bonus).
Nip and tuck (and duck, yet again).
Nip it in the bud (who's Bud?).
Nit-picking (see *Nose Picking*, yet again).
Nitwit (no wit).
No-brainer (tell that to the Scarecrow).
No doubt about it (no doubt).
No fuss, no muss (hate that muss).
No help from the audience (they hinder anyway).
No holds barred (hold on to those bars).
No ifs, ands or buts (there we go with butts again).
No man is as island (not even a really big man).
No news is good news (beats bad news).
Nook and cranny (watch out for those crannies).
No rest for the weary (that's why they're weary, silly).
No rhyme or reason (poetry style).
No siree Bob (leave Bob alone already)!
No skin off my back (peeling from sunburn).

No skin off my nose (make up your mind).
No spring chicken (or winter water buffalo).
No strings attached (don't believe it).
Not a happy camper (likely unhappy counselor too).
Not all it's cracked up to be (see *Asses*).
Not by a long shot (basketball term, I think).
Not by the hair of my chinny chin chin (see *Double Chins*).
Not giving 'em the time of day (not yours to give).
Not firing on all cylinders (don't fire the cylinders).
Not for the faint of heart (cue the Tin Man).
Nothing to write home about (oh at least write something).
Nothing up my sleeve (what about your arm?).
Not hitting on all eight (stop hitting).
No tickie, no washie (no thank you).
No time like the present (I always like a present).
Not in the cards (use a trick deck).
Not just whistling Dixie (whistle a happy tune).
Not my cup of tea (then try decaf).
Not on the radar (see *X-ray*).
Not out of the woods yet (follow the bread crumbs).
Not playing with a full deck (trickier deck).
Not pulling any punches (don't you throw a punch?).
Not seeing eye to eye (different heights, I guess).
Not seeing the light of day (open your eyes).
Not setting the world on fire (good thing).
Not worth a plug nickel (or a wooden nickel).
Not wrapped too tight (we always need breathing room).
No way, Jose (which way to San Jose?).
Now or never (I'd go with now).
No worse for the wear (nowhere?).
Now you're talking (who's listening?).
Numbskull (no skill).
Odd man out (see *Sexist*).
Odds and ends (how about evens?).
Odds bodkins (very odd).
Offhand (underfoot?).
Off-limits (there are no limits).
Off the beaten path (see *Masturbation* again).
Off the cuff (up the sleeve?).
Off the mark (we really need to leave Mark alone).
Off the reservation (best to call ahead).

Off the top of my head (see *Haircuts*).
Off the wagon (on again, off again).
Off to the races (on to the races).
Off your rocker (and onto the sofa?).
Oh drat (a short draft?)!
Oh fiddlesticks (chopsticks?)!
Oh horse feathers (they have feathers?)!
Oh my goodness (yes, your goodness)!
Oh my merciful heavens (that would be our merciful heavens)!
Oh shoot (see *Guns*)!
Okie doke (Oklahoma baseball team, I think).
Okie dokie (another one).
OK, smarty-pants (maybe they self-clean).
Old bag (paper or plastic?).
Older than the hills (but younger than the mountains).
Old fogey (those fogeys are so old).
Old home week (probably like National Hot Dog Week).
Old Indian trick (Native American trick?).
Old maid (elderly housekeeper).
Old school (best school).
Old stomping ground (old Indian tricks).
On a bender (bend, don't break).
On a fool's errand (and off your rocker).
On a level playing field (lousy pitcher's mound).
On a lighter note (soprano?).
On an even keel (uneven may hurt).
On a power trip (blast off!).
On a roll (I'd rather eat a roll).
On a shoestring budget (keep those shoes tied).
On a slippery slope (whoops!).
On a slow boat to China (now that may really take a while).
On a tear (tear it up).
On a whim (I can't fit on a whim).
On a wing and a prayer (Amen).
Once in a blue moon (some reference to mooning, I guess).
Once upon a time (in no time).
One for the ages (I think that's images).
One good turn deserves another (be careful or you'll go in circles).
One hand washes the other (that's how they get clean).
One-shot deal (it only takes one).
One to a customer (one is enough).

On pins and needles (use a mattress instead).
On the back burner (still hot, right?).
On the ball (see *Penis Envy*).
On the bandwagon (I'm with the band).
On the chopping block (karate, I think).
On the cutting edge (not a good place to sit).
On the double (off the triple?).
On the edge of your seat (see *Butt*).
On the fence (ouch!).
On the fly (baseball term).
On the front burner (make up your mind).
On the gravy train (I'll take the slow boat to China).
On the home front (or the backyard).
On the hook (that's gotta hurt).
On the inside track (outdoor inside track?).
On their last legs (you only get one set).
On the lam (get off the lamb, you pervert).
On the level (very plumb).
On the make (make it last).
On the mark (lucky Mark).
On the mend (sewing reference).
On the move (off the mark).
On the one hand (which one?).
On the other hand (oh, the other one).
On the outs (is it like off the ins?).
On the prowl (still searching).
On the QT (you're such a cutie).
On the right track (what's with all the tracks?).
On the rocks (use the ropes).
On the ropes (see, much better than on the rocks).
On the same page (that might get crowded).
On the same wavelength (it's a swimming thing).
On the short end of the stick (wouldn't that be either end?).
On the skids (skid row?).
On the straight and narrow (straight and narrow what?).
On the tip of your tongue (kinda crowds your mouth, doesn't it?).
On the up and up (not down and down).
On the wagon (which is it—on or off?).
On the warpath (that's the old stomping ground).
Oopsy daisy (oopsy?)!
Opening up the floodgates (do we like floods?).

Open season (spring, I think).

Open sesame (why not poppy, plain or cinnamon raisin?)!

Opportunity knocks (I typically wait for the doorbell to ring—long wait, huh?).

Out of kilter (must be a kilter shortage).

Out for blood (my blood stays in hopefully).

Out for the count (Count who?).

Out in left field (better than left out).

Out like a light (must need a new bulb).

Out of bounds (think outside of the box).

Out of gas (see *Farting*).

Out of line (no cutting in line).

Out of line (or out of whack—I hate when that happens).

Out of the clear blue sky (it's all so very clear).

Out of the loop (and very dizzy).

Out of the blue (and into the green).

Out of the question (no more questions; only answers are left).

Out of the woods (so what were you doing in there anyway?).

Out of the frying pan and into the fire (another reason to stay out of the kitchen).

Out of the woodwork (must be termites).

Out of thin air (as opposed to thick air?).

Out of this world (see *Aliens*).

Out of whack (don't you just hate running out of whack?).

Out on a limb (or out to lunch).

Out to lunch (must be at a launch).

Over a barrel (talk about a prone position).

Over hill and dale (look for Chip and Dale).

Over my dead body (that can be arranged).

Over the hill (but under a mountain).

Over the top (I prefer under the bottom).

Owning up to it (looking up too?).

Painted with a broad brush (much less work than using a small brush).

Painting the town red (you would need a very broad brush).

Paperwork (it's all work).

Par for the course (partake?).

Party pooper (see *Shit*).

Passing around the hat (another new Olympic sport).

Passing the baton (already an Olympic sport).

Passing the buck (beats passing gas).

Pass muster (pass the ketchup, while you're at it).

Pawning it off on someone (chess move, I think).
Paying through the nose (I use my hands; much cleaner).
Peachy keen (very peachy?).
Peanut gallery (part of the elephant house).
Pee like a racehorse (see *Penis Envy*).
Peeling rubber (like peeling onions?).
Pencil pusher (lotta lead).
Penny-pincher (that explains her sore tush).
Penny wise and pound foolish (see *Pennies*; they are foolish).
Penultimate (must be a good pen).
Per se (per who?).
Phony as a three-dollar bill (I'll take any dollar bill).
Phony baloney (that makes a bad sandwich).
Phooey (I think it's spelled fooey)!
Picking a fight (see *Nose Picking*).
Picking up the pieces (poor Humpty).
Picking up the slack (way too much slack around).
Picking your brain (sounds painful).
Pick of the litter (no, you pick up the litter).
Pick your poison (I'll pick lemonade).
Picture-perfect (wouldn't that be perfect picture?).
Piece of cake (who doesn't like a piece?).
Pie in the sky (look out below).
Pig in a poke (don't poke the pig).
Pigging out (keep the pigs out).
Piggyback (you look so silly with a pig on your back).
Pigtails (not a great visual).
Pigsty (oy, enough with the pigs).
Pinhead (a lot can fit on the tip of a pin, you know).
Pining away (how about oaking away?).
Pinning one's ears back (see *Face-Lift*).
Pinning the blame on (pinning the tail on the donkey is much easier).
Pipe down (my pipes only go up).
Pipe dreams (who dreams about pipes—plumbers, maybe?).
Pipsqueak (ever hear a pip squeak?).
Pissant (like a carpenter ant?).
Pissing and moaning (STD?).
Pissing contest (what are the rules?).
Pissing in the wind (see *Urinating*).
Pissing match (see *Competition*).
Pitching a fit (baseball term).

Pizazz (see *Urinating*—yet again).
Plain as day (slow day).
Playing it close to the vest (pocket pool?).
Playing hooky (not yet an Olympic sport).
Playing phone tag (how do you know who wins?).
Playing possum (now that's acting).
Playing second fiddle (at least it's playing).
Playing the devil's advocate (I'd choose a better role).
Pleased as punch (must be some good punch).
Poetic justice (just another rhyme).
Poetic license (you need a license to be a poet?).
Point well taken (must be a tennis term).
Poison pen letter (better not open it).
Polly wolly doodle (that little Polly).
Pony up (more horses?).
Poop deck (don't ask).
Pooped out (see *Shit*).
Pooh-poohed (Winnie?).
Poopsie (I guess that's endearing to someone).
Poppycock (see *Penis Envy*).
Potbelly (quite unattractive).
Pounding the pavement (best to use a jackhammer).
Pound of flesh (do they sell that by the pound?).
Pouring your heart out (I guess that means bleeding a lot).
Powdering your nose (see *Drugs*).
Pray tell (Amen).
Preaching to the choir (it distracts them from their singing).
Pressed into service (ironing task).
Price of tea in China (bet it's cheaper there).
Prima donna (easier to just call her Donna).
Pros and cons (does that include ex-cons?).
Pulled a boner (see *Masturbation*).
Pulled a fast one (better than being pushed).
Pulling in the reigns (when it reigns, it pours).
Pulling my finger (surprise!).
Pulling my leg (as long as it's not my finger).
Pulling out all the stops (how about the go's?).
Pulling rank (smelly).
Pulling strings (just don't pull my string).
Pulling the plug (and down the drain it goes).
Pulling the rug out from under 'em (whoops).

Pulling the wool over their eyes (just spinning yarns).
Pulling yourself up by the bootstraps (what if you wear sandals?).
Punching their lights out (easier to just turn them off).
Puppy love (love those puppies).
Pure as the driven snow (how pure can it be after you drive on it?).
Purple people eater (never saw purple people).
Pushing the envelope (heavy envelope).
Pushing your luck (always try to get lucky).
Pussyfooting around (see *Kinky Sex*).
Put a cork in it (see *Diarrhea*).
Put a fork in it (it's done).
Put a lid on it (especially Pandora's box).
Put a sock in it (no, you put a sock on it).
Put 'em in a rubber room (bounce away).
Put it on ice (it's usually best cold).
Put it on my tab (put it on ice too).
Put out to pasture (that's where they send cow's milk).
Put that in your pipe and smoke it (see *Drugs*).
Put the hurt on (yeah, can you turn that off?).
Put the pedal to the metal (the pedal is already metal, right?).
Put the screws to 'em (go ahead and nail it).
Put the wood to (it's for the ark).
Putting a damper on it (let the air in).
Putting all your eggs in one basket (what are you—the Easter Bunny?).
Putting 'em in orbit (what goes up, comes down).
Putting in your two cents (see *Pennies*).
Putting it off (oh go ahead and put it on).
Putting it on the line (long line).
Putting it to bed (sleep tight).
Putting it to rest (sleep even tighter).
Putting on a full-court press (something about ironing).
Putting on airs (gotta be lighter than air).
Putting on the dog (I'd leave the dog alone).
Putting on the Ritz (always tastes better when it's on a Ritz).
Putting our heads together (someone would be short one head now,
    wouldn't they?).
Putting on your game face (just another mask).
Putting the cart before the horse (again with the horses).
Putting the kibosh on it (put relish in it too).
Putting them on (or off).
Putting them on a pedestal (pick 'em up when they fall).

Putting them on notice (as long as it's not a pedestal).
Putting them on the map (did they fall off?).
Putting them to shame (what a shame).
Putting the whammy on 'em (leave my whammy alone).
Putting words in their mouth (stay out of other people's mouths).
Putting your head in the sand (can't see much from there).
Putting your foot in your mouth (not very tasty, I'm sure).
Put-up job (put up or shut up).
Put up your dukes (or your earls or kings).
Put your best foot forward (is that right or left?).
Put your money where your mouth is (mine is more comfortable in my
    wallet).
Quaking in your boots (would that be an earthquake?).
Quiet as a mouse (mine's always clicking).
Quitting cold turkey (I like my turkey warm).
Racking my brain (rack 'em up).
Ragtag (children's game).
Rain check (what's that—something like a coat check?).
Rain dance (outdoors only, please).
Raining cats and dogs (umbrella probably won't cut it).
Raining on my parade (better keep my umbrella handy).
Rainy day fund (spend it on a sunny day).
Raise a red flag (better than a white flag).
Raising Cain (he's very dead).
Raising hell (leave hell where it is).
Raising holy hell (that sounds rather confusing to me).
Raking in the dough (all I ever get to rake is leaves).
Ramping it up (or sliding down).
Ratcheting up (maybe pumping up).
Rat fink (what's a fink?).
Rat race (don't bet on the big fat one).
Rattling their cages (give them a saber).
Rattling their sabers (that's the way to rattle).
Razzle-dazzle (some kind of drink, I guess).
Reached the end of the line (real lines don't end).
Read 'em and weep (sad story).
Read 'em the riot act (Act One).
Read my lips (are they spelling something?).
Read the writing on the wall (graffiti).
Ready, willing and able (I guess they can).
Real McCoy (I hate those fake McCoys).

Red herring (have a knish with that).
Red-letter day (Valentine's Day).
Red Rover (come on over).
Remember the Maine (I forgot).
Resting on their laurels (I prefer a bed).
Rigmarole (some kind of pastry).
Right hand not knowing what the left hand is doing (hands should be
    in constant communication with each other).
Right off the bat (or left off the bat).
Right on (something like right arm).
Right on the money (it always gets back to the money).
Right out from under your nose (don't sneeze).
Ringing off the hook (hang up already).
Ringleader (ring bearer?).
Rinky-dink (I think it's rinky-drink).
Robbing Peter to pay Paul (what about Mary?).
Robbing the cradle (leave the baby).
Rocking the boat (sit down already).
Rolling out the red carpet (let it roll).
Rolling the dice (always blow on them first).
Rolling up your sleeves (still nothing there, right?).
Roll in the hay (watch out for the needles).
Roll with the punches (I prefer mine with butter—rolls, that is).
Roly-poly (very poly).
Rome wasn't built in a day (really?).
Rootin' tootin' (see *Farting*—not for the last time).
Rubbed the wrong way (is there a right way—see *Sex,* also not for the
    last time).
Rubbing their nose in it (use a tissue).
Ruffling their feathers (only birds have feathers).
Rule of thumb (the rule is no thumb sucking).
Rules the roost (is that a rule?).
Rumpus room (that's where you find all the rumpuses).
Run amok (like a 5K, I think).
Run of the mill (see *Bull Running*).
Running around in circles (that will get you nowhere fast).
Running around like a chicken with its head cut off (I'd like to see that).
Running circles around 'em (and getting very dizzy).
Run for the hills (walk, don't run).
Running it into the ground (again, best to walk).
Running like clockwork (how does a clock work anyway?).

Running neck and neck (and arm in arm?).
Running on empty (it won't run on empty).
Running on fumes (it will run on fumes though).
Running the gamut (special course).
Running them ragged (both Ann and Andy).
Run of the mill (is that still running?).
Run it up the flagpole (better to use the rope).
Run the gamut (I prefer to walk mine).
Saving for a rainy day (do you spend it when it rains?).
Say cheese (eat cheese).
Say the word (which one?).
Scared to death (what a way to go).
Scared the bejesus out of me (shouldn't be Jesus anyway).
Scaredy-cat (I still hate cats).
Scaring the living daylights out of 'em (where's that flashlight again?).
Scaring the dickens out of you (how did the dickens get in there anyway?).
Scaring their pants off (see *Exhibitionism*).
Scatterbrain (mine is always scattered).
Schoolboy crush (lose some weight).
Schoolgirl crush (you too).
School of hard knocks (WWF Academy).
Scissor happy (mine are very happy).
Scram (rugby term?)!
Scraping the bottom of the barrel (think of all that gross stuff down
    there).
Scratching the surface (see *Itch*).
Screaming bloody murder (I get the bloody murder part, but
    screaming—it may be too late).
Scuttlebutt (I'm working on that visual).
Search me (not a smart invitation).
Seesaw battle (playground war).
Secondhand (that's as far as hands can go, right?).
Second nature (what would first nature be?).
Seeing eye to eye (shouldn't that be eyes to eyes?).
Seeing the light (not too hard; it's that real bright thing).
See you later, alligator (I'll stay away from alligators).
Selling 'em a bill of goods (don't you want a receipt?).
Selling 'em down the river (better than up river).
Selling yourself short (shorts on sale?).
Separating the men from the boys (look for the razors).
Serves them right (don't serve them wrong).

Serving two masters (better serve them right).
Set in stone (stones break, you know).
Setting 'em up (rack 'em up).
Setting the stage (like setting the table).
Setting the world on fire (pyromaniac).
Setting your hair (ready, set, go).
Settle down (where?).
Shake a leg (don't dogs do that?).
Shake your booty (usually happens by itself).
Shaking like a leaf (leaf it alone).
Shell-shocked (too many seashells).
Shenanigans (the little people in *The Wizard of Oz?*).
Shape up or ship out (see *Dieting*).
Sharp as a tack (pinhead).
Shindig (my shins can't dig).
Ship of fools (on a slow boat to China).
Shipshape (see *Overweight*).
Shiver me timbers (brrr!).
Shooting the breeze (aim high).
Shooting yourself in the foot (bad aim—real bad aim).
Shoot the works (see *Guns*).
Shorthanded (maybe compensate with longer legs).
Short shrift (I'll keep mine long, thank you).
Shot in the dark (you really need to duck again).
Showstopper (intermission).
Show them the ropes (oh go ahead and show them everything).
Shrinking violet (don't you just hate it when they shrink?).
Shucks (corny term)!
Sick as a dog (they're rarely sick, right?).
Sick 'em (not the dog)!
Sidetracked (single tracked).
Silver bullet (Hi-yo, Silver).
Singing a different tune (name that tune).
Sink or swim (pick swim—trust me).
Sit tight (some may not have a choice).
Sitting ducks (there we go with ducking again).
Sitting on a powder keg (powdered beer?).
Sitting pretty (sit up straight).
Skating on thin ice (can't you read the sign?).
Skedaddle (and scram too)!
Skyscraper (like an ice scraper?).

Sky's the limit (no limits).
Slam dunk (you'd know it if you saw it).
Sleeping like a baby (no snoring).
Slim pickings (slim is better than none).
Slinging mud (or hash).
Slip of the tongue (my tongue is very slippery).
Slow on the uptake (much faster on the down low).
Slowpoke (what's a fastpoke?).
Smack dab in the middle (just a dab).
Small potatoes (one potato, two potato....).
Smart alec (leave it to Alec).
Smart as a whip (are whips that smart?).
Smegma (I don't think that's a word).
Smooch (one of the few times that getting beats giving).
Smooth sailing (no waves).
Snake in the grass (get out that lawnmower).
Sneaky Pete (oh that Pete!).
Snowing to beat the band (battle of the bands?).
Snow job (not a sex act).
Snookums (you can have her).
Snug as a bug in a rug (get the bugs out).
Soaked to the skin (wet skin).
So far, so good (so what?).
So help me (can So help me too?).
Sold me a bill of goods (don't pay the bills).
So mad, you're spitting bullets (cover your mouth).
Something is rotten in the state of Denmark (must be those bad apples).
Something to hang your hat on (that would be your head, right?).
Something up your sleeve (still your arm?).
Son of a gun (that's what happens when you play around with guns).
So on and so forth (so?).
So on and so on (maybe they mean sew on).
Sound asleep (that sound must be snoring).
Sound like a broken record (they don't sound like anything if they're broken).
Sour grapes (don't they make wine from those?).
Sourpuss (be nice—get your head out of the gutter).
Sowing their wild oats (sewing?).
Space cadet (new military school).
Spearheading (spear chucking?).
Spill the beans (then clean them up).

Spill your guts (better clean them up too).
Spinning tales (see *Asses*).
Spinning your wheels (hate those ruts).
Spitting image (see *Hygiene*).
Splitting hairs (easier than splitting atoms).
Spoiled to death (what a way to go).
Spreading like wildfire (fight fire with fire?).
Spreading your wings (I only have arms).
Spring a leak (because it's springtime?).
Spunk (use your imagination).
Square meal (my plate is round).
Squeaky-clean (clean is clean).
Squirreled away (yes, keep the squirrels away).
Stamp of approval (sold at your local post office).
Stand up and be counted (I guess it doesn't count if you're sitting down).
Stand-up guy (comic).
Starting from ground zero (it's a beginning, right?).
Starting from scratch (it starts with an itch).
Starting off on the right foot (what's the matter with the left foot?).
State of the art (where is that state?).
Stay tuned (see *Couch Potato*).
Stealing one's thunder (see *Ten Commandments*).
Stealing them blind (maybe they didn't see you rob them).
Stemming the tide (good luck).
Step in the right direction (see *Left-Hand Turns*).
Stepping out (better than stepping in it).
Stepping up to the plate (batter up).
Stick it in your ear (never know what you'll find there)!
Sticking out like a sore thumb (probably because it is a sore thumb).
Sticking to your guns (I can think of better things to stick to).
Stick in the mud (clear as mud, yet again).
Sticking your neck out (what are you, a giraffe?).
Sticker shock (call the EMTs).
Sticky wicket (I hate it when my wicket gets sticky).
Stinks to high heaven (don't stinks go to hell?).
Stop fiddling around (unless that's your instrument of choice).
Stop on a dime (I would stop *for* a dime).
Stop 'em in their tracks (railroad tracks?).
Stop the presses (they stop at stop signs)!
Storm's a-brewing (turn off that coffee maker).
Straight answer (like there's a curved answer).

Straight as an arrow (boring heterosexual?).
Straight as the crow flies (crows don't deviate).
Straight from the horse's mouth (you wouldn't catch me in there).
Straighten up and fly right (can you really fly wrong?).
Straight scoop (gotta involve either poker or ice cream).
Straight shooter (see *Gay*).
Straw that broke the camel's back (must have been that last straw).
Street-smart (my street is a genius).
Strike up the band (what, the band is on strike now?).
Strike when the iron is hot (I stay away from hot irons).
Striking gold (gold goes on strike too?).
Stubborn as a mule (or smelly as a mule).
Stuck holding the bag (old bag).
Stuck in your craw (my craw hurts).
Stuffed to the gills (stuffed gills are delicacies).
Suit yourself (bathing suit?).
Sunday driver (driver's license restrictions, I guess).
Super (not supper)!
Super-duper (very duper)!
Surefire way (they call that arson).
Swallowing a bitter pill (not a happy pill).
Swan song (can you hum it for me?).
Sweating bullets (deadly).
Sweating like a pig (I'd rather not do anything like a pig).
Sweeping it under the rug (better to use a vacuum).
Sweeten the pot (as long as the pot's not calling the kettle black).
Sweet pea (not like sweet tea).
Sweet tooth (I can't taste my teeth).
Swell (oh well)!
Swept off your feet (very thorough cleaning).
Ta-da (doo-da)!
Tag team (you're it).
Tag, you're it (you're still it)!
Ta ta (CU)!
Take a back seat to (use those seat belts).
Take a nose dive (follow your nose).
Take another crack at it (how do you take a crack?).
Take a number (any number).
Take a page from their book (don't rip it out).
Take a shot (of what?).
Take a stab at it (just don't take a stab at me).

Take it to the bank (I'm much better at taking it from the bank).
Take it up a notch (it's a belt thing).
Take it with a grain of salt (I typically need more than one grain).
Take the bull by the horns (stay away from horny bulls).
Take your breath away (see *Bad Breath*).
Take your lumps (one lump or two?).
Take your money and run (as long as it's your money).
Taking flack (giving is better).
Taking it on the chin (best not to have a double chin).
Taking its toll (oh just pay the toll).
Taking no prisoners (jails are overcrowded anyway).
Taking off the gloves (especially inside).
Taking the world by storm (they call that a hurricane)
Talking it out (better than keeping it in).
Talking out of both sides of your mouth (ventriloquist?).
Talking trash (trash should be seen and not heard).
Talking turkey (special language).
Tallyho (and ta ta too)!
Tearing your hair out (see *Baldness*).
Tearing your heart out (talk about heartless).
Teensy-weensy (weensy?).
Teeny weeny (I'm not touching that one).
Teetotaler (I told you to stick with decaf).
Telltale sign (just what we need—talking signs).
Tempest in a teapot (go with decaf instead—didn't we already talk
   about this?).
Testing their mettle (hope my mettle passes).
Thank your lucky stars (they are all lucky).
Thar she blows (give her your hankie)!
That feeling in the pit of your stomach (stop eating the pits).
That'll fix their wagon (stay on the wagon).
That rings a bell (ding-dong).
That's a dilly (what's a dilly?).
That's a doozy (or is that a dilly?).
That's a kick in the pants (you'd know it if you got it).
That's all folks (it's never all).
That's all she wrote (not much of a writer, huh?).
That's all well and good (very well).
That's another story (Book II).
That's a lot of hooey (is that Baby Huey?).
That's a lulu (no, she's a Lulu).

That's a real toe-tapper (or knee-slapper).
That's a tall order (stick with the light beer).
That's for the birds (the birds can have it).
That's going to backfire (see *Farting*).
That's horse hockey (special sport)!
That's just chicken feed (what do chickens eat anyway?).
That's just ducky (oy, more ducks).
That's life in the fast lane (pass on the left).
That's no way to run an airline (up?).
That's old hat (trash that old hat).
That's right up my alley (right alley).
That's the bee's knees (do they even have knees?).
That's the bomb (stay away from the bomb)!
That's the cat's pajamas (do they wear pajamas?).
That's the last straw (don't you just hate it when someone takes the
    last straw?).
That's the name of that tune (that's what I want to know).
That's the name of the game (that's a silly name for a game).
That's the $64,000 question (must be an expensive answer).
That's the ticket (I hate getting tickets).
That's the way it goes (where did it go?).
That's the way the cookie crumbles (I don't like crumbled cookies).
That's the whole ball of wax (it's a wax ball).
That's the whole shooting match (see *Guns*).
That takes the cake (I'll take the cake).
That will tide you over (is the tide over?).
The ball's in your court (my ball, my court).
The customer's always right (whose idea was that?).
The devil made me do it (gotta blame someone).
The fix is in (or out).
Their days are numbered (all days are numbered, aren't they?).
Their goose is cooked (at least it's not duck).
Their heart is in the right place (where else would it be?).
The jig is up (put it down already).
The more, the merrier (Robin Hood and his Merry Men?).
Them's fightin' words (oh give peace a chance, will ya?).
The natives are restless (try sleeping pills).
The plot thickens (the soup thickens).
The proof is in the pudding (no, I like pudding in my pudding).
There are bigger fish to fry (doesn't matter to me—not a fish fan).
There are more fish in the sea (like I said, I don't care).

There'll be hell to pay (use your credit card).

There's a new sheriff in town (or old sheriff in a new town).

There's more than one way to skin a cat (how many do you need?).

The rest is history (it's all history).

The show must go on (sometimes on and on and on).

The whole enchilada (no holes).

The whole shebang (or hebang).

The whole shooting match (see *Guns*, yet again).

They're going at it (or on it).

They've got moxie (maybe they should give it back).

Thick as thieves (fat crooks?).

Thingamabob (poor Bob).

Thingamajig (woodworking term).

Thingamajiggy (very special woodworking tool).

Things of that nature (so natural).

Thingy (unique thing).

Thinking cap (mine is shrinking).

Thinking long and hard (see *Penis Envy*).

Thinking out loud (that would be talking, right?).

Think tank (do they swim in the think tank?).

Third time's the charm (three strikes and you're out).

This hurts me more than it does you (yeah, who are you kidding?).

This, that and the other (all three).

Thorn in your side (ouch!).

Threading the needle (it's a sewing thing).

Three-ring circus (who doesn't like it?).

Three's a crowd (it always comes in threes).

Three sheets to the wind (air dry).

Throwing a monkey wrench into it (not the best way to fix things).

Throwing caution to the wind (different than pissing in the wind).

Throwing cold water on it (fighting fire).

Throwing good money after bad (who's got bad money?).

Throwing in the towel (throw it in with the laundry).

Throwing out the baby with the bath water (save the baby!).

Throwing their weight around (don't throw it here, please).

Throwing your hat in the ring (great use for hats).

Thrown for a loop (baseball term).

Thrown to the wolves (throw it back).

Throw the book at 'em (that may hurt).

Thumbing your nose at (see *Nose Picking*).

Thumbs down (but keep your chin up).

Thumbs up (make up your mind).

Tickled pink (that's a lot of tickling).

Tickle your fancy (now where exactly do you suppose your fancy is?).

Tick off (yes, get that tick off me).

Tidbit (don't bite).

Tight-lipped (see *Face-Lift*).

Tightwad (I hate it when my wad gets too tight).

Time flies when you're having fun (time doesn't fly; flies fly).

Time is of the essence (essentially).

Time is on your side (it take sides?).

Timetable (very large table).

Time to shove off (just shove it).

Time will tell (mine keeps secrets very well).

Tip of the hat (no tip policy).

Tip of the iceberg (cold as ice.)

Tip-top (very top).

Tit for tat (what's a tat; see *Breasts*).

To be perfectly frank (I'd rather be me; and what makes Frank so perfect?).

To boot (or not to boot).

To each his/her own (my own).

Toe the line (maybe tow the line).

To hell and back (what a ride).

To make a long story short (see *Long Sentences*).

Tomfoolery (good old Tom).

Tongue-in-cheek (hard to talk that way).

Tongue-lashing (I'm working on that visual).

Too big for your britches (see *Dieting*).

Too close for comfort (give me space).

Toodle-loo (some kind of British bathroom, I think)!

Toodles (special noodles)!

Too hot to handle (use oven mitts).

Tooling down the road (don't use tools while driving).

Tools of the trade (tool trader).

Too many irons in the fire (fire irons).

Too pooped to pop (see *Shit*).

Tooting your own horn (see *Farting*).

Tootsie wootsie (wootsie?).

Top banana (they all look the same to me).

Top dog (what ever happened to Top Cat?).

Top-notch (belt term).

Top of the morning to you (is there a bottom?).

Topsy-turvy (very turvy).
Tote that barge (lift that bale—then take a nap).
To the nth degree (what number is nth?).
Touch and go (look but don't touch).
Touching base (see *Sex*).
Touchy-feely (stop touching already).
Tough act to follow (so don't).
Tough noogies (I like mine more tender).
Tough nut to crack (then pick another one).
Tough as nails (try a manicure).
Track record (LP?).
Treated like second-class citizens (coach?).
Treat with kid gloves (what a treat).
Trial by fire (I'll stick with a jury).
Tricks of the trade (only works for magicians).
Trigger-happy (must be something about Roy Rogers' horse).
Tripping the light fantastic (no idea; sorry).
Trouble in River City (that's why they need a new sheriff in town).
Tsk-tsk (vowel shortage).
Tugging at your heartstrings (no strings attached to my heart; just veins).
Turf battle (why would anyone fight about grass?).
Turn a blind eye to (blind ambition?).
Turning over a new leaf (leave the leaves alone).
Turning over in their grave (talk about bad sleeper).
Turning point (points don't turn).
Turning the corner (until the next corner).
Turning the tables on 'em (does that really shake 'em up?).
Turning the tide (I think a washing machine does that).
Turning the other cheek (see *Asses*).
Turning the screws (nails may work way better).
Turning up the heat (stay out of the kitchen).
Turning up your nose (it pays to be double-jointed).
Tut-tut (King Tut's son?).
Twiddling thumbs (mindless activity).
Twinkle toes (must be very clean toes).
Twisting my arm (and pulling my finger).
Two heads are better than one (except it looks very weird).
Two-pronged approach (I wouldn't even like one prong approaching me).
Two thumbs up (then you're all thumbs).
Two wrongs don't make a right (they just make it more wrong, right?).
Under penalty of death (better pay attention).

Under the gun (or over a barrel).

Under the weather (how low can you go?).

Under wraps (not wrapped too tight).

Under your breath (what's under there—another breath?).

Until kingdom come (I'm waiting for my kingdom to come).

Until the cows come home (where'd they go—probably out to dinner).

Until you're blue in the face (blue blood?).

Up a creek without a paddle (better get an outboard motor).

Up for grabs (see *Groping*).

Up in arms (or down in legs).

Up in the air (everything is up in the air).

Upsetting the apple cart (my apple cart doesn't get that sensitive).

Up the wazoo (I don't think I'd like anything up my wazoo).

Up the ying yang (or down my ying yang either).

Up to snuff (how high is snuff—I guess it's 'snuff).

Up to your ears (but not over your head).

Up to your eyeballs (which is higher?).

Up your nose (I'd stay out of there).

Use your noodle (or eat your noodles).

Vegging out (yes, get them out and off my plate).

Vim and vigor (the V brothers).

Voilà (as in presto)!

Waiting in the wings (I'd be floating on the wings).

Waiting for the dust to settle (then you clean it up, I guess).

Waiting for the smoke to clear (another reason not to smoke).

Waiting for your ship to come in (if you're way inland, you've got a really long wait).

Waiting with bated breath (is that like bad breath?).

Wait till your father gets home (worth waiting for?).

Wait till your mother gets home (which is worse?).

Walking all over you (watch for skid marks).

Waking up the dead (good trick).

Waiting for the other shoe to drop (watch out).

Walking on eggshells (another reason to wear shoes).

Walking wounded (toughness).

Warm and fuzzy (I'm not big on being fuzzy).

War of words (low on destruction).

Wash your mouth out with soap (better than brushing?).

Waste not, want not (I always want plenty).

Watched pot never boils (only if you haven't put the heat on).

Watching me like a hawk (better to watch the hawk).

Water under the bridge (damn).
Water under the dam (or damn bridge—something like that).
Wearing out the welcome mat (you're welcome).
Wearing your Sunday best (or Monday worst).
Weathering the storm (isn't the storm part of the weather?).
We'll cross that bridge when we come to it (what else would you do—
    jump over it?).
Well, I'll be a monkey's uncle (that would be a step up for some)
Well, la-di-da (do-re-mi?)!
Well, shut my mouth (gladly)!
Well-wishers (probably wish they had a well).
Went belly-up (mine hangs down).
Wet behind the ears (at least it's not a wet willy).
Wet nurse (she should get out of the rain).
Wetting your whistle (nothing worse than a wet whistle).
What a drag (push or pull?)!
What a motley crew (some kind of haircut, I think)!
What a train wreck (another reason to stay on track)!
Whatever floats your boat (mostly water).
Whatever tickles your fancy (I love to have my fancy tickled).
Whatever turns you on (the light switch works).
What have you (I don't have it).
What in tarnation (where is Tarnation?)?
What in the Sam Hill is going on (why does Sam Hill care?)?
What's all the hubbub, bub (who's Bub?)?
What's all the hullabaloo (that's a hell of a baloo)?
What's cooking (those olfactory bulbs should give you a hint)?
What's good for the goose is good for the gander (yeah, take a gander
    at this).
What's happening (best to open your eyes)?
What's the game plan (just play already)?
What the hey (or hay)?
Whatchamacallit (you call it).
Wheeler-dealer (big deal).
When all is said and done (then what?).
When it rains, it pours (no shit).
When pigs fly (then it's time to wake up—or lay off the drugs).
When the chips are down (is that the way the cookie crumbles too?).
When the dust settles (settle outside).
Where's the fire (where are your glasses?)?
Where the rubber meets the road (see *Condoms*).

Where there's smoke, there's fire (even if you get fired?).
Wherewithal (fashion statement).
While away the hours (takes a while).
Whipped into a frenzy (whipped cream?).
Whippersnapper (snap to it).
Whipping boy (if you like that kinda thing).
Whirling dervish (dervish?).
White as a ghost (now do we really know what color ghosts are?).
Whiz-bang (see *Urinating*).
Whoa (there's that horse thing again)!
Whoa, Nelly (stop already)!
Whoop-dee-do (some kind of hair style, I think)!
Whoopee (see *Urinating,* again)!
Whoopee cushion (use the toilet).
Whooping it up (I guess that's coughing a lot).
Whoopsie (run when the doctor says this)!
Whosie (who?).
Whosie-whatsit (thingamajig?).
Who struck John (poor John)?
Who was that masked man (he's the guy in the mask, silly)?
Widget (ever see one of those?).
Wigged out (or out of wigs).
Wild blue yonder (very wild).
Wild-goose chase (or any goose chase—find something better to do).
Wild, wild West (one wild isn't enough?).
Willy-nilly (who's he?).
Wine, women and song (in that order?).
Wingding (not to be confused with a Ring Ding).
Wiseacre (half-acre).
Wishbone (I'd wish for something else).
Wishful thinking (always wishing).
Wishy-washy (stay clean).
With both feet on the ground (can't get very far that way).
With both guns blazing (shooting or blazing?).
With your tail between your legs (I don't have a tail—or an ass, for
    that matter).
Woke up in a cold sweat (don't you sweat when you're hot?).
Woman's prerogative (see *Sexist*).
Won't see the light of day (use a flashlight).
Working around the clock (hard to do with a digital timepiece).
Working banker's hours (still 60 minutes).

Working feverishly (now that's working too hard).
Working on the railroad (at least it's work).
Working the graveyard shift (sixth gear?).
Working your ass off (now don't you look funny).
Working your fingers to the bone (wear gloves).
Works like a charm (Lucky Charm?).
World-class (first-class, coach…?).
Worst-case scenario (scene one?).
Worth a shot (see *Guns*).
Wouldn't hurt a fly (I would definitely hurt a fly).
Wouldn't that be a fine how-do-you-do (how do you do?)?
Wrapped around their finger (either little you or big finger).
Wreaking havoc (poor havoc).
Wrong side of the tracks (so is that right or left?).
X marks the spot (thank you, Mark).
Yanking your chain (see *Masturbation,* yet again).
Yessiree (yes is best)!
Yesterday's news (old papers).
Yes, we have no bananas (any oranges?).
Yikes (not whoops)!
Yippee (kind of hippy)!
Yippie ki-yay (yea!)!
You bet (no, you bet).
You betcha (cha?).
You bet your ass (don't risk what you can't afford to lose; although I
    guess we can all afford to lose some).
You bet your sweet ass (what have you been sitting in?).
You can dress them up (girls only).
You can kiss that goodbye (depends what it looks like).
You can lead a horse to water (no more horses, I promise).
You can take that to the bank (usually money).
You drive me to drink (bring your ID).
You had to be there (I'm there).
You lie like a rug (rugs always tell the truth).
You look like a ragamuffin (and you smell like one too).
You missed the boat (where did that boat go?).
You missed your calling (take a message).
You're a silly goose (not a serious goose).
You're not a spring chicken (nor do I want to be).
You're on another planet (not well grounded).
You're such a stuffed shirt (use less starch).

Young buck (Uncle Buck?).
Young Turk (old buck).
You're a sight for sore eyes (use those eye drops).
You're toast (Halloween costume, I guess).
Y2K (why not?).
Zoning out (land planning term).
Zounds (sounds?)!

SINCE

Worst hurricane since 1972; biggest plane crash since 1985; driest month since 1960. Who cares, and what difference does it make? Even if the 1985 crash was worse, if this one makes the news, it must be pretty bad, right? Records and comparisons—they don't really change the here and now, do they?

SINCERITY

There's no sin in sincerity, so please be sincere with your comments and promises. Sorry, but yes, people judge you; and they judge you by what you do and what you say (see *Reputation*). Stand behind it and mean it.

SINGING

Admit it: we all think we've got great singing voices and are the next Paul McCartney or Barbra Streisand. Well, guess what? Likely not so much. If you're singing away and people around you cringe, it's a dead giveaway that you should limit your singing to the shower, where we think we sound great. Other venues would include your car (with the windows tightly rolled up) or very alone in your house (with the doors and windows closed, please).

SINGING IN THE RAIN

It's pretty stupid to sing in the rain. You'll get sick, for goodness' sake. Didn't your mother ever teach you anything? And don't forget to bundle up and put on your galoshes. And stand up straight.

SINS

We all commit sins, although some of us go way overboard in the sin department. Seeking forgiveness and atoning are the ways to go. Be careful of committing the really big sins, though (see *Ten Commandments*), as you may be risking some very serious consequences.

SIZE

Does size matter? Only if you're very, very big or very, very small (see *One Size Fits All*).

SKIDILLION

Skidillion—now that's a lot. It's even more than a bazillion.

SKID MARKS

Skid marks should only be left by tires. You really don't want to leave your own trail, do you (see *Wiping*)?

SKINNING A CAT

How many ways can there possibly be to skin a cat? I'm thinking only one really matters. However, I don't care (see *Cats*).

SLEEP

Your body clearly does need eight hours of sleep each night. Otherwise your well-oiled machine will begin to fall apart—really. Now too much sleep can lead to a big problem, as sleep breeds sleep (see *Depression*).

SLEEPING WITH SOMEONE

OK, I get the cuddling, canoodling and post-sex embracing and caresses. But sleeping together? Think about it. Isn't it more natural to sleep alone? Didn't we (mostly) sleep alone growing up? Sorry to be the spoiler here, but I find no big attraction to having someone tossing, turning and kicking next to me all night; not to mention the snoring and getting up to pee. And believe me, I'm sure it's no picnic sleeping next to my noisy hulk either. Sparkling personalities can only get you so far, you know. And waking up next to someone can be very scary: disheveled hair, gook in the eyes, bad breath (and that's just you). Sleeping is a bodily function. We don't share too many of our other bodily functions together, do we?

SLEEPING WITH THE ENEMY

Sleeping with the enemy is not a good idea. If there are sides to be taken, choose one and stick with it (see *Loyalty*).

SLINKY

A Slinky is just a big spring, right? It can bend over backwards and tumble down the stairs, but I can too. However, unlike me, the toy can do it without going to the hospital. Now what does that say?

SLOW AND STEADY

Yes, slow and steady does win the race. That doesn't necessarily mean you'll come in first, but in the end, you will ultimately win (see *Patience*).

SLOWPOKE

OK, so what's a fast poke?

SLUT

God knows where the word slut came from, but it's not something you should aspire to be, especially you girls. If you're well known as being easy, you probably want to find a different way to be popular with the boys (see *Reputation*).

SMART-ASS

Nobody likes a smart-ass? Nonsense; of course they do. Plenty of people like me, you know.

SMART-ASS ANSWERS

Everybody loves a smart-ass, so here are a few choice answers you may want to use:

> Are you done with that paper? (No, I left it on the floor for the dog to read—that is, while he's not answering the phone.)
> Did you get a haircut? (No, I got them all cut.)
> Did you just get off the boat? (Yes, and it was a wonderful trip; glad you couldn't make it.)

Don't look at me in that tone of voice. (OK, that makes no sense.)

Every time I turn around, another bad thing happens. (So don't turn around.)

For those of you who don't know me, I'm the Vice President of…. (So who are you if we already know you?)

Get the fuck out of here. (Why, is there a fuck in here?)

Go fix your hair. (Is it broken?)

Go to hell. (Lead the way.)

I beg your pardon. (Oh, it's so unbecoming to beg.)

I can't pay you back; I'm a little short today. (Why, did someone cut your legs out from under you?)

I can't stand it anymore. (Then sit down.)

I'd like to see what you think about that. (I can hear what you think about that if you tell me, but I surely can't see it.)

I don't want to bore you, but…. (Too late.)

If you have any questions, my name is…. (What's your name if I don't have any questions?)

I have an idea. (Oh, I thought I smelled something burning.)

I'll talk to you soon. (Thanks for the warning.)

I'm fixing dinner. (Why, is it broken?)

I'm going out; want to join me? (Are you coming apart?)

I'm just not myself today. (Then who are you?)

I need to pick your brain for a minute. (Are you a neurosurgeon?)

I really worked my ass off yesterday. (So that's what happened to it.)

I think I just lost my head. (Trust me; you would know if you lost your head.)

Is the doctor in? (No, all of those patients are waiting for the next train.)

Is this seat taken? (I'm sure there are plenty of smart-ass answers to this; I just can't think of any right now.)

It was so funny I laughed my ass off. (Nope, it's still there; can't miss it.)

Man, I really busted my ass today. (Well that explains the crack.)

May I be frank? (Only if I can be Lester.)

May I have your name? (Well, then you'd have two names and I wouldn't have any now, would I?)

Oh, you're home? (No, that's the dog answering the phone.)

Pardon me. (Who do you think I am—the governor?)

See what I'm saying? (No, do you have letters coming out of your mouth?)

See you later. (Thanks again for the warning.)

So where is So-and-So (very common name)? (Don't know; not my day to watch him/her.)

This has been a very long day. (What, did they add a few hours to it or something?)

We're going to have to sit down and discuss this. (Can't you talk standing up?)

Were you born yesterday? (Yes, and I'm very mature for my age.)

What's up? (Whatever isn't down.)

Who died and left you boss? (Who cares; long live the king.)

Yawning. (Am I keeping you up?)

You can say that again. (Didn't you hear me the first time?)

SMELL THE ROSES

Yes, it's a good idea to stop and smell the roses (or potato chips) once in a while. The world passes us by way too quickly. So what's your rush? Go on, take a whiff, especially if those roses are in bloom. Whatever it is, it'll wait. It wouldn't hurt for you to listen to some nice soothing music as well (see *Stress*). Try it; you'll like it.

SMILING

You can open so many doors with a smile on your face. Some people have real killer smiles; but it doesn't matter if you've been kissed by the ugly stick—a smile is gorgeous on everybody. It's the prettiest part of anyone's face. A smile is a frown turned upside down (I read that somewhere). Anyway, when you smile, the whole world smiles with you (that's the law). It's very contagious, as most of us can't resist returning a smile. So go out and infect someone—everyone (see *Germs*). Smile; you'll like it.

SMOKE DETECTORS

The smoke detector is one of the best inventions of the twentieth century. But it will only save lives if the batteries are fresh. So change them at least every six months. You'd be wise to change your underwear even more often.

SMOKING

Let me get this straight. You take some crushed up tobacco rolled in paper, set it on fire and ingest it. The intense heat is sucked into your lungs and you exhale the smoke. And you do this because…? This all seems rather ludicrous to me.

Why not simply wrap your mouth around the tailpipe of a running car? Same thing, right? Do you smokers really enjoy having your breaks standing outside in the cold/rain/sleet/snow, just to maintain your habit? Don't be an idiot. Not only is smoking a very unattractive and smelly habit, but sucking down those cancer sticks is likely the most destructive thing you can do to yourself. If you've never smoked, don't start. If you smoke, stop. You can't fool yourself, because you know it will kill you (see *Addiction*). Find a way to get some help, and stop today. Besides, nobody wants to kiss an ashtray.

SMOTHERING

Yes, there is such a thing as loving someone too much. Smothering them with attention and affection could actually end up driving them away (see *Putting On A Pedestal*).

SNEAK A PEEK

What's the matter with you? Cover your eyes when discretion dictates it. Although it's so intriguing and tempting to try to get away with seeing something you're not supposed to see, right? OK, at least be discreet when you sneak a peek (see *Staring*).

SNEAKY

Even though it's sometimes fun, it's usually best not to be too sneaky. Unless you're a cat burglar, in which case you don't want to be too noisy. But who would want to steal a cat, anyway? Not me (see *Cats*).

SNEEZING

If you hold in a sneeze, your head will explode. Proven fact.

SNOB

Guess what? You're no better than anyone else—and the sooner you learn that, the better off you'll be. In the final analysis, we're all quite equal, actually. Remember: your shit stinks too (I'm just guessing here).

SNOOZE, YOU LOSE

If you sleep too much, the world will pass you by. So pay attention.

SNORING

Why don't you just put a sock in it? Oh, don't we wish it was that easy; but it would probably suffocate the snorer. This may seem to be the only fair thing for the snoree to do, but you're better off sending the snorer to a professional to get that condition alleviated.

SNOT

Snot—now here's a secretion we can easily live without. Does it really have a purpose? What can you do with dried up boogers anyway? Donate them somewhere? And who wants used boogers? You want to be careful here, because sometimes you might think it's a booger, but it's not (get it—it's snot).

SNOWBALL'S CHANCE

I'm guessing that having a snowball's chance in hell is not very good odds, so don't bet the ranch on it. Who's got a ranch anyway?

SNOW DAYS

Ah, there's nothing like an unscheduled day off. Snow's on the ground, you're warm and cuddly inside and enjoying family togetherness. That's good for about an hour, until cabin fever sets in. At this point you're climbing the walls, dying to get out. Want to find something to do? Try shoveling the damn snow (see *Exercise*).

SNUGGLING

Whoever invented the snuggle was a genius. It is so difficult to describe the emotions evoked by the full-body snuggle (when it's mutually desired, of course). The warmth, the security, the affection—what's not to like? (Yes, I'm a snugaholic).

S.O.B.

Sure, we all have some irreverent S.O.B. in us from time to time. Some of us relish this role (see *Pain In The Ass*). We can't be all good all of the time now, can we? But how come there are never any daughters of a bitch (D.O.B.)?

SOCIABLE

You can live your life like a hermit—or you can get to know people and make some friends. Your choice.

SOCIAL CLIMBERS

No, social climbing is not an innovative way to exercise. It's actually a complete waste of time. Just be you.

SOCIALIZATION

How on God's green earth will our children ever acquire any socialization skills? You watch them sit around with their friends, all with their earbuds and headphones on, independently participating in separate activities (music, video games, DVDs, TV, etc.). And as adults, what are we teaching them, as we sit with our friends at a restaurant, engrossed in our smartphones, checking our critically important e-mails instead of acting like human beings (see *Role Models*)? Simply breathing the same air with absolutely no interaction does not constitute doing something together. Go outside and play.

SOCK DRAWERS

Why do sock drawers get so messy? And whoever has time to clean them out?

SOFT TOUCH

Even those real big tough guys can be a soft touch, deep down inside. Everybody has a heart, right?

SOLDIERS

I have a tremendous amount of respect for soldiers, especially ours. Imagine your entire profession being centered on protecting all of us from our country's enemies. Soldiers have no say in the decisions politicians make requiring them to literally put their lives on the line, possibly making the ultimate sacrifice. And they are simply doing their job. Granted, they do this voluntarily, but that doesn't change the risks soldiers take. Once war is declared, they have to commit sanctioned killing. And their only real choice is to kill or be killed. Soldiers are our heroes, and we can't do enough to support them; we really can't. Thank God they do what they do.

SOLITAIRE

Solitaire is a good card game, and it isn't as mindless as you may think. Believe it or not, it takes a reasonable amount of skill and even some strategy, as the odds are always against you. Each game is very different, because it all depends on the cards you are dealt (same in real life, you know). Try some solitaire; it's relaxing and not too frustrating, and every game is a fresh start. Just like tomorrow, you never know what the next card will bring. Playing solitaire can really keep your mind sharp. Just remember to play by the rules (see *Cheating*).

SOLITUDE

I don't know about you, but I do some of my best thinking in solitude. It doesn't have to be such a lonely time and can often be very productive. Nobody to bother you—just you and your thoughts. (Well maybe that's not always so good.)

SOLUTION

Every problem has a solution. It may not be very palatable or staring you in the face, but there is always at least one. So don't be part of the problem; be part of the solution.

SOMEBODY

Somebody refers to someone. It's not typically a compliment (as in "Hey, that's some body you got there"). But everybody is a somebody—even you. Just be a good somebody.

SOMEDAY

Someday is not a day that's on a calendar, so it may never come (see *Procrastination*). But someday can actually creep up on you. Like today. Or maybe tomorrow.

SOMETHING

Something is way better than nothing (most of the time, anyway).

SOMETHING NICE TO SAY

Mothers (and sometimes fathers) are right. If you don't have something nice to say, don't say it. If your mouth engages before your brain has a chance to catch up, you'll likely get yourself into trouble (see *Discipline*).

SONG IN YOUR HEAD

Ever wonder why the most recent tune you heard stays in your head? All gosh darned day? Me too. And it's usually some nonsensical commercial jingle that keeps banging around and around. I'm convinced it's some terrorist plot to make us stupid—which may not be too difficult (see *Conspiracy Theories*). Naturally, my solution is to replace it with a song I like, so I can be stuck with that in my head the rest of the day. Too bad there is so much excess space in there. It's tough being me.

SONG IN YOUR HEART

Now having a song in your heart is completely different. It tends to make a happy day even happier.

SONGS

There has to be a finite number of combinations of notes that can create a melody. Sorry, but I think we've already reached the limit. My prediction is that from now on we'll just hear old tunes with different lyrics and call them new songs. Or we'll simply hear new tunes that just seem to all sound the same (see *Rap Music*). Lately, I'm afraid, it's been the latter.

SOPHISTICATED

Use your six senses here. If they look smart, smell smart and act smart, they probably are smart.

SORE LOSER

If you can't accept defeat, you've got no business being in the game. It's one thing to be gracious when you win, but it's much harder to be gracious when you don't. You can't win them all, and nobody likes a sore loser. Nobody. There, I said it.

SOUL MATE

They say that everybody's got a soul mate. Or is that cell mate? Same thing, I guess.

SOULS

I think there are a limited number of souls floating around in our universe. When we're done with them, they probably get passed on to someone else (like a baby). I think that's the way it works. However, I have no idea where the ones for shoes come from.

SOUL SEARCHING

We all have a soul, so you shouldn't have to search very hard. If you can't find it, the first place I'd check would be the lost and found. Now where did I leave that soul anyway?

SPACE

It's a crowded planet, and everyone needs his or her space sometimes. So back off and give them theirs. It usually has more to do with them than you.

SPANKING

A little swat on the tush once in a while is OK for our children, as it tends to add some punctuation to our disciplinary actions. But full bare ass, over the knee, wailing away spanking is a real no-no. Some think that there's a fine line between spanking and child abuse. THERE ABSOLUTELY IS NOT! If you're taking out your frustrations by beating your child (or anyone else, for that matter), go get some help. Right away. Now as for those kinky spankers and spankees—way too weird for me; but that's your business (see *Free Country*).

SPARE TIRE

Every car comes with a spare tire; so why are you carrying yours around? Do you think your car needs two? Don't sell the one in your car; just get rid of the one around your waist. It will only bring you trouble (see *Albatross*).

SPEAKERPHONES

Now why would anyone want the whole world to hear both ends of their phone conversation? And when the person talking to you is using their speaker, you don't really know who else is listening in (likely laughing at everything you say), right? Who needs their hands to be that free when they're on the phone anyway (see *Masturbation*)? Dumb invention.

SPEAKING

You always want to speak with conviction. That way people will think you know what you're talking about (see *Statistics*). Most think you speak from your mouth. Not so. The best communicators have learned to speak from their hearts, which typically have plenty to say. Try it; you'll like it. So will everyone else.

SPEAK SLOWLY

The world's best orators speak slowly. That way it's easier for others to understand and process; and it tends to keep you from stumbling over your words as you speak. It also helps to minimize airing stupid thoughts, as you have more time to think before you talk. However, speaking slowly is way different from speaking softly and carrying a big stick (see *Erection*).

SPEAK THE LANGUAGE

Now this may sound a tad intolerant (see *Politically Correct*), but if you plan to stay in this country, learn to speak English—or at least American. Our immigrant ancestors did, and there's no reason why current immigrants can't. God knows, my relatives practically butchered English with their strong accents, but at least they made the decision to speak the language. Most of us can trace our roots from other countries, and the English language is one of the things that unites us here. We don't need those bilingual signs (see *Enabling*). This is America, for God's sake, a nation of assimilated people. Assimilate away.

SPECULATION

Why so much time is spent speculating about all kinds of things is a mystery to me. Did he kill her, is she guilty, will they win the game, were they having an affair? Guessing and debating for hours on end seems to be a waste of time. All that talk and wasted energy won't affect the final outcome anyway, so why bother?

SPEECHES

Nobody wants to hear you go on and on forever about God knows what, so keep your speeches short. If you can't get your point across in a minimum amount of time (five minutes, tops), you're wasting everybody's time. (Remember: the Gettysburg Address was under 250 words and took less than five minutes to deliver.) Otherwise you windbags need to get someone else to deliver your message. And if you tend to stumble when reading your words, speak extemporaneously (look it up) from notes. You'll sound lots more sincere that way.

SPECIAL

Yes, everyone is special. But it's a special gift to be able to make everyone *feel* special.

SPEED

What's the hurry? Our society is obsessed with speed, as it seems to be of critical importance. We need faster computers, faster transportation, faster everything, to save time. And what do we do with all of this extra time? We sit in front of the TV and get fat. Speed kills, you know, and faster isn't always better; so cool your jets (see *Smell The Roses*).

SPEED DIALING

Don't get me wrong; I'm all for convenience. But hey genius, what do you do if you're using somebody else's phone (because your cell fell in the toilet) and forget the number you want to call? How much will it help if you can only remember the speed dial number from your phone? I dial numbers the old-fashioned way. So should you.

SPELLING

Spelling is way too complicated in the English language. I before E, except after C, blah, blah, blah. Who can keep track of all of these rules? Spelling is overrated, and those spelling bee-ers should get a life. What does it prove anyway? That you can memorize this atrocious language? So what? There is one drawback to lousy spelling though: think of all of the trouble you'd get into if you misspelled cooperate as copulate? Oh, just call it a typo. Good thing we have spell-check. Sorry, Noah.

SPENDING MONEY

Yes, sometimes you have to spend money to make money. They call that an investment. It's best, however, not to spend money you don't have.

SPERM

So why does it take a zillion little spermies to fertilize just one egg (see *Overkill*)? Is it because men have bad aim and can't shoot straight? Is it some feminist domination thing? Does it mean that women really are superior? Is this a way for them to get back at men for all of life's inequities? Or are sperm just so inept that only one knows what the hell it's doing and where it's going (see *Directions*)? Maybe it's a guy competition thing; you know, somebody wins and everyone else loses, like the lottery. Was Darwin right—survival of the fittest? While this is very perplexing to me, I'm not losing any sleep over it. Just another of life's unanswered questions.

SPINELESS

Your spine doesn't just keep your back erect; it also helps you to stand up for your convictions and beliefs. If you're going to be spineless, don't be surprised if people walk all over you. You'll be easy to spot, as you'll likely walk all stooped over.

SPIRITUALITY

We all need some spirituality in our lives. It can take the form of organized religion or be a free-form relationship with a higher power (see *God*). Many find opportunities to sit, reflect and commune with nature and/or intangible elements. Spirituality is good for the soul. Give it a try.

SPITTING

Only four things should ever come out of your mouth: words, vomit, gum and hairballs (very infrequently). Spit always stays in your mouth, until it goes down your throat.

SPLIT SECOND

Can anyone really tell the difference between a second and a split second? I sure can't.

SPLITTING HAIRS

I never understood the point of cutting up those poor little bunny rabbits.

SPOILED

We all want the next generation to have an easier life than ours, right? We want them to have fewer conflicts, a less difficult time growing up and fewer unmet needs. Although it's understandable to desire that, you're oftentimes not doing the young ones any favors. To shortcut the learning process by not having them do a lot for themselves will make it harder, not easier, for them in the long run. We hate to watch our children struggle, but sometimes it's best not to overdo the help, as then they may expect that all sorts of things will come to them, with little or no effort on their part (see *Taking It For Granted*). They may not like it, but it's never too late to unspoil them. Oh, and you can't spoil babies. Anybody that says so doesn't know what they're talking about.

SPONGING

Unless you're in serious trouble, nobody really likes it when you sponge off of them. Whether it's your parents, your friends or your lover, it gets old after a while (see *Taking Advantage*). Now sponging them off is a different story; most people like that.

SPORTS

Watching sports is supposed to be fun; that's why they call it playing. And nope, one play or player doesn't win or lose the game. There are lots of outs, shots, plays, goals, defenses, etc., in a sporting event, which means there are countless ways to win. Missing, dropping, striking out and the like all contribute to losing or winning the game. You just can't blame the one who dropped the last pass or missed the easy out. The outcome depends on the team, not one player (see *Sharing*).

SPORTSMANSHIP

Win or lose, it really is all about how you play the game. You want to look back at your days of playing your sport and be remembered for more than just your win/loss record, right (see *Class*)? Don't forget: it's only a game, after all.

SQUARE PEGS

No matter what you do, some things just won't work. So you can pound away all you want, but you'll never get those square pegs into those round holes. Face it: if it doesn't fit, it doesn't fit. This has nothing to do with giving up; it has to do with being realistic and practical. Oh, and it has nothing to do with Peg either. (I kinda like her.)

SQUEAKY WHEEL

Yes, the squeaky wheel does end up getting the grease. So that's good news for those of you who enjoy whining. If you complain long and loud enough, someone's bound to pay attention. Most of us will ignore you however.

STABILITY

We all need lots of stability in our lives. It tends to ground us and keep us going in the right direction.

STAINS

As with most things, it's best to blot first and rub later. Otherwise, get used to looking at that nasty stain from now on.

STANDARDS

It's good to have standards to live by, so try to keep them high.

STANDING ON CEREMONY

If you see something that needs to be done, just do it. Why wait around to be asked? It's oftentimes best to just ignore protocol (see *Do Something*).

STARING

So what are you looking at? Don't you know it's not polite to stare? Ever.

STARS

Go ahead and reach for the stars. You may only need a short ladder (thank you, Gary).

STARTING

You've got to crawl before you walk, and walk before you run. Getting started is usually half the battle, but you've got to start somewhere. It's much more important where you end up, rather than where you start, so anywhere is fine. One step at a time. There you go, one after the other; keep going. Just make sure you finish what you start.

STARTING FROM SCRATCH

Starting from scratch is usually the hardest way to begin (see *Reinventing The Wheel*). Same for starting over. Too bad, because sometimes it's the only way.

STATES

You think there are only fifty states in this country? Wrong again. Besides the great State of Iowa, for instance, there's the great state of:

Affairs	Emergency	Shock
Bliss	Flux	The art
Confusion	Health	The Union
Denial	Limbo	The world
Depression	Mass confusion	Transition
Despair	Mind	Undress
Disarray	Origin	War
Disbelief	Panic	
Disrepair	Remission	

And of course you've got your Altered State, Agitated State, Vegetative State, Blue State, Red State, Interstate and Tri-State; not to mention State Farm, Allstate and your basic In Test State.

STATISTICS

It's always good to use statistics to bolster your argument. You know, saying things like "Eighty percent of people with brown eyes only go to the bathroom three times per day." If those stats are not handy, just make them up. No one will know the difference (as you rarely see them challenged), and it'll make it sound like you really know what you're talking about. You never want the facts to get in the way of a good argument.

STATURE

Fortunately, stature is not a function of one's height. And it has nothing to do with your genes, as you don't inherit it; you earn it. You're never too old to grow your stature.

STATUS QUO

The world zips by at such a fast pace. Staying the same means you're actually falling behind. So there's really no such thing as status quo (see *Change*).

STATUS SYMBOLS

If you have to surround yourself with fancy materialistic things to show everyone how important you are, save your money. If that's what you're about, you're not that important.

STAYING PUT

We all have to weigh the value of relocating for better opportunities versus the need to have roots. Being or getting well established in an area is almost wasted if you have to move. A family needs a stable environment in which to live and grow, and staying in one area is part of that. Sure, we can be a phone call or e-mail away, but physical presence can't be replaced or duplicated.

STEALING

Stealing is one of the Ten Commandments you don't want to fool with. Never take things that don't belong to you. Sometimes it's easy to rationalize (like packing hotel towels—it's advertising, right?); but it's still stealing. You can, of course, steal the moment, steal a glance or even steal the show. Capturing the moment is OK too. However, stealing a kiss may get you into big trouble.

STEEL DRUMS

Wow, a steel drum is such a cool instrument; and to think they fashion it out of old oil barrels (see *Recycling*). It has such a distinctive sound. I'll bet it costs a whole lot less to make than a flute-a-phone. (I don't really know what a flute-a-phone is.)

STEP

Sometimes you've got to take a step back before you step forward. That's not so bad. It tends to give you some perspective.

STEPS

Given the choice, take the stairs rather than an elevator or other mechanical device, as stepping is very good for you (see *Exercise*). No, knucklehead, I'm not talking 14 flights, mind you.

STICK SHIFT

If you can't find 'em, grind 'em. Using a manual transmission is the best way to drive. You have so much more control over your vehicle, and it's easier on the brakes. Automatic transmissions are for sissies.

STIMULATE YOUR MIND

Stay stimulated; otherwise your brain turns to mush. You know what they say about an idle mind, don't you? I don't either, but I'm sure they say something.

STINKER

Being a stinker has little to do with causing an odor. It's often a term of endearment. Ask my son.

STINKY

If it smells, either cover it up or clean it up.

STOPGAP MEASURE

Remember that a temporary solution is only a Band-Aid. Don't use is as an excuse to put off finding a long-term answer.

STR

Is it so difficult for people to pronounce these words properly? I guess it is. For the record, it's:

Administration, not adminischtration
Chemistry, not chemischtry
Instructor, not inschtructor
Straight, not schtraight
Strange, not schtrange
Stranger, not schtranger
Strategy, not schtrategy
Street, not schtreet
Strength, not schtrength
Stress, not schtress
Strike, not schtrike
Strong, not schtrong
Structure, not schtructure
Struggle, not schtruggle

STRANGER

A stranger is just somebody who doesn't know you yet. That surely doesn't make them strange.

STREET NAMES

How cool would it be to live on a street with any of these names?

Alright Avenue
Career Path
Della Street
Determination Drive
Diane Lane
Easy Street
Everybody In A Circle
Inspiration Street
Jack La Lane
Lois Lane
Lost My Way
Lover's Lane
Loving Lane

My Way Highway
Observation Lane
One Way Street
Penny Lane
Primrose Path
Short People Street
Side Street
Smarts Street (OK, so it's backwards; work with me here)
Trustworthy Terrace
Wherethefuckarewe Road
Whoopee Cushion Court

And how about owning a street car named Desire?

STRENGTH

People tend to admire strength, whether it's real or perceived. You'd be amazed at how much strength you really have—that goes for physical, mental and emotional strength. When we really have to (or want to), we can do amazing things.

STRENGTHS

Know your strengths. Exploit them, maximize them and lead with them. The more you use your strengths, the less important your weaknesses become. And that's what makes you strong.

STRESS

It's not the stress in life that drives you crazy; it's your reaction to it. And the issue isn't necessarily trying to find a way to eliminate stress in your life, because that's impossible. It's all about attempting to find a way to deal with stress, so it doesn't kill you. There are lots of ways, and it's probably no coincidence that stressed spelled backwards is desserts (see *Moderation*). Remember: under stress, we regress.

STRETCH

Get up and stretch your legs (see *Walking*); and stretch your mind while you're at it. You ought to do this a few times every day, as it's very good for you. Many athletes stretch before exercise, but it's even better to stretch afterwards.

STRIKING OUT

So you strike out. Everybody strikes out. Good thing you'll always get another chance at bat (see *Go Down Swinging*).

STRUCTURE

Yes, we all live with plenty of structure in our lives. There's structure in our businesses, government, military and schools, for instance. We even live in a structure. So embrace structure, as it brings order to our lives. That's a good thing. Just don't let it hold you back or inhibit you.

STRUGGLE

For some, every day is a struggle. That's really too bad, so give them a hand when you can.

STUBBORNNESS

I kind of view having a hard head as an attribute. Go ahead, stick to your guns and hold your ground. However, you've got to know when it's time to be practical and walk away (see *Giving In*).

STUCK IN YOUR CRAW

Got something stuck in your craw? That sounds serious, so go unstick it, for God's sake, as it probably hurts. What's a craw, anyway? Must be something in your throat.

STUPIDEST

Stupidest is not a word; neither is irregardless. Look it up; although I guess you probably can't, if it's not there.

STUPID QUESTION

There are obnoxious questions, annoying questions and even rhetorical questions. But there's really no such thing as a stupid question. (Now if you keep asking the same question, that's stupid.) Remember: if you're ever in doubt, you're always better off asking. In hindsight, not asking can often get you into trouble, so ask away.

STYLE

No, you don't have to be wearing the latest, most fashionable clothes to show you have style (see *Class*). It's all about the way you carry yourself.

SUBSERVIENT

Don't ever act or feel subservient to anyone, as they are no better than you (or vice versa). Being submissive is not something to be proud of. At times, others have to be reminded that we're all equals in this world. Although there are those who think they are more equal than the rest of us.

SUBSTANCE

If you have no substance, then you are probably a rather shallow person (see *Superficial*). Would you be attracted to someone who didn't have any depth? Then guide yourself accordingly.

SUCCESS

Success isn't always measured by the size of your paycheck, the value of your house or the fancy car you drive. Some people can be very successful at making money, but are otherwise failures in life. Real success has to do with the type of person you are and the contribution you make to the world. The sweet smell of success breeds success, and inspires you to build on it. It's great to be on a roll.

SUCKER PUNCH

Worried about getting sucker punched? Then don't let your guard down, especially around those you don't know or trust.

SUFFOCATION

Yes, there are times when you could love someone too much. Often it's due to your own insecurity, when you are overly concerned that you might lose your loved one. Unfortunately, you could end up scaring them away by suffocating them with your love and attention. Have enough faith in yourself that they're not going anywhere and that they love you for you. Relax and have fun (see *In The Moment*).

SUICIDE

Suicide is rather final. Your lights are out, and you can't turn them back on. If you're thinking about ending it all, call a suicide hotline and talk to someone. Talk to lots of someones. You are never alone. Even if you think you've run out of people, strangers will often come to your aid. Every life is so very precious, and suicide is giving up. Don't give up.

SULKING

Funny thing about sulking: it rarely accomplishes anything. Because as much as you try, few people really notice. No one likes a Grumpelstiltskin. (You may want to file that away.)

SUNBATHING

Why do they call it sunbathing? It's nothing like taking a bath—unless you equate all of that moisture you generate with bathing. They should call it sticky, smelly sunsweating.

SUNBURN

Do you think your body is trying to tell you something? When it says ouch, it's usually for a reason. So use sunscreen, or you'll shrivel up like an old prune in no time and might cause some serious damage (see *Cancer*). Don't be an idiot. You can't replace your skin, you know.

SUNSHINE

You know, you don't have to be a star or supernova to spread some sunshine around. You can even spread it on a cloudy day (see *Smile*). You are my sunshine.

SUPERFICIAL

There's nothing super about being superficial. Plastic is usually quite thin and easy to see through. Sooner or later, they'll notice that there's not much to you (see *Substance*).

SUPERMAN

Yes, we are all supermen—except for those who are superwomen. Most of us can usually do whatever our minds are determined to do. We possess the ability to outfox a fox, outfish a fish and outwise an owl. That makes us all super. We can also outchicken a chicken, so be careful how you employ your vast powers.

SUPERSTITIONS

I don't believe in superstitions, as I consider them to be stupid-stitions.

SUPPORTIVE

Stay rock solid and support the ones you care about. It will always give them a lift to know you're behind them.

SURREAL

Boy, talk about odd situations. That's a real weird feeling, you know. Get it: 's a real?

SURVIVAL OF THE FITTEST

When it comes to the animal kingdom, I think old Chuckie Darwin was on to something. However, when it comes to humans, I've seen some of the un-fittest people survive just fine. Go figure. Do only the strong survive? Actually it's the adaptable ones who are able to thrive.

SUSPENSION

Now if you're very bad in school, they suspend you, right? The bad students probably don't like school anyway, so how is that a punishment?

SUSPICIOUS

It's a good idea to keep your eyes open and to be skeptical at times. However, it's a whole other thing to be paranoid and to assume the world is always out to get you. It's not (see *Moderation*).

SWAGGER

Walk with confidence, talk with confidence and keep your head up. Always. If you walk and talk with authority, they'll think you know what you're doing.

SWALLOWING A BITTER PILL

There are times when there is no way around it; you've just got to take it and swallow that bitter pill. Sorry. Just hold your nose and close your eyes, and you'll get through it.

SWEAT EQUITY

You don't always get credit for it, but using your sweat equity is the most satisfying way to build your assets. (I bet you expected me to make a joke about asses here, didn't you? Actually, I was going to say that it would help to build your abs too, but now I won't, thanks to you.)

SWITCHED AT BIRTH

There can only be one explanation as to why two children born of the same two parents, and brought up in the same environment, are as different as night and day. One of them must have been switched at birth.

SWORD

If you live by the sword, you die by the sword. This is a very good reason to stay away from swords. Way too sharp.

SYMPATHETIC

There's nothing pathetic about being sympathetic. It's a wonderful and very important quality to have. Cherish your ability to care about someone else, and teach others how to do it.

SYNERGY

The whole is often greater than the sum of the parts (see *Beatles*). Just listen to some good harmony sometime. It has lots to do with the group dynamic and teamwork, which makes collaboration that much more important in our world.

TAGS

You know how when you go to the store and the furniture has those tags that say: Do not remove under penalty of death? Well guess what? After you buy the stuff, you can remove them and you won't go to jail. It's the people in the stores who aren't supposed to take them off, silly, not you. Anyway, those tags look stupid hanging off your pillows.

TAKES TWO TO TANGO

There's a great way to irritate someone who is really looking for a fight when you're not so inclined. Simply disengage and walk away (not run away, as that's very different). Then they can just fight with themselves (since it takes two), which is much better for you.

TAKE THE MONEY AND RUN

Take the money and run? Really? If it's yours and you deserve it, then by all means, take the money. But if it's someone else's and you're not entitled those extra bucks, give it back. Right away (see *Do The Right Thing*).

TAKING A DEEP BREATH

OK, so someone really pissed you off, and you want to ring their neck. It's best, if possible, to invoke the 24-hour rule. Waiting makes your reaction that much more rational (and we all strive to be rational, right?). It also gives you time to plan your very special (read: devious) response, if you're so inclined (see *Getting Even*).

TAKING ADVANTAGE

An advantage is something you can give, but never, ever take. Don't take advantage of anyone or, just as important, let anyone take advantage of you (except in tennis, of course).

TAKING IT BACK

Sorry, once those words part from your lips, you can't take them back. They are absolutely out there, and whoever heard it, heard it. You may not have meant what you said, or you may wish you hadn't said it, but try as you might, you can't shove those words back into your mouth. Luckily, you can apologize; and if they're worth it, they'll forgive you.

TAKING IT FOR GRANTED

We all take basic things for granted, but we shouldn't (see *Democracy*). Don't forsake what you have, as someday you may have to live without it (or them).

TAKING IT OUT

You've got a problem? Don't take it out on someone who happens to be in the wrong place at the wrong time. Direct your anger to the source of your problem, even if it's yourself.

TAKING TURNS

When it's your turn, it's your turn—and not before (see *Cutting In Line*). Waiting your turn will help to keep the people around you calmer, which will also keep you from getting stepped on.

TAKING YOURSELF TOO SERIOUSLY

It's best not to take yourself too seriously. That will tend to keep you grounded (see *Humble*).

TALENTS

Always know your talents; cherish, share and celebrate them. Because you can have all the talent in the world, but if you don't use it, it's wasted. Just look at those gifted professional athletes who let their careers go down the toilet.

TALK

Try not to be all talk. Remember: talk is cheap, so you need some action to go along with it (see *Deeds*). Doing is a lot harder than talking, you know. If you're going to talk the talk, you've got to walk the walk. And talking (yak, yak, yak) and saying something are not necessarily the same thing.

TALKED INTO

Unless they are your parents or your parole officer, don't let anybody talk you into doing something you don't want to, or know you shouldn't do. If it doesn't feel right, it probably isn't right. Giving you a gentle nudge is something entirely different; that's OK. But ultimately, there's only one person who can talk you into anything—that's you (see *Accountability*).

TALKING IT OUT

When you have something on your mind, it's always best to talk it out with someone. Just verbalizing your problem with another person does wonders for understanding yourself. Now if you have a split personality, you don't need anyone else's help, right?

TALKING OUT OF BOTH SIDES OF YOUR MOUTH

Since I find talking out of both sides of my mouth a very difficult thing to do, I prefer just talking through the middle. So should you (see *Mixed Signals*).

TASTE

You always want to have good taste—and taste good (use your imagination).

TATOOS

Do you really want to be a walking billboard? Those things don't just wash off, you know. If you have something to say, say it. No need to print it on your body. So find a less permanent way to desecrate yourself and ruin your appearance.

TATTLETALE

It's hard to keep friends if you're constantly ratting them out. Yes, sometimes it's tough to decide if you're betraying a confidence or helping someone. Sorry, that's a call that only you can make.

TAXES

The average person is plagued with paying too many taxes. I understand that they are necessary in our society, but we don't have to like them. Here are just a few:

Ad valorem tax	Inheritance tax	State tax
Brass tax	Intangible tax	Surtax
Carpet tax	Local tax	Syntax
Estate tax	Luxury tax	Tea tax
Federal tax	Over tax	Thumb tax
Flat tax	Property tax	Value added tax
Foreign tax	Real estate tax	Value taken
Heart-a tax	Sales tax	away tax
Income tax	Sin tax	

Whew, that's a lot of taxes. Oy!

TEACHERS

Think about it. What would we be without teachers? We'd be dumb-asses, wandering around aimlessly, that's what we'd be. They're entrusted to teach us and our children, which is an awesome and daunting task. It's a profession they chose, which can really make a difference in students' lives. Teachers deserve our respect and support, and we owe them a lot. (I'm talking more than just an apple here.) Remember: teachers don't teach for the money; they teach for the outcome. You know that teachers have so much in common with doctors. They both have patience (or patients—sorry, I couldn't resist). The world is definitely a better place because of them. God bless our teachers.

TEAMWORK

The best way to get things done is through teamwork. You can get pretty far and be quite successful if you work together. And don't forget: there's no I in team (see *English Language*).

TEA PARTY

Do you think it's all fun and games in the Tea Party? Probably not.

TEARS

I have a theory about tears. I think we each have a limited lifetime supply of tears to use. Once we run out, we will be very dry and shriveled up. Now who wants that to happen? So here's my advice: conserve tears whenever possible. Don't waste them on silly things like movies, TV shows or commercials. Save them for the nachas (see *Yiddish Expressions*).

TEASING

Oh, a little gentle teasing here and there is OK; stop being so sensitive. As long as it's not meant to be malicious, embarrassing or degrading, it's alright.

TECHNOLOGY

Is it hard to keep up with new technology or what? It seems that someone's always trotting out some new way to make things faster, better or easier. (If you're lost, always ask a younger person to help, as they usually get it.) Things not only change hourly, but I think they change minutely, or even secondly (at least, it seems that way). Just another way to make us spend more money (see *Conspiracy Theories*). But you're better off embracing new technologies, as they're not going away.

TEDIOUS TASKS

The only way to get through a mindless job is to try to make a game out of it. I said try to; it doesn't always work. Even with repetitive tasks, at least there's a beginning and an end. Finding something to occupy your mind (like thinking) is also recommended.

TEENAGE YEARS

Good news for both sides: the teen years don't last forever.

TEETH

Your teeth are your friends, so be good to them and they'll be good to you. You only have one set, you know (well, children have two). Remember that they're not bottle openers, pistachio-nut crunchers or bag tearers. And don't forget to floss.

TELLING THEM WHAT THEY WANT TO HEAR

You're not doing anybody any favors if you just tell people what they want to hear. Being direct (and diplomatic) is best. You may sometimes have to question their sincerity when they ask for your honest opinion or advice, because they might not really want to hear it if they are just shopping for answers.

TEMPER

It's always a good idea to hold your temper, as it never helps to explode. This is easier said than done. Like holding your tongue, it so easily slips through your fingers.

TEMPORARY SETBACK

Oh lighten up! A temporary setback is only temporary (see *Plan B*).

TEMPTING FATE

Good luck with. Fate always wins.

TEMPTATIONS

Giving in to temptation doesn't always mean the end of the world. An occasional cookie or a little bit of ice cream once in a while isn't so bad (see *Moderation*). But resist temptations whenever possible, and don't get lured over to the dark side. Look what it did for Adam and Eve. (What did it do for them, anyway?) By the way the group was pretty good, too—The Temptations, that is, you nut.

542

TEN COMMANDMENTS

Following the Ten Commandments religiously (I couldn't help that) will mostly keep you out of trouble. If you keep track and your score is eight or above, you're doing pretty well. Stealing, murder—those are no brainers and not too hard to abide by (it's murder, by the way, as killing is sometimes OK; see *Soldiers*). Adultery—come on, you know you can control that one too (see *Temptation*). Honoring your father and mother isn't always so easy. Most people get tripped up on the coveting and bearing false witness ones. Just keep trying. Me, I covet sleep. Lots of sleep.

TERM LIMITS

How un-American—not to mention un-democratic—are term limits? Hello, that's what the right to vote is all about.

TESTS

Once you're out of school, the testing doesn't ever stop. Whether you know it or not, you're always testing yourself, and others are constantly testing you. So keep studying.

TEXTING

When did texting become a word (see *English Language*)? Is it anything like sexing? (I know what sexting is.) Isn't it more proper to say I sent a text?

THANKSGIVING

Thanksgiving shouldn't just be an American holiday; it should be universal. It has no religious overtones, you sit around and eat great food all day, not to mention watching football and indulging in plenty of other lazy activities. What's not to like? It should be celebrated and enjoyed by everyone. We all have at least something to be thankful for, even though it may not be the turkey. Gobble, gobble.

THANK YOU

"Thank you" are two words that still go a long way. I don't know if it feels better to hear it or say it, but unfortunately, it's not said enough anymore. So work on it, and show your gratitude. And it's never too late to thank someone. Never.

THANK YOU NOTES

You really want to follow up a good time at someone's house—or any act of kindness—with a thank you note, especially if they don't know you well. It shows good upbringing (see *Class*). That goes for gift getting as well.

THAT'S THE WAY IT IS

When you hear "that's the way it is" as an answer to a question (or "that's the way it's always been"), understand that this is not ever a reason. It's just an excuse, which isn't even close to being a valid answer. And it's a very lazy excuse at that.

THAT'LL

Here, take your pick:

Be the day.	Put a smile on your face.
Cure what ails you.	Put a spring in your step.
Do the trick.	Put a tiger in your tank.
Fill the bill.	Put hair on your chest.
Fix their wagon (don't you just hate broken wagons?).	Put some lead in your pencil.
Fix you right up.	Raise an eyebrow.
Get a rise out of 'em.	Rattle their cage.
Get their attention.	Separate the men from the boys.
Get you going.	Shake 'em up.
Get your blood pumping.	Show 'em.
Knock your socks off.	Take the cake.
Make them sit up and take notice.	Take your breath away (which may be a good thing; see *Bad Breath*).
Make your blood boil.	
Make your hair curl.	Teach 'em.
Make your head spin.	Tickle your fancy.
Make your nostrils flare.	Wake them up.
Put 'em to shame.	

THERE'S NOTHING LIKE

The good, the bad, the ugly—and the wonderful. I'm not saying I like all of these; I'm just saying that there's nothing like them.

A backache.
A back rub.
A bird dumping on your head.
A child's giggle.
A crisp apple.
A dame.
A dirty diaper.
A doctor's reassuring words.
A flat tire.
A giggle.
A good belly laugh.
A good cry.
A good dump.
A good steak.
A hug.
A kick in the ass.
A kiss on the forehead.
A long, hot shower.
A nap.
An ice cream cone.
A nice sunny day.
A pat on the head.
A sincere compliment.
A sweaty job.
A walk in the park.
A warm bath.
Basking in the sun.
Being on a roll (or eating a roll).
Children.

Cuddling.
French fries.
Getting some fresh air.
Going indoors wearing a wet bathing suit.
Having a baby fall asleep in your arms.
Having your back scratched (front scratched—not so much).
Hitting the ball with the sweet spot on the bat.
Putting a smile on someone's face.
Riding a bike.
Snuggling.
Staying under the covers on a rainy morning.
That new car smell.
The feeling of accomplishment.
Waking up on a bright new day.
Weekends.
Winning solitaire (without cheating).
Your child slobbering all over you.
Your dog slobbering all over you.

THE WAY THINGS ARE

If you don't like the way things are, change them. That task may seem rather daunting, but you never know how much of a difference one person can make. Start with you, and give it a shot.

THEY

They say you can't take it with you. They say it doesn't matter if you win or lose; it's how you play the game. (Oh, it matters, all right.) So who the hell are they? Some faceless, nameless experts on everything? Now I've never met them, but they seem to know something. On second thought, what the hell do they know anyway?

THEY ALWAYS GET THEIRS

It may take some longer than others, but they always get theirs. What goes around comes around; so all you have to do is sit and wait. Just be patient, as nasty stuff has a way of catching up with those who deserve it. As they say (there "they" go again) you reap what you sow. It will confirm your faith that there's still justice in the world. Karma can be a real bitch.

THEY'LL UNDERSTAND

As much as they know and care about you, don't be so sure they'll always understand (see *Taking It For Granted*). Sometimes you've just got to tell them and hope for the best.

THEY MADE ME

They can't make you. They can influence you, they can entice you, they can inspire, coax, intimidate and dissuade you; and they can even upset you. But only you can make you (that includes making you feel guilty; see *Blame*). No one else can control your feelings but you. However, if they tickle you, they probably can make you laugh—and maybe even make you happy.

THICK SKIN

If you don't have a thick skin, go get one, as they're not that expensive. If your feelings are constantly hurt, it's probably you, not them.

THINGS I DON'T UNDERSTAND

There are lots of things I ponder that don't make any sense to me. You're free to ponder yours, and I'll ponder mine. Here are some prime examples:

>   Air guitars. Does any music come out of them? I think they are fashion accessories to go with the Emperor's new clothes.
>   Am I the only one who gets mixed up on the times to call someone an overachiever or underachiever?
>   Bittersweet. Which is it? Sometimes you just have to make up your mind, right?

Can a gravy boat float?

Can anyone really tell the difference between a split second and a second?

Candy corn. It's really not corn, right?

Can go-karts stop?

Can you see through sheer determination?

Complimentary hors d'œuvres. What do they do—tell you how nice you look today?

Do butterflies make butter?

Do closet eaters really eat closets? (They must be very hungry.)

Do cobs make cobwebs? And what's a cob?

Does having an open mind mean you have holes in your head?

Does it ever get as cold as two below in Tupelo, Mississippi?

Doesn't the lion sleep every night? Not just tonight?

Does omnibus mean you're taking a bus?

Does uranium come from Uranus? Or maybe Myanus?

Do people from Hungary ever get filled up?

Do sweaters make you sweat?

Do you have to turn off electrolytes when you are done?

Do you need to be convicted to have convictions? That's not an affliction, right?

Do your taste buds have to be your friends?

Drunk as a skunk. Ever seen a drunk skunk? How would you know?

Electricity. No one could ever explain that to me. You plug it in and it works (see *Magic*).

Exactly how happy is a lark? What is a lark?

Exactly how neat is a pin?

Fantasy Football. Isn't real football good enough?

Getting that win under your belt. What's it doing under there, and how comfortable can that be? Isn't it kind of private under your belt? It is for me.

Grapefruit. Where's the grape part?

Gravity. Huh?

Having your cake and eating it too. What else would you do with cake?

How can Christmas Eve and New Year's Eve last all day? Doesn't eve mean nighttime?

How can there be four corners of the world? Isn't the earth round?

How can they have woman mannequins?

How can you have a small fortune? Isn't a fortune a lot?

How can you stare blindly? Blind people can't stare, right?

How come boys' bikes have a nut cruncher bar and girls' bikes don't? Shouldn't it be the other way around?

How come if you mix blue with yellow, you get green?

How come people tend to sit in the same unassigned seats when they go to recurring meetings?

How come they say "you better know which side your bread is buttered on"? Aren't both sides the same (except on the heel, of course)?

How come those big cranes have a ladder or toolbox attached to the chain at night? Are they afraid that someone will steal the tools, or do they need to weigh the chain down?

How come toenails grow more slowly than fingernails? Not enough sunlight?

How does grass know to grow green in the spring?

How do they get the salt into unshelled peanuts?

How do they shrink all of those pages into the scan and fax machines to fit them into the phone and Internet lines?

How do you break a sweat? And is there a way to fix it?

How many are countless?

How much is a tad? Or a tad more?

How many is umpteenth?

How much is x amount?

If an older person gets kidnapped, shouldn't they call it adultnapped?

If badminton is a good sport, why don't they call it goodminton?

If hell is very hot and heaven is the complete opposite, why don't they wear overcoats up there?

If necessity is the mother of invention, who's the father?

If pacifists don't fight, why do they have fists?

If someone tells you he's a liar, should you believe him?

If you have walking pneumonia, shouldn't you just sit down?

If you make something from scratch, do you have to start with an itch?

I know what a full moon is, but is there such a thing as an empty moon?

I never heard it through the grapevine. Vines just don't talk to me; must be malfunctioning grapes.

Insulated bags. They can keep things hot or cold. How do they know the difference?

Internal autopilot. How is it that we can be completely lost in nonsensical daydreams, but have no problem driving all the way home, negotiating traffic and not missing a single turn?

Is belittle the opposite of bebig?

Is it pandemonium when a bunch of crazy pandas run around?

Isn't awfully good a contradiction?

Is ozone the period of ecstasy during an orgasm?

Is there a difference between whoops and oops? How about whoopsie and oopsie?

Is there any money in a snow bank?

Is there such a thing as a fastpoke?

Lady-in-waiting. What is she waiting for?

Military terms like fire at will. So who is this poor bastard, and does it make sense for everybody to shoot at the same guy?

Misspelling and misuse of the words yeah, yea and yay.

Monty Python, or any British humor. I never really get that.

Pulling out all the stops. Huh? How can you pull out a stop? Can you push in a stop?

Reality TV shows. How real is it to have a camera following you all over the place?

Redoubling efforts. How do you do that? If you redouble, doesn't that mean quadrupling your efforts?

Rhodes Scholars. How smart to you have to be to drive on the street?

Roman numerals. Can't we just use regular numbers?

Shouldn't they call a hernia a himea?

Shouldn't you eat a crab cake for dessert?

Square inch. Is there such a thing as a round inch?

The whole nine yards. Doesn't it take ten yards to get a first down? What does nine yards get you?

Vegetable medley. What tunes are they supposed to know? My veggies never sing anything—and I feel cheated.

Velcro. Enough said.

Vincent van Gogh is dead. Shouldn't he be Vincent van Gone?

Was Marvin Gaye gay? (Not that there's anything wrong with that; just curious.)

What degree can you get from the Electoral College?

What do affairs have to do with adult trees? (Get it—adultery?)

What do naysayers actually say?

What do they wear in the warehouse?

What exactly is the nth degree?

What if there's a real fire during a fire drill? How would you know?

What if you bet your ass and lose?

What is a covert?

What is light about cellulite?

What kind of products are made in the olfactory?

What makes the Great Lakes so great?

What's the difference between slowing up and slowing down?

What's the difference between then and than?

What the hell does (sic) mean?

What was John Lennon thinking when he married a woman with the last name Oh No?

When a guy gets a vasectomy, they say he got fixed. Didn't he really get broken?

When do the cows come home?

When do you use affect, and when do you use effect? Can't we just use one?

When did actresses become actors?

When is the middle of the night? Doesn't it depend on your time zone?

When Rocky Raccoon went back in his room, did he die?

When the judge calls for a recess during a trial, does that mean it's time for dodgeball or the playground?

When they say this is the end of the line. A line never ends, does it?

When they tear down a building, why do they call it razing? Don't they have it backwards?

When you lose your virginity, you really win, don't you?

Where does mercury come from? The planet Mercury?

Which is the wrong side of the bed? It isn't the right side, so it must be the left, right?

Which side is the back of your hand?

Who is Mary Christmas?

Who lives at the Gettysburg Address? Why are bees kept in an apiary? Shouldn't apes be kept there?

Why are some people very tall, and some very, very tall?

Why can't you stop a yawn or a sneeze?

Why do birds suddenly appear every time you are near? And how do they figure out how to fly in those cool formations?

Why does a baseball game have nine innings? What's wrong with ten? Most everything else is a factor of ten, right? Anybody in baseball ever hear of the decimal system?

Why does the first bite always taste so much better than the last one?

Why don't psychics win the lottery?

Why don't they skin Douglas fir trees and make coats from them?

Why do Oldies radio stations keep advertising that they have the biggest tits?

Why do overlooking and looking over mean two different things?

Why do politicians run for election? Is that why some go to jail if they get caught?

Why do they all drive Hummers on CSI: Miami? Does it snow in Florida?

Why do they always talk about the four fathers who wrote the Constitution? You've gotta think there were maybe at least five or six, right? What about the four mothers?

Why do they call cologne toilet water? Doesn't toilet water stink?

Why do they call it rush hour if everybody sits in traffic and doesn't move?

Why do they call the 1900s the 20th century? Isn't it the 19th?

Why do they call them yard sales and garage sales? Are they selling their garage or yard? Of course not. They should just call it old crap that's lying around sale.

Why do they keep talking about peas on earth during the holidays?

Why do they lock toilet paper dispensers? Are they afraid of toilet paper theft cartels?

Why do they name all Cabinet positions Secretary (Secretary of State, Defense, Treasury, etc.)? Do they make photocopies for the president, take phone messages and open his mail? And what do they call their secretaries: secretary to the secretary?

Why do they say "goes in tight" when you sneeze?

Why do they say "he'll never live that down"? Aren't you supposed to live it up?

Why do they spell Shawn three ways: Shawn, Sean, Shaun?

Why do you have to keep your elbows off the table?

Why is Harry Reasoner the only journalist with a name that fits the profession?

Why is it so difficult to separate a stack of paper plates? Do they like each other so much that they have to stick together?

Why isn't it just dogs who are dogmatic?

Why is the devil a male?

Why is the last mile always longer than the first?

Why is the sky blue?

Why would anyone name a game craps? Yeech.

Why would a TV station advertise a program on another network? Aren't they looking to build up their own ratings?

You have two forearms. Does that mean you have eight arms?

THINK

Always be thinking, as that's what that big lump between your shoulders is for. But make sure you think *before* you talk. It's always better that way, rather than the other way around. And remember: it doesn't really matter what they think; it mostly matters what you think. Think away.

THINKING ALIKE

It may seem that two people think alike, but it's not really possible. You can have similar values and have a common way to solve problems, but thinking the same way in every instance? Doubtful. Remember that your frame of reference is your own way of thinking, and no one else can really think like you. (Good thing.)

THINKING OUTSIDE THE BOX

It pays to be innovative and to expand your mind when you're solving problems. The same old way doesn't always work.

THIRD TIME'S THE CHARM

Yeah, the third time may be the charm. Or maybe the fourth, or the fifth. Just keep trying.

THIRD WORLD

Boy, where have I been? I thought there was only one world (see *Self-Absorbed*).

THONGS

What's up with thongs? How comfortable can it be to have something sticking up your crack all day (see *Hygiene)*? Don't get me wrong; I understand the sexy part of it. But what if there's no romance on the agenda? Now granted, I don't have those parts, so maybe it's autoerotic to wear them. (Or is it aerodynamic? I always get those two confused). If some women think they won't have VPL (visible panty lines), they ought to worry more about TPIC (tight pants in crack). But again, I'm just a guy, so what do I know?

THOUGHT

Some of us are relatively clumsy about the way we do things, but it really is the thought that counts. (Try to keep that in mind the next time you receive some God-awful hideous gift.)

THOUGHTFULNESS

Thoughtfulness is a great character trait. Considering other's feelings before you act is the way to go. Sometimes you really have to swallow hard and forget about your ego, but it's worth it (see *Do The Right Thing*). Go ahead and go that extra mile; you won't be sorry.

THREATS

If you are going to threaten someone, you better be prepared to carry it out. You know—walk the walk. They may call your bluff, and if you budge (or blink), you lose. Idle threats won't get you very far either, so you may want to consider not making them in the first place.

THREES

So they say things come in threes. Who knows? The number three does have special significance to me (not that it matters). It's Babe Ruth's (and my) lucky number. That's the number he wore—which is the only thing we have in common. It never really helped my ballgame though.

THREE STRIKES

Three strikes and you're out? Not always. You're just down, not out. Get back up at bat and keep trying (see *Giving Up*).

THRONG

You don't want to confuse a throng with thong. They are entirely different things, and mixing them up can get you into all kinds of trouble.

THROWING UP

Ah, another lovely bodily function I can easily do without. Food sure tastes way better going down. Coming back up—not so much. Can't we just pick and choose, limiting ourselves to only the pleasant bodily functions (see *Napping*)?

THUMB SUCKING

Thumb sucking is a perfectly acceptable form of self-soothing. It's not recommended for adults, however. There might be some correlation between thumb sucking and breastfeeding, but I don't know what that is.

TICKLING

A tickle can usually get a rise out of children, especially the giggly ones. If they're not ticklish (or children), try to tickle their fancy. Where is that? Probably next to the humorous bone.

TIDES

High tide, low tide—why can't they just make up their minds and stay medium tide? Ocean-front property owners would be much happier.

TIGHT CLOTHES

Clothes getting too tight? Blame it on the cleaners. That's what I do (see *Fooling Yourself*).

TIME

I've got plenty of time to talk about time. They say that time is the great equalizer; I have no idea what that means. (They say that about death too, and I still don't know what that means either.) But it seems like you either have too much time or not enough. In reality, we all have the exact same amount of time. It's only when you don't notice time going by that it doesn't seem to matter. And no, time isn't always on your side; and you can't make up for lost time. But time can be a very precious commodity and (like your mind) a terrible thing to waste. Although we tend to use time (or the lack of it) as an excuse, most of us seem to have time to do the things we really want to do (see *Choices*). Oh, and I'd always bet on time in that race against time, as time usually wins. I can't explain why, but time seems to stand still when you're waiting to hear from your doctor about your lab results—then flies by when you're having fun, like during the summer. Actually, summers go by way too fast (which I think is another terrorist plot).

TIME HEALS

Does time heals all wounds? I don't know, but time will tell, as it tends to put things into perspective. Time certainly doesn't heal all of them, but it sure heals a lot of them.

TIME IS MONEY

Time isn't money. Money is money. Time is time, silly.

TIME MANAGEMENT

It's hard to manage time, as it mostly manages you.

Time Is Money

TIMING

Timing isn't everything, but it's a lot of things. Bad timing is asking someone about their dog right after it died.

TINGLING

When you get that tingling feeling, at least you know you're alive. That's tingling, not tinkling; although you know you're alive when you're tinkling too.

TIP OF THE TONGUE

Don't you just hate it when you can't get that word or name out (see *Frustration*)? You're so close, and you know it will find its way off the tip of your tongue before long. My solution: build longer tongues. Problem solved. Now if everything were that easy.

TIPPING

Of course you should tip, as the tippees depend on it. Just moderate your tip, depending on the service. Don't blame the wait staff if the food is terrible; just never go back there. If in doubt, overtip (see *Making Their Day*) and be a big shot; you can afford it. Let 'em keep the change. And here's a real tip: If you're having some work done on your house and such, tip the crew before they start. You'll get a better job that way. Otherwise, it's too late.

TIRED

Tired or exhausted? After groundbreaking research and centuries of study, scientists have finally discovered the cure for tiredness: it's called sleep. Now as for exhaustion, no one is really clear on the cure, but there are many likely causes (see *Overdoing It*).

TIRES

So why do all of the car tire sizes start with R? Does the R stand for round? Maybe your R size is directly proportional to the amount of road you think you own (see *Not-Me Syndrome*).

TODAY

If you spend too much time worrying about tomorrow, you'll miss today.

TOES

What useful purpose do toes serve? They get stubbed, they smell and they're ugly. You can't grab anything with them, so they have clearly outlived their usefulness. And what's with clipping those damn toenails all the time? How much fun is that? It's time to evolve away from toes. Maybe webbed feet would be the way to go. But since we're stuck with toes, remember: it's best to stay on your toes and not step on anyone else's.

TOGETHER

Yes, working together and making a concerted effort is the best way to get things done. United we stand, divided we fall.

TOGETHERNESS

It's always nice to spend that quality time with those important to you. However, there are times when a little too much togetherness will drive everyone crazy (see *Cabin Fever*).

TOILET HUMOR

You would be wise to keep toilet humor in the bathroom, right next to the toilet paper—especially when you're in mixed company.

TOILET PAPER ROLLS

They say that you can tell a lot about a person by the way they keep their toilet paper rolls—either top feeders or bottom feeders. God knows what this will tell you, but apparently it tells you something. Top feeder for me (probably more than you'd like to know).

TOILET SEAT

Why is it so impolite to leave the toilet seat up? Since this is only a problem for half the population, this is a very sexist issue. It sure is much more convenient for those of the male persuasion to leave the seat up, as we're always in a rush. But take good aim, fellas, as no one wants to see remnants of your handiwork (if you know what I mean) all over the place.

TOLERANCE

The T in United States stands for tolerance, which is the foundation of this country. Don't forget it. Don't ever forget it.

TOMORROW

Good thing someone invented tomorrows. Sometimes the best thing about today is that there will always be another day coming up. Remember this when you're having an especially bad one. Ah, what a difference a day makes. Some hope tomorrow never comes, but it always does; no one can stop it. However, you never know what tomorrow brings; that's what makes life so exciting. I've heard that if you take care of today, tomorrow takes care of itself. I don't know about that, but you certainly can impact your tomorrows. Just make them better than your yesterdays and you'll be fine. Keep those tomorrows coming.

TONGUE-TIED

Even the best orators stumble over their words from time to time. The problem is that the mind works a whole lot faster than the mouth. If your tongue gets stuck stumbling over your words once in a while, just sit back, compose yourself and speak more slowly. That's bound to untie it.

TOO GOOD TO BE TRUE

If it sounds or looks too good to be true, it almost always is.

TOO LATE

It can be late. It can be very late. It can even be very, very late. But it's really never too late (see *Forgive And Forget*).

TOO MUCH

Too much is better than not enough. I'm way too much.

TOOLS

Having the right tools for the right jobs makes all the difference. So if you need a hammer, don't use a stapler (see *Lazy*). And scissors are a poor excuse for a screwdriver.

TOOTH FAIRY

I'm not going to be the one who shatters a little child's dreams by telling them that there's no such thing as the Tooth Fairy. Next you'll be telling me that there's no Easter Bunny—or even Santa Claus. No way.

TOOTING YOUR OWN HORN

Leave the horn blowing to the qualified musicians. So don't bother blowing your own (see *Farting*).

TOUCH

If you ever touch someone's heart or soul, you'll never be forgotten. Never.

TOUCHÉ

The French have their own way, but I think you pronounce it tushie (you know—rhymes with mushy).

TOUCHING

How can you describe the human touch? The feelings you send through your fingers are the most genuine and unfiltered expressions you have (see *Honesty*). You can't fake or hide them, as they either reveal you or betray you. The touch you get from someone else's fingers are equally revealing. There is nothing like a gentle caress, as it can really touch your heart. Raise your hand if you love physical contact; I do. Just keep your touching appropriate.

TOUGH PROBLEMS

You know how some people try to answer difficult problems with simple, easy solutions? Things like: Just build more roads to alleviate traffic; or print more money if the economy is suffering. If it were only that easy. Unfortunately, tough problems usually require complicated solutions. I guess that's what the drawing board is for. Oh well.

TRACK RECORD

You don't have to be an athlete to have a track record, you know (see *Reputation*).

TRADITIONS

There are lots of good reasons to celebrate traditions and follow customs. Preserving your heritage and keeping your ethnicity and religion alive are some of them. But don't fall into the trap of simply doing things the same way because that's the way they've always been done. Just going through the motions without any real meaning attached is a waste of time. That requires no innovative thinking on your part (see *Easy Way Out*) and is just a default to old and outdated ways. There's a very thin line between honoring long-held traditions and questioning old customs. When you hear someone say that's the way we've always done it, remember: that isn't a reason; it's just an excuse. If you always do what you always did, you will always get what you always got.

TRAFFIC

Now there's not much you can do about traffic; it's the price of success. Unfortunately, most of us (me included) look as our cars as a way to be free and independent. Some of us have an unnatural aversion to public transportation, and we find a million reasons not to use it; so we see lots of one-passenger vehicles on the road (see *Selfish*). You do have a few choices:

> Deal with it.
> Listen to the car radio.
> Move to No-Where, USA.
> Take a nap.
> Walk.

TRAFFIC-LIGHT BUTTONS

Who believes traffic-light buttons really work? Hello? It's just a way to pacify pedestrians. Did you ever see the light change any quicker after you hit the damn button? Of course not.

TRAINING

On-the-job training is a good way to get experience and learn employment requirements and expectations. Pushing someone into a sink-or-swim environment is guaranteed to show them how to fail. Take the appropriate time, and train them well. Your boss will thank you.

TRANSPARENT

Most people can see right through another's thinly veiled motives (and sometimes clothes). They can spot a phony a mile away, so you're probably not fooling anyone.

TRAVELITIS

Some of us enjoy traveling, and some of us don't. I don't. You can keep all of that packing and schlepping. Staying put and enjoying my familiar surroundings are just fine with me. Even if I were to embark on a trip, I'd see America (the land of the free) first. The rest of you can go ahead and see the world. Besides, the earth may be flat after all, and I'd likely be the first one to fall off the end.

TREADMILLS

Talk about going nowhere fast (or slow). Walk or run around the block, for Pete's sake (see *Fresh Air*); you won't melt if it rains. Stationary bikes are right behind treadmills, you know. But then again, you shouldn't ride your bike in the rain, as you'll likely wipe out and get hurt. So that piece of equipment does serve some purpose.

TREATS

If you indulge yourself in something special too often, it's no longer a treat.

TREES

Here's the deal; if you cut down a tree, plant two new ones. We all come out ahead that way.

TRENDS

You want to be somewhat stylish? That's fine. But trying to keep up with every trend will typically make you shallow—and eventually broke.

TRIAL BY FIRE

Trial by fire isn't usually the best way to learn. Neither is the sink-or-swim approach. However, you won't easily forget the lessons learned that way. You won't forget that horrible experience either.

TRIOS

Yes, these all go together:

Alcohol, tobacco and firearms
Apples, peaches and pumpkin pie
Bewitched, bothered and bewildered
Bing, bang and boom
Blood, guts and gore (not Al Gore)
Blood, sweat and tears
Calm, cool and collected
Cheerful, bright and gay
Crosby, Stills and Nash
Dewey, Cheetam and Howe (it's a law firm)
Dewey, Fuckem & Howe (less prestigious law firm)
Duck, duck and goose
Ear, nose and throat
Earth, Wind and Fire
Eat, drink and be merry
Emerson, Lake and Palmer
Fame, fortune and glory
Father, Son and Holy Ghost/Spirit
Fee, fi, fo, fum (OK, so that's four—close enough)
Friends, Romans and Countrymen
Good, bad and indifferent
Good, bad and ugly
Hazy, hot and humid
Health, Education and Welfare
Healthy, wealthy and wise (two out of three aren't bad)

Here, there and everywhere
Hook, line and sinker
Hop, skip and a jump
Huey, Dewey and Louie
Jesus, Mary and Joseph
Judge, jury and executioner
Judge, trial and jury
Kukla, Fran and Ollie
Lazy, fat and happy
Lie, cheat and steal
Life, liberty and the pursuit of happiness
Lions, tigers and bears (oh my)
Lock, stock and barrel
Love, honor and obey
Manny, Moe and Jack
Man, woman and child
Me, myself and I
Moe, Larry and Curly
Morning, noon and night
Nina, Pinta and Santa Maria
Planes, trains and automobiles
Peter, Paul and Mary
Reading, writing and rithmetic
Ready, willing and able
Red, white and blue
Sex, drugs and rock and roll (so maybe that's four too—sue me)
Shake, rattle and roll
Snap, crackle and pop

Signed, sealed and delivered
Stop, drop and roll
Sun, moon and stars
Tall, dark and handsome
This, that and the other
Tom, Dick and Harry
Trains, planes and automobiles
Truth, justice and the
    American way

Up, up and away
Vera, Chuck and Dave
Waste, fraud and abuse
Wine, women and song
You, me and the lamppost
You, me and the phone
Yours, mine and ours

TRIUMPH

If you finish running a marathon, it's a huge triumph. Sure, only one person wins, but you don't have to be the winner to be triumphant. If you try (get it?) hard enough, you will be. By the way, it used to be a nice car too.

TRIVIA

I consider myself a veritable cornucopia of useless information. Just don't ask me about something important. Trivia is me.

TROPICAL FISH

Watching tropical fish swim around in an aquarium is very relaxing and therapeutic. It seems to be a great life: they just eat and poop and swim all day long. Watching and listening to the water is also very soothing and tends to calm you down. Yes, looking at a fish tank is very peaceful—unless the fish are fighting. Although sometimes it's hard to tell if they're fighting or mating. On the downside, you've got to clean the fish tank, and if you don't do it every couple of months, they'll die. Nothing is easy.

TROUBLE

Like most things, getting into trouble is a whole lot easier than getting out of it.

TRUMPET

What a clean, pure sound a trumpet makes. What do you suppose the players do with those lips when they're done, though? Or cheeks, for that matter?

TRUST

Being someone who can be trusted is such an honorable quality to possess. Find people who have earned your trust, and earn theirs; it just takes time. When in doubt, trust your instincts and trust your gut. But if you can't trust anyone, be prepared for a very lonely existence.

TRUST ME

When you hear those two words together, it's best to run like hell.

TRUSTWORTHINESS

It's no surprise that trustworthiness was invented. If people trust you, it makes you worthy. Very worthy.

TRUTH

There are times when it takes great courage to tell the truth. And sometimes the truth hurts. But never be afraid of it, because the truth really will set you free. At least be true to yourself.

TRYING

You may not always succeed, but at least be able to say that you tried. Don't try anything (or everything) once; that's stupid. But try a lot of things. And keep on trying (see *Giving Up*). Always remember that it never hurts to try. The old adage still works: if at first you don't succeed, try, try again. There is no shame in failure, you know; the only shame is in not trying.

TURNING AROUND

It seems that every time you turn around, it's always something else (whatever something else is). So maybe the solution is: don't turn around. Just not very practical, if you ask me.

TURNING OVER A NEW LEAF

Pledging to start over and do things differently is a noble task. Staying on course with these changes is the really hard part (see *Discipline*). If it's too drastic a change, it probably won't succeed. Gradual is typically the best way.

TURNING THE OTHER CHEEK

No, turning the other cheek has nothing to do with mooning. It's just a knack some people have of letting the indignities in life roll off them. It's a good quality to possess. The mark of a strong person is to show restraint, rather than overreaction.

TURNING THIRTY

If you're 30 and not married, attached or parenting, consider yourself lucky. So relax. You're in a much better position to be a good future spouse, mate and/or parent, as experience and maturity have their pluses. Now if you're turning 40 and are in the same situation, let's talk. Girls, the clock is ticking at that point, you know.

TURN SIGNALS

Stop being so lazy and use your blinker, as it's very hard for someone else to read your mind.

TURN UP

So you think you lost something. Don't drive yourself crazy looking all over for it. It'll likely turn up (see *Someday*); so relax.

TV

Does TV give you a jaded and unrealistic view of life today? Try growing up with *Leave It To Beaver* or *Father Knows Best*. Anyone born after 1950 knows that television has become the best unpaid babysitter there is. First we thought that everything was in black and white, and that everyone was white. And that all stories had a happy ending. Not very real-life, then or now. The Cleavers must have been terribly constipated, as you never heard June say: "Ward, answer the phone, I'm in the can." Or Ward say: "Now Beaver, I told you to stay away from your mother when she's got PMS." And what was up with June wearing those pearls and dresses all the time? No hair was ever out of place. I don't remember anybody's mother looking like that. One thing hasn't changed though: no one should ever aspire to be like the characters they see on television, good or bad. Why? Because they're not real, and life doesn't have all its issues resolved in a simple way, all tied up in a pretty box in an hour or less.

TWEAKING

At some point you're kind of tweaked out, and it's as good as it's going to get. It's very difficult for some to leave well enough (or good enough) alone, but try to quit while you're ahead (see *Perfection*).

TWINKLE

The eyes never lie. Those twinkles (not to be confused with tinkles) always mean something. It's usually a good thing.

TWISTING IN THE WIND

Either accept an apology or reject it. It may make you feel superior to keep someone hanging, but it's very unfair to the hangee. If they have the guts to apologize, have the common courtesy to accept it. And don't let them dangle or grovel. That kind of stuff has a way of coming back to you (see *Golden Rule*).

TWO-FACED

The problem with being two-faced is that no one will ever know which one they're talking to. One face is plenty for me.

TWO FIRST NAMES

You can have one first name and then a middle name, right? So you really can't have two first names, as there's only one to a customer. These people must have gotten special treatment (or had rich parents):

Anne Marie	Billy Ray	Linda Jo
Barbara Ann	Bobbie Jo	Lisa Marie
Barbara Sue	Bobbie Sue	Lou Ann
Becky Sue	Claire Ann	Lulu Belle
Beth Ann	Daisy Mae	Marie Claire
Betty Ann	Ellie Mae	Mary Alice
Betty Jo	Jim Bob	Mary Ann
Betty Lou	Jean Pierre	Mary Beth
Billie Jean	Jean Paul	Mary Catherine
Billie Jo	Joe Bob	Mary Claire
Billy Bob	John Paul	Mary Ellen
Billy Joe	Lee Ann	Mary Frances

Mary Jane	Mary Pat	Ruth Ann
Mary Jo	Mary Rose	Sally Jo
Mary Kate	Mary Sue	Sarah Jane
Mary Kay	Norma Jean	Sue Ann
Mary Lou	Norma Rae	Thelma Lou
Mary Margaret	Peggy Sue	Terri Lynn

TWO LAST NAMES

Ladies, names are too confusing and hard to remember as it is. Must you complicate things by using two last names? If you don't like his, use yours. But choose just one, please.

TWO-PIECE BATHING SUITS

Oh girls, there are some of you (and you know who you are) who should stick to one-piece bathing suits. Far be it from me to be critical, but some of you have got too much, and some of you don't have enough (if you know what I mean). Look in the mirror first, and if there's any question in your mind, don't wear that bikini (see *Modesty*). And what's with all that tugging, pulling and adjusting all the time? How comfortable can that be?

TWO SIDES

There are usually at least two sides to every story; sometimes even more. It's best to hear all of the versions before you come to your own conclusions. Employing this method tends to cut back in the looking like an ass department. And you don't want to look like that, right?

TWO-WAY STREET

It's so much easier to drive on a two-way street, as those one-ways get way to confusing. Anyway, life really is a two-way street, as you can come and go.

TY

We like these ty's:

Ability	Creativity	Dignity
Agility	Cutie (work with	Duty
Beauty	me here)	Femininity
Certainty	Dainty	Functionality

Generosity
Heredity (I think
  I like this)
Honesty
Humanity
Humility
Identity
Integrity
Likeability
Longevity
Lovability

Loyalty
Marketability
Masculinity
Morality
Nobility
Opportunity
Party
Pretty
Reality
Reliability
Respectability

Responsibility
Sanity
Security
Sensitivity
Serenity
Sincerity
Stability
Subtlety
Tranquility
Utility

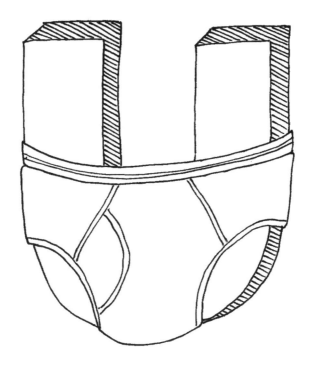

UFOs

Get real—we're not alone. We're not so important as to be the only beings in the universe. It's a big universe and we're a very little planet. Do you think the rest of the galaxies, solar systems and planets were created just to entertain us? Not likely. Go watch Star Wars. Or Star Trek (the TV show, not the movies— talk about dipping into the well too often; anyone hear of overkill? Sorry; just rambling.)

ULTIMATE PRICE

Paying the ultimate price is never worth it. You simply can't put a value on life itself.

UM

When you are at a loss for words and all else fails, um's the word (not mum's). Um, um, um….

UNAPPRECIATIVE

If you don't show your appreciation, others will stop doing things for you that you really enjoy.

UNAVOIDABLE

Some things are just going to get in your way, no matter what, and are unavoidable. It's best to prepare yourself.

UNCANNY vs. CANNY

I know what being uncanny is all about, but how does one become canny? Does that mean you have cans (see *Breasts*)?

UNCERTAIN FUTURE

Talking about an uncertain future is kind of redundant. The future is always uncertain, silly.

UNCLE SAM

Isn't it nice to know that we all have one relative in common? Nice hat, by the way.

UNCONDITIONAL LOVE

Unconditional love (otherwise known as no-matter-what love) is the way love is designed to work. This is the way parents are supposed to feel about their children. There shouldn't really be any choice with that.

UNCONVENTIONAL

It's OK to be unconventional. Who likes all of those boring conventions anyway?

UNDERARM HAIR

Listen, ladies: underarm hair is a real turn-off. Same with leg hair. No one's interested in how natural it is. Yeech! Guys, you don't have to worry about this. If you do, you've got something else to worry about.

Uncanny vs. Canny

UNDERCOOKED

Undercooked food will likely get you sick. Now having said that, I like my meat medium rare. (I'm quite the risk taker.)

UNDERCUTTERS

There are those who will always find something to complain about and will go out of their way to burst your bubble. They tend to be unhappy and love to spread their misery. The key words to listen for are "yeah, but." For example, when you say "I'm so happy; I got a raise today," they respond, "Yeah, but they should have given it to you a lot sooner." You want to stay away from undercutters.

UNDERDOG

Rooting for the underdog is lots of fun—especially when they win. It's so easy to back the favorite, and it's no surprise if they come out on top. But it's the underdog who really needs the support, and it's so exciting when they beat the top dog.

UNDERESTIMATING

Don't underestimate:

> The competition.
> The power of love.
> The power of one vote.
> The power of that electrical outlet.
> The power of the force.
> Your abilities.
> Your limits.
> Yourself.

UNDERSHIRTS

Girls, you don't need to pay attention here. But for you boys: always wear an undershirt *under* a dress shirt, sweater, etc. It helps absorb your stink. And Lord knows, we all benefit from that.

UNDER THE TABLE

The only things that should be under the table are your feet (and occasionally the dog). Being paid under the table, or paying someone under the table, causes the rest of us to pay your taxes. Nobody wants to pay someone else's taxes; it's hard enough to pay our own. And drinking somebody under the table isn't such a huge accomplishment either.

UNDERWEAR

Underwear shouldn't be worn as outerwear (see *Undershirts*).

UNDRESSING

Maybe it has to do with different body parts, but why do women take their shirts off by crossing their arms and pulling from the bottom? Mind you, I haven't seen any studies on this phenomenon, but most guys have already figured out that this results in inside-out shirts, which then have to be turned right-side out. Guys loathe this extra work (see *Easy Way Out*). And while we're on the subject, girls, what's with all of that wiggling around when you try to put your pants on? Must be some kind of ancient tribal dance. Different body parts too, I guess.

UNEXPECTED

If you expect the unexpected, then it wouldn't be unexpected, would it? It would be expected, right?

UNEXPECTED PREGNANCY

After years of exhaustive and extensive research, scientists have finally found the cause of unexpected pregnancies. The proper medical term is whoopsie-itis (see *Condoms*).

UNFINISHED BUSINESS

How many times at funerals have you heard people say: Gee I wish I would have told them blah, blah, blah? Hey genius, this is something you can get out of the way before they're dead, because you never know when their last day is coming. Make sure that the most important people in your life (and people who've been a great inspiration to you) know it. Tie up those loose ends today; tomorrow may be too late (see *Guilt*). It will make you feel good, and make them feel even better. Oftentimes they're not even aware of the impact they've had on you. If it's hard to tell them to their face, a letter or e-mail will also work. Just be sure to tell them. By all means, tell them.

UNFORGETTABLE

If you let people get to know the things that are unique and special about you, you'll never be forgotten.

UNGODLY

I don't know about you, but I'd rather be godly. Way too afraid of lightning hitting me.

UNGRATEFUL

Being or appearing ungrateful is not a redeeming quality, as it's best not to forsake your good fortune. If you don't show your appreciation (see *Magic Words*), you'll stop getting whatever it is that they give or do for you. That's usually not a good thing.

UNIBROW

Listen, guys. There's nothing appealing about having one long eyebrow over your eyes. Pluck it, shave it or (for you real bushy gents) take it out with the lawnmower. In any case, one (and only one) brow over each eye is what you want. Girls, what are you laughing at? You too.

UNIMPORTANT DAYS

How do you think days like July 5 or December 26 feel? Probably like January 2. How disappointing it must be to be those days, as it's got to be quite upsetting to be upstaged by your predecessor. And every year, no less.

UNIQUE

We're all one-of-a-kind, so go ahead and celebrate your uniqueness. Once we were made, they broke the mold. Aw, who wants moldy people anyway?

UNISEX NAMES

Gosh, don't children have enough identity issues to deal with as they grow up? Why start a child off with a name that will automatically confuse people? (As if we weren't confused enough already.) Therefore, you might want to consider avoiding the following when naming your offspring:

Abby/Abbe	Casey
Aaron/Erin (too close)	Cassidy
Addison	Charlie
Adrian/Adrienne	Chris
Al	Clare/Claire
Alex/Alix	Claude
Alexis	Connie
Alice (think Cooper)	Corey/Cory
Alison/Allison	Courtney
Andy/Andi	Dale
Angel	Dana/Dayna
Asa	Dandy
Ashley	Danny/Dani
Aubrey	Darby
Avery	Darcy
Bailey	Daryl
Bela/Bella	Dee
Bentley	Devon/Devin
Berle/Beryl	Dion/Dionne
Bernie	Dominique
Billy/Billie	Don/Dawn (way too close)
Blair	Dorian
Blake	Drew
Blanche	Dylan/Dillon
Bo	Evan/Evon
Bobby/Bobbi	Fay/Faye
Brady	Flo
Brett	Fran
Brook/Brooke	Francis/Frances
Brooks	Frankie
Cameron	Freddy/Fredi/Freddie
Carey/Carrie	Gabby/Gabi
Carmen	Gale
Carroll/Carol	Gene/Jean

Gladys (no; just making sure
    you're paying attention)
Glen/Glenn
Griffin
Hamilton
Jackie/Jacki
Jamie
Jan
Jerry/Gerry
Jess
Jessie
Jody/Jodi
Joe/Jo
Joey
Jonah
Jordan/Jordon
Josie
Jules
Julian/Julien
Kelly/Kelli
Kendall
Kerry/Keri
Kim
Kirby
Kristen/Kristin
Kyle
Laverne
Lee/Lea/Leigh
Lesley/Leslie
Lindsey/Lindsay
Lonnie
Loren/Lauren
Lyndon
Lynn
Madison
Mandy
Manny
Marcel
Marty/Martie/Marti
Marion/Marian
Marshall

Mason
Mattie/Maddy
Max
Mel
Meredith
Merl/Merle
Merrill
Michael
Michele
Mickey/Mikki
Monty/Monte
Morgan
Nat
Nicky/Nickie/Nikki
Noel
Parker
Pat
Patrice
Payton/Peyton
Perry/Peri
Phil
Randy/Randi
Ray/Rae
Reese
Rene/Renee
Ricky/Rickie/Ricki
Riley/Reilly
Robin/Robyn
Roman
Ronnie
Rory
Rudy/Rudi
Sal
Sam
Sandy/Sandi
Sasha
Sidney/Sydney
Sean/Shawn
Shane
Shannon
Shelby

Shelly/Shelley	Tony/Toni
Skylar	Tracy/Tracey/Traci
Sonny	Ty/Tai
Stacy/Stacey	Tyler
Steph/Stef	Uriah
Stevie	Ursula
Sue (you can thank Johnny Cash for that one)	Val
	Vic
Taylor	Whitney
Teddy/Teddi	Willie/Willi
Terry/Terri	Yves/Eve
Toby/Tobi	Zel

UNITED WE STAND

Yes, there is always safety in numbers. That doesn't mean you shouldn't stand on your own; you should. It just means that it's often easier if you've got others on your side.

UNKNOWN

Yes, we all fear the unknown. When we are out of our comfort zone, the future can be very scary and daunting. However, because we can't control the future, there really isn't any point in being afraid of it.

UNNATURAL

There's a reason you shouldn't screw around with the natural order of things. The reason is you're not supposed to; it's unnatural.

UNNECESSARY RISKS

Take a walk on the wild side? Do something really crazy? It's not necessarily recommended, as pushing things to the limit (or past the limit) is pushing your luck—and some of us aren't so lucky.

UNPLEASANT TASKS

Part of the human maturing process is learning to deal effectively with unpleasant tasks. Get used to it, because they are all over the place (see *Changing Diapers*). The sooner you get it over with, the better you'll feel. Grow up already.

UNPRETENTIOUS

Isn't it cool how those real down-to-earth, well-heeled types don't have to constantly show off their wealth? Having lots is a privilege, not a right, so be well-behaved if you come into bug bucks, and stay grounded.

UNREQUITED LOVE

Sorry. Sometimes if it's not there, it's just not there— and you can't do anything about it. You can't talk someone into loving you. Just move on.

UNSOLICITED ADVICE

Go ahead and give unsolicited advice to others (until you're told to mind your own business). Sometimes it's OK to be nosey. If you ever hear yourself say "I could've helped/saved/prevented them from...," then you didn't take *my* advice now, did you?

UNSOLVABLE PROBLEMS

There is no such thing as an unsolvable problem. Every problem has a solution. Of course, the solution may not be very pleasant or palatable. But if you can't find it, you're not trying hard enough.

UNSUNG HEROES

There are people who perform heroic acts all the time and no one knows about it. These can be as simple as helping an elderly person down the steps or as intense as actually saving someone's life. By far, this is the purest form of heroism. There's another word for these people (see *Angels*).

UNWORDS

Don't show your ignorance by using any of these. They're not words.

Bazillion	Fantabulous	Ironical
Brang	Gazillion	Irregardless
Brung	Gazinta	Stupidest
Fadoozled	Gigunda	

UPS AND DOWNS

We all have our ups and downs. You're better off if the downs aren't too low and the ups aren't too high (see *Balance*). Of course, whatever goes up must come down. However, whatever goes down usually comes back up again (see *Throwing Up*). And, you surely don't want to be upside down.

Here are the usual ups:

Ante up	Grow up	Own up
Batter up	Grown up	Pay up
Beat up	Gum up	Pick up
Belly up	Ham it up	Prop up
Blow up	Hands up	Puffed up
Boot up	Hang up	Ramp up
Break up	Heads up	Rest up
Buck up	Heat up	Rise up
Came up	Hiccup	Roll up
Catch up	Hold up	Round up
Check up	Hurry up	Run up
Chin up	Hush up	Saving up
Choked up	Jack Up	Screw up
Clam up	Jazz it up	Set up
Clean up	Jig is up	Settle up
Coming up short	Jump up	Shake up
Cover up	Keep up	Shut up
Dig up	Ketchup	Sign up
Double up	Knock up	Sit up
Dressed up	Last roundup	Size up
End up	Leg up	Slow up
Fatten up	Lighten up	Snap up
Fed up	Listen up	Sneak up
Fess up	Live it up	Speak up
Follow up	Lock up	Spit up
Foul up	Look up	Split up
Free up	Loosen up	Stand up
Fuck up	Make up	Stand-up guy
Get it up	Mess up	Start up
Get up	Mixed up	Step up
Giddy up	Mix-up	Stick up
Give up	Mount up	Stir up

Stuck up	Upcoming	Uptake
Suck up	Update	Up the lazy river
Sunup	Upend	Uptick
Tee up	Upfront	Uptight
Throw up	Up in arms	Up-to-date
Thumbs up	Up in the air	Upturn
Tied up	Uplift	Up, up and away
Time's up	Upload	Upward
Trumped up	Upright	Up yours
Up and up	Uproar	Wake up
Up and at 'em	Uproot	Walk up
Up and coming	Upset	Wind up
Up and running	Upside	Wrapped up
Up and up	Upstairs	
Upchuck	Upstate	

And of course, then you have your downs:

Blow me down	Dumb down	Rundown
Calm down	First down	Settle down
Chow down	Get down	Shot down
Countdown	Go down	Shut down
Down and dirty	Going down	Sit down
Down and out	Hand-me-down	Slow down
Down boy	Lay down	Smackdown
Down home	Lay me down	Turn down
Down low	Letdown	Upside down
Down payment	Lowdown	(that's up and
Downright	Mark down	down)
Downside	Pay down	Way down
Downtown	Pipe down	Wind down
Downturn	Play down	
Dress down	Quiet down	

URANUS

Wow, you'd think they'd have come up with a better name for that planet by now. How about Myanus or Hisanus? Or wouldn't it be cool if they just called the planet Fred or Bob or something like that? Or maybe the planet with the bad word in it? Or how about Urplanet? That would make it an equal opportunity place to go to, right?

URINAL ETIQUETTE

Like everything else, there are rules at the urinal (which mostly apply to you boys out there):

> Don't forget to flush.
>
> Eyes forward.
>
> No conversations between stalls.
>
> No creative acrobatics (no writing your name and all that).
>
> No peeking at the guy next to you (see *Penis Envy*).
>
> No talking (don't ask someone how he's doing; if you must talk, wait till you get to the sink).
>
> Only speak if spoken to (at the sink; if you have to answer, don't turn your body; that's bad form—and messy.)
>
> Take care of business and move on.
>
> Ten seconds in front of the mirror—max.

URINATING

There are not many instances where boys have the clear advantage over girls. Urinating is one of them. We can go anytime, anywhere, inside, outside, upside down, sideways, you name it. We can make designs in the snow (watch out for frostbite). We can go for target practice (it's a gift; see *Penis Envy*). If used properly, it can be a very useful tool. But listen, boys: no one really wants to watch you doing it, so save the special tricks. It's just a normal bodily function. Find something else to show off and be proud of. Anyway, make sure you pee before you go to sleep—which is always better than the other way around. However, girls have us beat in the speed department (unless you're waiting in those endless lines for the ladies room). All you have to do is drop trou and boom, you're done. We've got to first fumble with zippers, fish that thing out and then do our thing. It's a real production, because then you've got to shake it off and put it back, being oh-so-careful not to get tangled with Mr. Zipper. (Mr. Zipper can be very nasty.) But here's an important lifelong recommendation: never pass up a chance to pee.

USER-FRIENDLY

We should all like things that are user-friendly. Actually, we should like anything that's friendly, allegedly or otherwise.

USING

You can use a tissue; you can use a toothpick; you can even use a used car. But you can't use a person. A user is a loser, you know. And if you allow someone to use you, then you become the loser (see *Self-Esteem*). Don't ever let anyone chew you up and spit you out.

VACATION

Sure, vacations can be rather exhausting, and you really may need a vacation after your vacation. But there is a lot of benefit in getting away from it all to take a break and get some much needed rest. However, there is such a thing as too much vacation (see *Cabin Fever*); you do eventually have to return to reality at some point. Maybe all of those problems you left behind will be solved when you get back (probably not). OK, we can dream, can't we?

VACILLATING

Nobody likes a vacillator. So make up your mind already.

VAIN

Yeah, we're all vain. This is confirmed every time we look in the mirror.

VALENTINE'S DAY

Valentine's Day is a wonderful time to make a special expression of love to the important people in your life. Nothing wrong with sending flowers, candy, cards or gifts to your sweetie, children, friends and parents-in-law. It's a day to remember how special they are. I really like it (see *Hopeless Romantic*).

VALIDATION

Only you can validate you. Don't look to someone else to do it.

VALUES

We all need to have values and should try to stick to them. And it starts with respect. Too bad our society's values seem to keep going down—and down—and down.

VARIETY

Variety really is the spice of life (see *Food*). You should try it sometime.

VASECTOMY

A little snip here, a little snip there; and then you're done, right? No thanks. A vasectomy is way too permanent for me (see *Unnatural*). I sure don't want to mess with standard operating procedures. Let the boys swim.

VEGETABLES

Eat your vegetables and you'll live longer. Plain and simple. You may want to skip those nasty Brussels sprouts though; same with cauliflower and beets.

VEGETARIAN

It seems to be rather one-dimensional to be a vegetarian (not that there's anything wrong with it). I'd starve if I had to be a meatless kinda guy. Cavemen and cavewomen did just fine with meat and veggies. I'll sit at the carnivore table.

VEGETATE

There are times in life when you are completely spent and you just don't want to do anything. It really is OK to vegetate once in a while (see *Recharging Your Batteries*). Once in a while (read not very often) being the operative words here. You don't want to make a habit of it.

VEGGIE GARDEN

Growing veggies is a bit like raising children. First you search and search for some fertile ground. Then you clear and till the area. Next you poke the little seeds in and add some fertilizer. Make sure they get lots of sun and water, and before you know it, they start to sprout. As they grow, they have to be talked to, sung to, nurtured and protected. At some point, they are finally nice and ripe and ready to be picked and given to someone else to deal with as they may. The difference here, of course, is that you're not supposed to eat your children.

VEINS

Keep your veins unclogged. This is very important, as the more restrictions you put on your blood flow, the less time you'll be around. And you want to stick around, right?

VENGEANCE

You can try to get even, but vengeance will never take away the hurt and pain that was afflicted on you. The perpetrator may feel the consequences of your punishment, but it won't change the wrong they committed. Remember: vengeance is not justice; it's a primitive way to try to get back at someone.

VENTING

Picture yourself as a balloon. That pressure keeps building up; and if it doesn't have a way out, it explodes. You've got to find that safety valve to let the air out (see *Friends*).

VENTRILOQUISTS

Ventriloquists really scare me. They are the only ones I know of who make a living talking to themselves.

VICIOUS CYCLE

I think a vicious cycle is some stage the washing machine goes through. Anyway, if you're at that point in your life, you want to get out of it, which is often easier said than done. I get dizzy just thinking about it.

Vicious Cycle

VICTIM

You can't always be the victim. If you are, something is wrong—most likely with you.

VILLAGE

Yeah, it does take a village. We all need to chip in to help raise our young ones and try to save the world.

VINDICATION

Isn't it nice to be right? Sometimes euphorically right? Of course, that enthusiastic reaction is really internal and doesn't have to be shared with everyone (see *Rubbing It In*).

VIOLATED

Feeling violated is horrible. There's never a reason to cause someone to go through this. If you've been victimized, just remember: it's not your fault. Blame the perpetrators (see *Assholes*).

VIRGINITY

Your virginity is the only thing that you can lose and never, ever find again. (Once you lose it, you probably don't want it back anyway.) Sorry, but to me, virginity is overrated (see *First Times*). Where or how you start your sex life is way less important than how or where you end up. That goes for everything from playing video games to having babies.

VIRTUAL REALITY

I prefer real reality, thanks.

VIRTUE

Everyone should extol their virtues. Understand, of course, that I really don't know what extol means.

VISION

Having vision doesn't necessarily mean you see well. It also has lots to do with being a forward thinker. Remember that if you don't have your own vision, you will only see the world through someone else's eyes.

VISUAL LEARNERS

We're all visual learners, as it often really helps to draw a picture. Some of us may need to do it in crayon, but that's OK too. We'll get it eventually.

VITAMINS

With all of the crap we eat, it's a wonder that we still live as long as we do. God knows, we don't get the right vitamins from our food, so it sure can't hurt to take supplements. Just know what you're taking, as otherwise you may be creating some very expensive urine. Vitamins are vital, you know.

VOICE

Sometimes just hearing the voice of someone important to you can have a calming effect when you've got a problem. Don't underestimate the power of a short phone call or visit to settle you down.

VOICE-MAIL LADY

I swear that most people use the same lady to give you instructions on their voice mail. You know, press one for a directory, press two for English, etc. She must be one busy (and wealthy) woman. How come there's no universal voice-mail guy (see *Sexist*)?

VOLUNTEER

The words "I'll do it" can be music to the ears. Anybody can give money to a charity; but giving of yourself is something else altogether. Roll up your sleeves and lend a hand. Now you're not just anybody. You're somebody.

VOTING

Voting is a right, but it's also a privilege. (It should really be a law). Lots of people died protecting our right to vote. If you don't vote, you've got nothing to say about the taxes you pay or the decisions made by your government. The most important elections—the ones that directly affect your daily life—are usually the local ones. You know: mayor, school board, etc. Voting in the presidential elections will have very little impact on when your trash gets picked up. Sure, it often boils down to voting for the lesser of two evils, but your vote is still vitally important. Remember: everybody's vote counts (just ask Al Gore). What do you mean you're not even registered to vote? Are you kidding me? Wake up and join this great county. Vote early and vote often.

VULNERABLE

Be careful of people trying to take advantage of you when you're in a vulnerable state. And don't you dare kick someone when they're down either. Ever.

WADDLING

Unless you're a duck, you shouldn't be waddling around (see *Dieting*).

WAIT

Wait your turn. There's nothing worse than somebody cutting in line. What's your rush anyway? Got a plane to catch? Nobody really likes to wait, except maybe waiters and waitresses; and they may not even like it. Remember that good things are worth waiting for.

WAKE

So why do they call it a wake? Does anyone really expect the departed to wake up? You know, it's very hard to erase pictures from your mind. Is this the way you want to remember them: lying there dead? Not me.

WAKE-UP CALL

Sometimes wake-up calls are a little subtle, like a tap on the shoulder. Other times they're more obvious, like having a house fall on your head. Whatever the delivery method, always take heed, as you don't get too many warnings in life.

WALKERS, RUNNERS, BIKERS, DRIVERS

I'm a walker, and we sure don't like runners, as they almost knock us over and don't smile when they blow by us. I'm also a runner, and we don't like walkers, as they get in our way and expect us to smile at them. I'm a biker, and we don't like walkers or runners, as they don't understand that we own the whole damn road and they need to stay out of our way; we're in a rush and have no time to even smile at them. I'm also a driver, and we don't like walkers, runners or bikers, as they tend to cut in front of us or otherwise force us to pay more attention and slow down; we typically greet them in a very different way, without a smile (see *Gesturing*).

WALKING ON EGGSHELLS

Yes, once in a while, you'll have to be very delicate and treat hypersensitive people with kid gloves. Big deal. If they're worth it, step gingerly. If not, step away.

WALLPAPER

It's a lot easier to paint than hang wallpaper (see *Do It Yourself*). You can always paint over paint. But try to get that damn wallpaper off—forget it. If you insist, at least get the pre-pasted kind; it's much easier to use.

WANDERING EYES

Wandering eyes will only get you in trouble. If you're attached to someone and the temptation seems too hard to resist, you may want to rethink your relationship. If necessary, get unattached before you do something stupid.

WANT vs. NEED

We often get wants and needs mixed up, which is sometimes very convenient (see *Rationalizing*). While you may want a new car, you certainly *need* a shower (yes, you do). What we want, we don't always need. We also typically want what we don't (or can't) have, like vacation homes, fancy trips, elaborate bird feeders, etc. But we don't really need them, and we forget that most of our basic needs are already met, including food (usually too much), shelter, clothing, TV and more. Anyway, once we do get these wonderful extravagances, there's generally a letdown, as they're usually not all that they're cracked up to be. At that point we're still not satisfied, and we want something else. Oh well. Everyone needs a hug though.

WANTED

It's always great to feel and be wanted. To have someone desire your company can be such a rush. If it's mutual, it's even better. Let 'em know.

WAR

War represents humankind's resolution to conflict at its absolute worst. There is, without a doubt, no glory in war. Just blood, tragedy, hardship and pointless death. Haven't we evolved from this savage and heartless destruction resulting from cultural, political and racial hatred and disputes? It's the 21st century, for God's sake. Unless we find a way to end this barbaric reaction to a disagreement, we will never evolve past our current level. Don't forget that if we live by the sword, we die by the sword. War can only be justified as an absolute last resort to defend against blatant aggression. So here's my idea: Have the leaders of the nations involved in the disagreement fight it out themselves in hand-to-hand combat. We'll see how quickly they'll find another way to resolve their conflicts. War. What is it good for? Absolutely nothing (thanks, Edwin Starr). Absolutely nothing.

WARM

Warm is nice. Hot is not.

WARM SEATS

Don't you just hate sitting in a seat someone else just occupied? What a squishy feeling sitting in a pre-warmed chair is; way too intimate for me. (Worse yet are warm toilet seats.) Now how do you think they got warm in the first place? I know I don't want to know. Here's the dilemma: Do you wait for it to cool off and run the risk that someone else will beat you to it, or just plop down and forget about it (see *Choices*)?

WARNINGS

Heart attacks, accidents, meteorites falling on your head—we get warnings all the time. The trick is to heed them, as we don't get too many second chances.

WASH YOUR CAR

A clean car is a happy car. And don't forget the inside. A coat of wax once in a while wouldn't hurt either.

WASH YOUR CARES AWAY

So you're feeling kinda low and you just sit around feeling even more low, bordering on a vegetative state. Just by dragging yourself into the shower, you can often shake off those blues. It will wake you up and help to cleanse your body and mind. Try it; you'll like it. So will your family and friends (see *Hygiene*).

WASH YOUR HANDS

Washing your hands is the best way to keep from getting sick. However, you don't want to be obsessive-compulsive about this (see *Moderation*). No one likes a germ freak.

WASTE NOT

Waste not, want not? I don't know about that. I don't waste a lot, but I sure want a lot. Unfortunately, we are a country of wasters (see *Recycling*).

WASTING TIME

If you want to waste your time, that's your business (see *Free Country*). However, it's very hard to be forgiven for wasting someone else's time, as it's very precious and they can't ever get that time back. So don't do it. Tick, tick, tick….

WATCHED POT

Of course a watched pot boils, silly. It just seems to take forever when you're watching (see *Patience*).

WATCHING TV TOGETHER

Watching TV is not an interactive social activity. You stare blankly at a flickering screen, lost in your own thoughts. If someone is watching with you, anything they say is an interruption, not an accompaniment to your viewing pleasure. The best way to watch TV with someone is to both stay quiet and ignore each other. All you are doing is occupying the same space and sharing the same air. Going to the movies isn't quite as bad, except you get yelled at if you make any noise. If you want to do something together, go out to dinner or go for a walk outside; watching TV doesn't really do it.

WATCHING YOUR WEIGHT

Yes, we live in a society where most of us are watching our weight. Unfortunately, we typically watch our weight go up. So stop sitting around watching and do something about it already (see *Exercise*).

WATER

The world is made up of two things: dirt and water. Well, three things, if you include rocks. But there's water, water everywhere. Why? To drink, of course. You're not supposed to eat the dirt, but you should drink the water—lots of water. It's the key to life and good health. Don't drink the salt water though; it doesn't taste so good. Water can be very helpful, but it can be equally destructive, as in floods, hurricanes, etc.; too much of a good thing, I guess. Water flushes out all of the nasty stuff collecting in your body, so drink hearty, my friends. Water, water, water. See, it's not just good for your lawn.

WAVING

This could be embarrassing. Are they waving at me or the guy behind me? You probably know them, so wave back. Even if you don't think you know them, they likely know you, so wave back anyway. If you end up making an ass out of yourself by returning a wave meant for someone else, don't worry about it; that won't be the first (or last) time you do something embarrassing. When waving, try to use all five fingers. It's good form.

WAY

Yes, there's gotta be a way. Where there's a will, there's usually a lot of ways, you know; so keep looking even when you're stumped. You just have to find it. But it's best to start with a will. (What's up with Will anyway?) As you can tell, there are always lots of ways:

Byway (see *Gay*)	One way	Way to go
Highway	That way	Wrong way
My way	Two way	Your way
No way	Waterway	

WEAKNESS

Who said you should never show weakness? You don't have to hide it; just don't flaunt it. So you're afraid of heights? Who cares? We're all afraid of something. (For me, it's Brussels sprouts.)

WEAKNESSES

The real smart people know their own weaknesses and either try to improve on them or compensate for them (see *Strengths*). The best are simply secure enough to admit theirs.

WEALTH

Wealth doesn't always equate to the number of dollars you have in the bank. Ever hear of a wealth of knowledge? That's the best kind there is—and sure beats the hell out of monetary wealth any day. Which is yet another reason to spread the wealth around (see *Charity*).

WEAR

Don't know what to wear today? Try any of these:

Giftware	Software	Underwear
Nowhere	Tupperware	Wash-and-wear
Ready-to-wear	Somewhere	

WEARING THE PANTS

Anyone can wear the pants in the family. Just know which one it is. Or you can take turns (see *Cross-Dressing*).

WEARING YOUR HEART ON YOUR SLEEVE

It's perfectly OK for you to wear your heart on your sleeve. Let you be you. Just be careful to take it off when you put that shirt in the laundry.

WEATHER

It's too hot, it's too cold, it's raining, it's snowing…. No, there is absolutely, positively, nothing you can do about the weather. So deal with it and stop complaining. That is, of course, weather permitting.

WEATHER FORECASTERS

Please don't tell me about highs, lows, fronts or backs. I don't need to know how hot it got yesterday or if it's raining in China. El Niño, La Niña, El Nudnik, La Bamba—I'm not interested (see *Excruciating Details*). Just tell me how cold it will be tomorrow and if it's going to rain. And get it right once in a while, OK?

WEIRD

Well, who isn't a little cuckoo occasionally? So you may need to tighten up a couple of those loose screws here and there (see *Psychotherapy*). Just make sure you're still you; and don't let anybody change that.

WELCOME

Feeling welcome is such a wonderful emotion. And making others feel welcome is a sign of a very good host or hostess. So keep it up.

WELL-ROUNDED

Being well-rounded has nothing to do with your figure. A single-dimensioned person is exceptionally boring. You want to be as well-rounded as possible, with lots of dimensions (as in multidimensional).

WE'LL SEE

We'll see usually means no. Sorry.

WET WILLIES

Wet willies are fun to give, but nasty to get.

WETTING YOUR BED

So you're sound asleep and you have to pee. Except you probably don't know you have to pee because you're sound asleep. So you dream you're in front of (or on, for you squatters) the toilet, and whoops! It happens (or so I'm told), and it's nothing to get upset over. Now if it's a frequent occurrence, you better do something about it. But first, make sure that no one is putting your hand in warm water while you're snoozing. And lighten up on the liquid intake before going nighty-night.

WE/US

We and us are two of the biggest and most inclusive words in the English language. When you use them, you automatically imply collaboration and being part of something. (You may notice that there is no I in either word.) There's nothing like saying: We did it. As for wee-wee, that's something entirely different.

WHAT HAVE YOU DONE FOR ME LATELY

Damn, talk about short memories. How quickly they forget. If you have to continually prove yourself to someone, it's probably not worth the effort, as they'll never get it anyway (see *Superficial*).

WHAT IF

You can what-if yourself to death. You didn't, they didn't, it didn't. Who cares? Get on with it.

WHAT IF SOMEBODY TURNED OFF THE LIGHTS

What would happen if someone (or something) turned off the universal electric switch? Besides being in the dark, we would all be lost (hmm, that's redundant). No phones, no refrigerators, no can openers, no vibrators. And we'd run out of nonrechargeable batteries pretty fast. What would we do? We'd be completely paralyzed. So don't tell any alien life forms the secret to having us totally submit to them; they'd be having us for lunch. Shhh. It'll be our little secret, OK? I worry about stuff like that.

WHAT THEY THINK

Yes, we all worry about what people think about us. Too bad, as that's a complete waste of time. Ultimately, what they think isn't very important. It's what you think that really defines and drives you. That's what really matters.

WHAT WE EAT

When you think about it, we actually are what we eat, as we're the product of our own environment. Our food gets digested and our body absorbs the vitamins, minerals and nutrients. And that's what we become: a collection of all of that. Something to keep in mind the next time you're downing your third Big Mac. Do you want to end up looking like a Big Mac? Or worse yet, acting like a Big Mac?

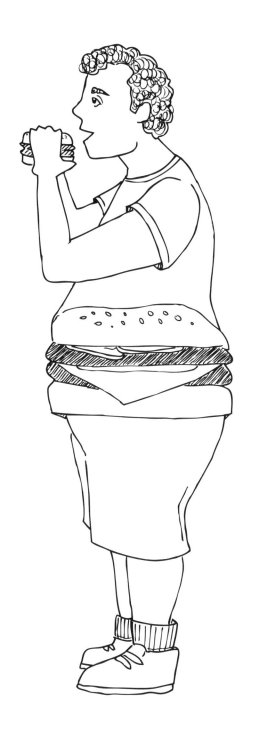

What We Eat

WHAT WILL THEY THINK OF NEXT

What will they think of next? Who knows? Just be glad that somebody's thinking. They often call that innovation and progress.

WHAT YOU DON'T KNOW

What you don't know won't hurt you? Ignorance is bliss? Hardly. Knowledge is power—and don't forget it.

WHEN ALL IS SAID AND DONE

When all is said and done, typically a lot more is ever said than done (see *Do Something*).

WHERE AM I'S

Having the "where am I's" is not to be confused with the deer caught in the headlights look. No, this is the reaction people have when they wake up from a very, very deep sleep—especially if it's in an unfamiliar bed.

WHET YOUR APPETITE

Don't you hate it when someone whets your appetite? That little tease just adds up to plenty of calories or trouble later. That's how the skillful can create and exploit pent-up demand.

WHINING

Whining is never allowed. That's the rule. Unfortunately, I break that rule a lot.

WHISPER

If you insist on having something stupid, rotten and nasty to say, at least be smart enough to whisper it into someone's ear. That way you only make a fool of yourself to one person, instead of a crowd.

WHITE-COAT SYNDROME

So the doctor wants to know why your blood pressure is high. See what happens to their blood pressure when they have to sit half-naked, waiting in a claustrophobic little room, anticipating life-threatening news from their friendly doctor. (And do they have to keep those stethoscopes in the freezer before they listen to your chest?) Anyway, after they are all done, leaving no stone unturned, and you're all comfy cozy finding out you're not dying, ask them to take your blood pressure again. It's guaranteed to be lower.

WHITE LIE

A white lie may be very convenient, unavoidable and the best thing to do at the time, but sorry, it's still a lie, no matter what color it is. Don't try to fool yourself. All lies tend to propagate, so you may want to watch out for those rolling snowballs (see *Truth*).

WHO'S GONNA KNOW

Who's gonna know? You are, silly. And you'll probably feel compelled to tell somebody, to ease your conscience. So save yourself some angst and embarrassment, and don't do it (whatever it is) when you know you shouldn't.

WHY

For such a small word, why sure asks a lot of questions. The world is full of why's, but I think the far better question is: why not?

WHY ME

No one is exempt from the trials and tribulations that go with life. Sometimes it may seem that we are being unduly put upon and challenged, but it's all part of that living your life business (see *Balance*). Deal with it.

WIFE BEATING

Do not pass go, do not collect $200. Go directly to jail. There is never an excuse for wife beating or any other kind of beating (like husband beating). Never. If you ever feel compelled to hit someone, hit the panic button and get some help.

WIGGLE

Adding a little extra wiggle to those hips is an ancient mating ritual. Girls, just know what you're doing, as it doesn't always pay to advertise (see *Cock Teasing*). Boys, you too.

WIGGLE ROOM

When you make a promise, you rarely have much wiggle room. After all, a promise is a promise. Instead, use the words maybe or I'll try, as these typically open up a safety valve. That's not a cop out; it's simply a way not to completely box yourself in and to be true to yourself.

WILLPOWER

We never seem to have enough willpower, do we? You can be the strongest person in the world, bench-pressing 500 pounds, and still have trouble saying no to things that aren't good for you (see *Discipline*). Apparently willpower takes a whole different kind of strength. But where there's a will, there's a way.

WINGING IT

Do the best you can with the information you've got. Winging it is not recommended, but if that's all you have, go with it.

WINNING

Winning is a lot of things, but it's not everything (see *Perspective*). And you definitely can't win them all, nor should you. Some get way too caught up in trying to win, and forget the whole point of the competition (see *Sports*). So relax. And keep in mind that no one can really be a good winner until they learn how to lose (especially gracefully), as losing is part of winning. So you win some and you lose some. Big deal; that's the way it goes.

WINTER

Warm winters scare me. It has to do with the natural order of things. Winters are supposed to be cold and snowy. A cold winter kills the bugs that are around during the rest of the year; that's a good thing. Cold weather also makes our nipples hard. Sometimes that's a good thing too, but I don't know why.

WIPING

Girls, front to back. Boys, your choice (see *Dingleberries*).

WISDOM

Wisdom is a very important asset to possess, as there's nothing dumb about wis<u>dom</u> (get it?). It's not very expensive and it pays great dividends, so you really want it in your portfolio. Unlike most things, the older you get, the easier wisdom is to obtain. It kind of comes with the territory—they call that experience. So hang around the wise ones; you might learn something. As for wise guys, you should probably stay away from them.

WISDOM TEETH

Do all of these extra teeth crowding your mouth make you any smarter? Maybe, so I'm holding on to mine. I'll take whatever wisdom I can get.

WISHFUL THINKING

Yes, it's best to stay reality based, but sometimes you just can't help letting your mind wander to better places. So what? Wishes can come true, you know. Just don't wish your life away. And be careful what you wish for.

WIT

You want to have a quick wit, not a dim one. It's a gift (see *Sure Dad, You Know Everything*).

WORDS vs. DEEDS

I'm going to bet on deeds, because they most often win over words. Remember: actions speak so much louder than words. If you can't back up your talk with deeds, they're just empty words. And make sure you chose your words carefully, as they can easily be misunderstood, and may even come back to haunt you. As for using hurtful words, these can be very dangerous weapons which should not be in your arsenal.

WORDS TO IMPRESS

If you sprinkle these words into your everyday language, people will think you know what you're talking about:

Abhor	Acute	Agog
Abrupt	Adapt	Alienate
Accoutrement	Admonish	Aloof
Acuity	Adversary	Altercation

603

Ambiguous
Ambivalent
Ameliorate
Amiss
Ancillary
Annoyance
Antic
Antithesis
Appalling
Arcane
Aroma
Arrogant
Articulate
Aspire
Astonishment
Astronomical
Astute
Aura
Awash
Betray
Blazé
Bodacious
Brisk
Buffoon
Cantankerous
Captivating
Cascading
Catapulting
Categorical
Cavalier
Charming
Cherish
Collaborative
Collegial
Colossal
Compelling
Complacent
Complex
Comply
Conjecture
Contemptible

Contrived
Conundrum
Convoluted
Copious
Coy
Dainty
Decadent
Decimated
Delicate
Delicious
Delightful
Demure
Denigrate
Depict
Descriptive
Despicable
Devour
Dichotomy
Dire
Discord
Discourse
Disdain
Disingenuous
Dongle
Effusive
Elated
Elegant
Elite
Eloquent
Elusive
Embark
Embellish
Embody
Eminently
Emit
Emote
Emphatic
Enamored
Enchanting
Encounter
Endure

Enlighten
Enmeshed
Enraptured
Ensconced
Ensure
Enthralled
Enthusiastic
Entice
Epiphany
Epitome
Erstwhile
Esoteric
Essentially
Euphoric
Exacerbate
Exalt
Exasperated
Exemplary
Exemplify
Exhilarating
Exonerate
Expediently
Expeditiously
Expressive
Extol
Exuberant
Exude
Fabulous
Fascinating
Fastidious
Faux
Feign
Fiasco
Flair
Flamboyant
Foe
Fortuitous
Frightening
Frivolous
Gallivant
Galore

Galvanize	Ludicrous	Proclivity
Gargantuan	Luxurious	Prolific
Glamorous	Majestic	Proper
Glum	Marginalize	Provoke
Glutton	Marvelous	Prowess
Gratitude	Mediocrity	Quibble
Haphazard	Mesmerize	Radiant
Hence	Meticulous	Radiate
Hideous	Mischievous	Rambunctious
Horrid	Mortified	Rapt
Horrific	Nefarious	Realm
Idyllic	Nitwit	Relinquish
Immense	Nomenclature	Remarkable
Imminent	Nuance	Reprehensible
Immodest	Oblivious	Resilient
Impending	Obscure	Resolute
Implore	Obtuse	Resounding
Imply	Odyssey	Reticent
Inconsequential	Oppressive	Rift
Inept	Orgasmic	Riveting
Innocuous	Ostentatious	Robust
Insidious	Outstanding	Sage
Insightful	Overt	Sashay
Insipid	Palatial	Saunter
Insufferable	Pamper	Savor
Interlude	Paradigm	Scant
Intuitive	Peak	Scion
Invoice	Peculiar	Scrumptious
Invoke	Pensive	Serene
Irascible	Perfunctory	Skedaddle
Ire	Perhaps	Sophistication
Irrelevant	Perilous	Spectacular
Jovial	Perplexed	Spellbound
Lackluster	Pert	Spontaneous
Lambaste	Picturesque	Stellar
Lament	Pivotal	Stoic
Languish	Poignant	Stunning
Leery	Poise	Stupendous
Lingering	Pompous	Stymy
Lithe	Practical	Suave
Livid	Presumptuous	Subversive

Succinct	Vague	Vivacious
Superfluous	Vary	Vivid
Surreptitious	Vast	Voluptuous
Tawdry	Venomous	Voracious
Thwart	Verbose	Wane
Treacherous	Vibrant	Wisdom
Trite	Vigilant	Yearning
Tutelage	Vigorous	Zenith
Typical	Vile	
Usurp	Vilify	

Don't bother with awesome; it's way too overused.

WORDS YOU DON'T WANT TO HEAR

When you hear anyone utter these words, it's best to be concerned:

Are you in yet?
I forgot my wallet.
I just want to be friends (see *Romantic*).
I lost my head.
Nice start (just when you thought you were done).
Oh no.
Uh-oh.
Whoops (real bad if coming from a doctor).

WORK

Most good fortune in life isn't the result of something falling into your lap. It's the result of work. And hard work usually pays off. It's important to know when you're knocking your head against the wall though. That isn't much fun.

WORKAHOLICS

We make many choices in life. Some people choose to be workaholics. If your job or career is the most important thing in your life, you're doing something wrong. You're probably doing a lot of somethings wrong. We should work to live, not live to work. You can love your job, but there's got to be more (see *Balance*). Go smell some roses, and get a life.

WORK IN PROGRESS

Every last one of us is a work in progress. Good thing (see *Hope*).

WORK OUT

Things tend to have a way of working out, although it may not seem so when we're in the middle of some nasty trauma. But in the long run, they mostly do.

WORLD

Don't just wait around for the world to change. Get up and change it yourself.

WORLD COMING TO AN END

When faced with any sort of challenge, some people act like the world is coming to an end. Few things are really that urgent. It's unlikely that the world will end any time soon, so find something else to worry about.

WORLD HUNGER

World hunger is an international disgrace. I'm not talking about missing a meal once in a while here. There is no excuse for anyone to be hungry in this world today. No excuse.

WORLD RECORDS

Do you really care who holds the world record for cramming the most hot dogs into their mouth in 60 seconds or for packing the most naked people on a theme park ride? You'd think some people would have more important things to aspire to. Get a life. (On second thought, I might be interested in some of those naked people.)

WORRYING

OK, I'm a real expert on this. And take it from me, worrying is an absolute waste of time. First, we spend most of our worrying time contemplating things we can't control or change anyway. Second, it seems that a majority of the things we worry about never even happen. It's best to lighten up, sit back and enjoy the ride. Now if you thrive on worrying and run out of things to worry about, let me know, and you can have some of mine, as I'll gladly share my list.

WORSE

Things can always be worse. It may not seem like it, but they always can (see *Holocaust*).

WORST ENEMY

It's not smart to be your own worst enemy. Leave that to somebody else, and learn to be your best friend instead.

WORST PEOPLE EVER BORN

Maybe God did make some mistakes, as these people (and I use that term loosely) never should've been born:

Adolph Hitler	Idi Amin	Pol Pot
Hideki Tojo	Joseph Stalin	Saddam Hussein
	Osama bin Laden	

WORTH DOING

If a task is worth doing, do it right (see *Half-Assed*).

WORTH IT

When you come right down to it, there isn't much that is ever really worth it. That goes for those fancy dinners, Corvettes and hot fudge, among other things.

WORTHLESS

Nobody is ever worthless. Useless, maybe, but not worthless.

WORTHWHILE

If it's worthwhile, then it's worth working hard for.

WRAPPED

Some people are wrapped way too tight, and some not tight enough. That's what makes the world go around.

WRINKLES

You'll get more wrinkles if you keep worrying about them (see *Old Wives' Tales*). Sure, you can protect yourself from the sun, but wrinkles are a sign of maturity. Some call them laugh lines, which may actually end up defining the amount of life you have enjoyed. You want to be distinguished anyway.

WRITING

Writing is rapidly becoming a lost art. E-mails are OK (see *Group E-mails*), but with smartphones being so cheap and accessible, people are just too lazy to write. It's a shame, because writing can be so much fun. Nothing like going to the mailbox and finding a letter from someone. So go ahead and write to somebody; you'll make their day. And the pen really is mightier than the sword. You can do a lot of damage or create a lot of neat feelings with it. Anyway, how can you read something between the lines when you're just talking?

WRONGS

No, two wrongs don't make a right (or a left). Even five wrongs don't make a right. They just make you very wrong. So you never want to use that as an excuse to get even.

XEROX

Wow, what a stroke of genius to name your company after a photocopier. It sure opened plenty of doors for them. The possibilities are endless. I was actually thinking of naming my son Kleenex, but his mother wouldn't let me. Just imagine all the attention he would have gotten every time someone sneezed.

XENOPHOBIA

It's very sad to realize that even in today's world of mega information (which is at almost everyone's fingertips), there is still so much ignorance, fear and hatred. Sure, hatred itself is ignorant, but to hate a class of people, an entire culture or a nation, without knowing anything about a single individual, is just plain stupid. Most of this fear tends to be based on stereotypes and a lack of understanding other's cultures. You can't simply paint an entire group with a broad brush and assume they're all bad. Or all good for that matter (see *Bad Apple*).

X MARKS THE SPOT

Even for people like me who get lost going around the block (see *Directions*), it's hard to miss that X. Hide some buried treasure under there, and even I can find it.

X-RATED

Poor X. I think as a letter, it gets a bad rap. Why would they assign this letter to a rating with such a negative connotation (see *They*)? X-rated is used to describe a nasty, dirty, sex-filled, violent movie. If that's the worst rating, I suggest calling it Z-rated instead. After all, Z is the last letter in the alphabet, and nobody really likes that letter anyway. Just a thought.

X-RAY

Geez, talk about no secrets—or privacy. The x-ray is a great diagnostic tool, but if you have something to hide, don't get one. They can see everything in there.

XYLOPHONE

Did you know that the xylophone was invented in 500 A.D.? That's a very long time ago. Just think: someone was trying to make some kind of telephone and instead came up with this cool instrument. The sound is so distinctive and unique. I marvel at the people who can play it. Way cool.

YARD/GARAGE SALE

Who are they kidding? They're not selling their yards or garages. Why don't they just call it junk–that-you-don't-need-anymore sale?

YAWNING

What kind of a wasted effort is yawning anyway? Our bodies spontaneously cause us to uncontrollably and involuntarily react. And of course it's contagious, so someone else yawns when they see you yawn. I'm sure there's a point to yawning; however, that point completely escapes me. If it's to tell us that we're tired, we already know that, right? That's why we're yawning.

YELLING

There's no point in yelling (unless the other person is very far away or otherwise couldn't hear you). You should always use your indoor voice. Screaming bloody murder will get someone's attention, but you will look like an idiot. If you can't communicate without raising your voice exponentially, you're doing something wrong (and you may want to consider working on your communication skills). Yelling is especially unbecoming on you girls, as it's not very ladylike (see *Sexist*).

YELLOW TRAFFIC LIGHTS

Do you know what the yellow traffic light is for? It's for caution. Do you know what that means? It means slow down, not speed up.

YES DEAR

Every man should learn to say these two very important words: "Yes dear." They are bound to keep you in the good graces of your lifemate. And you want to stay in her good graces—trust me.

YES MEN

If you surround yourself with people who always tell you what you want to hear, you not only become deaf to the realities of life, you become blind to your own faults as well.

YESTERDAYS

If your yesterdays are better than your todays, you need to work on your tomorrows. We tend to embellish the past, which is OK. Just don't live there.

YET

The best is yet to come. It really is. So stay tuned, as we've all got plenty to look forward to.

YIDDISH EXPRESSIONS

Here, use these words even if you don't know what they mean. You'll impress your friends:

Altacocker (old fart)
Bissel (little bit)
Boychik (boy; it's a Yiddish oxymoron)
Bubala (little bubby)
Bubamisis (babble)
Bubby (big bubala)
Bupkis (nothing)
Chaim Yankel (some famous nobody)
Chazer (pig)

Chazeri (some kind of bread, I think)
Chutzpah (guts)
Cockamamie (no idea what this means)
Conniver (schemer)
Dreck (trash)
Eppes (somewhat)
Facacta (fucked up)
Fagala (gay boy)
Fahkemp (not so fucked up)
Farmisht (confused)
Fartumult (more confused)
Feh (disgust)
Finagle (trying to get away with something)
Fumfer (stutter)
Fustunkin (super confused)
Gatkes (underwear)
Gantseh k'nacker (big shot)
Gonnif (thief; not to be confused with Ray Conniff)
Gonsa k'nacken (bigger big shot)
Go schloffen (go to sleep)
Hocken (nagging)
Hocking me a chinik (driving me crazy)
Kaka (shit, in the universal language)
Keppie (head)
Kibitz (fool around)
Kina hora (knock on wood)
Kinder (children)
Kishkes (insides)
Kitsel (tickle)
K'nacker (not-so-big shot)
Kniver (schemer)
Kreplach (dumpling)
Kvell (beaming with pride)
Kvetch (pest)
Landsman (fellow Jewish guy)
Loch in kup (punch in the nose)
Mama loshen (mother tongue, as in language)
Maven (expert)
Mazel tov (congratulations)
Meeskite (ugly person)
Megillah (long book)

Mensch (this author, as in me)
Meshugass (nonsense)
Meshugeneh (a character)
Mishpacha (family)
Momzer (bigger pig)
Nachas (personal pride—not knockers)
Nachatumin (in-laws)
Nebbish (mousy kind of guy)
Nervous chalaria (crazy woman)
Noodge (pain in the ass)
Nosh (snack)
Nu (what's new?)
Nudnik (nice pain in the ass)
Oy (oy)
Oy gevalt (very oy)
Oy vey (more oy)
Oy vey iz mir (even more oy)
Oy yoi yoi (way too much oy)
Patschkie (play)
Patschkie around (play more)
Pisch (pee)
Pischer (little one)
Pisser (not Yiddish, but refers to a funny and unique person or experience)
Plotz (sit)
Potch (spank, as in Chief Potchontuchus, a very famous Native
    American)
Pulkie (belly button)
Punim (cheek)
Pupik (also a belly button)
Putchuch (fussy one)
Putz (wiener)
Rachmanus (sad sack)
Schissel (some)
Schlemiel (knucklehead)
Schlep (drag)
Schlock (see dreck)
Schlong (see you later)
Schlub (slob)
Schluffing (sleeping)
Schlump (bigger slob)
Schmaltz (cooking fat or drama)

Schmancy (pretentious, as in fancy schmancy)
Schmatta (rag)
Schmear (spread)
Schmeggie (my son)
Schmendrick (jerk)
Schmo (sucker)
Schmoosh (crush)
Schmooze (kiss ass)
Schmuck (see Putz)
Schmush (squash; almost Yiddish)
Schmy (stroll)
Schnook (simpleton)
Schnozzola (nose; probably not Yiddish, but sounds like it)
Schnurer (hog)
Schtick (modus operandi or style)
Schvitz (sweat)
Sechel (common sense)
Shanda (something scandalous)
Shaygetz (non-Jewish guy)
Shayna punim (pinchable cheeks)
Shiksa (non-Jewish girl)
Shmutz (dirt)
Shpiel (story)
Shpilkes (ants in your pants)
Shmegegge (anything you want it to be)
Shpritz (spray)
Shtup (stick in; see *Sex*)
Shyster (almost Yiddish for con man)
Simcha (blessing)
Smidgen (not Yiddish, but it should be)
Taka (really)
Tatala (term of endearment for a man)
Tchotchke (keepsake)
Traif (un-Kosher food)
Tsatsgulah (endearing term)
Tsurus (angst)
Tuchus (tushie)
Tuchus facious (ass face; I made that up)
Ungapatchket (too much)
Vonce (pest)
Vos tust du (what's happening?)

Whole megillah (all)
Yenta (gossip/gossiper)
Yuckaputz (big putz)
Yutz (bigger putz)
Zaftig (pleasantly plump)
Zetz (punch)
Zie gezunt (good health)

Y'KNOW

Y'know, it was snowing outside, and y'know, the cable went out, and y' know, y'know, y'know…. If I knew, then you wouldn't have to tell me now, would you?

YOGA

There are people way smarter than me who tout all of the physical and mental benefits of practicing yoga. They are entirely right. Don't knock it till you try it.

YOU

Remember: the world would be lost without you. If you're not happy with yourself, who else will be? So please be happy and enjoy the ride. Here, these should boost your ego.

You:

Are a pisser (that's a compliment).
Are a riot.
Are my special angel.
Are so cool.
Are the best.
Are too funny.
Are too much.
Hang the moon.
Kill me.
Light my fire.
Light up my life.
Make me feel brand new.
Make me smile.
Make me so very happy.
Rock.
Rock my world.
Rule.

YOU ARE WHAT YOU ARE

There are few givens in this world, but when it comes right down to it, you are what you are. Maybe you can't play professional basketball, were not born into royalty or aren't God's gift to the opposite (or same) sex. Accept and embrace yourself, and be very proud.

YOU CAN BRING A HORSE TO WATER

You can bring a horse to water but you can't make him drink? Oh, if he's thirsty enough, he'll drink. Don't you worry.

YOU CAN'T ALWAYS GET WHAT YOU WANT

No, you can't always get what you want, but you can get and do a lot of things if you keep at it (see *Giving Up*).

YOU CAN'T TAKE IT WITH YOU

They say you can't take it with you, but I'm not so sure about that. If this is true, they can't come after you to get it either, right? Just to be safe, I'm always keeping some money in my pockets; so should you. You may have to make a call from up there. Or down there.

YOU CAN'T WIN 'EM ALL

So you can't win 'em all; but if you win most of them, you're doing better than most of us.

YOU GET WHAT YOU PAY FOR

Don't those bargains look great at the dollar store? What do you think that stuff is worth? A dollar, silly. That's why it's junk. Believe me, even at a dollar, those merchants are still making money on you. Try parting with a little more cash and getting something that will last more than five minutes. Although I'm not suggesting you pay full retail either (see *Stupid*).

YOU HAD TO BE THERE

Even the best storytellers can't recreate all of the details of an event. And sometimes, try as they may, you still won't get it. You probably had to be there.

YOU KNOW WHAT THEY SAY

You know what they say about blah, blah, blah. I don't know, but they always seem to have something to say.

YOUNG AT HEART

We all have a chronological age, which typically has no logic to it at all. The key is to always be young at heart, as that's what really counts.

YOU'RE NOBODY

You're nobody 'till somebody loves you? Wrong. You're nobody until you love you—or until you at least like you.

YOU'RE RIGHT

Sure, you're right and the world's wrong. It's good to be an individual and a free thinker, but you've got to know when to be realistic and practical. Odds are, you've got to be wrong sometimes, right (see *Balance*)?

YOU'RE WELCOME

If someone is nice enough to say thank you, make sure you acknowledge it with a you're welcome.

YOURSELF

Always be yourself, and always believe in yourself. After all, no one else can be *your* self.

YOUR WAY

So, it's your way or the highway, huh? Well, your way may be one way, but it's not the only way. It's always best to consider others' ideas as well (see *Open Mind*).

YUM

It's a shame that so much of what's bad for you is so yummy.

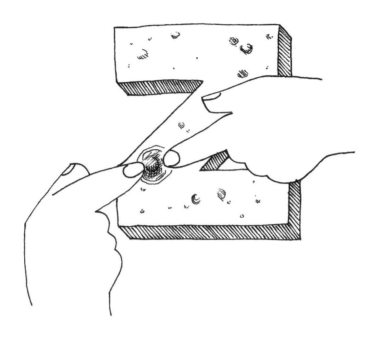

Z

The Zs are kinda light, which is fine, as I'm not a big fan of them anyway. And I'm getting kind of tired at this point.

ZEBRA

There's an old question as to whether a zebra can change its stripes. Although that causes much debate and ensuing long discussions, the clear answer is no. If a zebra could change its stripes, it would be a chameleon, silly.

ZERO

How can anything be less than zero? You see temperatures that are defined as below zero, and hear people talk about less than zero tolerance. Zero is zero, right? It's the rock bottom of rock bottoms. Things can't get any lower than zero, as that would make them less than nothing. And something can't be less than nothing, can it?

ZIGZAG

Try not to zig when you're supposed to zag.

ZIPPER

Whoever dreamed up that marvelous invention the zipper clearly was not considering a man rushing to get dressed. I'm guessing a woman developed this wonderful device to keep her wares all tucked in, so to speak. Great for her. However, we careless guys can do some painful damage using that "convenience," especially when time is not on our side. Ouch!

ZITS

Ah, the age old question: to pop or not to pop those zits. Go ahead and pop them, as they're ugly to look at. Just make sure you keep the area clean, or you may wind up with an ugly infection instead. And don't you just hate those undergrounders?

ZODIAC

 For some, studying the signs of the zodiac is a very interesting exercise. Your sign is determined by the time and date of your arrival into this world. Allegedly, I'm a Gemini, which means, as I understand it, that there are two of me. And according to many that have crossed my path during my life, that would make exactly one too many of me (one being way more than enough). Fortunately I don't subscribe to the science of astrology and the like. I have developed my own system—and by my calculations, I was born under the sign of the Jerk. Are you surprised?

ZOOS

Where do they find all of those lovely exotic animals—with all of their authentic smells, no less (see *Sarcasm*)? They sure don't look very happy locked up in those cages all day, which is why you never see them smile. I don't think I'd like it; would you? No privacy and no bathrooms, while people observe their every movement, so to speak. (Hey, this is the last chapter—were you really expecting something groundbreaking here?)

ZYZZYVA

This is the last word in the dictionary, and I really have no idea what it means. I never thought it would happen, but it appears that I have run out of things to say. A temporary situation, I'm sure (see *Tired*).

AFTERWORD

So there you have it: my masterpiece, my manifesto. That sounds so cool, but I really don't know what that means. It's a veritable treasure trove of my incessant (or insightful) ramblings, and lots of semi-important information. I've spilled my guts, and I feel much better (not that you should be so concerned). But this was all about stuff I learned and ideas I have that I wanted to share with the immediate world. Again, I'd be happy if only my children read it. If I got hit by lightning tomorrow and didn't get a chance to impart my wisdom and share my philosophies, passions and random thoughts, I'd feel cheated. (I'd be dead, but I'd be cheated.) Some say that this book is too revealing and self-deprecating. It probably is, but so what? And yes, the puns were intended.

All of this writing has been great therapy for me, and I highly recommend it, as it's a good exercise and a fulfilling release. Very cathartic. I really poured my heart and soul into this, and it was a lot of fun. (Sometimes I even cracked myself up.) I just never realized how much I had to say.

So how did I manage to write about all of these obscure topics? Everywhere I went, I'd jot down notes on stupid and not-so-stupid subjects to write about. I used a tape recorder for a while, but I put it in such a safe place, even I couldn't find it.

These are just one guy's opinions and not really open for debate. You disagree? Then write your own damn book, and maybe your children will read it someday. Just put plenty of surprises between the lines.

Do I follow my own advice and suggestions? Well, not always (see *Hypocrites*). Do I practice what I preach? Sometimes. If I did everything I recommend, I would probably be a saint (and the first Jewish one at that). Do as I say, not as I do. I figure if I followed 50 percent of my good advice, I'd be doing pretty well. Half the battle is knowing what you should do. The other half is knowing your faults and weaknesses, and trying to do better. The last half (shades of Yogi Berra) is to set some goals and work at it every day.

The cool thing for me is that my lovely children don't have to go very far to get my advice on things. If I'm not around, they can pick up this book (or trip over it) and feel me jump out and keep them company. This book *is* their crazy dad (sure Dad, you know everything), and speaks to them—and to you, if you're paying attention.

THE END

This page intentionally left blank

(So what are you looking here for?)